```
786.5 Arc              216030
Archbold.
Style and structure in the
 praeludia of Dietrich...
```

The Lorette Wilmot Library
Nazareth College of Rochester

WITHDRAWN

Style and Structure in the
Praeludia of Dietrich Buxtehude

Studies in Musicology, No. 82

George Buelow, Series Editor

Professor of Music
Indiana University

Other Titles in This Series

No. 79	*Tonal Coherence in Mahler's Ninth Symphony*	Christopher Orlo Lewis
No. 80	*Viennese Harmonic Theory from Albrechtsberger to Schenker and Schoenberg*	Robert W. Wason
No. 81	*Roger Sessions and His Music*	Andrea Olmstead
No. 83	*Schoenberg's 'Moses und Aron': Idea and Representation*	Pamela White
No. 84	*Thorough-Bass Accompaniment According to Johann David Heinichen*	George Buelow
No. 85	*The Orchestra in the Nineteenth Century: Physical Aspects of its Performance Practice*	Daniel J. Koury
No. 86	*Lowell Mason: His Life and Work*	Carol A. Pemberton
No. 87	*Bach-Quellen in Amerika—Bach Sources in America*	Gerhard Herz

Style and Structure in the Praeludia of Dietrich Buxtehude

by
Lawrence Archbold
Assistant Professor and College Organist
Carleton College
Northfield, Minnesota

UMI RESEARCH PRESS
Ann Arbor, Michigan

Copyright © 1985, 1981
Lawrence Leo Archbold
All rights reserved

Produced and distributed by
UMI Research Press
an imprint of
University Microfilms International
A Xerox Information Resources Company
Ann Arbor, Michigan 48106

Library of Congress Cataloging in Publication Data

Archbold, Lawrence, 1951-
  Style and structure in the praeludia of Dietrich Buxtehude.

  (Studies in musicology ; no. 82)
  Revision of dissertation—University of California, 1981.
  Bibliography: p.
  Includes index.
  1. Buxtehude, Dietrich, 1637-1707. Organ music.
I. Title. II. Series.
ML410.B99A87   1985   786.5'092'4   85-1064
ISBN 0-8357-1646-5 (alk. paper)

Contents

Acknowledgments   *vii*

Introduction   *1*

Part I: Style

1   Texture   *9*
    Textural Styles
    Historical and Critical Evaluation

2   Harmony   *31*
    Harmonic Styles
    Historical and Critical Evaluation

3   Rhythm and Meter   *49*
    Rhythmic and Metrical Styles
    Historical and Critical Evaluation

4   Thematic Variation   *63*
    Thematic Variation in Fugal Subjects
    Thematic Variation throughout the Praeludium
    Historical and Critical Evaluation

5   Expression   *93*
    Movement and Climax
    Expressive Form
    Historical and Critical Evaluation

Part II: Structure

6 The Opening Free Section   *109*
    Style Analysis
    Structural Analysis
    Historical and Critical Evaluation

7 The First Fugal Section   *129*
    Style Analysis
    Structural Analysis
    Historical and Critical Evaluation

8 The Remaining Sections   *159*
    Style Analysis
    Structural Analysis
    Historical and Critical Evaluation

9 Coherence   *209*
    Synthesis and Closure
    Middleground and Background Form
    Historical and Critical Evaluation

Conclusion: Chronological Considerations   *235*
    The Sources
    Previous Attempts at Chronology
    A Proposed Chronology

Notes   *301*

Bibliography   *339*

Index   *343*

Acknowledgments

I would like to express my profound gratitude to Dr. Lawrence Moe of the University of California, Berkeley, whose help with the preparation of this project was enormous, and who, indeed, has been an unfailing source of support throughout my career. I would also like to thank Dr. Kerala J. Snyder of Hartt College whose lively interest in my work and many helpful suggestions for its present revision have been a great source of encouragement.

Introduction

It has now been over one hundred years since Dietrich Buxtehude's organ music first appeared in print, under the editorship of Philipp Spitta.[1] That Spitta's edition was published in the same decade as his monumental biography of J.S. Bach is no coincidence, for that work contains the first — and in many ways still impressive — critique of Buxtehude's organ works.[2] The Spitta edition, revised and augmented by Max Seiffert in 1903 and again in 1939,[3] remained unchallenged until the appearance of Josef Hedar's edition of 1952,[4] which was prepared at the same time as his dissertation, *Dietrich Buxtehudes Orgelwerke*.[5] Because Hedar was able to draw upon several significant manuscripts that were unknown to Spitta and Seiffert,[6] his edition clearly supersedes their efforts.[7]

In 1971, yet another edition of the Buxtehude organ works appeared, edited by Klaus Beckmann.[8] Certainly the most important addition to the study of these pieces since Hedar's dissertation and edition, it embodies a new approach to the problems of editing this music. For the first time, a text-critical, rather than an *Urtext*, method was adopted.[9] As none of the sources we possess is an autograph, and most are not in organ tablature (as the autographs would have been), our knowledge of Buxtehude's organ music is far from first-hand.[10] Moreover, some of the sources have been dated considerably after Buxtehude's time. Realizing that the sources may well contain numerous errors of transcription, Beckmann has viewed them with an eye towards reconstructing the readings of the original tablatures.[11] The result is a fresh view of the works — one which is at times significantly different from that presented by Spitta or Hedar.[12]

This new text-critical methodology does not significantly challenge the current state of these works from the standpoint of musical style. Buxtehude's position has been clear for some time, and remains so: "The evolution of North German organ music reaches its peak with Dietrich Buxtehude."[13] "Buxtehude was to the north what Froberger was to the south. In them, and only in them, was the art of Frescobaldi brought to fulfillment."[14] "In the north, continuing the tradition established in the early part of the century by Sweelinck and Scheidt, the chief figures were Georg Böhm at Lüneburg and Buxtehude at Lübeck."[15] Buxtehude's position at the apex of both the Italian tradition of Frescobaldi and Froberger and the northern tradition of Sweelinck, Scheidt, Scheidemann, and the rest of the north German organists is undisputed; so too is his direct influence on the early organ music of J.S. Bach.[16]

Our understanding of this music from a closer, more intimate point of view, however, is significantly challenged by the Beckmann edition. By showing the curious and often inexplicable details of Buxtehude's writing to be the product of garbled sources rather than a garbled mind, the Beckmann edition reveals Buxtehude to be a composer of far more elegance than had ever before been believed.[17] Indeed, with Buxtehude's organ music, we are faced with the somewhat paradoxical case that *Urtext* editions have hindered as much as helped our understanding of his genius. In short, Beckmann gives us not only the composer of power, brilliance, and rhapsodic effusion which we have known since Spitta, but also a composer of remarkable refinement hitherto unrecognized. No longer repelled by surface curiosities, we can now approach these pieces from a more sophisticated point of view than in previous attempts that only determined the number of figural and fugal sections and charted obvious thematic relationships. As certainly the most impressive organ music of its century, a century rich indeed in organ music, Buxtehude's works do not stand in need of defense or justification. They do, however, by their ability to engage and entrance both the player and the listener, call for explanation and illumination. In light of the new view of these works made possible by the Beckmann edition, this book seeks to meet that challenge at a level of detail and with a variety of means not previously attempted: both stylistic and structural analysis, as well as historical and critical observations, are brought together in the quest.

This study is limited (in the interests of presenting a detailed examination of a small number of pieces rather than a more cursory view of many) to the group of twenty-two works of Buxtehude which can be considered as *pedaliter-praeludia*, that is, a praeludium with pedal parts.[18] Table 1 presents a concordance of their appearance in the various editions. In studies and editions previous to Beckmann's and the Karstädt catalogue of

Table 1. Concordance of Editions

BuxWV[19]	Title	Spitta[20]	Spitta-Seiffert-Kraft[21]	Hedar[22]	Beckmann[23]
136	Praeludium in C	. . .[24]	II/20	II/2	I/1
137	Praeludium in C	I/4	I/4	II/1	I/2
138	Praeludium in C	. . .	. . .	. . .	I/3
139	Praeludium in D	I/11	I/11	II/11	I/4
140	Praeludium in d	I/10	I/10	II/19	I/5
141	Praeludium in E	I/8	I/8	II/14	I/6
142	Praeludium in e	I/6	I/6	II/9	I/7
143	Praeludium in e	I/13	I/13	II/10	I/8
144	Praeludium in F	. . .[24]	II/19	II/16	I/9
145	Praeludium in F	I/15	II/15	II/15	I/10
146	Praeludium in f#	I/12	I/12	II/13	I/11
147	Praeludium in G	. . .	. . .	II/7	I/12
148	Praeludium in g	I/5	I/5	II/22	I/13
149	Praeludium in g	I/14	I/14	II/24	I/14
150	Praeludium in g	I/7	I/7	II/23	I/15
151[25]	Praeludium in A	. . .	II/21	II/12ab	I/16, Anhang 1
152	Praeludium in a	. . .[24]	II/17	II/6	I/17
153	Praeludium in a	I/9	I/9	II/4	I/18
154[26]	Praeludium in B♭	. . .	. . .	II/21	I/Anhang 3
155	Toccata in d	. . .[24]	II/30	II/20	I/19
156	Toccata in F	I/20	II/26	II/17	I/20
157	Toccata in F	I/21	II/27	II/18	I/21
158	Praeambulum in a	. . .[24]	II/18	II/5	I/22

Buxtehude's works,[27] such pieces were generally termed preludes and fugues for organ.[28] Of these works, however, three are labeled toccata, and one praeambulum. None of these works exhibits characteristics which would prevent it from being termed a praeludium, and indeed they are formally indistinguishable from those which are actually called praeludium.[29] These twenty-two works make up only a fraction of Buxtehude's organ compositions. The study omits all of his works based upon chorales or other liturgical themes (the chorale fantasias and chorale preludes of which a total of forty-seven survive).[30] Also omitted are the *manualiter-praeludia*. These works, similar in form to the *pedaliter-praeludia*, are usually on a smaller scale and do not have pedal parts.[31] A number of other *manualiter* works survive under the titles of canzona, canzonetta, and fuga. These are also not a part of this study.[32] Finally, the three great ground bass pieces for organ (with pedal parts) — the Ciaconas in c and in e, and the Passacaglia in d — are also omitted because of the substantial difference in form from the praeludia. The numbering of the works established in the Karstädt catalogue (abbreviated BuxWV) is adopted here. The readings of the Beckmann edition, including measure numbers, have also been adopted here unless otherwise noted.

Part I of the current study ("Style") isolates and examines in detail individual stylistic elements of the praeludia. It also places the topic in its historical context regarding Buxtehude's immediate predecessors and incorporates critical judgments of the composer's work. The view of form developed in this part is largely the traditional one defined by these stylistic features; the alternation of free and fugal textures, harmonic articulations, changes of meter, and thematic links constitute the approach to form used by Spitta, Hedar, and other scholars.[33] Only the inclusion of expression goes beyond their canon.

Part II ("Structure") explores the works by formal section. While considering form as defined by stylistic analysis, these chapters also look to a different definition of form, that which "depends on the conception and the working-out of the prolongations,"[34] as defined by structural analysis. Again, historical and critical evaluation is included. These three chapters consider various parts of the praeludia separately rather than considering the works as whole compositions. The background harmonies and fundamental lines discerned in them become middleground phenomena when the works are discussed as complete compositions in the ninth chapter.

The Conclusion considers the findings presented here in view of establishing a proposed chronology of the works. A survey of the sources and previous attempts at chronology form the first two sections; the third section presents the proposed chronology. With little real evidence for a precise chronology forthcoming from the sources, most evidence has to be gleaned from stylistic and structural analysis. While the findings presented here cannot be considered definitive, they refine previous attempts at chronology and provide a far more detailed discussion of the stylistic and structural aspects of the praeludia which can be considered relevant to such an undertaking.

Another possible approach to form in the praeludia, one which is not explored here, is the parallel which can be discerned between the musical forms and the rhetorical conventions of the day.[35] Harald Vogel has applied the concept to Buxtehude's praeludia in various workshops; and Lena Jacobson has provided an extensive analysis of the praeludia in this manner.[36] Harald Vogel has also recently proposed that some, if not many, of the praeludia survive in the "wrong" key: that they could not have been conceived in the keys in which they come down to us because they are not playable in meantone in those keys. He has suggested the transposition of such works to keys in which the music is acceptable in meantone yet which does not violate the range of the composition in view of the compass of the instrument. Such transpositions are sometimes but not always possible. Indeed, Kerala J. Snyder has recently suggested that Buxtehude's organ in the Marienkirche could have been adapted to some form of well-tempered tuning in 1683. These and related questions were explored in detail recently at Wellesley College.[37] Some years ago, Kenneth Powell suggested that the use of unusual keys might indicate a later origin for those praeludia which employ them.[38] This view has recently generated considerable interest. Yet such a criterion is not sufficient in itself to construct a chronology of the works. It is evident that much more needs to be learned about the history of the tuning of the organs of north Germany in the seventeenth century.

Part I

Style

1

Texture

Textural Styles

Texture is the traditional approach for style analysis to the Buxtehude praeludia.[1] The variety and imagination of these works can hardly fail to capture a commentator's attention:

> Passage work of great brilliance, dramatic pedal solos, breathtaking rests, obstinate ostinatos, expressive recitatives, boldly traced fugal subjects, massive chords, and sustained pedal points as bases for lively motivic play or for gently flowing sicilianos are some of the multifarious ideas that come and go. . . .[2]

Yet for purposes of formal analysis, this multitude of devices is reduced to two textures: free (or "toccata")[3] and fugue. Grout likens their formal scheme to a realization, "on a grand scale," of "the Baroque conflict between impulse [free sections] and order [fugal sections]"; and describes the process of joining the two opposing kinds of textures as the "effort to discipline the freedom of the toccata, and in the most dramatic manner possible, by yoking it with the ricercare . . . in a union of musical opposites."[4] It is not only, then, the various kinds of textures themselves that have interested analysts, but also their alternation and juxtaposition.

Hedar divided the praeludia into three categories: "toccatenfuge," "toccatenvariantenfuge," and "toccata."[5] The first has but three examples. The dividing line between his next two categories, however, is unclear.[6] Furthermore, one work in each of these last two groups could belong as easily in the first group.[7]

Apel omitted whatever distinction there might be between these forms and schematized the form of these works as "T F T . . ."[8] ("T" for toccata, or free section; "F" for fugal section). Thus many forms are possible as this string could be, theoretically, extended indefinitely. (In reality these works never include more than four fugal sections.) The situation is more complex, however, because such forms as T F F T occur, without the central T section. Apel also simplified the nomenclature, for all of these praeludia are called "toccatas" except for BuxWV 144 (whose form is T F), which he refers to as "the only genuine prelude and fugue."[9]

Powell draws on both these approaches, but chiefly on that of Apel. Like Apel, he sees the "toccata" as a genre set apart from the few examples in the north German repertory which end with the first fugal section.[10] Powell, however, adds several works whose form is T F T to the "genuine prelude and fugue" type (for example, the Toccata in F, BuxWV 157). And since Powell's study concerns only the works he calls toccatas, it does not include these works. Powell does, however, make several contributions. First, his definition of the toccata form:

> To say that the north German organ toccata has a specific form would be erroneous. To say that it has a set of basic characteristics from which the composer selects what he needs, would be more to the point.[11]

He rightly emphasizes the fluidity of the "form," so much so as to imply "formal possibilities" as an alternate concept. Powell prefers an archetypal form of free/fugue/interlude(s)/fugue/other,[12] of which any section but the first two can be omitted. (Again, works which end after the first fugue, or after the interlude, are not included in his study.) Like Hedar, Powell is sensitive to the role of these sections beyond just that of alternation: witness his terminology "interlude" and "other." (He usually further clarifies "other" as "coda.") He further defines the types of interludes, establishing a useful distinction between those which are "dependent" and "independent"[13] (sections which are either joined to the preceding fugue, as a short ending in a free style, or which stand separate of the preceding fugue). Also like Hedar, he is careful to distinguish between fugue and fugato, the latter being understood as an interlude rather than as a true fugal section.[14] Traditionally, then, analysis has relied on the distinction between free and fugal textures to determine the formal structure of these works. However, it is important to observe the real diversity of textures within these two basic groups.

There is a vast range of free textures in the praeludia, from passages in a chordal style to those in rhapsodic, figural, and modular styles. Purely chordal writing is perhaps the simplest found in the praeludia. Most often, however, chordal passages are lightly decorated with ornamentation. A more rhapsodic style features richly elaborate flourishes, trills, and passagework. When these elements are combined with extreme registers, dramatic disruptions, and Buxtehude's taste for daring musical gestures, the result is a texture which is flamboyant (at times even capricious) in effect.

The chordal-rhapsodic branch of the free music is very different from the two other important free textures, the figural and the modular styles. Both these styles, unlike the chordal and rhapsodic, tend towards equality of the individual voices. In the figural stye, all the manual parts may participate in a dialogue consisting of small figures used in a freely imitative way. This figural style results in a texture which is extremely flexible but one which moves in spurts: a figure is introduced and (although rarely presented more than a few times) treated intensively. Its potential is quickly exhausted, at which point a new figure appears.[15]

Free textures cast in modular forms are a specialty of Buxtehude. These repeating structures set up a pulse of their own, often that of a measure, within which a harmonic progression is contained. All this music is strongly tied to the barline and yields an intense, sometimes tenacious music; occasionally, the repeated patterns "get stuck" and seem to grip the musical fabric. There are many forms of repetition, ranging from simple reiteration to sequence, ostinato, and full-fledged ciaconas. Passages which employ simple repetitions and sequences are particularly associated with the free endings which close many of the fugues. The *grave* fugue of the Praeludium in f♯, BuxWV 146, ends with a free extension of two nearly identical measures: | $-i_6-iv-V_{-7}$ | $VI-i_6-iv-V_{-7}$ | i.[16] The *vivace* fugue of the same work, which follows immediately, ends in a similar manner with four measures, the first two of which parallel the second two.[17] Such structures are an important feature of a number of the praeludia. Repetitions, however, more often involve sequences. While such passages are usually of only a few measures' duration, several large-scale sequential passages can be found.[18]

Ground bass structures are the second main type of modular constructions and are generally found in the last section of the praeludia. They are often associated with subdominant harmony, as Apel has suggested.[19] These ostinatos can be a short figure of perhaps no more than two or three notes which merely bounce back and forth between the tonic and dominant, or between the subdominant and its own dominant.[20] Figures which are somewhat longer can embody a more extended progression, and may begin to resemble ciaconas in their effect. They can range from the two small hints of ciacona in the last section of the Praeludium in a, BuxWV 153, to the clearly ciaconalike construction after the second fugue of the Praeludium in g, BuxWV 149. Both of these examples elaborate the subdominant:

12 Texture

Praeludium in a, BuxWV 153

Praeludium in g, BuxWV 149

A ciacona effect is equally pronounced in the free ending to the fugue in the Praeludium in C, BuxWV 138. This imaginative passage resembles a ciacona, but it is treated with unusual freedom. It lies in the tonic, as do all three of the large, genuine ciaconas in the praeludia:

Praeludium in C, BuxWV 138

The ciacona from the Praeludium in g, BuxWV 148, may be taken as an example of the large-scale ciacona sections.[21] It stands as the praeludium's closing section and is replete with intricate figurations which rival the most impressive moments of the figural style.[22]

There is also diversity within the fugal textures. Fugues which consist of an exposition with paired entries, codettas, and then, typically, further expositions can be contrasted with those fugal sections which present only a part of such a fugue, namely just the exposition. In these latter cases, the entrances of the subject are usually tightened up by the omission of the codettas, giving the effect of dense imitation rather than real fugue. The result is a modular construction, making this technique the fugal style's parallel to the ostinato passages of the free style. These fragmentary fugues, or fugatos,[23] have a characteristic breathlessness which contrasts with the poise of a true fugal section.

Recognition of the various types of textures makes possible a more refined view of the form of these works. The opening free section chiefly relies on figural texture, with all but four of them being organized around it. Some are entirely figural, while others either precede or follow figural texture with others. The fugal section which follows the opening free section is the second pillar of the form. The use of the free ending is virtually standard and a great variety of free textures can comprise them. The remaining free and fugal sections are by far the most complicated to schematize. The alternation of free and fugal textures after the first fugue is not a rigid scheme; in fact, it breaks down some fifteen times in seventeen works. The procedure should be regarded as an archetypal form. A basic distinction, however, can be made between those works which end with a free section and those that end with a fugal one. The works which end with a fugal section are of two basic types: those which end with triple-time fugues and those which end with gigue fugues. See table 2 (in which "dependent interludes"[24] following fugues have been termed "free endings").[25]

The norm of four-part writing is generally maintained throughout Buxtehude's praeludia. On occasion in the free style the number of parts is temporarily increased to five for the emphasis of added sonority, but an entire passage $a5$ is rare. Another alternative to four-part writing is a reduced texture in three parts. It is found in many works, most often in the opening free sections. Two-part writing is much less common; an entire passage $a2$ is extremely rare. Scalar passagework, runs, and flourishes $a1$, however, are a frequent feature in these works. An important use of $a1$ texture is the opening flourish.[26] All of the praeludia begin with a texture in less than four parts, usually with a single-line flourish in the manual part or rarely a pedal solo. On occasion it becomes a double flourish when another, usually imitative, part is added to it. The material of the flourish is sometimes extraneous to the main thematic material of the opening section, and at times is incorporated into the first section in various ways.[27]

The various textural sections of the praeludium can be grouped in a hierarchical manner even though the principle of alternating textures would suggest a nonhierarchical form. Indeed, the form of the praeludium is not a single-level phenomenon. The relative stability of the opening free section and the first fugal section vis à vis the variability of those sections which follow suggests that the sections can be grouped into three parts:[28]

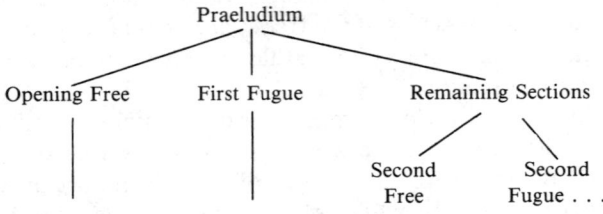

Further, the free endings which close most of the fugal sections can be added to the schema:

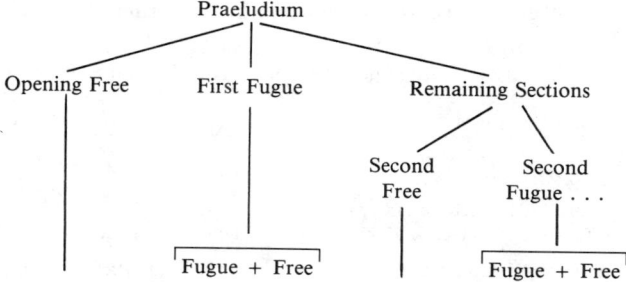

Both the nature and the clarity of the structure depend in large part on the joints between the sections. Strong, stable, well-prepared tonic cadences create the strongest demarcations between the sections.[29] These are most often found at the ends of the opening free section and the first fugue, and, of course, at the end of the last section. In a form with so many sectional divisions, the cadences must be given different amounts of weight to avoid too great an effect of starting and stopping between each section (which would give the effect of an undifferentiated string of sections). There are many ways to downgrade the force of such cadences and preserve forward momentum. The note value of the cadence chord need not be a stable whole or half note, but can be reduced to a quarter or even an eighth. Another way to weaken the arrival is the feminine cadence, although it is not frequently used. Cadences on chords other than the tonic, however, are very often found, particularly between the remaining sections. So, too, are sectional transitions which involve harmonic dissociation. Sectional divisions can be blurred simply by halting a textural section, without a real cadence, and beginning a new section in a kind of run-on effect.[30] Sections are frequently overlapped, though usually only to a slight degree. This effect is usually associated with the joining of a fugue and its free ending; it is also associated with the carry-over of thematic material.[31] Actual textural modulation is quite rare. The most impressive example occurs in the Praeludium in g, BuxWV 149, between the second fugue and the beginning of the closing free section.[32] A change of texture which is articulated by an interruption rather than an actual cadence is another effect which is sometimes used to join a fugue and its free ending. Paradoxically, such a dramatic heightening softens the joint between the sections because of the very strong forward impulse which is created.[33] These expressive, even violent, moments are prime characteristics of Buxtehude's intense musical language.

Table 2. Textural Sections in the Praeludia

Opening Free Section

Key	BuxWV	Opening Free Section	Key	BuxWV	Opening Free Section
C	136	Figural	g	148	Figural/Fugato/Flourish
C	137	Rhapsodic/Imitative/Rhapsodic/Figural	g	149	Ciacona
C	138	Figural/Pedal Point	g	150	Pedal Point (Fugato)
D	139	Figural	A	151	Rhapsodic/Imitative/Chordal
d	140	Figural			
E	141	Rhapsodic/Figural	a	152	Rhapsodic/Figural
e	142	Figural	a	153	Figural/Pedal Point
e	143	Pedal Point/Fugato/Ostinato	B♭	154	Rhapsodic/Imitative/Rhapsodic (Fragment)
F	144	Figural	d	155	Figural/Overlegato/Pedal Point/Fugato
F	145	Figural/12/8 Ostinato Pedal Point	F	156	Figural/12/8 Broken Chords/Pedal Point
f#	146	Pedal Point/Chordal/Pedal Point	F	157	Rhapsodic/Figural
G	147	Rhapsodic/Imitative/Rhapsodic/Figural	a	158	Figural

(Table 2 continued)

First Fugue

Key	BuxWV	Fugue		Free Ending
C	136	Common-Time		Chordal-Figural
C	137	"	"	Modular
C	138	"	"	Modular/Rhapsodic (end)
D	139	"	"	Modular/Ostinato
d	140	"	"	Rhapsodic
E	141	"	"	Rhapsodic
e	142	"	"	Short Extension
e	143	"	"	Modular
F	144	"	" (end)	
F	145	"	"	Rhapsodic (end)
f#	146	"	"	Modular
G	147	"	"	Rhapsodic (end)
g	148	"	"	Chordal
g	149	"	"	Chordal
g	150	"	"	. . . . .
A	151	"	"	Chordal
a	152	"	"	. . . . .
a	153	"	"	Rhapsodic
d	155	"	"	Overlegato/Figural
F	156	"	"	Figural/Overlegato
F	157	"	"	Modular (end)
a	158	"	"	Short Extension

(Table 2 continued)

Remaining Sections

Key	BuxWV	Second Free Section	Second Fugue	Free Ending
C	136	. . . .	Fugato	Canon/Ostinato
C	137	Figural	. . . . . .	. . . . . .
D	139	Chordal	. . . . . .	. . . . . .
d	140	Chordal-Rhapsodic	Imitative	Rhapsodic
E	141	Chordal-Rhapsodic	Fugato	Rhapsodic
e	142	. . . .	3/2	Short Extension
e	143	. . . .	3/4	Extension
f#	146	. . . .	Common-Time	Modular
g	148	. . . .	3/2	Extension
g	149	Basso Continuo Style/Modular	3/2	Short Extension (Textural Modulation)
g	150	Chordal	Fugato	Modular
A	151	. . . .	Common-Time (end)	
a	152	. . . .	3/2	Figural (end)
a	153	. . . .	6/4	. . . . . .
d	155	Chordal	3/4	Sequential/Chordal
F	156	Rhapsodic/Imitative/Pedal Points	Common-Time	Flourish
a	158	. . . .	6/4	Extension/Figural (end)

(*Table 2 continued*)

Key	BuxWV	Third Free Section	Third Fugue	Free Ending
C	136	. . . .	Gigue	Extension (end)
C	137	Ciacona/Extension (end)		
D	139	Closing Free Section (end)		
d	140	. . . .	3/4	Modular
E	141	. . . .	Gigue Fugato	Extension
e	142	Chordal	Gigue	Extension (end)
e	143	Closing Free Section (end)		
f#	146	Chordal-Rhapsodic	. . . . .	. . . . .
g	148	Ciacona (end)		
g	149	Closing Free Section (end)		
g	150	. . . .	3/2	Extension (end)
a	153	Closing Free Section (end)		
d	155	Closing Free Section (end)		
F	156	Closing Free Section (end)		

Key	BuxWV	Fourth Free Section	Fourth Fugue	Free Ending
d	140	Closing Free Section (end)		
E	141	Chordal	Common-Time	Modular (end)
f#	146	Closing Free Section (end)		

Historical and Critical Evaluation

Several peculiarities of the kinds of textures used in Buxtehude's praeludia can be explained on historical grounds. These works pointedly avoid the textures which are characteristic of the organ music of the preceding generation of north German organists. The north German repertory of the early seventeenth century is best typified by the works of Heinrich Scheidemann (ca. 1595-1663), who, from 1629 until his death, was the organist at the Katharinenkirche in Hamburg.[34] Scheidemann's relaxed and spacious style consists of simple yet refined harmonies and smooth, flexible figures. Quarter-note chords either stand unembellished or have an overlay of flowing eighth-note figurations. Sixteenth notes are relatively rare. Sequences, however, are frequently used, sometimes to the point of exaggeration. These textural characteristics are largely missing from Buxtehude's praeludia. Only a very few passages evoke that "scheidemannische Lieblichkeit" of which Mattheson wrote,[35] and those that do have a distinctly archaic character.[36]

An important link between the Scheidemann tradition and Buxtehude are the works of his immediate predecessor at the Marienkirche in Lübeck, Franz Tunder (1614-67).[37] The imitative sections of Tunder's praeludia stand close to Scheidemann; and, like Scheidemann's most progressive works, Tunder's fugal sections are truly fugal and not just imitative. They are still, like most of Scheidemann's, stodgy in comparison to the music of the next generation. The free sections, however, reveal a much bolder, impassioned style than Scheidemann ever achieved in his free organ works. They also have new textural devices, including the flourish opening. The last sections provide some important examples of modular construction, as well as the pedal points and subdominant harmony which are typical of Buxtehude's closing free sections. What is perhaps Tunder's most impressive passage in his praeludia, the opening of a fragmentary Praeludium in g,[38] resembles very closely the dynamic music of Buxtehude.

Buxtehude's figural style is more intense and rigorous than that of Scheidemann or Tunder, and can even seem cramped by comparison. ("Lieblichkeit" was hardly Buxtehude's aesthetic goal.) His figurations rely almost exclusively upon sixteenth notes and faster harmonic rhythms, and upon a richer harmonic language—all of which evoke the Italianate sound of Frescobaldi and Frescobaldi's pupil, Froberger. Neither of these composers, of course, was active in north Germany. While it seems certain that Buxtehude had access to at least some of their works, their influence may have come indirectly as well, through Matthias Weckmann (1619-74).[39] A member of Froberger's circle,[40] Weckmann was acquainted with Scheidemann and was himself the organist of the Jacobikirche in Hamburg from

1655 until his death.[41] Many textural characteristics of his music anticipate those of Buxtehude (Apel notes the long fugal subjects in sixteenth notes and the dramatic use of rests.)[42] The "recitative-like exclamations"[43] of the Toccata in e,[44] as well as the sudden, dramatic disruptions with which they are associated, can also be mentioned.[45] There is even evidence of direct modeling relationships: the rather peculiar passage in the Praeludium in D, BuxWV 139, mm. 70–86, for example, was clearly inspired by a similar passage by Weckmann.[46]

The form of Buxtehude's praeludia derives from two main sources: the north German praeambulum as developed by Scheidemann and Tunder (Tunder used the term "praeludium" instead), and the toccata and canzona of Frescobaldi and Froberger. Both of these traditions were cultivated by Weckmann.[47]

The fourteen praeambula of Scheidemann are generally works of modest proportions (from about thirty measures in common time upwards to sixty; only a few approach or exceed one hundred measures). They are cast in a simple, three-part form which consists of an opening free section, followed by either an imitative section or a fugal one (or both), and finally closing free material.[48] The Praeambulum in d, WV 36,[49] can serve as an example:

Scheidemann: Praeambulum in d, WV 36

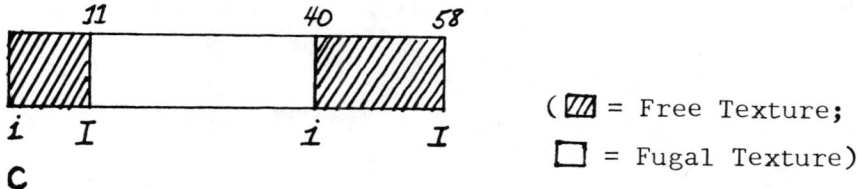

Tunder's four surviving praeludia[50] all resemble Scheidemann's Praeambulum in d in form and clarity of formal articulation:

Tunder: Praeludium in F[51]

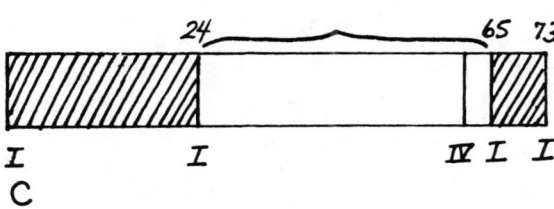

22   Texture

Praeludium in g[52]

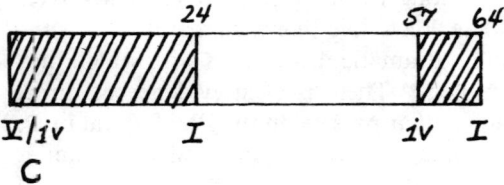

Praeludium in g[53]

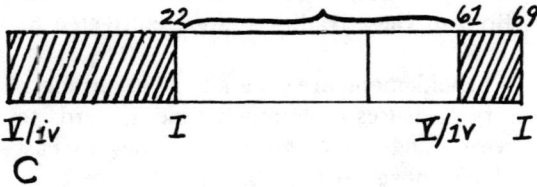

Praeludium in g[54]

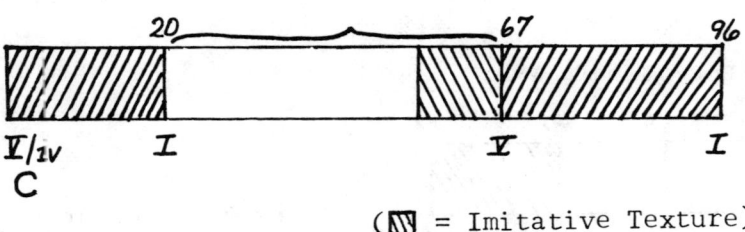

(▨ = Imitative Texture)

A larger, more ambitious opening free section, however, is typical of Tunder's works. Another important innovation made by Tunder is the clarification of the hierarchical organization of the sections. The first formal articulation (between the opening free section and the fugue) is consistently made the primary one of the work; the second formal articulation (between the fugue and the closing free section) is less forceful:

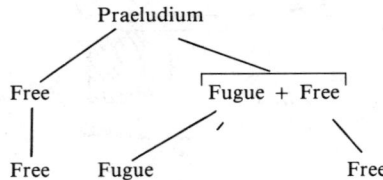

Three large organ works of Matthias Weckmann survive: a Fantasia, a Fuga, and a Praeambulum, all in d:[55]

Weckmann: Fantasia in d

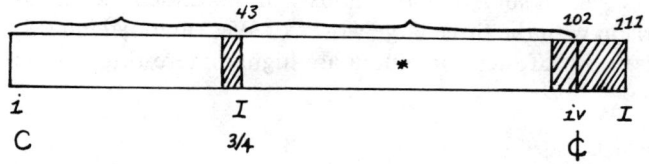

(* = Subject Derived From Previous One)

Fuga in d

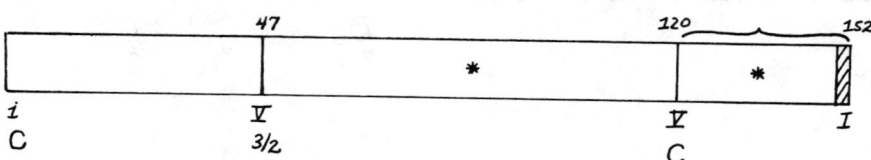

Praeambulum in d

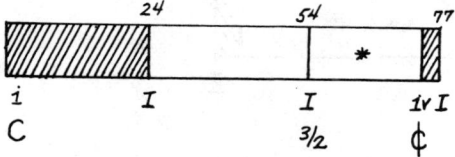

All three of these works demonstrate a synthesis of elements from both the traditional north German praeambulum/praeludium and the Italian/south German toccata and canzona. As such they are crucial precedents for Buxtehude's praeludia. Of the three works, the Fuga stands closest to the southern style. It is a large-scale canzona,[56] but is unambiguously for organ.[57] The Fantasia incorporates a Tunderian closing free section into the canzona scheme. Its prominent use of free endings derives from Frescobaldi and Froberger; they are here handled with greater clarity than in any other north German predecessor of Buxtehude. As its title suggests, the Praeambulum stands closest of all to the north German style. It has a large opening free section and a closing free passage. Yet unlike Tunder's works, it has a second fugal section in triple time with a subject derived from the first one as is typical of the toccata and especially the canzona.[58] The balance between free and fugue in the praeambulum is typical of Tunder, as are the clarity of the sectional divisions and the rudiments of a hierarchical organization of the sections.[59]

Two other works (which survive anonymously in the Lüneburg Tablatures) stand comparison with the three large works of Weckmann;[60] indeed, they may well be his. Both of these praeludia are highly interesting works:

Anonymous: Praeludium in G

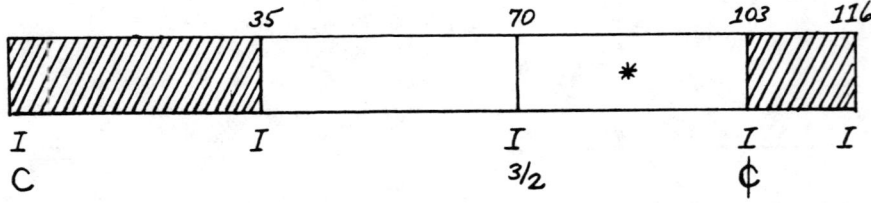

Praeludium in F

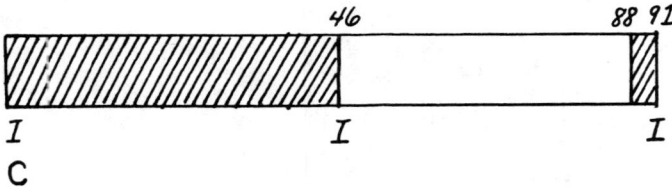

The Praeludium in G[61] is significantly larger than either Weckmann's Praeambulum or any of Tunder's praeludia, but is comparable in size to Weckmann's Fantasia or Fuga. Yet it is cast in essentially the same form as Weckmann's Praeambulum with a closing free section as extensive as that noted in his Fantasia. The Praeludium in F[62] is a more modest work midway between Weckmann's Praeambulum and Tunder's praeludia. Its extremely large opening free section—more expansive than that of Weckmann's Praeambulum, which it closely resembles, and almost twice the size of Tunder's opening free sections—suggests a balance between free and fugue with the emphasis on free textures. This tendency can also be observed in some of Buxtehude's praeludia, but realized within a somewhat different formal scheme.

Weckmann also composed in the style of Froberger. In spite of the fact that these works (five canzonas and six toccatas) were probably intended for harpsichord (they have no pedal parts), their influence on Buxtehude's style is enormous. Their form is much more fluid than that of the preambulum/praeludium, even though it, too, depends on the alternation of free and fugal textures. The alternation procedure, however, is less architectural, more improvisational, and certainly more dramatic. In comparison to the north German tradition, the toccata lacks a real clarity of form, at least in the hands of Weckmann. He exaggerates the contrasts found in Froberger; and while Weckmann may demonstrate a "dreamy, romantic expression,"[63] his toccatas completely lack Froberger's overrefined elegance. Indeed, Weckmann's toccatas can even seem crude by comparison. Yet Buxtehude must have regarded Weckmann's works as some of the most provocative, if not polished, keyboard music he knew; and he learned much from them. A comparison of Weckmann's Toccata in d[64] — and its transition from a sequential passage to a chordal one and, finally, to a closing rhapsodic flourish — with the similar flow of textures in the free sections after the fugue in the Praeludium in D, BuxWV 139, shows just how much Buxtehude owed to Weckmann's (and Froberger's) more flexible way of linking textural sections.[65] And certainly the dramatic gestures found in the Toccata in a[66] (especially the abrupt breaking-off of the upward rush of sixteenth notes for a sudden change of texture), must have captured Buxtehude's imagination. By comparison they make the dramatic gestures of Tunder seem formal and wooden. The Buxtehude praeludia achieve their distinctive mark by combining the extremely improvisatory toccata, with its almost ad hoc form and multiplicity of sections, with the more rigid and formalistic praeambulum (or praeludium). They are not just toccatas in the Froberger style. Rather, they preserve the architectural grandeur of the old praeambulum while transforming it and making it more subtle by crossing it with the newer Italian style.

Several works demonstrate Buxtehude's search for this ideal. The Praeambulum in a, BuxWV 158 — the only praeludium which preserves this archaic title — is an example:

Praeambulum in a, BuxWV 158

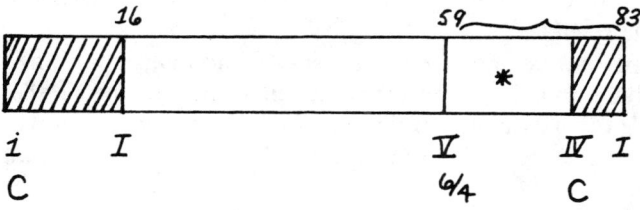

It has a modern, rigorously figural opening free section (though a rather expressionless one in comparison with some of his other works), and old-fashioned fugues: the first, with its plodding quarter-note subject, is reminiscent of Scheidemann and Tunder;[67] the second, in 6/4 time with its subject an obvious derivation of the first, follows the practice of Weckmann. Buxtehude's subject in flowing eighth notes, however, is an advance over Weckmann's halves or quarters in such fugues.

The Praeludium in a, BuxWV 152, is a similar piece: it is the only praeludium of Buxtehude with a strongly modal harmonic language (phrygian), which in itself would indicate an early origin. The form of the Praeambulum in a is followed quite closely:

Praeludium in a, BuxWV 152

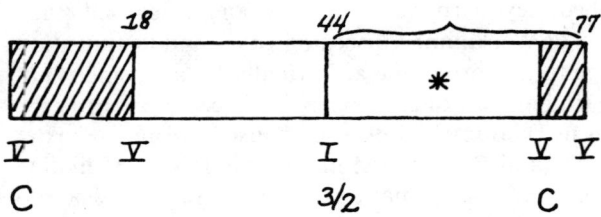

Several aspects of this work, besides its more modern title, indicate a later origin than that of the Praeambulum in a. The opening free section is longer and much more impressive, the first fugue longer and livelier. The free ending of the second fugue, while exactly the same length as that of the Praeambulum in a (six measures), is considerably more flamboyant, with bolder, less routine figures. The penultimate measures are especially revealing: the quarter-note motion of the Preambulum seems stark indeed set against that of the Praeludium.[68]

Few other praeludia are so clearly transitional; most are mature examples of the genre.[69] Yet the form of these works varies widely; each praeludium gives a more or less individual interpretation. However, there are several formal considerations which span the entire corpus, and which invite critical evaluation. Chief among these are the balance of the sections and the clarity of the form.

The balance between free and fugal sections can find many solutions. Certain works exhibit particular, even extreme, tendencies in one or the other direction, while others seem carefully balanced. A few works consist of predominantly free textures. The Praeludium in D, BuxWV 139, can serve as an example:

Praeludium in D, BuxWV 139

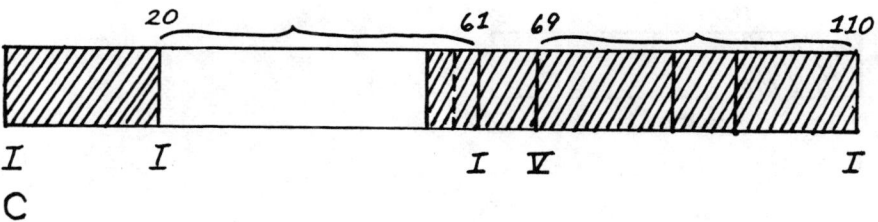

The single fugue coupled with an extensive free close gives this work its particular tilt in the direction of free textures. This tendency can be seen in details as well: the fugue ends with an elaborate free ending. Beginning in measure 70 is an example of a free passage (a sequential texture strongly influenced by modular construction) which appears in a context where a fugato (also modular in construction) might have been expected.

Some praeludia strain the form in the direction of fugal saturation. The Praeludium in g, BuxWV 150, for example, has very little free texture at all:

Praeludium in g, BuxWV 150

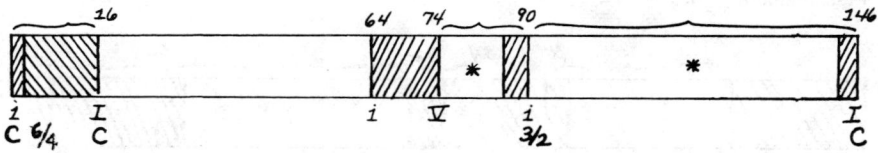

Fugue even invades the opening free section, which is a unique example of an entirely imitative opening section (over a pedal point).

Several works seem quintessentially balanced. This is perhaps easiest to perceive in those which have only one fugal section. The pair of Praeludia in F, BuxWV 144 and 145, provide an interesting comparison. Both seem carefully balanced, though the first is a miniature, and the second is one of the largest of the praeludia. Note how the size of the parts increases proportionally:

28   Texture

Praeludium in F, BuxWV 144

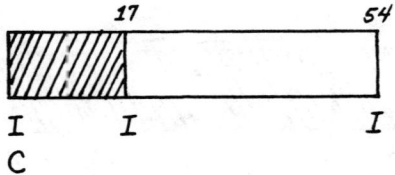

Praeludium in F, BuxWV 145

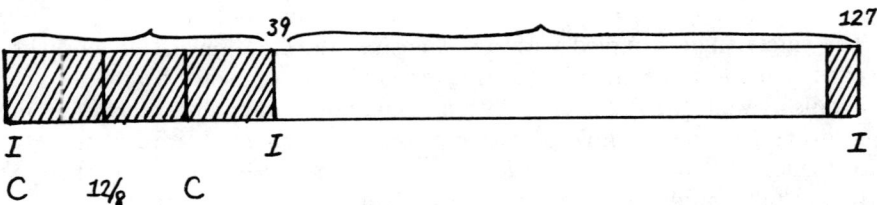

Some works have a multitude of free and fugal sections which likewise demonstrate a careful balance. The Praeludium in d, BuxWV 140, is an example:

Praeludium in d, BuxWV 140

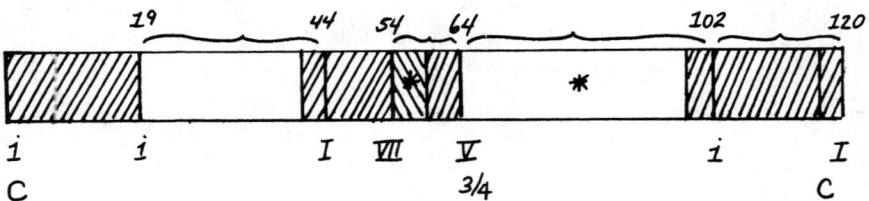

There is also another spectrum, one between works which balance several large sections and those which balance a multiplicity of smaller ones. Works such as the Praeludium in e, BuxWV 142, the Praeludium in F, BuxWV 145, the Praeludium in g, BuxWV 149, and the Toccata in F, BuxWV 157, are all poised, grandiose compositions, with large but relatively few sections. A balance can also be achieved through the juxtaposition of many smaller sections, with no one section outweighing the others.

The Toccata in F, BuxWV 156, is the most jumbled and capricious in form of any of the praeludia:[70]

Toccata in F, BuxWV 156

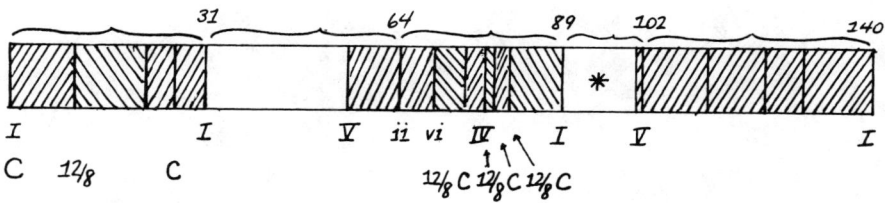

The clarity of the form also varies considerably. Some of the works stress clear articulation of form, with a correspondingly clear hierarchical grouping of the sections.[71] Other praeludia are less clear sectionally. The Praeludium in d, BuxWV 140, is a work which particularly exploits blurred formal articulations.[72]

The function of texture in the praeludia, then, is one of alternation and juxtaposition; the chief role of the free and fugal sections is to contrast. Yet, the textures can also be considered to be progressing. Their function, like that of harmonic function, is one of implication and resolution within the expectations of the style. The logic of this progression, however, is not entirely a matter of texture: there is the intertwined aspect of harmonic form, and ultimately the question of expression. How aspects of texture relate to expression, and how the ultimate logic of textural progressions can be linked to it, will be considered in detail in chapter 5.

2
Harmony

Harmonic Styles

The harmony of the Buxtehude praeludia has received far less attention from scholars than has the texture of these works.[1] Several aspects of Buxtehude's harmonic language have been pointed out: Apel has noted the use of the subdominant in the closing portions of the works;[2] Powell has discussed influences of modality;[3] and recently Shannon has written about tonal orientation:

> By the late seventeenth century tonal harmony is the conditioning factor of keyboard figuration. Such sections can be reduced to strong, chordal progressions against which the figurative patterns move.[4]

The peculiarities of Buxtehude's use of harmony need to be more thoroughly investigated before a comprehensive view of his praeludia can be attained.

The harmonic language of the praeludia consists almost entirely of the diatonic chords of the key in which they are written and their secondary dominants. Occasionally secondary subdominants are used as well, although this is unusual. Any move farther outside the tonality is very rare. As the chords of the key itself constitute the bulk of the harmonies employed, the expressive weight of the harmony—that which is especially rich and full of tension—falls on the secondary dominants. This is true not only because the secondary dominants introduce tones outside the scale of the key, but also because they are often seventh chords. The secondary dominants are also the usual source of chromaticism in these works.[5]

The praeludia lie almost exclusively within the major/minor tonal scheme; only the Praeludium in a, BuxWV 152, has a strongly modal character (phrygian). However, occasional details in other praeludia suggest modal influence.[6] The use of the sharped fourth degree as a cadential decoration is one such case.[7] It is a coloristic device which embellishes the

32   Harmony

cadence chord itself, $\substack{6-5-\#4-5 \\ 1\text{-}\text{-}\text{-}\text{-}\text{-}\text{-}}$ or $\substack{4-\#4-5-(6-5) \\ 1\text{-}\text{-}\text{-}\text{-}\text{-}\text{-}\text{-}\text{-}\text{-}\text{-}}$, and is found in six of the praeludia.[8] When it is used at the cadence of the opening free section, it emphasizes the starting note of the coming fugue subject (5), and/or prefigures the subject in some way.[9] A particularly ingenious use of this cadential decoration occurs in the Praeludium in E, BuxWV 141, where the sharped fourth of the cadence ending the first fugal section is made motivic at the beginning of the following free section, effecting a tonicization of the dominant:

Praeludium in E, BuxWV 141

A variety of harmonic styles appear in the praeludia. These range from those which rarely proceed beyond the chords of the key at hand to those which feature secondary dominants and tonicizations. The pace at which the harmonies change also varies, as does the relative regularity of such change. However, central to the understanding of these harmonic styles is the way in which they establish harmonic areas. The harmonies of these works, as in all tonal music, are organized into a hierarchical structure which reaches from the musical foreground into the background. The progressive reduction of detail from level to level reveals deeper and deeper structures. This process can be observed at the foreground level when various harmonies are grouped around a central harmony to form a harmonic area.[10] The other harmonies of the area elaborate this basic harmony, beginning the hierarchical organization of the music. Not surprisingly, these harmonic styles are intimately associated with textural styles, and—in the praeludia—can best be understood in relation to them.

The simplest kinds of harmonic areas in the praeludia are found in free textures in a slow harmonic rhythm. Perhaps the simplest of all is the pedal point. While pedal points by definition support various harmonies, it is equally clear that they actually support only one basic harmony—that for which the pedal point note is the root. The other harmonies over the pedal point play a decorative role; in various ways, they prolong the basic harmony.

Pedal points are especially useful at cadences, both to prepare the arrival (the dominant pedal), and to discharge energy after the arrival (the tonic pedal). In the following example of a dominant pedal point, more than one harmony occurs over the sustained note, even though it is only two measures long:[11]

Praeludium in C, BuxWV 136

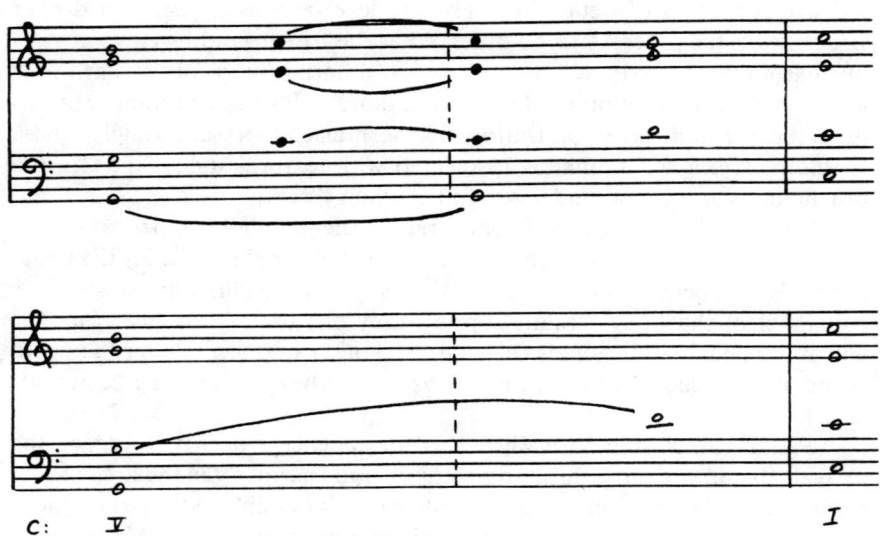

Progressive reduction of the content reveals that the G-major harmony is prolonged through a $^6_4$ chord elaboration (a double neighbor note): $^{3--4--3}_{5--6--5}$. This simple way to create a pedal is the structural basis of all the dominant pedals.[12] This gesture implies a move to the tonic, but in $^6_4$ position, which invalidates it as an arrival. The music must then return to the dominant, from which a proper arrival on the tonic can be effected (thus its appropriateness for the creation of tension just before a cadence).

Tonic pedals also prolong a single harmony, but not in anticipation of another harmony. Their function is to diffuse energy after the cadence has occurred, rather than to build tension towards a release. The diffusion of energy usually involves a change in register of the chord of the basic harmony. While such a change of register of the basic harmony can be found in several dominant pedals,[13] it is not their fundamental aspect. The manipulation of register, however, is an important part of the tonic pedal as it is one way that the energy is actually dissipated:

Praeludium in F, BuxWV 145

The structural line of the passage, beginning in measure 123, is c″–bb′ (initially displaced by bb″)–ab′–g′–f′. The f′ arrives with the tonic cadence at measure 126, and structurally the composition could have ended at this arrival. Over the tonic pedal which follows, however, a flourish tosses f′ up an octave to f″, which discharges energy.[14]

The most impressive tonic pedals are those in which the pedal point is approached from the subdominant rather than the dominant, and the entrance of the tonic pedal is made a dramatic event. The last passage of the Toccata in d, BuxWV 155, is an example:[15]

Toccata in d, BuxWV 155

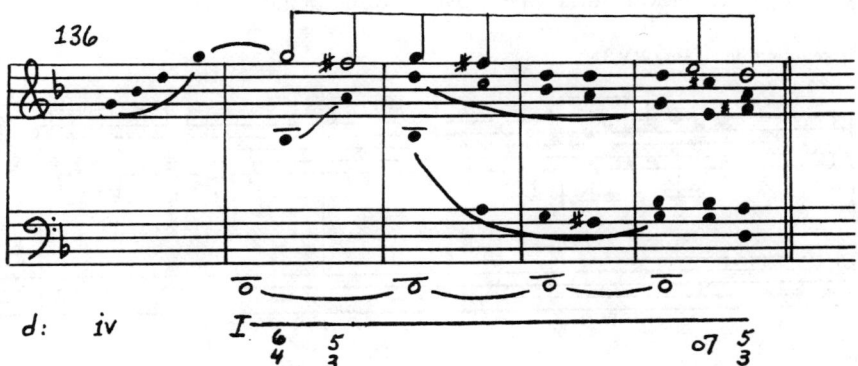

36   Harmony

A large area of subdominant harmony (measures 129-36) precedes the tonic pedal, and an extreme range is attained in the soprano (g″) before the tonic pedal enters. When it does enter, however, it is a powerfully dramatic gesture (not only because g″ and D are separated to the greatest degree possible for G and D on the organ, but because the entrance of the pedal alone articulates the harmonic change to the tonic). The entrance of the tonic pedal and the tonic (plagal) cadence are not simultaneous at the foreground level; this is the structural basis for the dramatic effect associated with this type of pedal. Since the moment of entry of the pedal point is in fact no cadence at all (at the foreground level), a cadence (or several) needs to occur later over the pedal. In this example, a vii°–I cadence (measure 140) is coordinated with the arrival of the final note of the soprano line, d″, which has fallen over the course of the pedal point from the g″ with which it began.[16]

Another important use of the tonic pedal is associated with the beginning of the work, rather than with its final cadence. In several of the praeludia, the opening section includes a tonic pedal point.[17] The pedal may be of relatively modest proportions, supporting figural texture, or arpeggiations. Larger pedals, which may dominate virtually the entire section, support imitative passages. Pedal points which are at the beginning of a praeludium obviously are not the resolution of a cadence nor do they diffuse energy. Some of the simpler examples of these pedals do little more than serve as a focus for the organization of figural texture. The large pedals which support imitative passages, however, paradoxically create energy through the conflict between imitation (and the harmonic patterns it implies) and the persistent pedal. Opening tonic pedals appear several measures into the opening free section, after the flourish. One work, however, actually places the flourish itself over a tonic pedal:

Praeludium in d, BuxWV 140

Using this as a model, a similar pedal can be extrapolated underneath the opening flourishes of other works:

Praeludium in e, BuxWV 142

Implied pedal points, such as that illustrated above, are one step in complexity beyond the harmonic area as defined by an actual pedal point; the "pedal point" (or harmonic area) has to be extrapolated from the context. While these flourishes (under an imaginary pedal point) may not in themselves define a harmonic area, they do begin the first harmonic area of the work which is extended by the tonic pedal (if the section employs one). Implied pedal points are also suggested in other kinds of passages, which do define their own harmonic area, such as the subdominant area typically found in closing free sections. Although none of these sections rely on an actual subdominant pedal, the subdominant area can readily be understood as having an implied pedal point:[18]

38   *Harmony*

Praeludium in d, BuxWV 140

Tonicization (the dominant of the subdominant) is employed to expand the content of these subdominant harmonic areas. In the harmonic language of these works, tonicizations are decorative chords. They are rarely structural, that is, established as a harmonic area themselves. However, in their role as decorations of chords of the key, tonicizations are essential in the expansion of content. An implied pedal point can be enriched in the following manner: IV becomes IV–V/IV–IV–V/IV–IV . . ., while a progression of chords of the key can be enriched with tonicizations: III–IV–V–I becomes V/III–III–V/IV–IV–V/V–V–I, resulting in what can be termed a chain of tonicizations. Tonicization chains are the basis for many passages in the free style, and often are found in conjunction with figural texture:

Praeludium in C, BuxWV 136

Such chains can be incorporated into larger passages (as in the Praeludium in C illustrated above where the chain leads to the dominant pedal, which closes the section). They can also be the basis of an entire passage, as in the subdominant areas described above.

Free passages in faster harmonic rhythms, such as modular textures, are not generally associated with actual pedals or chains of tonicizations. Modular textures are more tightly organized than rhapsodic or figural music, and their harmonic areas reflect this greater degree of textural coherence: they are more bland than those based on tonicization chains, but they are also more stable. Modular textures are based upon simple progressions which define a harmonic area. These progressions are usually chords of the key rather than tonicization chains. The progression is then repeated several or numerous times, extending the harmonic area. The simplest modular textures are synonymous with some of the implied pedals discussed above.[19] With a genuine progression, however, the passage can no longer be considered an implied pedal point. A passage with numerous repetitions becomes a ciacona. In the most elaborate modular textures, the progression may appear in more than one key.

Fugal sections are even more tightly organized than modular textures, and the analysis of their harmonic areas is inseparable from that of their fugal form. The alternation of subject and answer produces either a large tonic area (if the subject does not modulate) or an oscillation between tonic and dominant harmonies (if the subject does modulate).[20] The actual progressions which comprise the harmonic areas are as simple or as complex as the harmonization of the subject demands. A diatonic subject (by far the most common) will have a simple progression; a chromatic subject (which is unusual) will have a rich, complex one. After the exposition, fugal sections often continue with more expositions and other added entries in the original key. Episodes are rare. Thus an entire fugal section can be in a tonic harmonic area, or exhibit only an oscillation between tonic and dominant areas.[21] An actual exposition outside the tonic (rather than just one or two entries) is found far less frequently; the mediant is the most likely choice.[22] In this way, harmonic areas other than the tonic or dominant are introduced into fugal sections.

Harmony not only exhibits hierarchical structures within sections, but also plays a major role in creating the sections themselves through cadences. Well-prepared tonic cadences create the strongest sectional articulations; their force penetrates deepest into the background of the work and farthest in the hierarchical organization. Nontonic cadences, no matter how strong their preparation, have less sense of resolution and stronger forward momentum.

The boundary between the opening free section and the first fugal section is always a tonic cadence, though the cadence chord itself may vary from a strongly prepared, whole-note arrival to an eighth note which implies an *attacca* continuation:

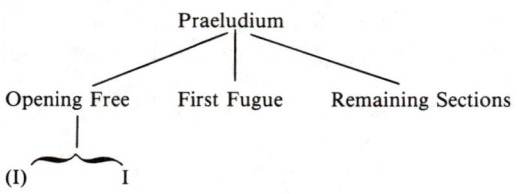

Harmony   41

The cadence between the first fugal section and the following free or fugal section is usually a tonic cadence:[23]

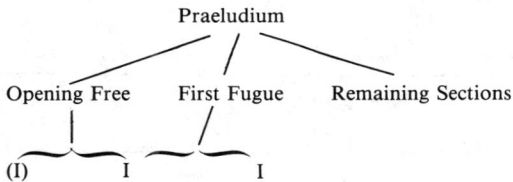

The remainder of the sections which follow may end with either tonic or dominant cadences (or, rarely, with subdominant or subtonic ones), except for the final cadence, which is always tonic. Thus in the archetypal scheme of these works, the sections after the first fugue are tied together more closely than the first to the second, or the second to the third. The result is the three-part form of the opening free section, first fugue, and the remaining sections:

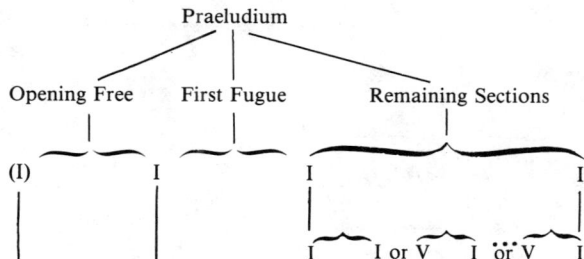

Some works, such as the Praeludium in C, BuxWV 137, use tonic cadences exclusively at sectional divisions:[24]

Praeludium in C, BuxWV 137

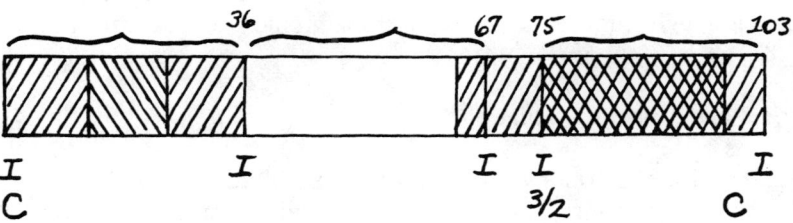

Other works, such as the Praeludium in C, BuxWV 136, use a dominant cadence once after the first fugue:[25]

Praeludium in C, BuxWV 136

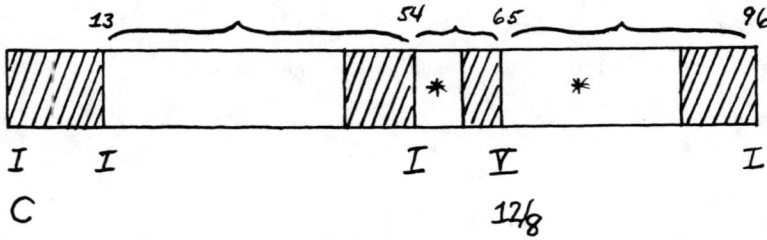

The Praeludium in e, BuxWV 142, uses two dominant cadences:

Praeludium in e, BuxWV 142

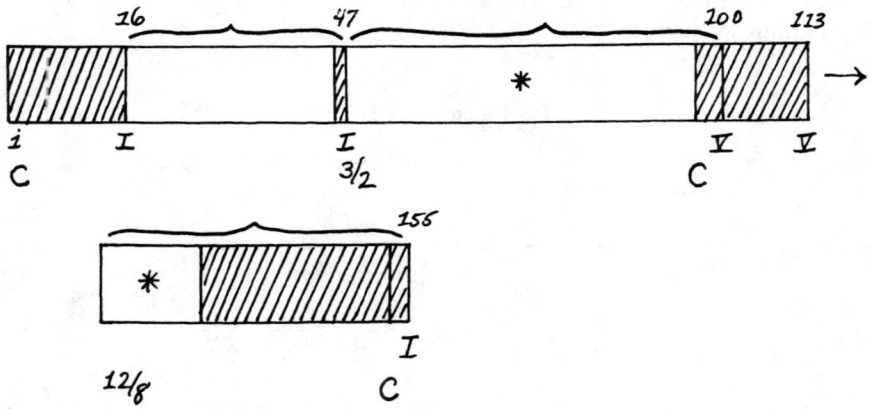

The Praeludium in d, BuxWV 140, can serve as an example of those praeludia with more unusual schemes. This work uses two nontonic cadences, one of which is a highly unusual cadence on the subtonic (see the illustration on page 28).

Historical and Critical Evaluation

Buxtehude's use of harmony can be illuminated by that of his immediate predecessors in north Germany. While the influence of modality is strongly felt in the works of Scheidemann, in the praeambula and praeludia of Tunder and Weckmann the tonal cogency of the harmony is much more pronounced.[26] These two composers also enriched the harmonic language of north German organ music, especially in the music of the free sections. It is especially the opening free sections of Tunder's praeludia that show him reaching out for a richer harmonic style. However, the harmony rarely goes much beyond an emphasis on the dominant of the subdominant or the dominant of the dominant.[27] Weckmann went further in his Praeambulum in d.[28] It also stresses the subdominant at the beginning, but has large tonicizations of the mediant and the dominant as well. In the opening free section of the anonymous Praeludium in F,[29] which is very similar to Weckmann's Praeambulum, the harmonies are even richer, reaching $V^{\flat 6-5}_{4-3}/V$; a large arrival on the dominant of the mediant also occurs. Buxtehude, taking advantage of this increased tonal cogency, enriched the harmonic language of north German organ music even more. For this he drew upon the toccata tradition of Froberger which Weckmann also cultivated. From these works come the large role played by secondary dominants and chains of tonicizations in his praeludia.[30] However, the use of secondary dominants (as a rule rather than as an exception) is his own innovation. Also new is his frequent use of seventh chords. Indeed, it is the rich sound of secondary dominants, which themselves usually appear as seventh chords (often in Buxtehude's favorite $^6_5$ position), that most noticeably distinguishes his music harmonically from that of his predecessors. As was true of Weckmann and Tunder, this increased harmonic richness comes primarily in the free sections. With Buxtehude, however, this trend leads to genuinely different harmonic styles for the free and fugal sections.

The various techniques of prolongation found in Buxtehude's praeludia derive from both the praeludium and the toccata traditions.[31] Works by Tunder and Weckmann in the praeludium tradition always end with a free section, and it is here that pedal points are generally employed.[32] Moreover, the closing tonic pedal is usually preceded by an even larger subdominant pedal. Buxtehude preserved and expanded the role of the closing tonic pedal and the traditionally large role for the subdominant, but eliminated the actual subdominant pedal in favor of an implied pedal point. These passages are often modular in texture. For this, too, there are precedents in the praeludium repertory: in several works subdominant pedals are preceded by modular textures which circle around the subdominant.[33] The implied subdominant pedal of Tunder's Praeludium in g can be compared with the analogous passage in Buxtehude's Praeludium in d, BuxWV 140.[34] None of these earlier works, however, employ the dramatic use of a suspension of which Buxtehude was so fond: IV (implied pedal point)–I^{6-5}_{4-3} (pedal point).[35]

The opening free sections of Buxtehude's praeludia also show the influence of the north German praeludium. The opening flourish, which is the standard way for Buxtehude to begin a praeludium, is directly traceable to Tunder's works. The toccatas of Weckmann and Froberger also have a traditional opening gesture: the sustained and, by implication, rolled tonic chord. This kind of opening is not employed in the Buxtehude praeludia with pedal parts, but significantly, it can be found in one of his keyboard works without pedal.[36] Thus to begin his organ works, Buxtehude follows the more specifically organistic tradition of the praeludium with its rhetorical shape of a flourish leading to a strong tonic chord (or even a cadence). The use of pedal points in the beginning section of his works can also be traced to earlier praeludia, but none of his predecessors employed them as boldly as Buxtehude did.[37] Most of the praeludia, however, do not proceed after the opening flourish to pedal points. The figural style, with its secondary dominants and chains of tonicizations, generally follows the flourish, and this style of prolongation comes from the toccata.

The role of harmony in the sectional articulation of the works derives from both the preambula/praeludia (of Scheidemann, Tunder, and Weckmann) and the toccatas (of Weckmann as well), for both these forms are multisectional. Scheidemann's praeambula generally exhibit a three-part form. The opening free section may end on the tonic or dominant,[38] or simply evade a cadential articulation. Scheidemann usually does not provide a clear cadence to mark the end of the second section; when there is one, it is usually a tonic cadence.[39] Harmonic articulation in his praeambula can be summarized as:

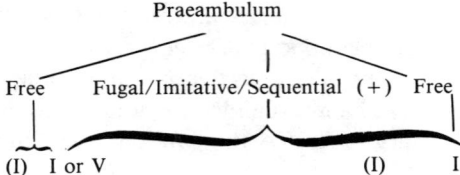

Tunder established the tonic cadence as *de rigueur* to end the opening free section but avoided that kind of cadence at the end of the fugal section: all the second sections of his praeludia end with cadences on the subdominant or the dominant of the subdominant.[40] His works demonstrate the following form:

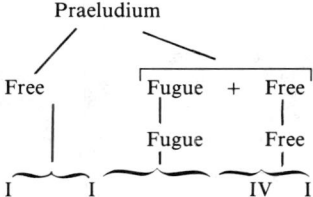

Weckmann's organ works (the Praeambulum, Fantasia, and Fuga) present a more varied picture. In each, more than one fugal section is included.[41] Of the three, the Praeambulum stands closest to Tunder; the other two lack opening free sections, and the Fuga does not have the strongly subdominant ending typical of Tunder's praeludia and Weckmann's Fantasia and Praeambulum. The dominant cadences at the end of two fugal sections in the Fuga, however, are strongly suggestive of Buxtehude's practice. Such cadences cannot be found in the two anonymous praeludia from the Lüneburg Tablatures. While the Praeludium in G has two fugues like Weckmann's authenticated works, the Praeludium in F has only one.[42]

While Weckmann's three organ works incorporate elements of both the north German praeludium and the Italian/south German toccata and canzona,[43] his six toccatas for harpsichord are unambiguously in the second category. They are also far more irregular in form: only one, the Toccata in e,[44] emphasizes clear sectional articulations with tonic cadences at each important textural change:

Weckmann: Toccata in e

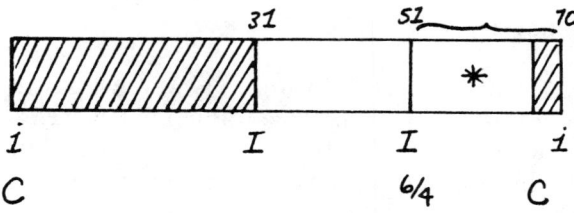

The others frequently evade clear cadential articulations at sectional divisions, a technique which helps create their fantasylike character.

The harmonic shape of Buxtehude's praeludia,

Harmony

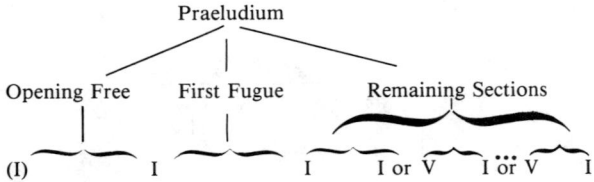

owes much to both Tunder and Weckmann. From Tunder came the tonic pillar which closes the opening free section, and from Weckmann the use of dominant cadences farther along in the form. Buxtehude's reliance on another tonic pillar to end the first fugal section,[45] however, does not derive from either Tunder or Weckmann: Tunder closes the single fugal section of his form on the subdominant; only Weckmann's Praeambulum in d and the anonymous Praeludium in G are predecessors of this procedure. Buxtehude's insistence on this feature stabilized the first fugal section, and gave it a structural status comparable to that of the opening section.[46] Buxtehude reserved the more complex aggregates of textural sections for what follows. After the first fugue, the stability of sections is routinely undermined through nontonic cadences or textural devices. An overall three-part form is created as a result.[47]

The relatively great degree of sectionalization in the praeludia presents special problems for harmonic balance. Since the three main sections of the form each generally begin and end in the tonic, tonal movement away from the tonic can only be short-lived. Rather than one large gesture, the works contain several tonal motions of varying lengths:

>   Opening Free Section: I--- . . . ---I
>   First Fugue: I--- . . . ---I
>   Remaining Sections: I--- . . . ---I

Each praeludium's elaboration of this archetypal form, however, leads to equally individual possibilities for harmonic balance within the scheme.

In spite of the great number of possible solutions to the problem of harmonic balance, several generalizations are possible. Fugal sections, due to their structure, are likely to be tightly organized around a tonic/dominant polarity. Free sections, which are uninhibited by such strict organization of their texture, can circulate more widely through the chords of the key. The only other harmony which regularly asserts its force is the subdominant. It does not usually find a role in fugal sections nor in the opening free section, but is generally reserved for the closing one. This is especially true if the work ends with a closing free section. Thus the archetypal harmonic scheme of the praeludia can be further detailed:

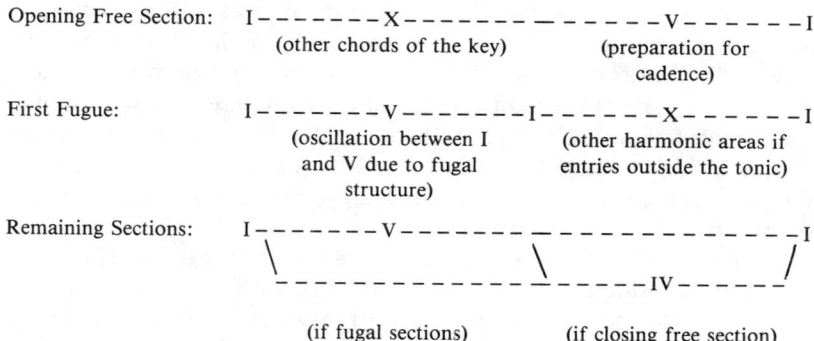

Harmonic balance is perhaps most easily observed in those works in which only a few large sections are juxtaposed. In the Praeludium in F, BuxWV 145, an unusually large and harmonically rich opening free section is balanced by an unusually long (and harmonically bland) fugue with which the work closes. Praeludia in which many smaller sections are juxtaposed have a necessarily more complex scheme. In the Praeludium in E, BuxWV 141, the second fugal section, a fugato, is unusually wide-ranging; the fourth fugal section, which ends the work, includes several entries in the subdominant, as if to compensate for the lack of a closing free section (and its usual emphasis on the subdominant). As there are numerous sectional divisions, several after the first fugue have dominant rather than tonic cadences. Works with a preponderance of free music have the possibility of easily maintaining harmonic richness through most of their duration. One such work, the Praeludium in D, BuxWV 139, presents a typically rich opening free section followed by a fugue which is hardly harmonically reticent. After a short *adagio* chordal passage, a large closing free section begins; the first passage is in modular texture and employs sequential harmonic patterns. The turn towards the subdominant which precedes the final tonic pedal is one of the largest such events in any of the praeludia. A work with a large amount of fugal writing would seem predestined to harmonic poverty. Such a fate can be avoided, however, through the use of special harmonic effects such as a chromatic fugue subject. In the Praeludium in e, BuxWV 142, the second fugal section, placed directly after the first fugue (in a position which is often a harmonically rich free section), is the boldest example of Buxtehude's harmonic daring within fugal structure.

Other works evidence solutions of a more individual character. For example, in the Praeludium in C, BuxWV 137, the submediant plays an unusually important role, and is stressed in several sections of this otherwise rather harmonically bland work. The Praeludium in f♯, BuxWV 146, has a pair of fugues, each stressing different harmonic areas, followed by several free sections. A similar scheme can be found in the Praeludium in a, BuxWV 153. Works in which the first fugue ends with a dominant cadence, and thus alters one of the major pillars of the form, create new possibilities for harmonic balance. The Toccata in F, BuxWV 156, for example, delays a return to the tonic with a large central section (of rhapsodic, imitative, and pedal point textures) which circles through several other keys, notably the submediant and the subdominant.

Harmony in these works, then, is closely tied to texture. The alternation and juxtaposition of textures is coordinated with the harmonic schemes of the works, not only in the placement of important cadences, but also in the juxtaposition of harmonic styles. Like textural schemes, harmonic schemes are not entirely self-sufficient: their logic, even when considered in conjunction with texture, remains somewhat elusive. This is because harmony, like texture, cannot be fully understood apart from expression and the expressive forms embodied in the praeludia. These aspects of harmony will be considered in chapter 5.

3

Rhythm and Meter

Rhythmic and Metrical Styles

Rhythm and meter are two important aspects of the praeludia which, like texture and harmony, help shape these works and articulate their form.[1] Of the two, meter has received more historical and analytical investigation.[2] Rhythm, which is characterized by several styles, has received less attention. These styles can be elucidated according to regularity or irregularity at the rhythmic foreground. Rhythmic regularity is clearly the norm for Buxtehude, and it dominates most of the music of the praeludia. The direct result of constant rhythmic regularity or irregularity at the foreground level is uniformity of rhythmic style. Since rhythmic patterns are closely associated with texture, they are apt to change only when textural sections do; radical changes within a section are not generally found. Even such relatively simple rhythmic variances as the juxtaposition of sixteenths, eighths, and quarters are unusual. Only within rhapsodic sections are such rhythmically irregular passages to be expected.

Rhythm at the foreground level is the duration of individual pitches. Rhythm at higher levels, however, is the duration of structures: harmonic structures, textural structures, and the product of their coordination. Harmonic structures establish a rhythm of their own chiefly through cadences. It is the cadences, which confirm (or reconfirm) harmonic arrivals, that articulate these larger rhythms. The harmonic areas of these works are of various lengths, from small-scale tonicizations to large pedal points and even larger fugal expositions; cadences are often, but not always, coordinated with a change of harmonic area. Cadences create a sense of phrase, and it is these phrases which form the structural basis of rhythms at a higher level.[3]

The phraseology of the praeludia can be either regular or irregular. They do not consistently show the kind of foursquare melodic and harmonic framework which lies behind so much later music. Tonicization chains, for example, can yield both square and supple phrase structures.

50 Rhythm and Meter

Passages in rhapsodic style create a meandering, quasi-improvisational effect, and completely evade regular phrase structures. Modular textures exhibit rigid phrase structure; so too implied pedal points, which are similar in rhythmic design. True pedal points most often consist of a single phrase. Fugal sections are characterized by many small phrases, the result of subject and answer entries.

These phrases join to form the textural sections which are the formal basis of the praeludia. The ciaconas, which have the most rigidly square phrase lengths of any texture, also exhibit the most rigidly hierarchical structures at higher levels. In the ciacona which opens the Praeludium in g, BuxWV 149, the six repetitions are clearly grouped in twos by the figural style of the variations. This leads to a clear phrase structure and also to a regular high-level rhythm:

Praeludium in g, BuxWV 149

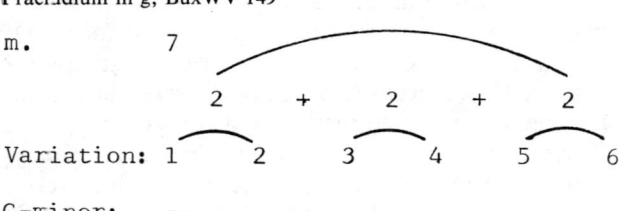

In the ciacona which ends the Praeludium in g, BuxWV 148, this 2 + 2 structure is even clearer, for the statements of the theme alternate between the pedal part and the manuals. Its first twelve statements group in the following pattern: 2 + 2 + 2 + 2 + 2 + 2. The final two statements which follow are irregular; both come in the pedal part, and the second is modified to lead to the final cadence. This ciacona, unlike the one from BuxWV 149, is long enough to suggest further grouping beyond the 2 + 2 level. Such grouping at a higher level is accomplished through different harmonic areas. The first six statements are in G-minor, and the remaining ones in B♭-major:

Praeludium in g, BuxWV 148

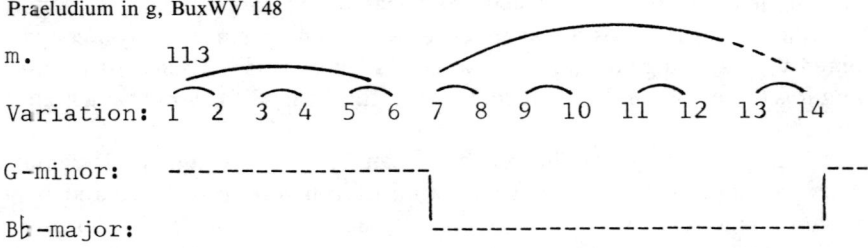

The higher-level structure is not perfectly symmetrical, however; and neither is the move from G-minor to B♭-major very graceful. (A better articulated transition from the tonic to the mediant would have strengthened the sense of grouping.)[4]

Most textures do not provide these same possibilities for symmetry in hierarchical grouping; the high-level rhythm and phrase structure of most sections is less regular. In the opening free section of the Praeludium in C, BuxWV 136, the figuration pushes relentlessly forward, and strong cadences within the section are avoided, as is a sense of clear phrase structure. The entire section is essentially one large phrase, with a minimum of articulation at any lower level. Only rarely does the figuration actually suggest grouping by measure: the suggestions of sequence in measures 4–5 and 6–7 lead towards the dominant of the supertonic and the supertonic which precede the subdominant and dominant:

Praeludium in C, BuxWV 136

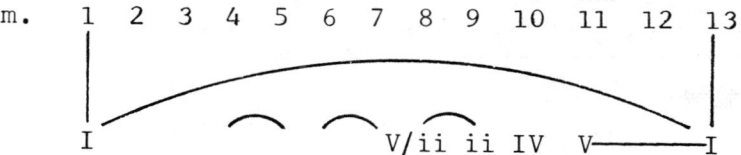

The opening free section of the Praeludium in d, BuxWV 140, however, has a highly developed phraseology. The cadential arrivals are clearly of different weights (those in measures 13, 16, and 19 being the strongest):

Praeludium in d, BuxWV 140

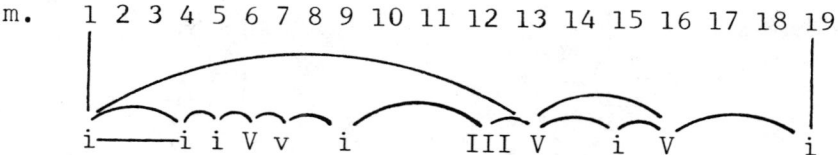

The closing free section of the Praeludium in f♯, BuxWV 146, provides examples of modular texture and pedal points. The lower-level phrases move in groups of two and three measures. The next highest level is articulated by large cadences on the dominant, the subdominant, and the final tonic cadence:

52 Rhythm and Meter

Praeludium in f#, BuxWV 146

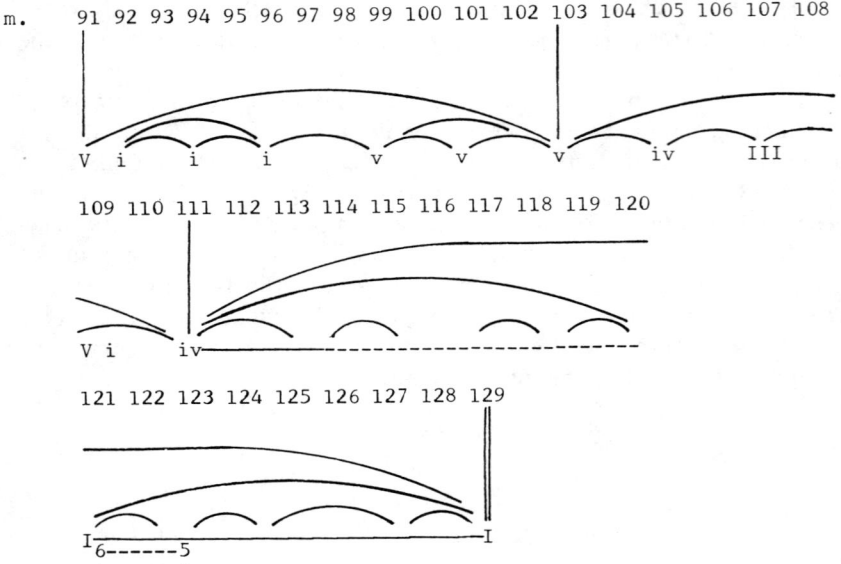

Fugal sections can also exhibit similar hierarchical construction. The lower-level phrases formed by the subject and answer are joined into the higher-level rhythm of the expositions. This is especially clear in the fugue from the Praeludium in C, BuxWV 137:

Praeludium in C, BuxWV 137

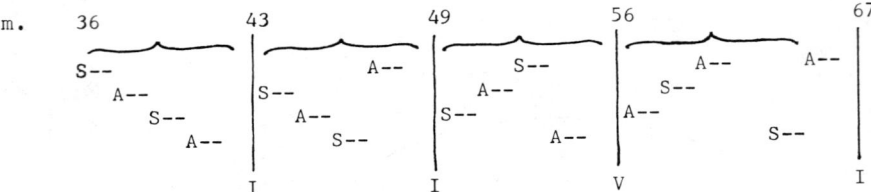

Rhythm is also created by the textural sections themselves. In terms of duration, the opening free section is usually shorter than the first fugue, and the first fugue virtually always shorter than the remaining sections. The remaining sections, however, may contain a variety of textural sections, and its individual members range from those that are quite short to some that are even longer than the first fugue:

Opening Free Section   First Fugue   Remaining Sections

This suggests that the remaining sections, usually the largest of the three parts and occupying the climactic position, bear the most weight in the overall scheme.

The characteristic meter of these works is common time. Each work begins with it, and the vast majority end with it as well.[5] Common time dominates virtually every praeludium; very few present more music outside this meter than within it. Any other meter serves as a contrast to common time, and other meters have fairly standard functions in the praeludia. Of these standard functions, the triple-time fugue is the most common, accounting for well over half of the metrical sections in the praeludia which are not in common time. The meter most often used is 3/2; 3/4 and 6/4 are less frequent.[6] Several indications suggest that the half note of 3/2 equals the quarter of common time.[7] The relationship between common time and 3/4, however, is not so certain.[8] Other uses of triple time include passages which would otherwise have been written in common time with triplets. However, these passages are also usually imitative in nature.[9] Very few cases of genuine nonimitative music occur in triple time. Other meters are used only rarely in these works. There is only one instance of cut time, and only one instance each (and of only one measure's duration) of 6/8 and 2/4.[10]

The presence of a meter signature does not always indicate a clear meter; some passages in the rhapsodic free style, especially when found at the beginning of a praeludium, evade a clear sense of meter. The various attempts to bar the opening of the Toccata in d, BuxWV 155, provide an example. While the manuscript of the work is undoubtedly corrupt, it is presented in a metrically vague way.[11] Other works which are preserved in a better state also reflect the same kind of metrical ambiguity at their beginning.[12] There are also several passages which have a strong metrical sense, but one which is at odds with the marked meter.[13] This effect, however, is relatively unusual; often, when the metrical sense is not that of the marked meter, it is because the music simply lacks a strong metrical sense.

Meter at the foreground level is by definition the regular recurrence of accent. At middleground levels, however, metrical structure can be more flexible, more problematic. Metrical patterns eventually merge into what might be termed rhythmic shapes, or simply irregular metrical formations.[14] Such rhythmic shapes generally occur unusually near the foreground in the praeludia.[15] As has already been pointed out, the phrase structure of these works is often irregular; the metrical structure is usually not able to sustain regular patterns at that, or any higher, level. Textures with regular phraseology are those which are the most metrically stable at higher levels.[16] The alternation of strong and weak measures is most noticeable in tonicization chains where the harmonies directly encourage such an effect:

Praeludium in C, BuxWV 136

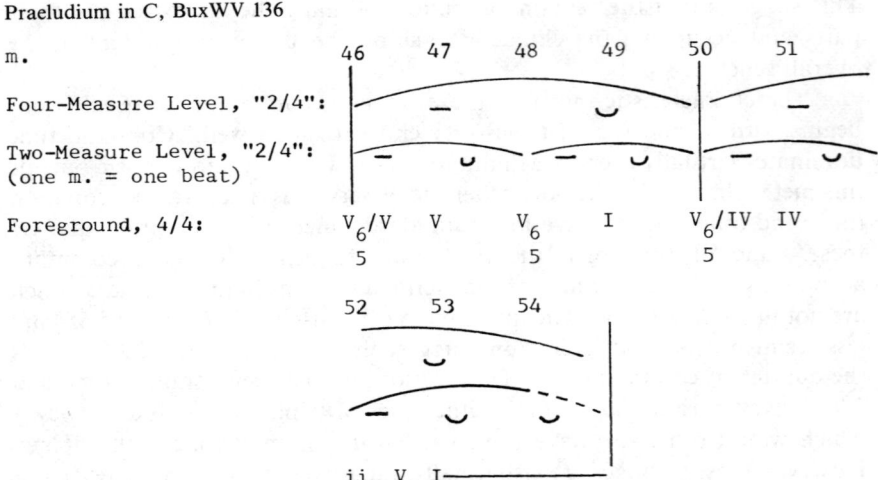

This passage has a very orderly metrical hierarchy; tonicization chain technique, however, does not always lead to such metrically clear passages.[17]

The pattern of subject and answer entries and cadences in fugues is usually very regular at lower levels. However, fugues are often metrically irregular at higher levels. The fugue of the Praeludium in C, BuxWV 137, is one of the most regular:

Praeludium in C, BuxWV 137

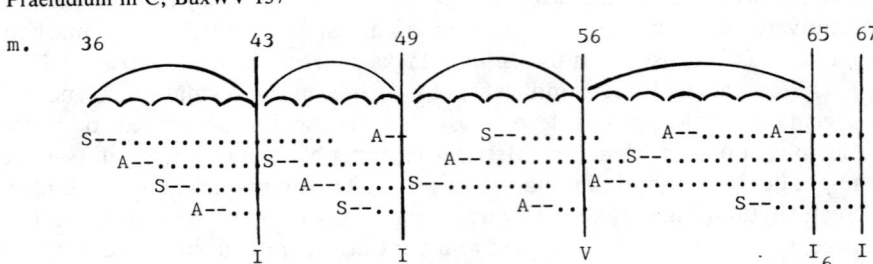

Rhythm and Meter   55

The subject and answer create phrases of one and one-half measures; extensions which lead to the cadence of the first and third expositions, as well as a codetta between the third and fourth entries of the fourth exposition, are the same length. Only the extension (free ending) which closes the last exposition breaks the pattern by its organization in half-measure units.

Large free sections, particularly at the end of a work, are the most irregular of all. The closing free section of the Praeludium in D, BuxWV 139, includes changing textures with corresponding shifts in metrical regularity. Note especially the modular structure of the sequential passage (beginning at measure 70); clear four-measure groups frame the section. The nine measures in between do not consist of three three-measure groups, but contain an "extra" measure (measure 76). The following chordal passage (a tonicization chain) has a simpler overall metrical scheme. The final portion contains first an implied subdominant pedal and then a real tonic pedal. The texturally dramatic entrance of the tonic pedal is metrically dramatic as well: it enters in the last measure of a four-measure group rather than at the beginning of a new group:[18]

Praeludium in D, BuxWV 139

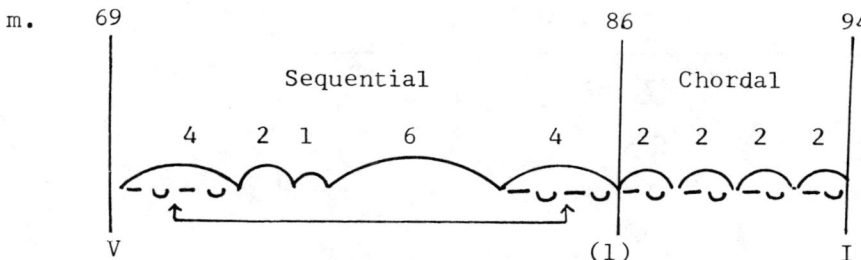

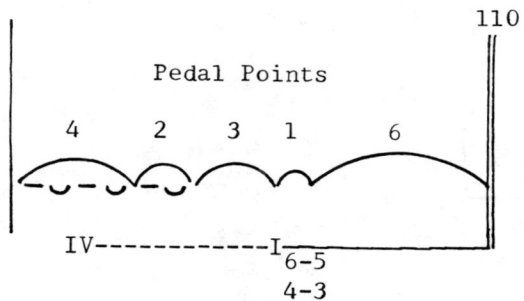

It is the rhythmic structure (phraseology), then, which dominates the middleground of the praeludia, rather than strictly regular metrical formations. And it is the rhythmic structure of sectional juxtaposition, rather than an overriding metrical structure, which forms the high-level rhythmic/metrical shapes of these works.

Historical and Critical Evaluation

Aspects of Buxtehude's use of rhythm and meter in the praeludia can be directly traced to the keyboard music of his immediate predecessors.[19] The special role of triple-time sections and the use of phrases of irregular length are found in earlier works. The provenance of the sections in triple-time is the variation canzona.[20] While none of Scheidemann's praeambula (or fugas, toccatas, or fantasias) have triple-time sections, his Canzon in F, WV 44, does:[21]

Scheidemann: Canzon in F, WV 44

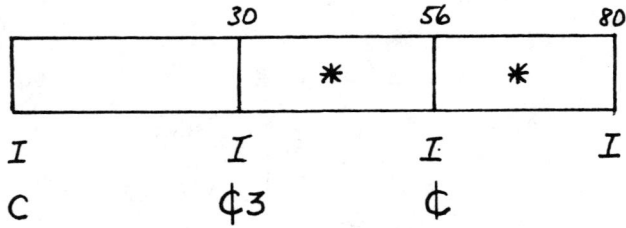

Likewise, all four of Tunder's praeludia do not change meter, but his single Canzona in G has a triple-time section:[22]

Tunder: Canzona in G

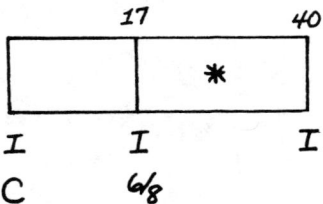

All five of Weckmann's canzonas have triple-time sections.[23] Unlike Scheidemann and Tunder, however, Weckmann incorporated canzonalike triple-time sections into the praeambulum/praeludium genre. While both his Fantasia in d and his Fuga in d stand close to the canzona, the Praeambulum in d provides a clear example of the intermixture of the canzona and the praeambulum/praeludium.[24] (See the illustration on page 23.) Weckmann's six toccatas present a different situation.[25] Only three have triple-time sections; two employ such sections in the manner of a canzona, while one other has a nonimitative triple-time passage in the opening free section:

Weckmann: Toccata in d[26]

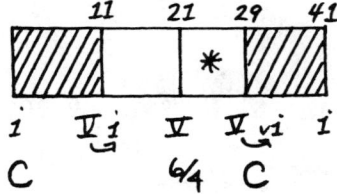

Toccata in a[27]

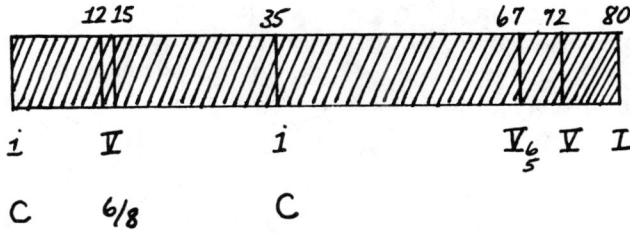

(See also the illustration of the Toccata in e[28] on page 45.) Both of these uses of triple-time meter, in fugal sections with thematic variation and within the opening free section, are used by Buxtehude in his praeludia.

Irregular phraseology can be found in both the north German praeludium and the Froberger-style toccata. The opening free section of Scheidemann's Praeambulum in d, WV 35,[29] has two large phrases of ten and seven measures:

58 Rhythm and Meter

Scheidemann: Praeambulum in d, WV 35

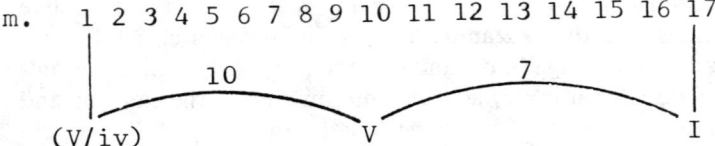

A similar opening, on a somewhat larger scale, can be found in Tunder's Praeludium in g:[30]

Tunder: Praeludium in g

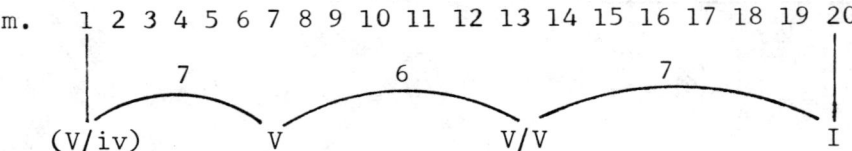

Infrequently, there are passages in the free style by these two composers with a more regular phrase structure, particularly in closing sections. The last ten measures of the Preambulum in d, WV 34,[31] by Scheidemann provide an example. Here, strong and weak measures are suggested:

Scheidemann: Praeambulum in d, WV 34

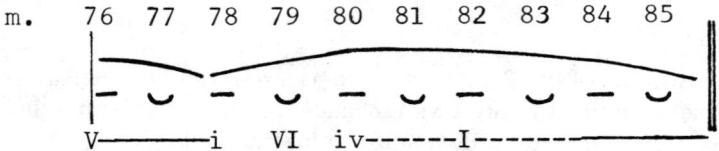

The last eight measures of another Praeludium in g[32] by Tunder are similar in design:

Tunder: Praeludium in g

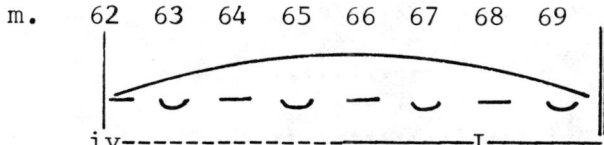

Weckmann's free sections are likewise irregular in phraseology, as the opening of the Praeambulum in d demonstrates:[33]

Weckmann: Praeambulum in d

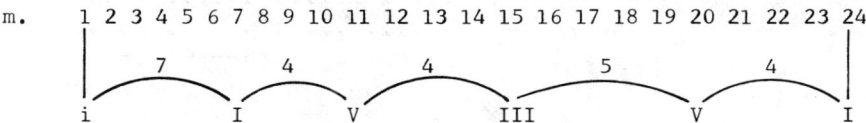

His works in the toccata style have a similarly irregular phrase structure, as, for example, the opening of the Toccata in e:[34]

Weckmann: Toccata in e

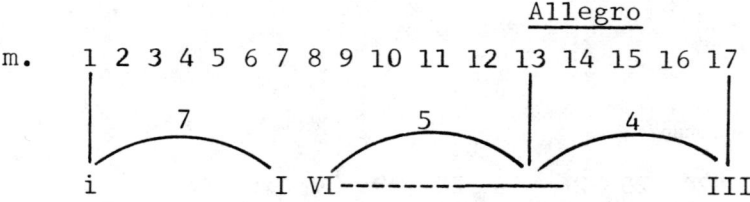

The fugal sections of Tunder and Weckmann are often noticeably irregular in phraseology as well, as some entry patterns from their expositions indicate:

Tunder: Praeludium in g[35]

```
m.    22   23   24   25   26   27   28   29
                          S-------........
                      A-------..........
          S-------....................
                                A-------
```

Praeludium in g[36]

```
m.    20   21   22   23   24   25   26   27   28   29   30
                              A-----------...........
              S-----------......................
              A-----------........................
                                          S----------
```

Weckmann: Fantasia in d

```
m.    1    2    3    4    5    6    7    8    9    10   11   12
                   A-------.................        A------
          S-------.............................................
                              A-------.................
                                   S------...
                                        A------........
```

Praeambulum in d

```
m.    24   25   26   27   28   29   30   31   32
              A---------.......A--------
          S----------.....................
                   A--------..................
                              S--------........
                                        A--------
```

Even when the entry pattern is more regular, as in Tunder's Praeludium in F[37] or Weckmann's Fuga in d, it is not sustained, and the modular precision typical of Buxtehude is never achieved.[38]

While Buxtehude used the irregular phraseology of both the north German and the toccata styles in his free sections, he also used free sections which were more regular than those of his predecessors. These include free sections in modular textures, and especially the ciacona movements which he incorporated into the praeludium. Likewise his fugal sections are more regular in construction, generally yielding a more highly organized metrical structure (and phraseology) at middleground levels.

Rhythm and meter raise critical questions at both low and high levels of structure. When Edward Cone writes concerning the form and style of the late baroque, he is describing a very different kind of music, even though it follows the praeludia by only a generation:

> Certainly the style of [the late baroque], the age of Bach and Handel, is most memorably characterized by an important rhythmic feature: the uniformity of its metrical pulse. This is in turn but one facet of a regularity that pervades the texture of the music. As a result the typical movement of this period is indeed a *movement*, i.e., a piece composed in a single unvarying tempo. To be sure, there are exceptions duly labelled as fantasias; yet the rule remains that each tempo should be represented by an extended, relatively self-contained unit. Even when a movement juxtaposes two or more such units in clearly contrasted tempos, there is often an underlying arithmetical relation that, if observed in performance, unifies them. . . . In this music, events of the same kind tend to happen either at the same rate of speed, or at precisely geared changes of rate, whether these events are cycles of keys, short-range harmonic progressions, or sequences of melodic motifs. In the best of this music, the contrapuntal texture, either actual or implied, sets up a hierarchy of events, each proceeding at its own rate, yet all under a strict metric control that extends from the entire phrase down to the smallest subdivision of the beat.[39]

It is hard to avoid the conclusion that the style traits described by Cone can also be grounds for critical evaluation. But the mature music of Bach and Handel does not stem from the same tradition as the praeludia of Buxtehude; the north German praeambula and praeludia, and especially the toccatas of Frescobaldi and Froberger, are far more loosely organized that the concertos of Vivaldi and the other Italian models from which Bach and Handel worked. The increased coherence of this later style is due as much to its emphasis on rhythmic/metrical regularity as it is to its more highly developed tonal focus. But Buxtehude's rhythmic style embodies its own critical criteria; certainly the important question is how and under what circumstances this flexibility is an asset.

The aesthetic goal for Buxtehude was not rhythmic regularity but, rather, improvisational spontaneity and its re-creation in the praeludia. It is in the free music, where this effect is most noticeable, that Buxtehude's musical language is most impressive. The opening of the Toccata in d, BuxWV 155, for example, is gripping music. However, it derives its effect not from gripping rhythmic order and coherence, but precisely from the lack of it. Its rhythmic freedom, joined with powerful harmonies and arresting motives, re-creates the drama of spontaneous music. Such drama can also be found in the closing free sections, as those of the Praeludia in D, BuxWV 139, and in f#, BuxWV 146. The fugal sections, however, do not strive for the drama of spontaneity. While they are generally simple in design, and are usually close to the kind of fugue which would result from improvisation, they cannot capitalize on the possibilities of rhythmic flexibility as can music in the free style. Perhaps to heighten this tension, Buxtehude moved away from the more irregular phraseology typical of the fugal sections of his immediate predecessors. Yet his fugues do not approach the intensely regular late baroque style, which was to develop from a different source.

Rhythm at the highest level, that of the sections themselves, is an aspect of the flexibility of the style that Buxtehude turned to credit. In the works of Scheidemann, Tunder, and Weckmann in the north German tradition, the central fugal section is usually the most extensive: it bears the most weight, and the free close functions like a coda. Though Buxtehude experimented with this pattern and created many designs, he most often shifted the weight of the form to the sections after that fugue. In his hands the remaining sections became the longest and most unstable part of the form, with their potential as the climactic portion of the work fully realized. The relationship between rhythmic and metrical structures at various levels and the expressive shape of the praeludia is explored in chapter 5.

4

Thematic Variation

Thematic Variation in Fugal Subjects

The use of thematic variation in the praeludia chiefly occurs in the fugal sections. When there is more than one fugal section in a praeludium, subsequent fugal subjects as a rule derive from the subject of the first fugue. There can be no doubt that this practice was an old one by the time it reached Buxtehude; numerous examples exist in the variation canzonas of Frescobaldi and Froberger.[1] Closer to Buxtehude, Weckmann also employed this idea. Significantly, this is true not only in his canzonas, but also in his larger organ works.

The thematic derivation of the fugal subjects in the praeludia has been discussed by several scholars. While its presence has never been in doubt, the extent of its application has been. Further, the kinds of variation techniques used have not been thoroughly investigated. While the process usually occurs in an immediately obvious way, occasionally thematic connections are suggestive rather than blatant. This has led to considerable confusion concerning thematic variation in Buxtehude's praeludia. That the practice was not new with Buxtehude has been largely ignored; indeed, in his hands, it was in a relatively late stage of development. While Buxtehude played the major role in bringing this technique into the praeludium, in multifugal keyboard works of any sort, thematic variation was a standard procedure. It is reasonable to assume that the question was not so much whether or not the technique was to be employed, but how and to what degree. It has been suggested by Apel that:

> When a work contains more than one fugue, Buxtehude often uses variations of the first fugue subject [for subsequent fugue subjects] . . . but Hedar definitely goes too far in his analyses when he considers every such subject a variant of the main subject.[2]

This view has been considerably expanded by Powell.[3] He echoes Apel's opinion that not all of the works incorporate thematic variation; he goes farther, and quite clearly asserts that a large number of the multifugal praeludia do not employ this technique.[4] Powell makes his criteria clear for judging what constitutes thematic variation: the relationship must be obvious and unmistakable in order for him to acknowledge a connection. He presents examples of several fugal subjects from different praeludia to demonstrate that their thematic relationships can be as convincing as other relationships in the same work.[5] It is at this point that the dangers of his position become obvious. To believe, as Powell apparently does, that intrawork thematic relationships and interwork ones can be equated, is to misapprehend seriously the aesthetic significance of such phenomena. The meaning of a particular theme, motive, or even interval within a work is simply not comparable to its meaning within a repertory of pieces.

Buxtehude's fugal subjects themselves are relatively short and simple; their interest lies not so much in their intrinsic qualities as in their potential for variation. Thematic variation is closely linked to a change to triple meter; and, as Powell points out, "The subjects of the second and succeeding fugues have much more rhythmic variation within themselves and thus more motion and vitality."[6]

This effect, and several others in Buxtehude, can be traced to Weckmann.[7] Shannon points to another, more important one:

> A new type of fugal theme appears in Weckmann's works. This type has none of the square and stodgy shape of those by Tunder and his predecessors. Instead it has a light, percussive quality and depends for its shape on the outlines of rudimentary harmonic motion.[8]

These themes often employ repeated notes, another feature which probably originated with Weckmann, as Apel suggests:

> A new type of fugue subject, which came into much favor during the second half of the 17th century, makes its first appearance in [Weckmann's] canzona no. 7. It consists of long stretches of running sixteenth notes, often starting with a tone repetition . . . .[9]

Apel may be a bit hard on Buxtehude in lamenting his frequent use of such subjects:

> The repercussion subjects . . . which are characterized by tone repetitions, are purely of historical interest. In the second half of the 17th century this type achieved a popularity that is difficult to explain and hardly justified aesthetically.[10]

Admittedly Buxtehude's fugal subjects do not stand comparison with those of Bach's organ fugues,[11] but they are apt musical ideas for the kind of variation process which is used in the praeludia. The "square and stodgy shape" of the fugal subjects of Scheidemann and Tunder has limited appeal for variation. It is the livelier subjects of the Weckmann canzona that most readily provide Buxtehude with possiblities for inventive variation. A subject with an outline based on harmonic motion can have notes readily added or subtracted without losing its overall coherence; a string of repeated notes which begins a subject is not only easily transformed into a triple-time version, but can also be decorated with neighbor note motion. A subject which is built with several ideas rather than just one is another feature that can be traced to Weckmann's thematic invention. Such a subject allows variations to proceed from either the beginning of the subject or its continuation. The inclusion of a characteristic interval may lead to variations which preserve simply that element. Weckmann also anticipated Buxtehude in the use of the tonal answer of the first fugue as the basis for variation rather than the subject.

Buxtehude clearly possessed a rich array of techniques for thematic variation which can best be demonstrated by a survey of his works. Praeludia which have two fugal sections, the first in common time and the second in triple meter, offer the simplest and most frequent scheme for thematic variation. (Six of the fifteen multifugal works employ it.) The phrygian Praeludium, BuxWV 152, and the Praeambulum, BuxWV 158, both of which have already been described as archaic works,[12] are of this type. Thematic variation is obvious in both works, yet each is an instructive example of Buxtehude's techniques. In the Praeambulum, the second subject is not only in a new meter (6/4 instead of common time), but adds neighbor notes to the original subject for a livelier, more complex theme:

Praeambulum in a, BuxWV 158

In the second fugue of the Praeludium in a, BuxWV 152, the original pitch series is more strictly maintained; however, the first fugue's answer, rather than its subject, becomes the model for the second fugue's subject:

66   Thematic Variation

Praeludium in a, BuxWV 152

Works which closely follow these models are the Praeludium in e, BuxWV 143 (comparable to the Praeambulum), and the Praeludium in a, BuxWV 153 (comparable to the Praeludium).

Two remaining examples of works having only two fugues with the second in triple time offer more complex cases of thematic variation. In the Praeludium in g, BuxWV 148, the second subject is derived from the first in a considerably more subtle way. The opening note of the first subject, D (repeated six themes), is transformed into D-E♭-D-E♭-C-D; three of the six original D's are replaced by neighbor notes. The opening interval of the first subject, D-B♭, is preserved in the new subject, but after that the new theme is on its own:

Praeludium in g, BuxWV 148

The Praeludium in g, BuxWV 149, also preserves the outline of its original in its second subject. However, instead of adding notes here, the composer subtracts them: (G-D)-E♭-C-A-D-C-B♭-F♯-G-A-B♭ is reduced to (D-B♭)-E♭-A-D-F♯-G-A-B♭ (repeated notes omitted):[13]

Praeludium in g, BuxWV 149

This work illustrates one more important aspect of Buxtehude's art of thematic variation: the derivation is not always based upon the head of the subject, but sometimes on the subject's continuation.

Two praeludia have two common-time fugues. In the Praeludium in f♯, BuxWV 146, the two fugues have contrasting tempi, *grave* and *vivace*, instead of contrasting meters. The second subject embodies the descending fifth (C♯-F♯) of the first subject, while the new countersubject contains the diminished seventh of the original subject:

Praeludium in f♯, BuxWV 146

It comes as no surprise, perhaps, that his rhythmically awkward second subject is broken down into motives and is virtually abandoned after its exposition.[14] In the Praeludium in A, BuxWV 151, the derivation of the second subject involves a reordering of the pitches of the original pattern: E-C♯-A-E becomes E-C♯-E-A. But a similar rhythmic pattern and metric placement reinforces the relationship:

68   *Thematic Variation*

Praeludium in A, BuxWV 151

The seven remaining multifugal works all have more than two fugal sections. Three works follow the scheme of common-time fugue, fugato, and triple-time fugue (which is the two-fugue scheme with a fugato inserted between them). In the Praeludium in C, BuxWV 136, the three subjects are obviously connected thematically. Note the derivation of the fugato subject from the first fugue's answer. For the final gigue fugue, the original subject is the model:

Praeludium in C, BuxWV 136

Thematic Variation 69

Two Praeludia, in d, BuxWV 140, and in g, BuxWV 150, also follow this form. The Toccata in F, BuxWV 156, is somewhat similar. It has two common-time fugues, with a complex of rhapsodic, imitative, and pedal point passages in between. The second fugue follows the outline of the first fugue but omits the opening triadic figure:

Toccata in F, BuxWV 156

The imitative passages which are included in the intervening section also suggest the original subject. The first imitative passage uses the 1-3-1 pattern of the opening of the original subject, but at a different pitch.[15] The second imitative passage uses the same 1-3-1-(5) at yet a different pitch. The third, however, uses A–D–C–B♭, which is the continuation of the original subject, after the 1-3-1 has been heard (twice):

70   *Thematic Variation*

Toccata in F, BuxWV 156

Three final examples all present unusual situations. The Toccata in d, BuxWV 155, has three fugal sections, but in the following order: fugato (within the opening free section), fugue in common time, and fugue in triple time. All three share clearly related thematic material.[16] The Praeludium in e, BuxWV 142, is the only work with three real fugues. The subjects of these fugues are connected, but in subtle ways. The second subject preserves not only the opening fifth motion (using 5–1 instead of 1–5) but the descending 5–4–3 motion (with the 5–4–3 found in the answer and 1–7–6 in the subject), the octave leap, and also the use of chromaticism. The 5–4–3 motion and the octave leap, however, are reversed. The final gigue fugue also employs an octave leap and the 5–4–3–(2–1) motion:

Praeludium in e, BuxWV 142

The final work, the Praeludium in E, BuxWV 141, has four fugal sections: fugue (common time), fugato, fugato (in gigue rhythm, 12/8), and fugue (common-time). The opening third of the first subject, B–G♯, is the only thematic link to the second subject:

Praeludium in E, BuxWV 141

72 Thematic Variation

The subject of the second fugato also uses the opening third, B–G#:

Praeludium in E, BuxWV 141

The fourth subject is clearly derived from the gigue fugato's subject; the outline of the subject of the gigue (B–C#–B–A–G# . . . A) becomes the fourth fugue's answer; the gigue's answer (whose overall motion is E to E) becomes the new subject:

Praeludium in E, BuxWV 141

In all the multifugal praeludia, then, Buxtehude uses some degree of thematic variation;[17] the degree, of course, is a matter for critical evaluation.

Thematic Variation throughout the Praeludium

The derivation of fugal subjects from common thematic material represents only one aspect of thematic variation in Buxtehude's praeludia. Buxtehude often used thematic relationships in other ways, such as between free and fugal sections.[18] In works with interconnections such as these, the thematic web can be significantly more complex than those which employ connections only between fugal subjects. The typical plan of subjects linked by thematic variation:[19]

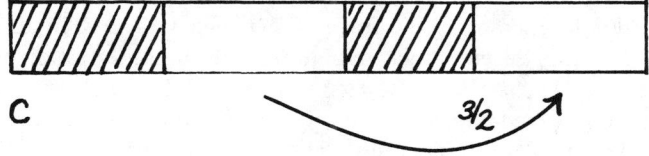

contrasts with much denser ones when all of the sections participate:

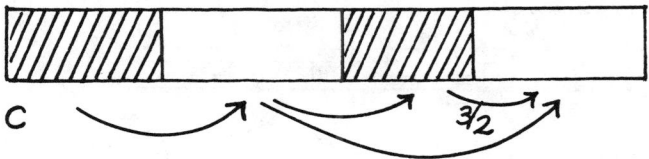

These latter relationships go beyond the traditional investigations of style analysis, which is chiefly concerned with the thematic relationships of fugal subjects. The wide-ranging and often subtle thematic relationships beyond those of just fugal subjects reveal another layer of thematic sophistication in these works.

The most obvious thematic relationships between a free and a fugal section approximate those between fugal subjects as outlined above. The Praeludium in C, BuxWV 137, provides an example. This work has only one fugue; however, the ciacona with which it closes uses a theme clearly derived from the fugue's subject:

Praeludium in C, BuxWV 137

In this work, the ciacona is clearly analogous to the triple-time fugues which sometimes occupy the closing portion of the form held here by the ciacona.

74   *Thematic Variation*

More often, however, thematic relationships between free and fugal sections are subtle and suggestive rather than obvious. Interconnections between the opening free section and the first fugue, which appear in a number of the praeludia, are examples of such linkage. Again, the Praeludium in C, BuxWV 137, provides an example. The fugal subject is anticipated in the opening pedal solo flourish:

Praeludium in C, BuxWV 137

The Toccata in F, BuxWV 157, contains another example of the foreshadowing of the subject in the opening free section:[20]

Toccata in F, BuxWV 157

Thematic Variation 75

Such thematic links, however, can range within the entire form of the praeludium. Again, the Praeludium in C, BuxWV 137, provides an example; it includes a link between the opening free section and the second free section which follows the fugue. Note the similarity of canonic treatment in both passages, as well as similar figuration; each passage then leads to a second figure which is also shared:

76   *Thematic Variation*

Praeludium in C, BuxWV 137

The thematic web of the work is far more elaborate than might be imagined if only fugal subjects are considered:

Praeludium in C, BuxWV 137

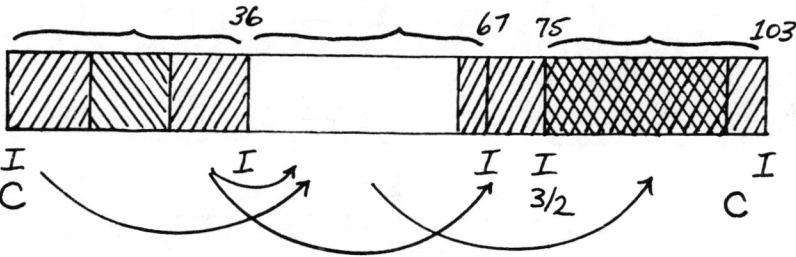

In some works, free floating motives unrelated to the fugal subjects appear in several sections. The Praeludium in E, BuxWV 141, provides an example. A cadential figure in the counterpoint of the first fugue reappears in two other contexts: at the dramatic juncture between the first fugato and its free ending and in the free ending of the final fugue:[21]

Praeludium in E, BuxWV 141

78   Thematic Variation

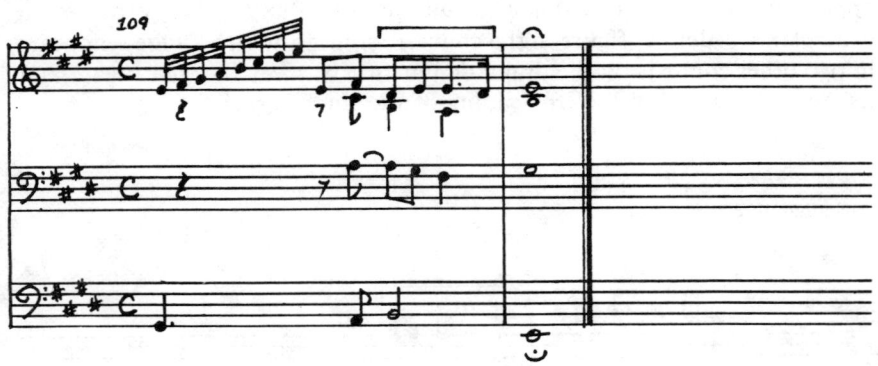

A more substantial link can be found in the Praeludium in f#, BuxWV 146. A sixteenth-note figure, part of the second fugal subject, becomes associated with a quarter-note motive which appears later during the section. Together, they play an extensive role in the closing free section:[22]

Praeludium in f#, BuxWV 146

Thematic Variation 79

A few of the praeludia suggest a *grundgestalt* conception: an initial idea serves as the basis for many, if not all, of the thematic ideas which follow. The Praeludium in d, BuxWV 140, is an example. The main figure of the opening free section, d–C–B♭–A, and its answer, a"–g"–f"–e"–d", (while the section is not a fugue, the idea is developed in imitation), provide the material for not only the three subjects which follow (common-time fugue, imitative quasi fugato, and triple-time fugue) but also for thematic ideas in the closing free section:

80   Thematic Variation

Praeludium in d, BuxWV 140

The descending scalar motion implicit in the figure of the opening free section appears unadorned in eighth notes in several sections.[23] This further development of the original motive becomes another element of thematic unity.

The most impressive web of thematic connections is found in the Praeludium in g, BuxWV 149. The opening free section is a ciacona;[24] repeated six times, the them becomes the basis of the fugal subject which follows:

Praeludium in g, BuxWV 149

The core of the fugal subject comes from the second half of the ciacona theme. The relationship is strengthened considerably by the dramatic statement of that part of the theme to close the ciacona:

Praeludium in g, BuxWV 149

82   *Thematic Variation*

Following the first fugue, a free section (marked *allegro*, in an unusual basso continuo texture) opens with a figure clearly derived from the first fugal subject:[25]

Praeludium in g, BuxWV 149

The thematic material of the second half of this free section also derives from the ciacona theme:[26]

Praeludium in g, BuxWV 149

The thematic ideas of this work are passed from section to section, irrespective of whether or not they are fugal:

Praeludium in g, BuxWV 149

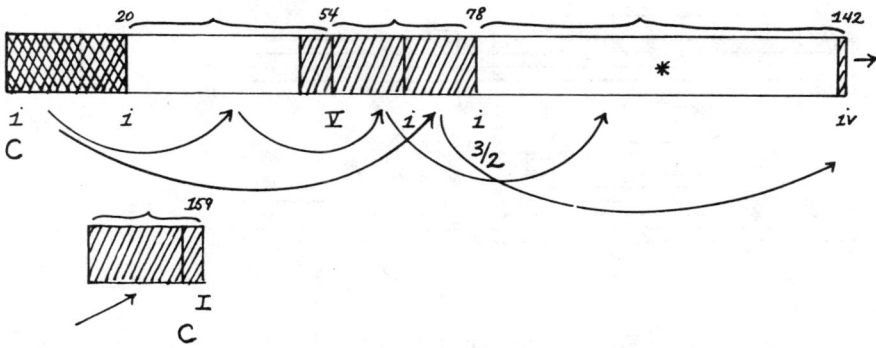

As these praeludia demonstrate, thematic variation is not simply a question of fugal themes. It is a technique that Buxtehude occasionally extended to include free sections (most notably ciaconas) as well, and sometimes used in a very free way to create a multitude of interconnections between many sections of a work. The result was a new dimension in thematic structure within the tradition of the praeludium.

Historical and Critical Evaluation

Thematic variation in Buxtehude's immediate predecessors can be found in those works which use triple-time sections.[27] Scheidemann's Canzon in F, WV 44,[28] his only free organ work which has a triple-time section, is also his only work which employs thematic variation:[29]

Scheidemann: Canzon in F, WV 44

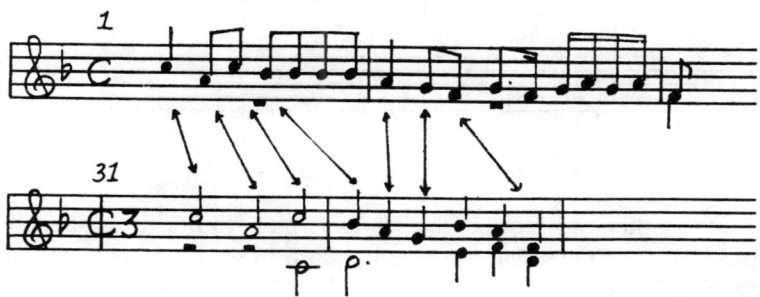

84   Thematic Variation

Tunder's Canzona in G[30] is likewise that composer's only example of either triple time or canzonalike thematic variation in his free organ works:

Tunder: Canzona in G

It is only with Weckmann that triple-time sections linked with thematic variation become more common in the north German repertory, and are transferred from the canzona to the preambulum (or praeludium). With fugal subjects which are clear examples of thematic derivation, his Praeambulum in d[31] is an important predecessor of Buxtehude's praeludia:

Weckmann: Praeambulum in d

Of Weckmann's other two large organ works (which do not have opening free sections like the Praeambulum), the Fantasia in d[32] presents a similar case of thematic derivation:

Weckmann: Fantasia in d

The Fuga in d,[33] has three thematically connected subjects:

Weckmann: Fuga in d

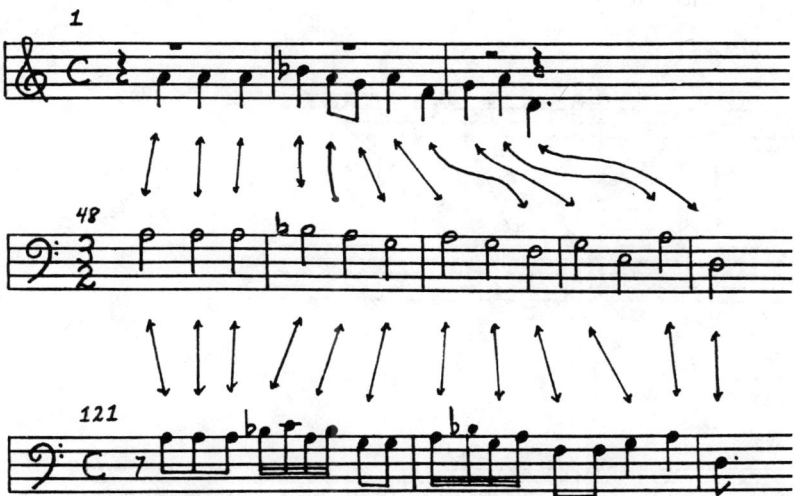

The anonymous Praeludium in G[34] (which may be by Weckmann) also has a similar kind of thematic link between its fugal sections:

86   Thematic Variation

Anonymous: Praeludium in G

Thematic variation is also characteristic of some of Froberger's toccatas,[35] and two of Weckmann's toccatas also employ this technique. Both the Toccata in d and the Toccata in e[36] begin with somewhat livelier subjects than those in his larger organ works:

Weckmann: Toccata in d

Toccata in e

Weckmann's canzonas offer the most sophisticated examples of thematic variation. They anticipate many of Buxtehude's more subtle uses of thematic derivation, and were likely significant models for him. While the Canzon in d[37] has the most obvious thematic links of any of the canzonas,

Weckmann: Canzon in d

the return to the original theme in the third section is an unusual procedure. Similar examples cannot be found in Buxtehude's praeludia, but are approximated in several of his works for keyboard without pedal.[38] The Canzon in c[39] has several interesting features, including the use of a subject in gigue rhythm.[40] This anticipates several works of Buxtehude, notably the Praeludia in C, BuxWV 136, and in e, BuxWV 142. The gigue subject is derived from the answer of the original fugue rather than from the subject itself, another technique which anticipates Buxtehude. The third subject is the original answer, but with a new countersubject:

Weckmann: Canzon in c

88   Thematic Variation

The Canzon in C[41] has subjects which seem only loosely connected. This is because the second derives from the latter portion of the first subject:[42]

Weckmann: Canzon in C

An even thinner thread of thematic logic is used in Weckmann's Canzon in G.[43] In this work only a single interval, D-B-D, from the head of the original subject, links the three themes:

Weckmann: Canzon in G

Such a technique directly anticipates some of Buxtehude's most subtle uses of thematic variation between fugal sections, such as in the Praeludium in E, BuxWV 141.

There are very few precedents, however, for thematic connections between free and fugal sections. The two anonymous praeludia offer examples.[44] In the Praeludium in G, there are links between the fugal subject and the closing free section:

Anonymous: Praeludium in G

90 Thematic Variation

In the Praeludium in F,[45] the opening free section anticipates the (single) fugal subject:

Anonymous: Praeludium in F

But even these two examples are tame in comparison to the far more daring application of this technique by Buxtehude, especially in such a work as the Praeludium in g, BuxWV 149.

The evaluation of Buxtehude's use of thematic variation ultimately hinges on a critical issue: how minimal can thematic links become before the clarity and audibility of the process break down? In view of the stylistic expectations associated with the long tradition of thematic derivation in these multifugal forms, it seems that thematic links could indeed become suggestive rather than blatant. Thematic derivation is a relatively simple matter when there are only two fugal sections: the second fugue adopts a new, triple-time meter, and the pitch set of the subject is altered as needed. Buxtehude's replacement of the second fugue in a two-fugue scheme with one in common time was clearly an innovation. But he more often addressed the problem of incorporating three (or even four) such transformations, and in these cases, new techniques obviously had to come into play. Buxtehude's solution in several works, such as the Praeludia in C, BuxWV 136, in d, BuxWV 140, and in g, BuxWV 150, was to make the second fugal section a fugato. This heightens the contrast by textural means. Derivations from the original answer rather than the subject also complicate the scheme without jeopardizing its effect. However, such slender connections as are found in the Praeludium in E, BuxWV 141, in its two fugato sections, seem to strain the limits of the technique. Such thematic links are not only suggestive, but are easily missed.[46]

Only the Praeludium in e, BuxWV 142, has three real and very different fugues. While the thematic links are indeed suggestive rather than obvious, they are made through several motives rather than a single interval. Weckmann offered many cogent examples of thematic derivation for a second fugue, though when he tried a third his solutions were not remarkable. The three fugues of the Fuga in d are simply too similar; and in several of his canzonas he reverts to the original subject or answer—but with a new countersubject—for the third fugue. Buxtehude's solution in the Praeludium in e is a very different, and considerably more sophisticated, one.

Equally innovative is Buxtehude's linking of free and fugal sections.[47] This impressive new concept of thematic interconnection within the praeludium represents an entirely new thematic logic within this tradition, and it yields several important examples. The thematic derivation of the ciacona from the fugal subject in the Praeludium in C, BuxWV 137, is as undeniably clear as the usual triple-time derivation of a second fugal subject. The use of thematic links between the opening ciacona of the Praeludium in g, BuxWV 149, and the following fugues and free sections, however, is a much more advanced scheme. With its thematic logic embracing all of its sections in direct but not too obvious ways, it is Buxtehude's most significant achievement in thematic variation. The relationship between thematic variation and expression is further investigated in the following chapter.

5

Expression

Movement and Climax

> *They [Buxtehude's praeludia] have a wonderful sense of movement and climax....*
> Donald Jay Grout[1]

The sense of movement and climax embodied in these works is an important element of their nature, style, and form. Movement, a point of climax, and the concomitant patterns of musical energy — that is, the accumulation and release of tension — create much of the expression which is communicated by the music. With these elements of the piece under consideration, it is possible to unite the various aspects of the style (texture, harmony, rhythm, meter, and thematic variation) in a meaningful synthesis. Indeed, the elements of style can best be understood as functions of expression.

A sense of movement is created by many elements of the praeludia: the alternation of textures, the unfolding of harmonic plans, changes in rhythmic style and meter, and the progress of thematic development through variation. Considered apart from expression, movement can seem static and formalistic, its function one of contrast rather than of progression. While the contrast that alternations and changes provide is without doubt an important aspect of praeludia, such a concept misses the sense of directed forward motion, the dynamic quality of the music.

The motion of Buxtehude's praeludia is remarkably unidirectional; it is not circular, nor is there any sense of recapitulation. While thematic ideas do unite these works, they do so through the process of variation rather than return. A fugal theme, when it reappears in later sections, does so in a new guise. The original form does not reappear; and it remains only as a memory while its structuring force is transferred to its new version and is subsumed by the variation process. The same principle of nonrepetition can be observed in other stylistic features as well. Rarely do textural sections repeat in such a way as to suggest a textural recapitulation. While the alternation of free and fugal styles is basic to the form of the praeludia, it is

94 Expression

usually a new kind of free or fugal texture which appears in each succeeding section. A second fugal section is almost without exception in a different meter and rhythmic style than the first. Even when three or more fugal sections occur, each is very different from the others. (The same holds true for the free music.) Changes in rhythm and meter are essential in maintaining the ever-new quality of the succeeding sections of the praeludia. Harmonic plans also contribute: various sections stress different harmonies, with dominant, subdominant, mediant, and other harmonic areas characterizing different sections.

In addition to its unidirectionality, the movement is directed towards a goal. The goal is the point of climax, the moment in the work toward which movement drives, and beyond which it relaxes. The sense of climax can be understood as a two-part event: a point of maximum tension followed by a point of resolution:

$$\begin{bmatrix} \text{Accumulation} \\ \text{of Tension} \end{bmatrix} \Big/ \begin{matrix} \text{Point of} \\ \text{Maximum Tension} \end{matrix} \Big/ \begin{matrix} \text{Point of} \\ \text{Resolution} \end{matrix} \Big/ \begin{bmatrix} \text{Relaxation} \\ \text{of Tension} \end{bmatrix}$$

These two elemental phenomena of climax can be regarded as the fundamental inhalation and exhalation of the work:

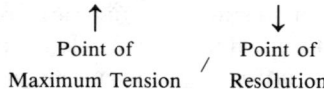

Points of climax are created through various means: high register, a dramatic change in texture, an unusually forceful gesture, or a strongly articulated return to the tonic may all play important roles. The Praeludium in d, BuxWV 140, can serve as an example. The sections after the first fugue are all relatively short, strongly contrasting, and unusually intense. As the piece moves from a chordal-rhapsodic section to an imitative (quasi-fugato) one with an elaborate free ending to a triple-time fugue (all knit together by nontonic cadences), tension mounts—especially as successive pitch peaks are reached (g″ in the free ending of the imitative section and a″ in the triple-time fugue). In the free ending of the triple-time fugue, c‴, the highest note available to Buxtehude on the organ, is attained for the first and only time in the work. This motion is directed towards the tonic cadence (measure 102) which forms the articulation point between the free ending of the triple-time fugue and the beginning of the closing free section.[2] With the pitch peak in the free ending of the triple-time fugue as the point of maximum tension, the tonic cadence then marks the point of resolution from that tension:[3]

Praeludium in d, BuxWV 140

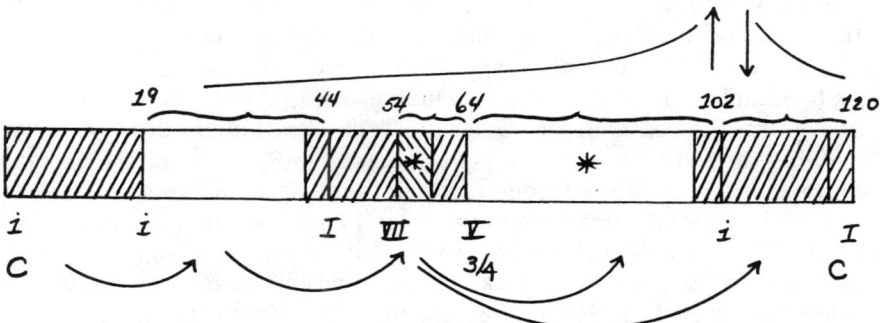

Beyond this arrival, the music moves in fudamentally different ways. The texture becomes strongly modular (and as a result more static), and the figuration speeds to sixteenth-note motion, but does not really lead anywhere, for the tonic cadence is repeatedly confirmed (measures 103, 104, and 105). The eventual drift of the harmonic motion is to the subdominant (which arrives in measure 111); during the subdominant harmonic area, especially static sixteenth-note figuration in quasi-canonic style spins out energy over an ostinato figure in the pedals (measures 111–13, extended through measure 116). With the energy of the work virtually depleted, the music broadens to common time and the figurations relax into scalar eighth notes. The final cadence, a plagal one, arrives directly from the subdominant harmonic area.[4]

While each work provides a unique solution to the coordination of climax with texture, harmony, and form, certain patterns can be discerned. In addition, some works (like the Praeludium in d) have a highly developed sense of climax, and precise points of maximum tension and resolution can be isolated. Other works have a considerably weaker sense of climax. In most cases, the penultimate textural section will contain the point of maximum tension, and the last section the point of resolution. This is true whether or not the penultimate section is fugal and the last section free, or the reverse. A few works which have exceedingly large closing free sections locate both the point of maximum tension and the point of resolution within that section. However, in these works the closing free section is a combination of various kinds of free textures, and the two aspects of the climax are divided between two of them. Works which have only an opening free section and the following fugue (and do not proceed to further free or fugal sections) have a somewhat different scheme: both parts of the climax are necessarily contained within the fugal section. As fugal sections usually close with a free ending, the two elements of the climax are generally distributed between them. (The point of maximum tension occurs near the end of the fugue, with the point of resolution in the free ending.)

Works which end with a large closing free section offer some of the best examples of climax. The Praeludium in d, BuxWV 140, discussed above, may be considered paradigmatic.[5] The Praeludium in f♯, BuxWV 146, has an unusually strong sense of climax; both aspects of the climax, however, occur after the second (and last) fugue. The impressive chordal-rhapsodic section, which follows the second (*vivace*) fugue, contains some of Buxtehude's boldest harmonic writing. Its point of maximum tension (measures 85-90, especially measure 88), finds its resolution within the following (modular) closing free section. The dominant close of the chordal-rhapsodic section is the upbeat (on a large scale) for the powerful tonic arrival several measures later at the peak of the ascent of the ostinato figure (measure 96).[6]

The five praeludia which end after the first fugal section[7] also embody aspects of this pattern. In these works, the two aspects of the climax are divided between the fugue itself and its free ending (which leads the fugue to a satisfactory tonic cadence).[8] The Praeludium in C, BuxWV 138, can serve as an example: the modular free ending of the fugue, a miniature ciacona, directly follows the climax of the fugal section (occurring with the peak of the sequence from measures 50-52 and the pedal entrance of the subject in the submediant in measure 53).

Works which proceed beyond the first fugue, but end with a fugal rather than a free section, also exhibit patterns of maximum tension followed by a resolution. In these works, the point of maximum tension falls in a penultimate free section and the point of resolution in the final fugal section. This is most clearly demonstrated in the Praeludium in E, BuxWV 141. The last fugal section, with its emphasis on subdominant harmony, serves as a point of resolution for the accumulated tension of the work; the point of maximum tension can be located in the *adagio* chordal passage which immediately precedes it. A similar pattern can be discerned in the two praeludia which end with gigue fugues. Especially in the Praeludium in e, BuxWV 142, the greatest tension—the center of gravity of the work—occurs before the gigue. Its chromatic second fugue (in 3/2) builds to a powerful climax (with c''' in measure 97); the high level of intensity continues through the following chordal section. It is only when the gigue fugue begins that the tension is relieved.[9]

Expressive Form

The expressive form which is the pattern of energy creation, transformation, and dissolution extends over the entire work as a powerful force binding together the various parts of these multisectional forms. The logic of textural alternations, harmonic plans, high-level rhythm, changes of meter, and thematic variation can better be understood by realizing the dynamic nature of the praeludia in conjunction with the formalistic aspects of their construction. It is the expressive conception that provides not only the logic behind these various stylistic elements, but also the power to join them into a meaningful progression of events.

The drive towards the climax is by far the more extensive aspect of expression in the praeludia. As the climax is invariably located towards the end of the work, the anticipation which precedes it is longer and more complex than the concluding relaxation. All of the elements of the style contribute to the drive towards the climax in various ways. The opening free section, whether short or long, texturally single-minded or boldly variegated, is chiefly anticipatory to the first fugue. The first fugue is generally more focused than the opening free section, and normally builds to an internal climax. If the work ends with this section, that climax serves as the point of maximum tension and resolution for the entire work. If, however, the work continues with further free and/or fugal sections, such a climax becomes only one step on the way towards an even larger climax. It is the final accumulation of tension near the end of the work which is the most impressive and which gathers the energy of the preceding sections into its own. After the first fugue, the alternation of textures may become more rapid and the textural sections themselves more fragmentary. It is in these remaining sections that such textures as fugatos and chordal-rhapsodic passages are generally found. Fugatos are shorter than real fugues, and their strettolike construction gives them a greater sense of energy and forward motion (and less sense of poise). Broken off soon after their exposition, they give the effect of a fragmentary gesture. Chordal-rhapsodic sections are also often fragmentary in construction and gesture. (Their intensity, however, is harmonic rather than entirely textural.) Fugues which appear in the remaining sections are never as poised or relaxed as the first fugue; for harmonic, rhythmic, or metric reasons they are more intense and animated. The high level of excitement which these textures generate is an important resource in the creation of the drive towards the climax and the climax itself. Thus textural sections which might, in a strictly formalistic analysis, be considered as only one of many textural sections after the first fugue, or simply as a linking passage between others, may have importance for the expressive shape of the work far beyond their function indicated by formal analysis.

Harmony also contributes in important ways to the drive towards the climax. The opening free section and the first fugue are both tonally closed and harmonically relatively stable.[10] Various parts of the remaining sections, however, may be tonally open, with nontonic cadences (except, of course, for the final cadence). It is in this part of the praeludia that the richest and most intense harmonies are usually found. These especially powerful harmonies help build the tension and energy necessary for achieving the climax.[11]

Rhythm and meter provide another important aspect of expression. A change in meter, from the common time typical of the opening free section and the first fugue to a livelier triple-time meter, is an important device which raises the energy level of a work as it progresses. Second (or third) fugal sections in 3/2, 3/4, or 6/4 provide not only an important contrast, but also the added rhythmic vitality needed for intensification. Closely allied is thematic variation. As the fugal subjects undergo successive transformations, they are not only varied, but are enlivened in their new guises as subjects for fugatos or triple-time fugues. Thematic variation, more than any other element of the style, establishes the unidirectional aspect of the works: the praeludia move forward in ever new sections and guises towards their climax and conclusion.[12] That the climax is not articulated through recapitulation, either sectional or thematic, but rather through the intensification of material confirms the crucial role of these elements of the style in the creation of tension and its resolution.

After the climax is achieved, stylistic elements also act in various ways to reduce the energy level of the work and to release the accumulated tension so that the work can come to a convincing close. An important resource for the dissolution of energy is modular texture. Following the climax in most free endings, the texture soon shifts to ostinato passages. The repetitive pattern of the ostinato allows for the gradual dispersal of energy. In two works the entire closing free section is a large ciacona;[13] these sections function in an analogous way, but on a larger scale. Other resources of the free style are also employed after the climax, such as pedal points (especially tonic pedal points), flourishes, and other figurations (such as static, shimmering figures).[14] These textures, in various ways, serve a similar function of discharging the accumulated energy of the work. Two other works end with gigue fugues.[15] Just as in a suite, the gigue does not bear the expressive weight of the whole, but serves as a lighter, final movement in which the tensions already accumulated can be dissolved.

Harmonically, postclimax passages rely chiefly on subdominant areas. This is especially noticeable in the modular textures which follow the climax, for they are closely associated with subdominant harmony.[16] Even when a work ends with a fugal section, the subdominant may still be stressed within the fugue.[17] The subdominant, then, is used in opposition to the dominant: the dominant builds tension and leads to the climax, while the subdominant releases tension after the climax. The subdominant often leads directly to the tonic for the final cadence, an event which may occur at the beginning of a large tonic pedal.[18] Over the pedal, various kinds of figuration release excess energy as the middleground harmonic motion slows to the pace—that is, no pace at all—of the pedal point itself.

Rhythm and meter do not play as great a role in the relaxation of tension after the climax as they do in the preparation of it. There is usually, however, a noticeable change of rhythmic pattern following the point of climax, as in the Praeludium in d, BuxWV 140, described above. As in that work, there is generally also a return to common time (and the stability it represents) after triple-time sections have led towards the climax. Thematic variation also does not play a significant role. Except for those works which use a fugue or ciacona as the last section, passages after the climax are generally not thematically connected with previous sections.

The basic scheme of points of tension and resolution, ↑↓, generally associated with first a fugal section, ↑, and then a free section, ↓, is a model which can help to explain several aspects of the praeludia. The fact that the point of maximum tension and the point of resolution are located in different textures partly explains why Buxtehude's fugues are either broken off or abruptly concluded. This also helps explain the dependence of the fugues on a free ending of some sort, and why so few do not use one. Buxtehude virtually always called upon the free style for the resolution of a climax. This also suggests why the works emphasize closing sections: they are not merely postludes, but have an integral role in the expressive shape of the works. The overall pattern of expression can be summarized as follows:

Opening Free Section	↑	↓
Anticipatory	Fugue	Free
	Increase of Tension	Release of Tension

There is no better evidence for the interrelationship of various sections and textures than that the means of tension accumulation and release are generally not associated with the same textural section. The archetypal scheme, however, is subject to numerous complications in the actual praeludia. However, it is in conjunction with this basic plan that the logic of the various elements of the style can best be understood.

Historical and Critical Evaluation

The degree to which Buxtehude's sense of movement and climax is an innovation in north German organ music can be demonstrated by a survey of the works of his immediate predecessors. Many of the elements necessary for the creation of movement and climax are often clearly present in the works of Scheidemann, Tunder, and Weckmann.[19] Yet for several reasons, the expression which they generate is considerably less impressive than that of Buxtehude. Not only are the praeambula, praeludia, and toccatas of these earlier composers usually shorter than Buxtehude's, but the resources for building such climaxes as their forms allow are generally not used to their maximum potential.

The praeambula of Scheidemann rarely demonstrate a convincing sense of climax. The fugal sections are usually too stodgy to build much momentum, and the changes from one texture to another are often not clearly articulated. This is especially true of the change from the fugal section to the closing free section,[20] an apt location for the climax. A heightened expressivity within this scheme can be found in the praeludia of Tunder, which represent an important link between the works of Scheidemann and Buxtehude. In Tunder's works, the textures following the end of the fugal section are clearly suggestive of Buxtehude's typical methods of releasing tension after the climax. In all four of Tunder's praeludia, there is a clear impression that the closing free section dissolves the preceding accumulated tension. The sudden shift from the typical eighth-note motion of the fugal section to the figural patterns in sixteenth notes of the free section is a clear point of articulation in each work. Modular textures, pedal points, and, perhaps most importantly, subdominant harmony can also be found.[21] What works against these passages, however, is the lack of both momentum and drive to climax in the preceding fugal section. The diminution of the subject, which is typically introduced near the end of the fugue, generally fails to achieve this end. Probably the most cogent sense of climax of the four is found in the Praeludium in g.[22] The diminution of the subject in the second part of the fugal section leads to a strong cadence on the tonic major, an articulation which marks the beginning of the closing free section:

Tunder: Praeludium in g

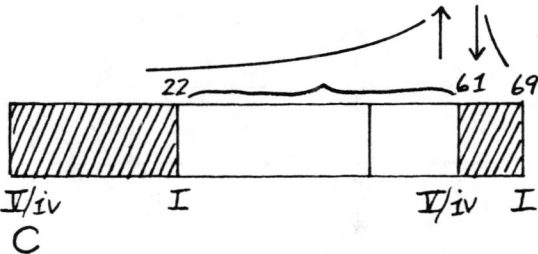

Weckmann's large organ works, the Fantasia, Fuga, and Praeambulum, all in d,[23] each have at least two fugal sections, the second of which is in triple time. The fugal sections of these works, and particularly the first ones in common time, have a far greater sense of movement and climax than do Tunder's.[24] The triple time fugues, however, are often disappointing; they are either too short or too tame to develop the same degree of movement which characterizes the first fugues. As a result, the sense of climax at the end of the work, and the drive towards it, are significantly weaker than might be expected. This tendency can be observed in the Praeambulum as well as in the Fantasia, where the second fugue turns towards the subdominant before the drive to a climax has begun. The Fuga has three fugal sections, the third of which returns to common time; the third fugue manages to create considerable forward momentum, but it does not have a subdominant harmonic area after the last fugue. (A dominant pedal keeps the energy level from falling until the final cadence.) Weckmann's toccatas and canzonas are similar to the Fuga, for an emphasis on the dominant (and the building of tension) is maintained up to the final cadence.[25] Several of the toccatas, however, provide excellent examples of the use of sequential rather than fugal passages to create a drive towards the climax.[26] Buxtehude's Praeludium in D, BuxWV 139, is a direct descendant of such works. In general, however, Weckmann's toccatas have a far less structured expressive form than Buxtehude's praeludia. While they do contain passages which drive towards a climax, what energy is built is too often lost when a passage which might capitalize on this power does not materialize. However, a fine example of a drive to the climax and its resolution at this time can be found in the anonymous Praeludium in G:[27]

102 *Expression*

Anonymous: Praeludium in G

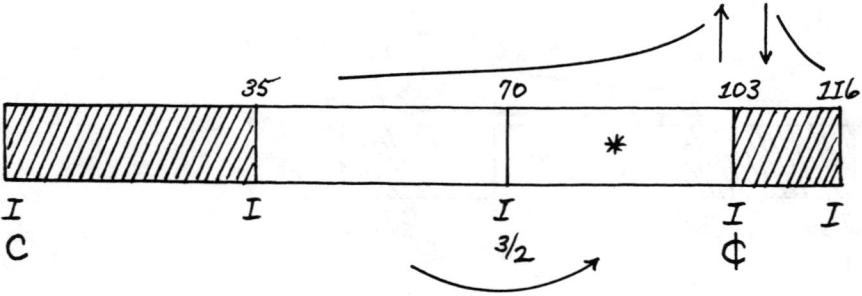

The second fugue, in triple time, builds towards a clear climax at its close on g″. In the following free section (which resembles analogous passages in Tunder's praeludia), sequences and hints of ostinato provide a resolution to the fugal tension and climax. A subdominant pedal with new canonic figuration, similar to that in Buxtehude's Praeludium in D, BuxWV 139, leads to the final cadence:

Anonymous: Praeludium in G

Praeludium in D, BuxWV 139

These works of Buxtehude's immediate predecessors help illuminate the degree of his innovations. Yet if the overall trend from Scheidemann through Tunder and Weckmann to Buxtehude is one of intensification of material, heightening of character, and more elaborate forms, this very transition can be observed in Buxtehude's works themselves. The Praeludium in a, BuxWV 152, and the Praeambulum in a, BuxWV 158, which are both in various ways old-fashioned in form,[28] have a clear (if rudimentary) sense of drive, climax, and resolution. But with means similar to those of Tunder, Buxtehude achieves a greater sense of movement and especially of climax. Unlike Tunder, Buxtehude does not rely on diminuition to intensify the central fugal section as it proceeds. Rather, a new fugal section, with the fugal subject recast in triple time, creates a larger form in which to build towards a climax. These triple-time sections create more momentum as they reach for higher and higher registers.[29] With a more cogent and expressive fugal structure, the tension becomes more powerful and its resolution clearer in the free sections which follow. But Buxtehude went far beyond this relatively modest scheme. In his larger works, there is not only a sense of forward motion, but also a clear and powerful expressive form encompassing the whole work.

The most convincing climactic structures in the praeludia occur in those works with large closing free sections. Together with the increased expressive power of his fugues, these expansive free sections are a most important development for achieving cogent expressive form.[30] In these large free sections the expressive power of the resolution of tension is perhaps even more impressive than the preceding fugal climaxes. In a work such as the Praeludium in d, BuxWV 140, discussed above, the progression of textures, harmony, meters, and thematic derivations is clearly directed towards achieving an overall, coherent, and expressive shape. Works which

104   *Expression*

locate the climax entirely within free textures, such as the Praeludium in f#, BuxWV 146, can be equally impressive. In this work, the free section after the second fugue builds towards a grandiose climax which is resolved in the huge closing free section which follows:

Praeludium in f#, BuxWV 146

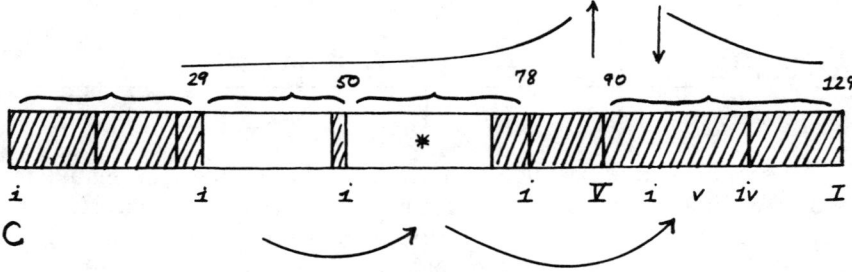

More problematic are those works which end with a fugal section or a ciacona. For example, in those works which close with a ciacona, a specific point of resolution in that section is difficult to isolate. A similar situation is found in those works which end with a fugal section. Even if a precise point of resolution is not clear (as in the Praeludium in e, BuxWV 142), the sense of drive towards a climax and resolution is still very real:

Praeludium in C, BuxWV 137

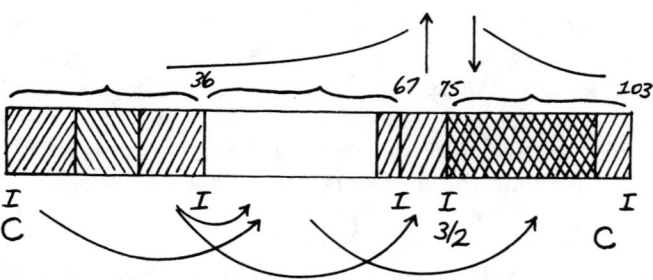

Praeludium in e, BuxWV 142

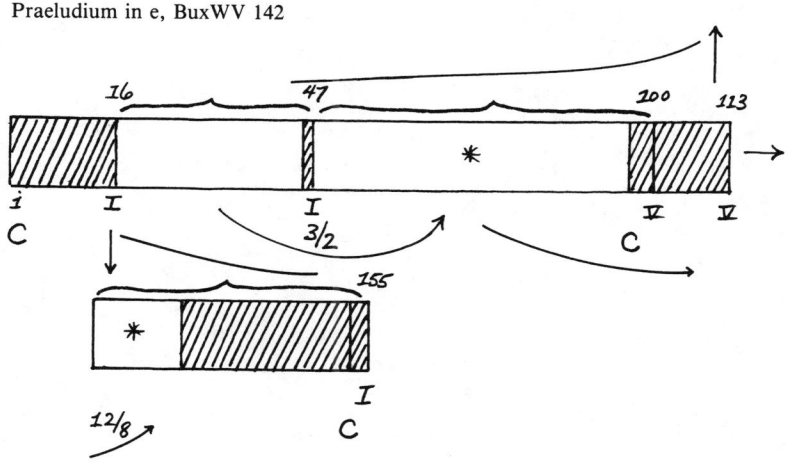

A more highly developed sense of climax and resolution is arguably Buxtehude's most important contribution to the praeludium tradition. It is to this end that his other stylistic innovations were directed, and a more cogent expressive form is one way that Buxtehude achieved a greater sense of coherence within these multisectional forms. Yet, other means of coherence are not lacking in these works. Buxtehude brought to the praeludia an equal sensitivity to the coherence provided by harmony, counterpoint, and line. Like the kind of coherence created by expression, such coherence also transcends textural alternations, harmonic areas, rhythmic and metric contrasts, and thematic transformations. Moving beyond the foreground level into the middleground and background, harmonic/linear coherence represents a second facet of analytical investigation and provides new insights about the nature of coherence in the praeludia.

Part II

Structure

6

The Opening Free Section

Style Analysis

The first section of Buxtehude's praeludia is always a free section. These sections encompass various styles and forms. Several basic features, however, have already been noted.[1] The harmonic plan is always closed (I-----I), and is elaborated with a dominant area and usually others as well (I---X---V---I). The final cadence of the opening section is often the strongest and most stable internal one of a praeludium. The most prominent texture of the opening section is figural; virtually all such sections use it. Some are entirely figural, while others either precede figural texture with rhapsodic and perhaps imitative texture, or follow it with some other type of texture(s).[2]

Texture and harmony are the two most important style features which determine the shape of the opening sections. The coordination of textural progressions and harmonic plans occurs in several specific ways. When an opening section consists of only figural texture, the basic harmonic motion is of course contained in that texture:

```
        Figural  --------------------------
        I----------X----------V----------I
```

The opening section of the Praeludium in C, BuxWV 136, is paradigmatic.[3] The simple harmonic plan is one large gesture. After an elaboration of the tonic followed by a move to the dominant (measures 1-4), a tonicization chain leads to the supertonic (measures 5-9); tonicizations then disappear and motion towards the cadence (measure 13) begins:

Opening Free Section

Praeludium in C, BuxWV 136

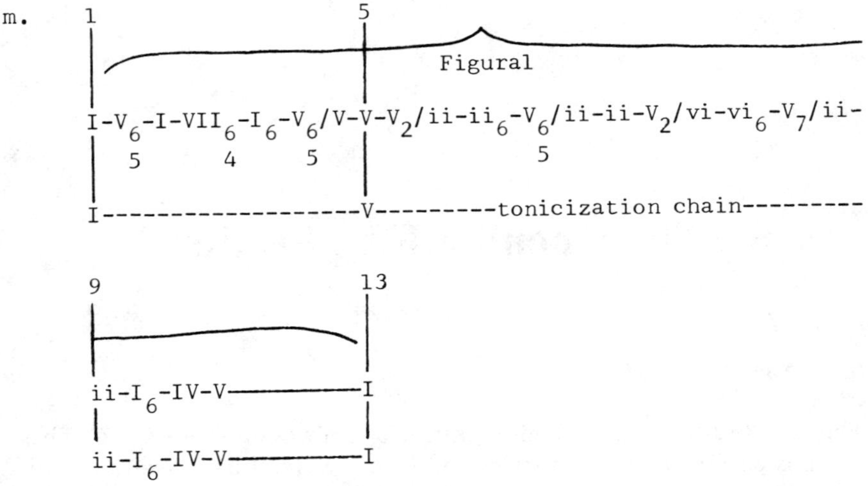

m. 1   5
                       |⌒‾‾‾‾‾‾‾‾‾‾‾‾‾‾‾‾‾‾‾‾‾‾‾
                       | Figural
$I-V_6^5-I-VII_6^4-I_6-V_6^5/V-V-V_2/ii-ii_6-V_6/ii-ii-V_2/vi-vi_6-V_7/ii-$

I--------------------V---------tonicization chain---------

9   13
|‾‾‾‾‾‾‾‾‾‾‾‾‾‾‾‾‾‾|
$ii-I_6-IV-V$————————I
|
$ii-I_6-IV-V$————————I

In one type, anticipatory textures generally elaborate the tonic; the basic harmonic motion is reserved for figural texture:

Rhapsodic-- (Imitative)--Rhapsodic--Figural ---------------------
I --X------V------I

In a second type, other textures (pedal points, fugatos, ostinatos, or 12/8 passages, etc.) follow the figural section; they generally prolong the dominant:

Figural ----------------Other ------
I----------X----------V----------I

The Praeludium in C, BuxWV 137, provides an example of the first type.[4] The harmonic plan consists of three gestures: the first (measures 1-11), is a rhapsodic pedal solo and flourish (I-----I); the second (measures 12-22), an imitative section (I-----I); the third (measures 23-36), a rhapsodic passage which soon gives way to figural texture (vi---iii---V---I):

Praeludium in C, BuxWV 137

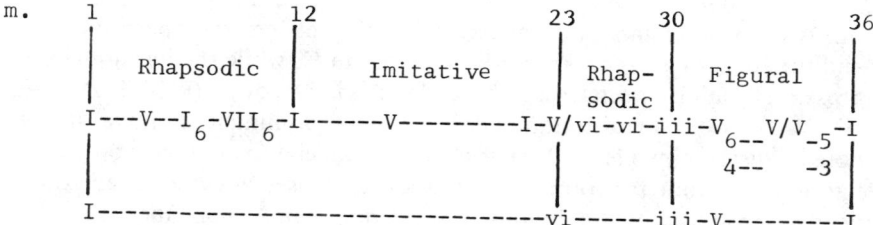

The Praeludium in a, BuxWV 153, provides an example of the second type; a large dominant pedal point follows figural texture:

Praeludium in a, BuxWV 153

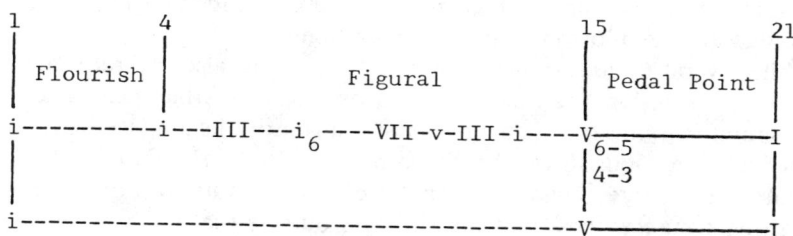

The cadence which ends the opening section is usually well prepared: a cogent harmonic formula provides a drive towards the cadence and such cadential preparation is usually enhanced by the broadening of the harmonic rhythm. A dominant pedal point of one or several measures is a frequent feature of the penultimate harmony; it is generally accompanied by a concomitant weakening of figural texture (if the section ends with that texture), which emphasizes the increasing importance of harmonic function as the cadence draws near.[5] The Praeludium in E, BuxWV 141, presents a typical example. In its simple but strong cadential preparation, vi–I_6–IV–(IV_6)–V-----I, the chords which prepare the dominant (vi–I_6–IV) are each of half-note duration; the penultimate dominant is three times as long.[6] A more frequent solution, however, is to subsume the entire preparation for the cadence within a large dominant pedal point. Such pedal points are not the product of a cadential drive, but generate the cadential gesture themselves. In the Praeludium in a, BuxWV 153, for example, the pedal point is six measures long; it alone signals the approaching cadence.[7]

Only two works utilize an especially weak cadence to end the opening section. In both of these works, the Praeludia in C, BuxWV 137, and in d, BuxWV 140, there are unusual thematic links between the opening section and the following fugue. In the Praeludium in C, while the harmonic progression which prepares the cadence is strong (ii–V–I–IV–ii–I$_6$ –ii$_7$–V/V–V–I), its realization is not. The final dominant is only a quarter note in duration, while the final tonic is only an eighth note. Not only is the harmonic rhythm far too swift for a strong close, but the raised fourth degree introduced by the dominant of the dominant is not cancelled by the natural fourth degree before the tonic arrival.[8] The Praeludium in d contains the most radical, that is, the least forceful, cadence of any opening section. The thematic link of the falling octave (d–D) to the following fugal subject outweighs the use of a strong cadence.[9] For this highly unusual gesture, Buxtehude creates a cadence which, throughout its entire preparation (measures 16–19), releases energy rather than building towards a climax. A rare feminine cadence, which is no match for the very strong arrival on the dominant in measure 16 three measures before, leads as seamlessly as Buxtehude's art can allow into the following fugue.

While several basic textural/harmonic forms (and also several examples of unique solutions) can be discerned, one aspect of the opening sections is common to all: the opening gesture is a flourish leading to the first tonic arrival. The flourish can be either short or long, a1, a2, or even a pedal solo. In its largest manifestations, it even creates its own quasi section.[10] In no instance does the flourish begin outside the tonic; rather, it elaborates the tonic as it leads to the first tonic arrival. At the arrival, the other voices and the pedal generally enter, and proceed in a full-voiced texture (usually figural). The opening flourish has the character of an upbeat; rarely does it enter on the first beat of the first measure, but often as | C ♪ ♫♪ . . . |. The first tonic arrival becomes the first real downbeat of the praeludium.[11]

Neither the flourish nor the opening section as a whole generally participates in the overall thematic web of the praeludium in its entirety.[12] Usually the opening section represents a self-contained thematic area. (Only occasionally do opening sections introduce thematic material which becomes significant for the praeludium as a whole.) The opening section, however, is not without its own thematic logic. The logic is that intrinsic to the figural style: small, flexible figures or motifs form a succession of thematic ideas (ABC . . .). Such a procedure, it should be noted, is strikingly similar to the overall thematic logic of the praeludium as a whole, which lacks recapitulation of thematic material and emphasizes the continuous variation of material as the sections proceed.

The opening flourish introduces the first thematic material of the praeludium. Though usually containing at least one serviceable motive, the

Opening Free Section 113

thematic material of the flourish is often not incorporated into the remainder of the section. Sometimes it is discarded immediately after the tonic arrival and the entrance of the other voices: A (flourish) BCD . . . ; occasionally, however, it becomes a significant thematic element, in which case the logic of the section approximates A (flourish) A'A"A''' . . . , as in the Praeludium in e, BuxWV 142:

Praeludium in e, BuxWV 142

114   Opening Free Section

However, both schemes are open-ended, and neither suggests a rounded thematic structure (ABC . . . A). In none of the opening sections with several textures is there any significant thematic link between the various passages; the thematic logic of figural texture (ABC . . .) remains undisturbed by preceding or following textures and becomes characteristic of the entire opening section. The archetypal form of the opening section can thus be summarized:

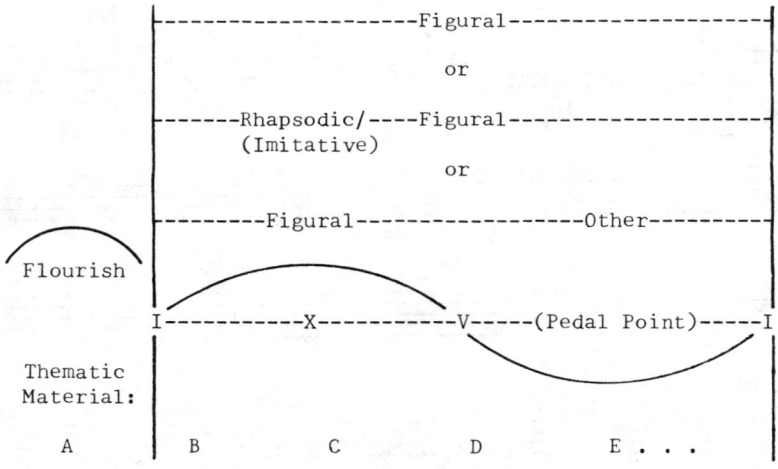

The shape of the section is controlled, then, largely through texture and harmony; the degree to which thematic material and the logic of its deployment controls its course is usually not large. The role of texture and harmony, and especially harmony at higher levels, is explored next.

Structural Analysis

The opening free sections join various and sometimes disparate harmonic areas, tonicization chains, pedal points, rhapsodic, figural, and other textures. All are united to form some degree of wholeness. Such a process of synthesis can be observed not only at the foreground level, as various gestures combine to form an opening section, but also, and more importantly, at higher levels. At such levels, texture becomes less important, and the interaction of harmony and counterpoint increasingly more so. Large-scale harmonic/contrapuntal motion, as the single most powerful means of synthesis, ultimately governs the progress of a section. Such background motion is a cadence which extends over the course of the section, and as such is crucial for the sense of closure achieved in the section.[13] While the actual cadence and its preparation at the foreground level are important elements of closure, at higher levels the drive towards the cadence can be observed to extend over most, if not all, of the section.

Synthesis and closure are achieved through the coordination of the background harmonic progression and a fundamental line.[14] This coordination can take many forms; indeed, each section has a unique solution. A survey of the typical background and middleground structures of the opening sections can begin with the Praeludium in C, BuxWV 136, which is one of the simplest.[15] A middleground sketch reveals an opening tonic elaboration ($I-I_6$) followed by a prolongation of the dominant ($V-ii_6-ii-V_{-7}$) leading to the return to the tonic. The first four measures (the tonic elaboration) establish $\hat{3}$ (e″) as the fundamental soprano note:

Praeludium in C, BuxWV 136

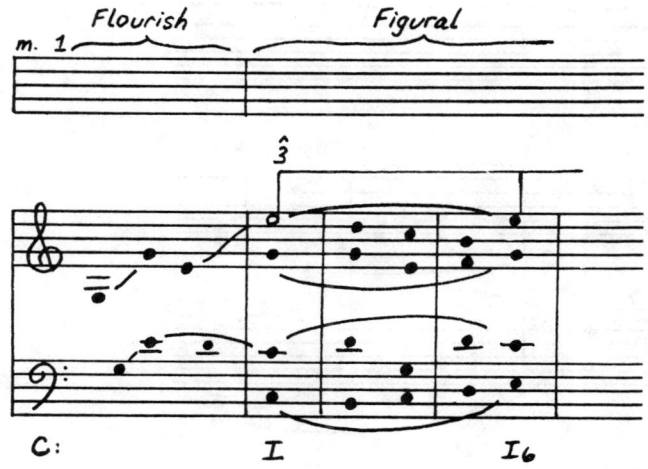

116   Opening Free Section

From the I_6 in measure 4 the dominant is easily reached by way of its own dominant in measure 5:

Praeludium in C, BuxWV 136

This tonicization begins a series of such progressions which results in a tonicization chain; it moves to the supertonic and prolongs that arrival:

Praeludium in C, BuxWV 136

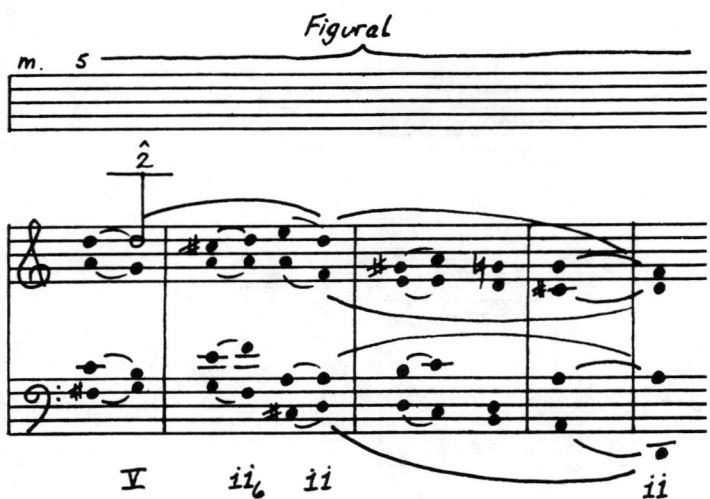

Parallel rising motion in the outer voices returns the music to the dominant:

Praeludium in C, BuxWV 136

Together with the preceding tonicization chain, these motions can be considered, at a higher level, as a prolongation of the dominant:

Praeludium in C, BuxWV 136

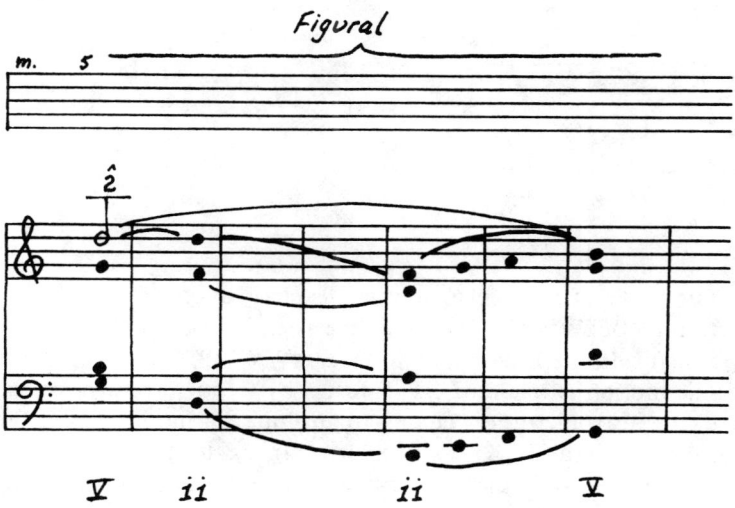

118   Opening Free Section

The fundamental line falls to $\hat{1}$ (c″) at the final cadence of the section as the overall $\hat{3}$-$\hat{2}$-$\hat{1}$ / I-V-I motion is completed:

Praeludium in C, BuxWV 136

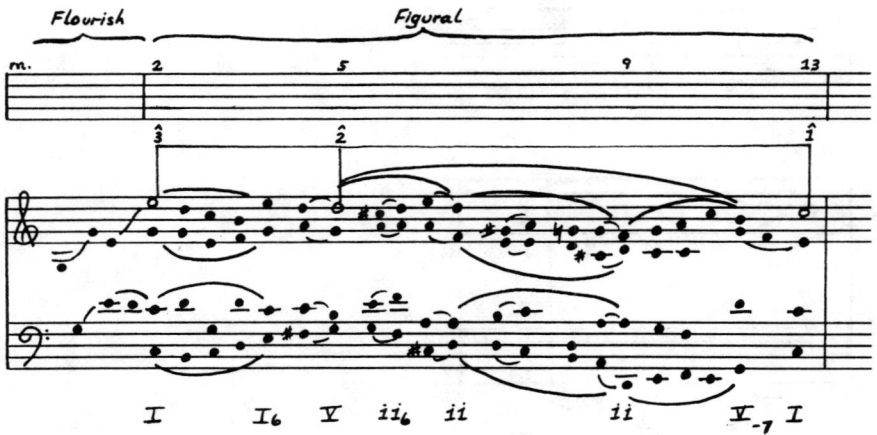

A further reduction demonstrates the basis of the section in an archetypal background form:

Praeludium in C, BuxWV 136

Buxtehude's style of coherence, however, is rarely as crystaline as in the opening section of BuxWV 136, where synthesis and closure are especially clear and powerful. In the Praeludium in D, BuxWV 139, for example, the basic harmonic motion is rendered less forceful by frequent returns to the tonic. There are no tonicization chains to prolong harmonic areas; the section is instead several I–(X)–V–I gestures strung together. After an unusually long flourish, full-voiced figural texture begins in measure 7. The first I-V-I gesture, created by voice interchanges, establishes f#' (3̂) as the beginning of the fundamental line. In the next I-X-V-I gesture, f#' is transferred up an octave to f#", and sustained at that register. In the following I-V-I motion, f#" descends through e" to d" (3̂-2̂-1̂) effecting closure of the fundamental line. In the final two I-V-I motions, the line at first hovers around d", and then, in an almost plagal, codalike gesture, f#' is regained (d"-c♮"-b'-a'-g'-f#'). The movement of the fundamental line (3̂-2̂-1̂) is confined to just the third I-V-I motion, a fact which substantially weakens its power. Likewise, the repeated I-V-I gestures, all relatively equal in strength, weaken a sense of overall harmonic motion. There is no dominant area at all comparable to those in BuxWV 136 or 153; the section is entirely centered on the tonic. The isolation of one I-V-I motion as the carrier of essential harmonic/contrapuntal motion is not arbitrary only to the extent that it manifests linear closure. Yet the 3̂-2̂-1̂ descent occurs at a register at odds with f#'. Decorated with a characteristic 5̂-4̂-3̂ motion (a'-g'-f#'), f#' occurs at three important moments in the section (measures 7, 12, and 20). The register of the 3̂-2̂-1̂ descent does not dominate the entire section as in BuxWV 136; indeed, f#' is a significant challenge to the overall strength of the fundamental line. The note f#' itself is an important aspect of coherence, especially to join the various harmonic motions. It is as much a reference point in the linear coherence of the section as the 3̂-2̂-1̂ descent itself:

Praeludium in D, BuxWV 139

Opening Free Section

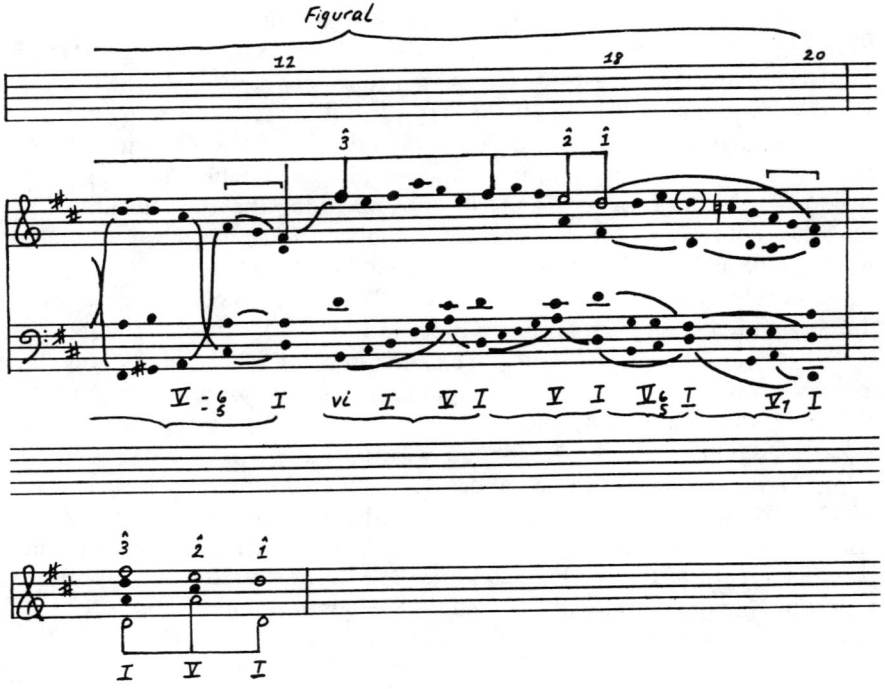

A $_{\text{I-V-I}}^{\hat{3}\text{-}\hat{2}\text{-}\hat{1}}$ construction is not the only possible background structure. While the basic I-(X)-V-I motion is always present, the counterpointing fundamental line can take several other forms. One such form is a $\hat{5}$-$\hat{4}$-$\hat{3}$-$\hat{2}$-$\hat{1}$ descent (which incorporates the simpler $\hat{3}$-$\hat{2}$-$\hat{1}$ into a larger motion). The opening section of the Toccata in F, BuxWV 156, is an example. It consists almost entirely of large pedal points, first on the tonic, and then the dominant. (The final tonic is not elaborated by a pedal point but is simply a cadence chord.) During the opening tonic pedal, a' ($\hat{3}$) rises through b♮' to c''; that note ($\hat{5}$) is prolonged throughout the first (imitative) section of the dominant pedal. The dominant pedal is then interrupted by four measures of lively harmonic rhythm at the quarter note. When the pedal resumes, c'' descends through b♭', a', and g' to f' ($\hat{5}$-$\hat{4}$-$\hat{3}$-$\hat{2}$-$\hat{1}$). An important aspect of the second dominant pedal is the addition of a voice above the descending $\hat{2}$-$\hat{1}$ motion; the insistence of $\hat{5}$-$\hat{4}$ above it (especially in measures 29 and 30), and finally $\hat{5}$-$\hat{4}$-$\hat{3}$ at the cadence substantially weakens the effect of the fundamental line's descent to $\hat{1}$:[16]

Toccata in F, BuxWV 156

122   Opening Free Section

The third standard formation of the fundamental line, $\hat{8}-\hat{7}-\hat{6}-\hat{5}-\hat{4}-\hat{3}-\hat{2}-\hat{1}$, can also be found. The Praeludium in f♯, BuxWV 146, presents an example. The opening tonic pedal point establishes f♯″ ($\hat{8}$) as the beginning of the line. The descent is found in the following chordal passage.[17] When the $\hat{1}$ arrives at the cadence, it is f♯″, the original $\hat{8}$, rather than an actual $\hat{1}$ (f♯′). Such an emphasis on f♯″ weakens the effect of the closure in the line and creates an overall static effect, f♯″–f♯″:

Praeludium in f♯, BuxWV 146

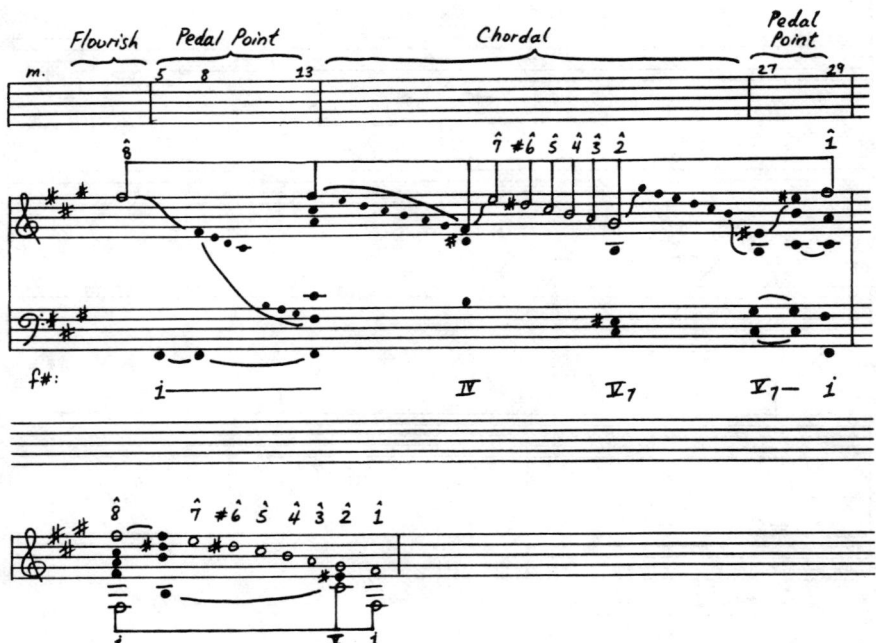

Not all of the opening sections can be reconciled, however, with the three types of fundamental lines. The Praeludium in g, BuxWV 150, with its unusual imitative texture over a tonic pedal point, is an example. With little if any background descent as a counterpoint to its I–V–I harmonic motion, the section seems static at higher levels. Whatever descent occurs is situated completely over the opening tonic pedal ($\hat{5}-\hat{4}-\hat{3}-\hat{2}-\hat{1}$ is suggested in measures 12–13); the dominant (measure 14) is counterpointed by ♯$\hat{7}$, not $\hat{2}$:

Praeludium in g, BuxWV 150

The structures in the opening free sections clearly depend on the cadential gesture. The fundamental line consists of the stepwise descent to the cadence, whether such a descent occurs over virtually the entire course of the section or only over a portion of it. As most of the opening free sections are relatively small, the cadential gesture can easily encompass much if not all of the section, although this is not always the case. The structures can be further characterized as lacking strong support for each member of the descending line. Indeed, often one or more scale degrees in the line is weakly supported. Also, altered scale degrees appear occasionally in such lines.[18] Movement of the line may also be concentrated near the cadence, with its initial note prolonged throughout much of the section.[19] These characteristics are prime elements of the style of these structures and they mark an important aspect of the nature of the opening free sections. And as similar formations are also found in the sections which follow the opening free section as well as at a higher level in the works when considered as wholes, they are a significant part of Buxtehude's structural style.[20]

Opening Free Section

Historical and Critical Evaluation

Various aspects of the style and structure of the opening free sections can be found in the works of Buxtehude's predecessors. The opening sections of the praeambula, praeludia, and toccatas of Tunder and Weckmann exhibit a wide variety of forms.[21] Those of Tunder's four praeludia have two basic schemes. The opening section of the Praeludium in F[22] has a I-----I (I-X-I-V-I-IV-V-I) harmonic plan. As in Buxtehude's Praeludium in D, BuxWV 139, there are frequent returns to the tonic. The three remaining praeludia, all in g, each begin with the tonic major (the dominant of the subdominant) rather than the tonic minor. Without an opening tonic pillar, their harmonic motion seems curiously unfocused.[23] Several exhibit an opening flourish and a thematic logic which anticipates Buxtehude's usual ABC... type. They have a strong close achieved through cogent cadential preparation which relies on a dominant pedal. A considerable command of figuration, particularly in sixteenth notes, intensifies the drive towards the cadence and the elaboration of the dominant pedal. But the sense of line and background coherence is not great. The opening on the tonic major in the Praeludium in g[24] seems to throw the harmonic motion off balance; only midway through the section does a fundamental line begin to exert real influence:

Tunder: Praeludium in g

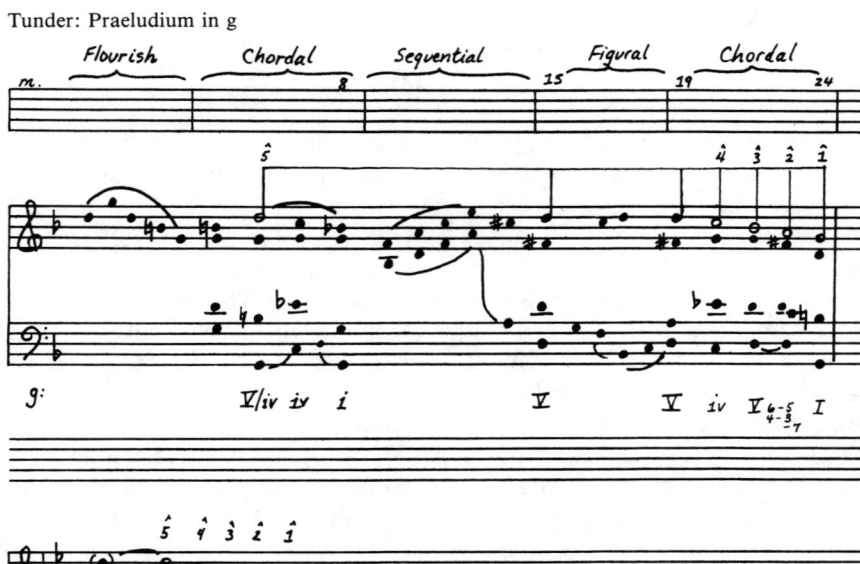

The opening free section of Weckmann's Praeambulum in d (his only organ work with such a section) and his keyboard toccatas demonstrate a less coherent style. While the opening section of the Praeambulum[25] has a I-----I plan, a well-prepared cadence, and a clear if not very cogent harmonic scheme, there is no overall sense of line:[26]

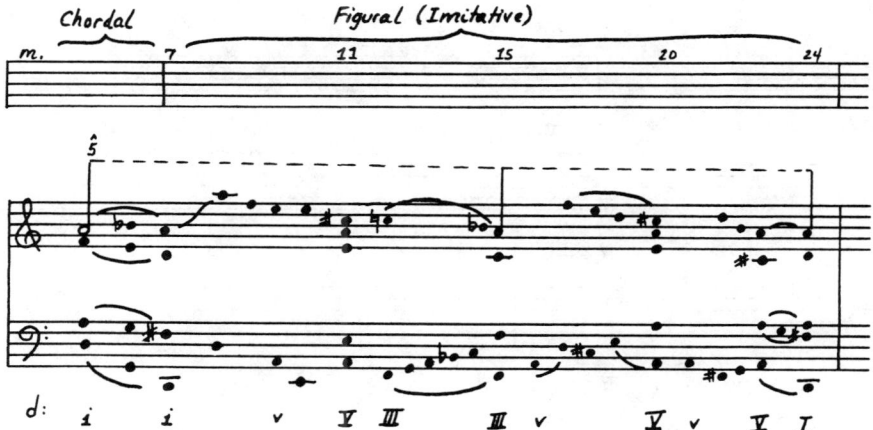

Weckmann: Praeambulum in d

Weckmann's toccatas betray a greater degree of structural chaos. Often lacking a clear cadence, their opening free sections fade into a following fugal or chordal section. (A close on the dominant is frequent.) These sections have very little sense of line, background coherence, or closure. To find convincing examples of synthesis within the toccata, it is necessary to turn to Froberger, the composer whose influence provoked these works. His toccatas demonstrate the elegant structures possible within the toccata style that eluded Weckmann. His Toccata in d[27] has a clear $\hat{8}$-$\hat{7}$-$\hat{6}$-$\hat{5}$ descent spanning the section: a very appropriate scheme for a section which closes on the dominant. Another Toccata, also in d,[28] closes on the tonic; an $\hat{8}$-$\hat{7}$-$\hat{6}$-$\hat{5}$-$\hat{4}$-$\hat{3}$-$\hat{2}$-$\hat{1}$ line encompasses the section and guides it towards a close:

126   Opening Free Section

Froberger: Toccata in d

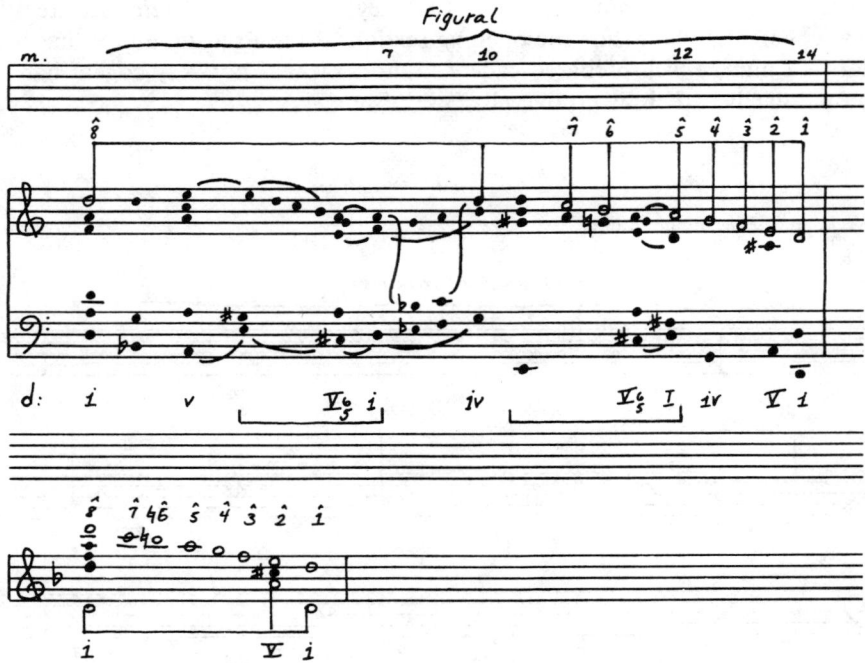

From the generation before Tunder and Weckmann to Buxtehude, the opening free sections of the praeambulum/praeludium became larger, bolder, and structurally more independent. In this development, Buxtehude relied heavily on the shapes provided by Tunder (the opening flourish, figural texture, and the dominant pedal around which harmonic closure is organized in addition to general size and expressive scope). Within Tunder's basic shape, Buxtehude expanded the sense of overall synthesis and large-scale closure. In both his greater sensitivity to background structure and more refined surface detail he approaches, more than any other north German, the elegance of Froberger. The formal stature of his opening sections was increased by solid tonic pillars at both the opening (after the flourish) and the ending. The equivocal tonic major opening in the minor mode frequently found in Tunder was abandoned, as were the open endings on the dominant often encountered not only in early north German praeambula (such as those by Scheidemann), but also in the toccatas of Weckmann and Froberger.

The degree of independence of the opening free sections within the praeludium depends on several factors. A cogent background structure, such as is achieved by most of Buxtehude's opening sections, argues for independence: it implies that each contains not only significant content, but most importantly, a drive towards closure. Ways in which the background formations and the fundamental line are weakened in their foreground realization, however, have already been mentioned. Moreover, background structure is not the only determinant of structural status: features at the surface level also affect the perception of structural integrity. While the extent to which the background controls the surface through harmonic areas, line, and register is considerable, not all that appears at the surface is a reflection of the background. The energy created at the surface by figuration and the sense of resolution of that energy within the section—what might be termed musical poise—is primarily an attribute of the foreground. Poise is not synonymous with elegance of structure; rather, the background is the framework which contains and directs surface energy. Moreover, poise is an important aspect of the integrity of a section or work. Without a balance between the accumulation and relaxation of energy (appropriate to the size of the section), the integrity of the section is compromised. With too little energy, a section will fall into fragments; with too much energy, it will strain its frame. Its close, no matter how well prepared, may sound at best inconclusive.

Buxtehude's opening sections often contain more energy and sheer exuberance than their relatively small size can contain. However, they still maintain a sense of equilibrium between the content and the form, or more importantly, between the surface and the structure. The result is the typical anticipatory sound of these sections; their energy is not fully resolved within their own frame, and a continuation of the praeludium is implied. Many opening free sections exhibit an extreme richness, even overabundance, of content and energy. The opening section of the Praeludium in d, BuxWV 140, is a notable example. So too is that of the Praeludium in g, BuxWV 149, with its ciacona texture. In this latter opening free section, the unusual repetition of the last section of the ciacona theme, unaccompanied in the pedal part, not only is an inspired link to the following fugal section, but also an attempt to modulate the high energy level of the opening free section into the more relaxed mood of the fugue which follows. The opening section of the Praeludium in f#, BuxWV 146, generates far more energy in its bold chordal passage than can possibly be reconciled with the short duration of the section; as a result, the passage casts a powerful shadow far into the rest of the praeludium. Even with less spectacular means, Buxtehude usually manages to fill to overflowing the content of the opening free sections: the rich figural style exemplified by such works as the Praeludia in C, BuxWV 136, in e, BuxWV 142, and in a, BuxWV 153, is another stylistic means to the same end. Similar results are also obtained in multitextural opening free sections. In the Toccata in d, BuxWV 155, for example, the rapid succession of figural, overlegato, pedal point, and fugato textures permits no relaxation in the level of tension, since each new texture is more intense than the previous. At the end of the section, the energy which has been generated is not adequately relaxed in time for the cadence. As a result, closure seems summary and incomplete.

Buxtehude faced the problem of how to create an opening free section that would both provide a stable, impressive first section but not be so independent as to split off entirely from the rest of the praeludium and break the momentum of the multisectional form before it even begins. The "genuine prelude and fugue"—a diptych of two structurally independent but grouped works—lay a generation beyond Buxtehude. To apply the term to those works of the north German organists of his generation (which, for whatever reason, employ only the opening free section and a following fugue)[29] is a serious misuse: it masks the fundamental difference between a praeludium and a prelude-and-fugue. As these opening free sections amply demonstrate, the first sections of the praeludium walk a tightrope between structural independence and dependence on the praeludium as a whole, between the status of a real piece and a fragment. While Buxtehude achieved a great deal of structural independence in his opening sections, their characteristic hyperexpressivity works against it. This balance was his solution to the dilemma of the opening free section in the multisectional praeludium. Ultimately, however, the complete analysis of the opening sections can only take place within the context of the praeludia as a whole. Following analysis of the first fugal sections and then those which appear after them, the independent/dependent status of the opening free sections, as well as the sectional/synthetic nature of the praeludium, will be further investigated.[30]

7

The First Fugal Section

Style Analysis

The second section of a praeludium is always fugal. As the opening section is always free, the fugue in the second section is the first fugue to appear in the praeludium.[1] While the sections which follow, if any, are texturally unpredictable, the first fugal sections are a standard element of the praeludium. They are the second most stable part of the overall form; their tonal plan is usually a closed one, I-----I.[2] (The opening free sections are always harmonically closed, and can thus be considered more stable.) In sharp contrast to the preceding section, the harmonic language of the first fugues is generally diatonic. Later in the praeludium, however, other fugal sections are apt to be in a richer harmonic style. The meter of the first fugues is always common time; succeeding ones generally employ contrasting triple-time meters. The first fugue, then, is both harmonically and metrically designed to allow contrasting and less stable sections such as those in triple time or with unusual harmonies to follow.[3]

The stability of the first fugal sections is also reflected in their overall shape. They are the most elaborately constructed and the most rigorously imitative of the fugal sections in the praeludia. The fragmentary nature of the fugatos and the structural looseness of the triple-time fugues, characteristic of second or third fugues, are avoided in the first one. At the highest level, the first fugues have a two-part structure, articulated by the following textural succession: fugue + free. The free ending is variable in style, usually short, and virtually never omitted. Within the fugue itself, shape is determined by harmony and fugal structure (exposition, succeeding expositions, extra entries, and entries outside the tonic). While harmony and fugal structure are highly interdependent, the cadences which articulate the harmonic plan are not always coordinated in the most obvious ways with the fugal structure. The result is a flexibility of form which yields many possible solutions.

First Fugal Section

In the first fugal section, the exposition always follows a subject/answer/subject/answer form.[4] Most frequently, the following pattern is used:[5]

>   S (soprano)
>   A (alto)
>   S (tenor)
>   A (bass)

The answer is virtually always a tonal answer; real answers occur only in the two archaic works, the Praeambulum in a, BuxWV 158, and the Praeludium in a, BuxWV 152. (These two works are also the only ones to present subdominant rather than dominant answers.) Countersubjects are sometimes found accompanying the entrances of the subject and answer.[6] Invertible counterpoint is also occasionally used, especially in connection with countersubjects.[7] If the subject does not modulate, the entire exposition is a tonic harmonic area:

>   S----A----S----A----
>   I----I----I----I----(I)

This simple solution occurs in six of the praeludia.[8] A modulating subject creates an oscillation between tonic and dominant:

>   S----A----S----A----
>   I----V----I----V----(I)

Such a solution is found in five of the praeludia.[9] Buxtehude's most frequent plan, however, is to emphasize the dominant tendencies of the tonal answer before the subject returns in the tonic:[10]

>   S----A----S----A----
>   I----I--V-I----I--V-(I)

Sometimes the harmonic motion is accentuated by a codetta:

>   S----A----...S----A----...
>   I----I-----V-I----I-----V-(I)

The actual shape of the subject, of course, is the chief determinant of which plan is used. Subjects which begin on $\hat{1}$ (and usually move towards $\hat{5}$) are generally modulating subjects.[11] The preponderance of Buxtehude's subjects, however, begin on $\hat{5}$ (and often move towards $\hat{1}$); they are either nonmodulating or, more frequently, use codettas.[12]

The exposition generally ends with a tonic cadence. The fugue of the Praeludium in C, BuxWV 137, offers an example unusual in its clarity:[13]

Praeludium in C, BuxWV 137

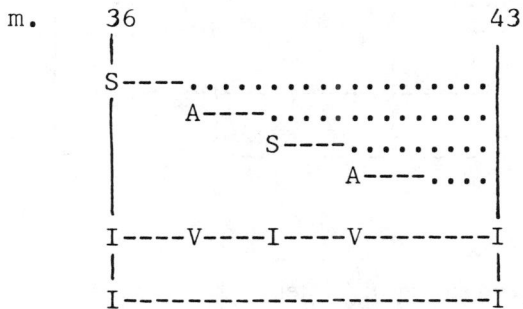

The end of the exposition and the first harmonic closure associated with it, however, are usually not so precisely coordinated. In most fugues an extra entry leads to the cadence. The fugue of the Praeludium in g, BuxWV 147, is an example:[14]

Praeludium in G, BuxWV 147

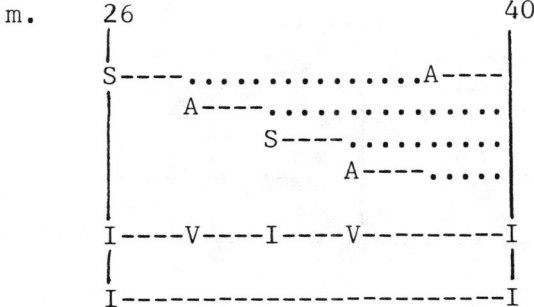

After the exposition, the fugues usually continue with another exposition.[15] Episodes and entries in other keys are unusual and, if they occur, generally follow the second exposition.[16] The second exposition may begin immediately after the first cadence, as in the Praeludium in C, BuxWV 137:

132 First Fugal Section

Praeludium in C, BuxWV 137

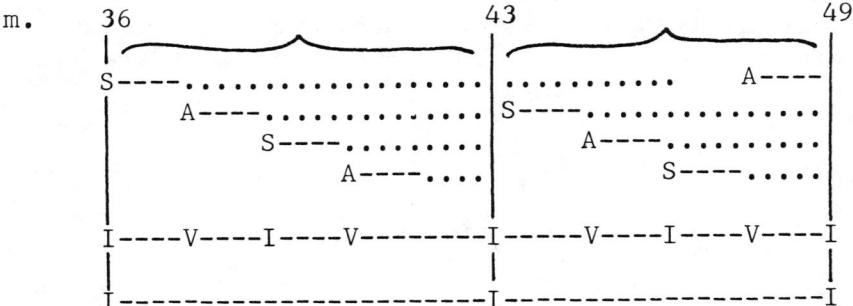

In many fugues, however, the extra entry which often leads to the cadence is actually the first entry of the second exposition, as in the Praeludium in f#, BuxWV 146:

Praeludium in f#, BuxWV 146

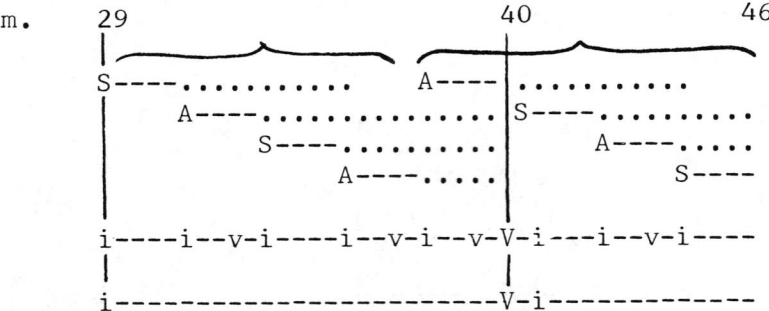

While there is no standard form for the second exposition, the entry pattern illustrated in BuxWV 146 is the most frequent type.[17] Occasionally, a special technique is used. In the Toccata in F, BuxWV 156, the entries of the second exposition are in stretto:

Toccata in F, BuxWV 156

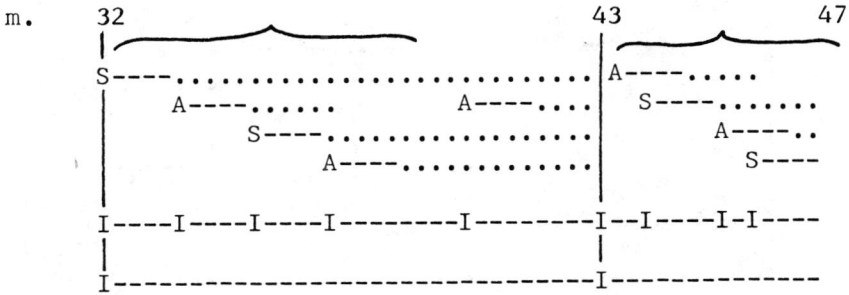

In the Praeludium in a, BuxWV 153, the entries of the second exposition are in inversion:

Praeludium in a, BuxWV 153

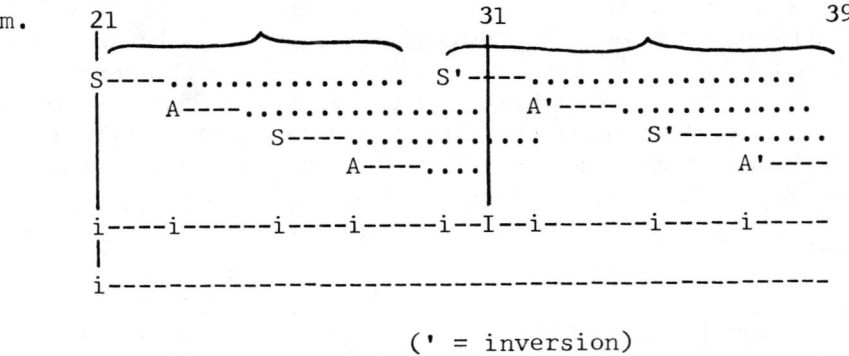

(' = inversion)

A third exposition follows the second in many fugues.[18] The Toccata in F, BuxWV 157, is an example:[19]

Toccata in F, BuxWV 157

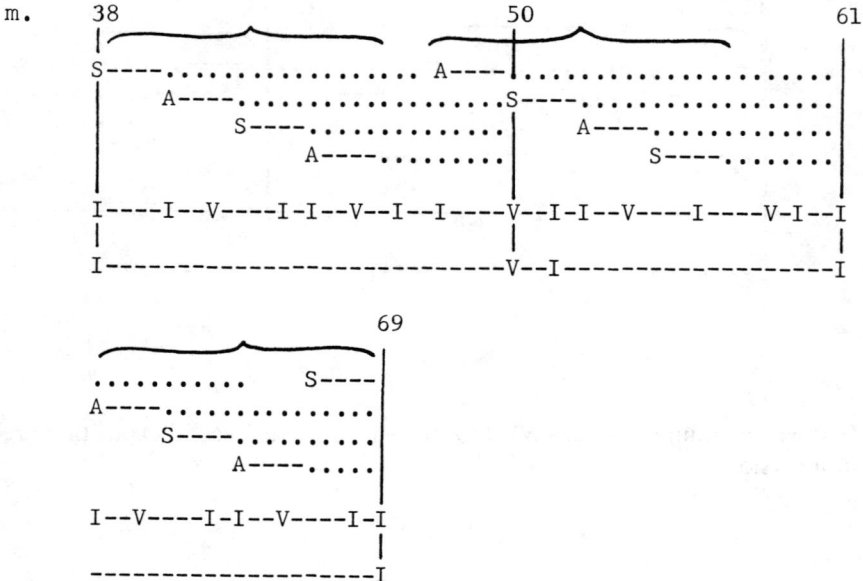

As in the second exposition, special techniques are occasionally used in the third one (for example, stretto is used in the Praeludium in G, BuxWV 147). In other fugues, entries after the second exposition do not take the form of a third one, but are simply extra entries; however, unlike those heard before, they often appear outside the tonic.[20] Such entries in the first fugues most often occur in the mediant, subdominant, or dominant, and less frequently in the submediant or subtonic.[21] The Praeludium in E, BuxWV 141, provides an example of entries in the dominant:

Praeludium in E, BuxWV 141

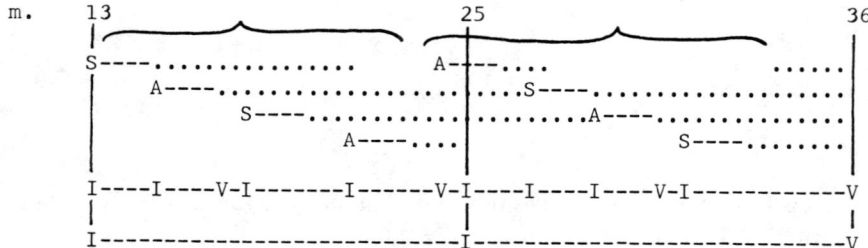

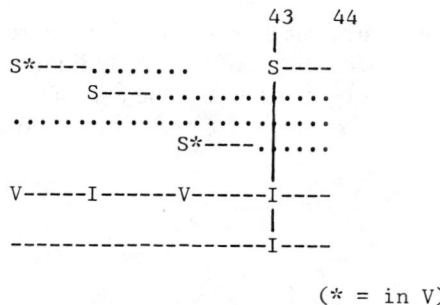

(* = in V)

The result of so great a dependence upon the technique of a series of expositions is a high-level modular form. An extreme example can be found in the Praeludium in C, BuxWV 137:

Praeludium in C, BuxWV 137

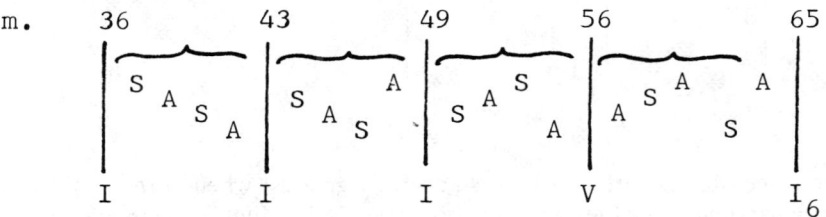

Such a high degree of modularity, however, is usually avoided through nonsimultaneous articulations of fugal form and harmonic arrival. This technique is applied throughout the fugue of the Praeludium in D, BuxWV 139:

Praeludium in D, BuxWV 139

m.   21   33   41   48   53   55
     ┌──┐   ┌──┐   ┌──┐   S*   S**   ┌──┐
      S A   S A   S A   S A
        S A   A S   A   A*   S
                   S   S A*

     I   I   I   iii   V   vi

(* = in vi; ** = in iii)

The ambiguity of an extra entry before a harmonic arrival is nowhere more elegantly realized by Buxtehude than in the first fugue of the Praeludium in f♯, BuxWV 146. In this fugue, a true extra entry occurs at the end of the second exposition to balance the effect of a pseudoextra entry at the end of the first exposition:

Praeludium in f♯, BuxWV 146

m. 29   40   50
    ⌒‾‾‾‾‾‾‾‾‾⌒ ⌒‾‾‾‾‾‾‾‾‾⌒
    | S   A   S |
    | A S   S A S |
    | S A |
    | |
    i   V   i

    [S   [A]   S]
    [A S   +   S A   +   ]
    [S A   S   ]

The force of these articulations is generally greatest when both fugal form and harmonic arrival are exactly coordinated. The highly sectional organization of the Praeludium in C, BuxWV 137, is a prime example. Emphasis on an internal articulation, however, can be obtained by other means. The large first fugue of the Praeludium in g, BuxWV 150, contains an unusually powerful internal articulation after the second exposition. A curious written out pedal trill contributes much to the effect.[22] Generally Buxtehude seeks to downgrade the strong sense of arrival within the fugue; forward momentum is preserved through the ambiguity of nonsimultaneous articulations and nontonic harmonic arrivals.

    A free ending is usually introduced several measures before the close of the first fugal section.[23] The free ending can be in any one of many various textures (chordal, rhapsodic, modular, and figural are the most frequently employed). These relatively short passages usually contrast quite forcefully with the preceding fugal texture. The fugal texture is generally interrupted, sometimes dramatically.[24] In only a few cases does the free ending seem to grow directly out of the preceding texture, either as a simple extension, or through actual thematic connections:[25]

Praeludium in e, BuxWV 142

The disjunction between the fugue and its free ending highlights the cadential function of the free ending. Some free endings elaborate the penultimate dominant, while others present an entire, cogent chord progression. They always contain the essential harmonic motion, V-----I, which closes the section, and are thus not codas.[26]

Five of the praeludia end after the first fugue.[27] They generally employ the same types of endings as do the majority, which continue with other sections. The Praeludium in C, BuxWV 138, and the Toccata in F, BuxWV 157, have unusually strong endings. The Praeludium in C ends with two free endings: first a modular passage which resembles a ciacona, and then a rhapsodic one. The first free ending, because of its ciaconalike construction, provides a number of internal tonic cadences in addition to its final cadence at measure 63. All of these cadences, however, occur on beat four of the measure. For this reason, a second free ending in another texture is used to lead to a more convincing closure in whole-note rather than quarter-note harmonic rhythm:

138   *First Fugal Section*

Praeludium in C, BuxWV 138

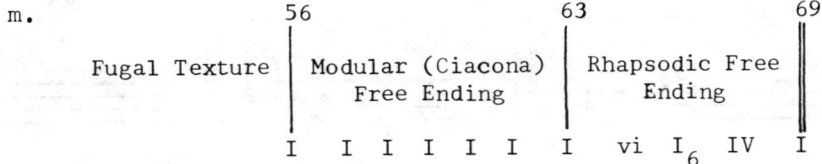

The Toccata in F closes with a large, complex section derived from many elements of the fugue including the subject and countersubject, plus free elements:

Toccata in F, BuxWV 157

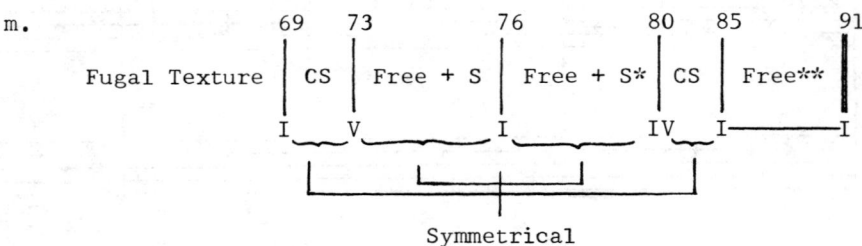

(CS = Countersubject; * = Fragment in IV; ** = Tonic Pedal)

The Praeludium in F, BuxWV 144, closes without a free ending of any kind; in this rare example, fugal texture leads to the end of the fugue and the praeludium as a whole. However, an exposition of fragments of the subject creates a strettolike effect just before the close:[28]

Praeludium in F, BuxWV 144

```
m.                  47                                        54
   Fugal Texture │ S*--...........        A*--..S*--......  ║
                 │       A*--.........S*--................. ║
                 │         S*--............................ ║
                 │           A*--          A*--............ ║
                 I                                          I
```

(* = Fragment)

An archetypal form of the first fugue can be approximated:

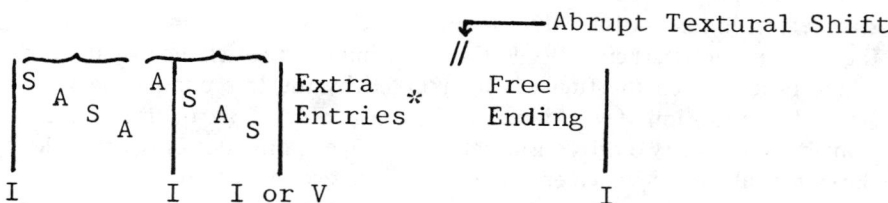

The shape of the first fugues, then, is largely the product of fugal form, harmony, and the free ending. The role of harmony, however, is larger than that delineated by style analysis alone. The organizational power of harmony (as well as line), particularly at higher levels, is discussed next.

Structural Analysis

Synthesis and closure[29] play important roles in the structure of fugal sections just as they do in free ones. Harmonic coherence in the fugues is particularly clear. The various kinds of harmonic plans created by the alternation of subject and answer,[30]

```
S----A----S----A----        S----A----S----A----
I----I----I----I----(I)     I----I--V-I----I--V-(I)

S----A----S----A----        S----A----...S----A----...
I----V----I----V----(I)     I----I-----V-I----I-----V-(I)
```

can all be easily understood at a higher level as a single tonic harmonic area:

```
      S----A----S----A----
      I----V----I----V----(I)
      I---------------------I
```

Generally, however, fugues are not built solely of tonic areas. For example, a second exposition will occasionally close with a nontonic cadence, or extra entries outside the tonic will create nontonic harmonic areas. These events, reflected in the middleground structure, are also easily integrated into the overall harmonic motion.

Closure in the fugal sections is more complex. While overall harmonic coherence may be easy to demonstrate, linear coherence, or the presence of a fundamental line which leads towards closure, is often less clear. The constant reliance on a series of expositions of the fugal material can create a static effect in terms of a large line. For the close of the section, therefore, the free ending is crucial. While the sometimes radical change of texture which occurs when the fugue is interrupted by the free ending seems to stress the opposition of the fugue and the free ending, the structural connections between the two are considerable. The free ending not only embodies the cadential motion which ends the fugue, but also in most instances brings the fundamental line of the fugue to its conclusion:

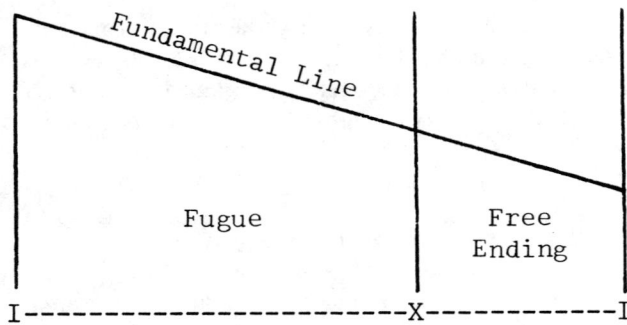

Rarely is the free ending simply a coda, uninvolved with the linear coherence of the section:

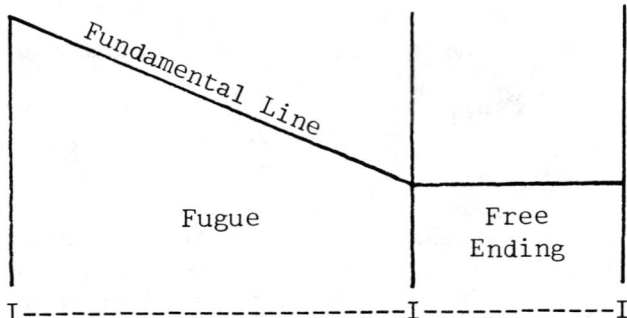

Rather, the movement of the fundamental line is often concentrated towards the end of the section; its descent may not commence until near the beginning of the free ending:

First Fugal Section 141

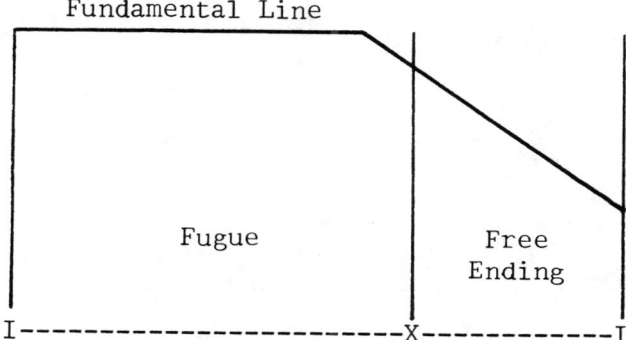

Closure is considerably more problematic when the fugue (or its free ending) does not end with a tonic cadence; the eventual resolution of the harmonic/linear background is then delayed until the following section:

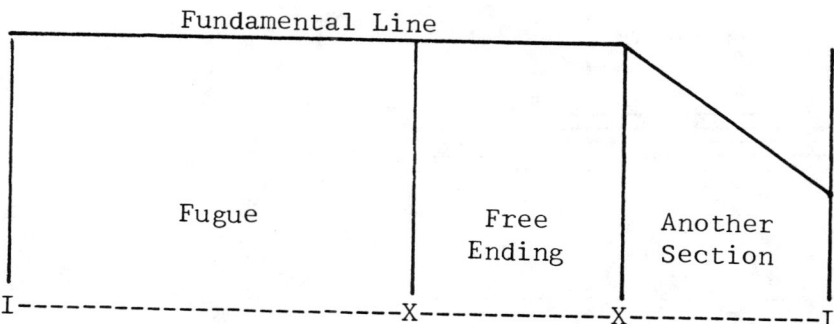

The fugue of the Praeludium in D, BuxWV 139, can serve as a typical example of synthesis and closure in Buxtehude's fugal style. The subject is based upon a descending motion of a third:

Praeludium in D, BuxWV 139

142   First Fugal Section

It is answered by a descending second:

Praeludium in D, BuxWV 139

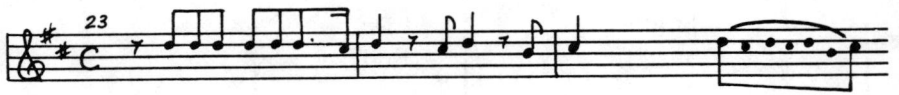

The alternation of these motions creates arrival points which constitute the harmonic framework:

Praeludium in D, BuxWV 139

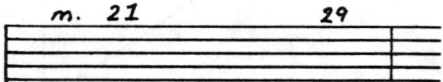

Occasionally short extensions are interpolated, as the one which ends the exposition with an elaboration of the dominant:

Praeludium in D, BuxWV 139

The second exposition, beginning with the dominant chord which ends the first exposition, follows a similar plan. The goal of the harmonic motion of the first exposition, however, is the tonic cadence in measure 33, which is not attained until after the second exposition is under way:

Praeludium in D, BuxWV 139

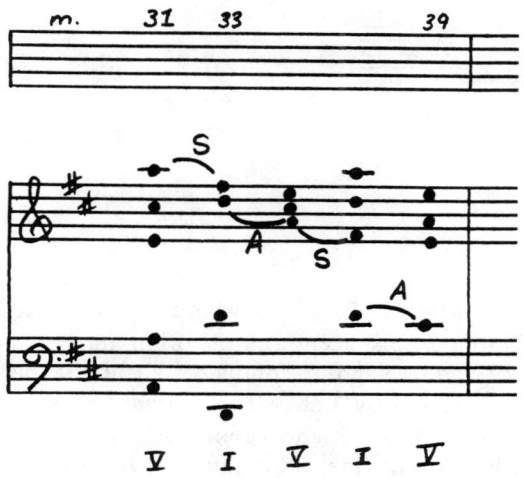

144   First Fugal Section

Throughout the fugue, $\hat{5}$ is prolonged in the soprano over the alternating tonic and dominant harmony:

Praeludium in D, BuxWV 139

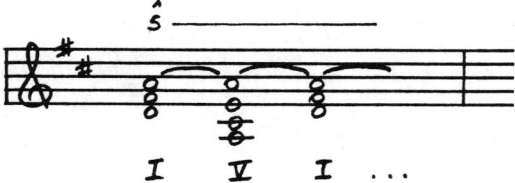

During the third exposition and the extra entries which follow, $\hat{5}$ is covered by other voices as the submediant and the mediant are employed:

Praeludium in D, BuxWV 139

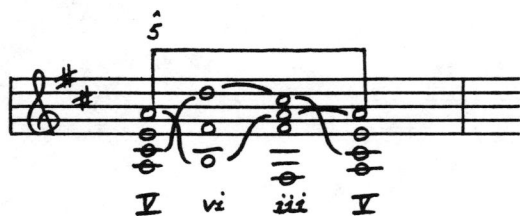

After the return of the dominant, $\hat{5}$ falls to $\hat{3}$, $\genfrac{}{}{0pt}{}{\hat{5}\text{-}\hat{4}\text{-}\hat{3}}{\text{V---vi}}$, where a deceptive cadence and a switch from eighth-note to sixteenth-note motion announce the beginning of the free ending. The free ending completes closure of the fundamental line, $\genfrac{}{}{0pt}{}{\hat{3}\text{-}\hat{2}\text{-}\hat{1}}{\text{vi-V-I}}$. The $\hat{1}$ is covered by $\hat{3}$ at its first arrival (measure 58), but an echo of this motion, an octave higher, confirms the descent (measure 61). The overall coordination of line, harmony, and fugal form can be summarized as follows:

First Fugal Section   145

Praeludium in D, BuxWV 139

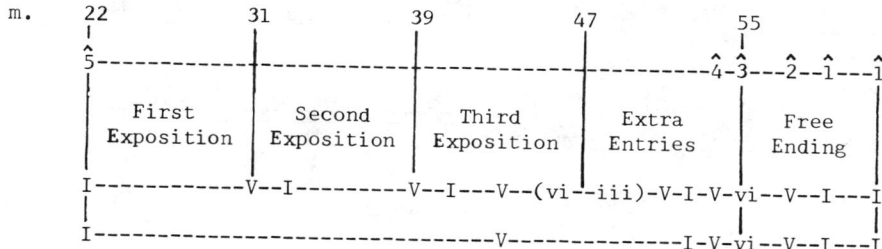

Details of the plan are presented on the following graph:

Praeludium in D, BuxWV 139

146   First Fugal Section

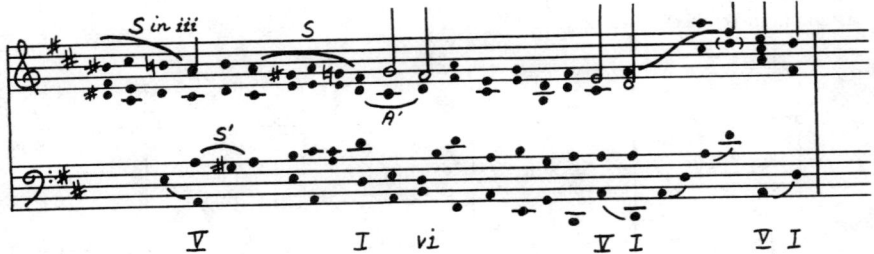

A stronger overall sense of line and a less modular form are found in the first fugue of the Praeludium in d, BuxWV 140. In this fugue the descent of the line, $\hat{8}$-$\hat{7}$-$\flat\hat{6}$-$\hat{5}$-$\hat{4}$-$\hat{3}$-$\hat{2}$-$\hat{1}$, spans a larger portion of the section. The exposition closes without a strong harmonic arrival; instead, the harmonic motion drives towards a cadence on the dominant at the close of the second exposition. The remaining extra entries and the free ending return the fugue to the tonic:

Praeludium in d, BuxWV 140

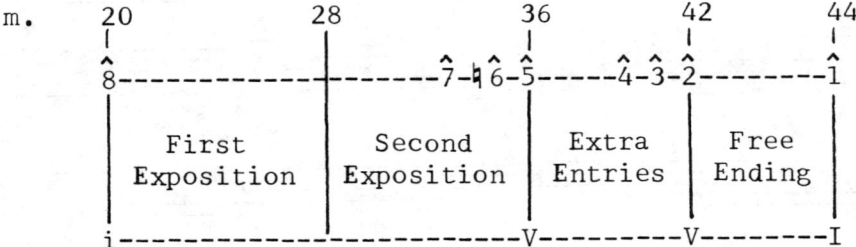

First Fugal Section 147

The $\hat{8}$ is prolonged as the subject and answer alternations proceed; only when real harmonic motion towards the arrival on the dominant begins does the line begin to move. The descent of the line continues during the extra entries and concludes during the free ending. The strong fundamental line, coupled with the clear harmonic scheme focused on its midway dominant cadence, make this one of the most powerfully coherent of the fugal sections:

Praeludium in d, BuxWV 140

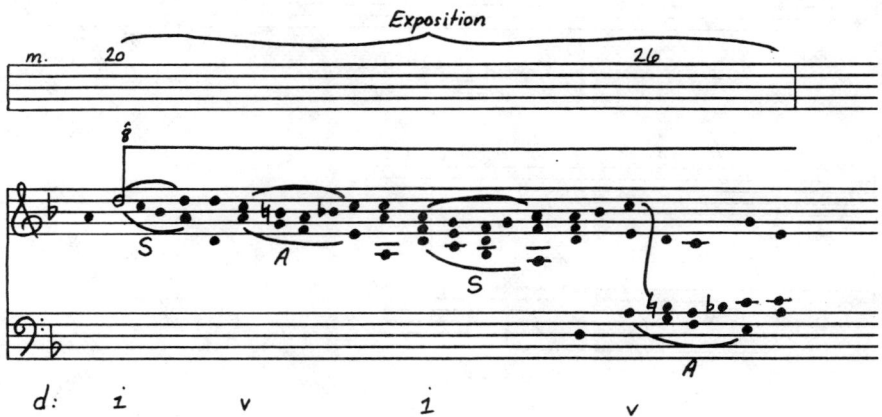

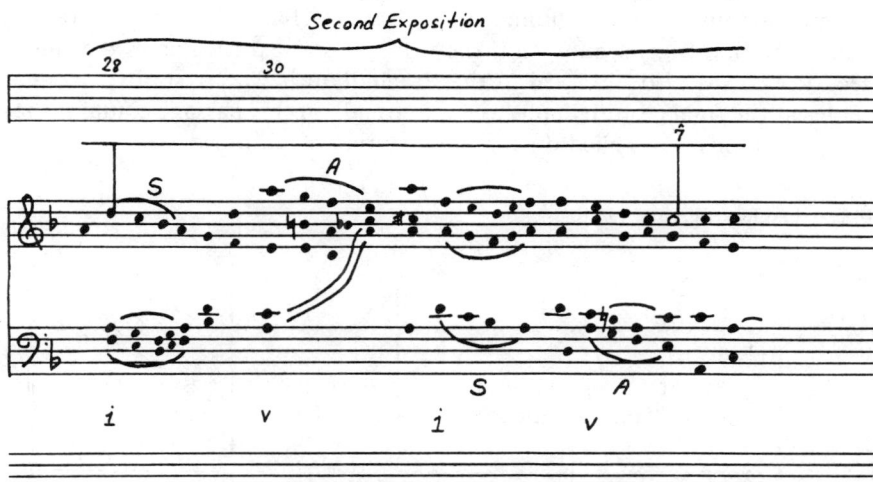

148 First Fugal Section

The characteristics of the first fugue are also found when it terminates the praeludium. The Praeludium in F, BuxWV 144, is one of several in which the first fugal section ends the work. A static $\hat{5}$ dominates the fugal section (as was also observed in the Praeludium in D). A stretto passage serves as the final gesture in place of a free ending; this passage contains the $\hat{5}$-$\hat{4}$-$\hat{3}$-$\hat{2}$-$\hat{1}$ closure implied during the material which precedes it:

Praeludium in F, BuxWV 144

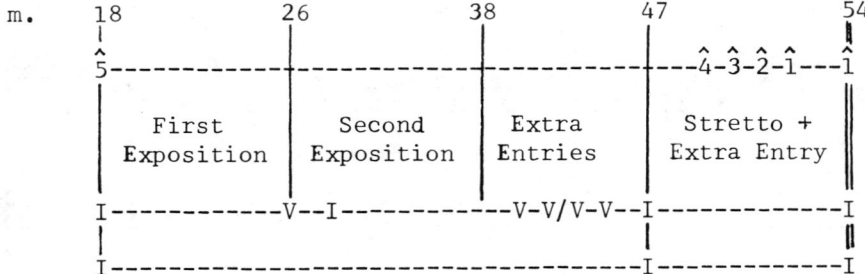

This fundamental line, however, is not nearly as powerful as that of the Praeludium in d, for example, in which linear motion spans the entire fugal section and is not concentrated in just one passage of it.

Other praeludia which end with the first fugue do employ the typical free ending. The Praeludium in F, BuxWV 145, is an example. As in the first fugue of the Praeludium in d, the fugue ends on $\hat{2}\atop V$; the free ending completes the fundamental line and brings a resolution to the tonic:

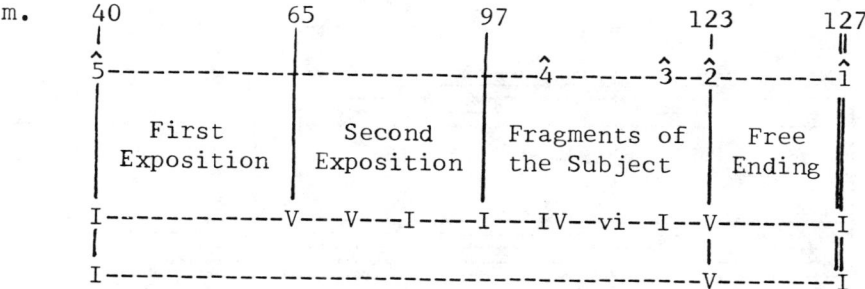

Fugues which end with a dominant rather than a tonic cadence do not resolve a fundamental line: a structure such as $\substack{5\text{-----}\hat{5}\\ \text{I\_\_\_\_V}}$ creates a strong implication of $\substack{\hat{4}\text{-}\hat{3}\text{-}\hat{2}\text{-}\hat{1}\\ \text{\_\_\_\_I}}$.[31] This concluding gesture, however, is left unrealized during the fugue and its free ending. The Praeludium in g, BuxWV 149, provides an example:

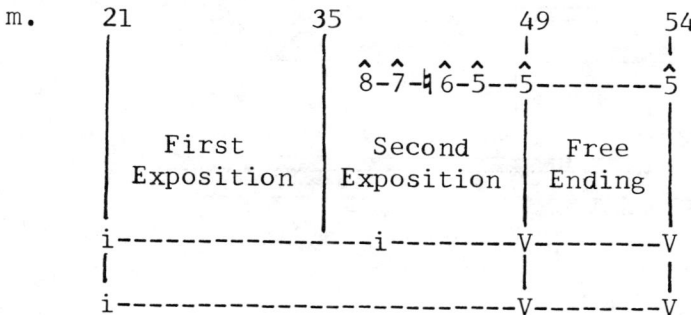

150   First Fugal Section

The following *allegro*, however, clearly and powerfully concludes the line, $\hat{5}$–$\hat{4}$–$\hat{3}$–$\hat{2}$–$\hat{1}$:³²

Praeludium in g, BuxWV 149

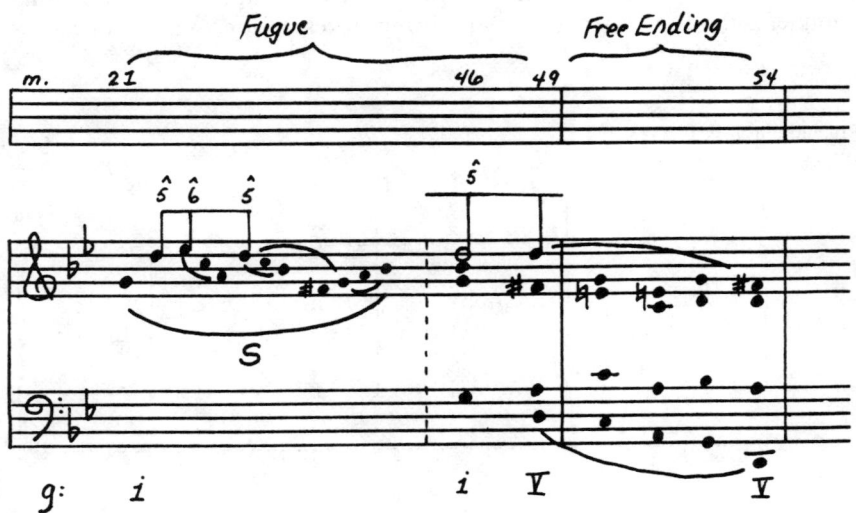

Historical and Critical Evaluation

The fugal techniques of Buxtehude's most important predecessors in north Germany stand in sharp contrast to his own usual procedures.[33] While Buxtehude relies on a series of expositions to build fugal form, Tunder, like Scheidemann before him, employs extra entries instead of a second or third exposition. Often these extra entries occur outside the tonic,[34] and may involve distortion of the intervallic shape of the subject or answer. Together with his stodgy subjects[35] and counterpoints, the result is a somewhat rambling effect and a shape with a weak sense of internal articulation. While Scheidemann's expositions usually exhibit Buxtehude's favorite S (soprano)/A (alto)/S (tenor)/ A (bass) scheme, they do so with an important difference: the entries come in stretto pairs:[36]

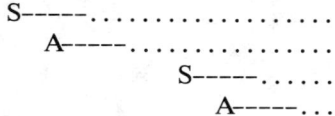

Tunder's expositions employ entry pairs less consistently. Moreover, the beginnings of a modular form can be observed in several of the fugues of his praeludia. In the Praeludium in g,[37] for example, the entries after the exposition can be grouped in fours, one entry each in the soprano, alto, tenor, and bass (in whatever order). However, in the second group of entries, the first four are all answers, and appear in three different keys. A final entry of a subject in the bass leads to another group of four entries, this time three subjects and one answer spread over three keys. Further extra entries end the section. While these groups of entries cannot be regarded as second or third expositions, their structure is delineated by similar harmonic articulations, in this case deceptive cadences:

Tunder: Praeludium in g

```
m.     24          31             36                        51
       ┌─⌢─┐      ┌─ ⌢ ─┐        ┌─── ⌢ ───┐                │
            S          A**         S***                A         S     │
          A        A*A         S****            A**                    │
       S                                                        S*
        A      A     A*      S              S                A*
                                                             
       │          │              │                           │
       i         D.C.           D.C.                        D.C.
```

(* = in v; ** = in ii; *** = in VII; **** = in III;
D.C. = Deceptive Cadence)

First Fugal Section

An actual second exposition is more closely approximated in another Praeludium in g.[38] As is typical in Buxtehude's fugues, an important harmonic articulation occurs within the second exposition. Here, however, it is placed after the second entry, while Buxtehude usually places it after the first. Several extra entries, including some in the subdominant and dominant, follow; the subject is then treated in diminution:

Tunder: Praeludium in g

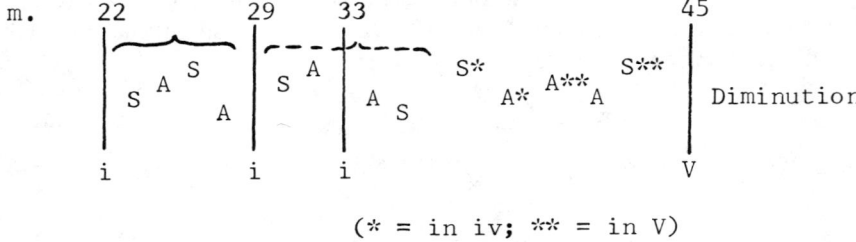

(* = in iv; ** = in V)

Weckmann's organ works exhibit characteristics of Tunder but more strongly anticipate many of Buxtehude. Weckmann's fugues have livelier subjects,[39] a more spacious size, and a greater sense of internal articulation. The Praeambulum in d[40] and its fugues stand closest to the work of Tunder. The Fantasia in d and the Fuga in the same key,[41] however, both more decisively demonstrate Buxtehudian techniques. As Shannon has pointed out, both owe much to the style of the canzona.[42] The first fugue of the Fuga is strikingly similar in its modular construction to those of Buxtehude; a second and third exposition follow the first, and its harmonic arrivals (all on the dominant) reinforce the fugal form:

Weckmann: Fuga in d

(F.E. = False Entry)

Its episode, rare in the north German organ fugal style of this time, strongly anticipates a Buxtehudian free ending in its sudden and unmotivated shift from a contrapuntal texture of quarter and eighth notes to sequential patterns of sixteenth notes. Indeed, this passage can be compared to the free ending of the Praeludium in D, BuxWV 139, a work already noted for its Weckmann-inspired section which follows the fugue.[43] The episode, of course, could have been a full-fledged free ending had the closing set of entries in stretto been omitted. The first fugue of the Fantasia in d also includes a sudden shift to free texture. In this work, the free passage does not lead to a resumption of fugal texture, however brief, before the close of the section, but clearly anticipates Buxtehude's free ending technique; it can be compared with the similar free ending of the first fugue of the Praeludium in C, BuxWV 136.[44]

The structural roles of the free sections in these fugues by Weckmann are also illuminating. The episode of the Fuga can be understood as a simple prolongation of the dominant, similar to several free endings of Buxtehude which also end on the dominant, for example, the first fugue of the Praeludium in g, BuxWV 149:

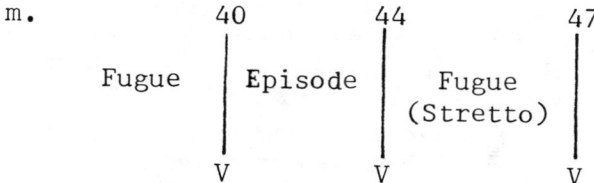

Weckmann: Fuga in d

Praeludium in g, BuxWV 149

The free ending of the Fantasia, however, like so many of Buxtehude's, participates in the essential harmonic/contrapuntal motion of the section; it completes not only the harmonic scheme of the section, providing the cadential motion, but also concludes the fundamental line which can be traced back into the fugue itself:

First Fugal Section

Weckmann: Fantasia in d

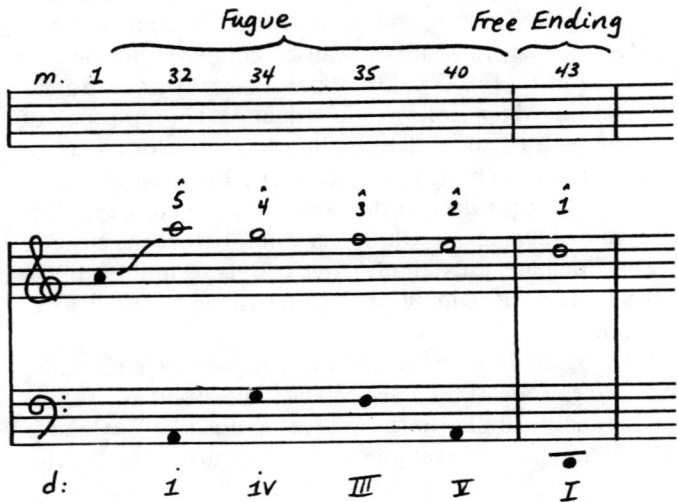

Although the free ending can in no way be understood as Weckmann's innovation (Froberger's keyboard works often employ such gestures),[45] it is the works of Weckmann which introduce the technique into the north German repertory.[46]

Several of the fugal sections of Buxtehude's praeludia exhibit characteristics typical of the fugues of Tunder and Weckmann. The use of entry pairs in the Praeambulum, BuxWV 158, is reminiscent of not only Tunder but Scheidemann as well.[47] After the exposition, this fugue also proceeds in a manner untypical of Buxtehude: stretto and casual part writing (voice entrances beginning neither with the subject nor the answer but simply with counterpoint) also suggest Tunder:[48]

Praeambulum in a, BuxWV158

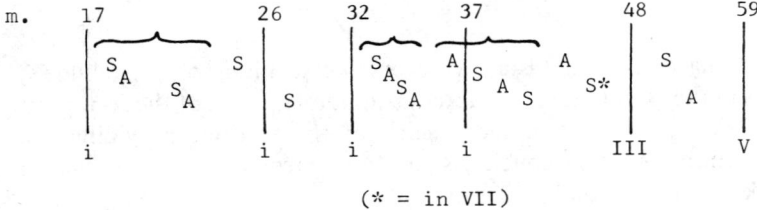

(* = in VII)

Several other fugues also have archaic elements. Casual part writing, including a broadening from $a4$ to $a5$[49] and entries in several keys, can be found in the Praeludia in e, BuxWV 143, and in g, BuxWV 150. In the Praeludium in e, a rather garbled set of extra entries, instead of an actual second exposition, follows the first exposition:[50]

Praeludium in e, BuxWV 143

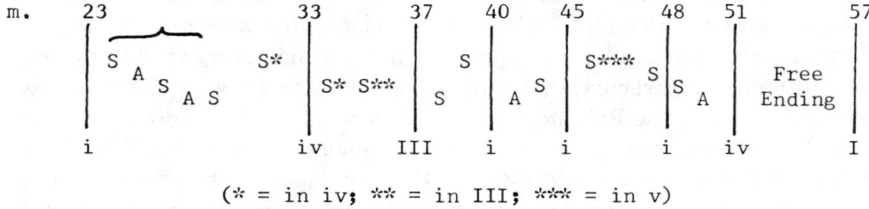

```
m.    23              33      37     40      45       48   51        57
      ┌─────┐         ┌──┐    ┌──┐   ┌──┐    ┌───┐    ┌──┐ ┌──┐      ┌──┐
      S                S*            S        S***          S         Free
        A                   S*  S***      S                    S      Ending
          S  A S                    S     A                 A
      A S
      i               iv      III    i      i        i    iv        I

              (* = in iv;  ** = in III;  *** = in v)
```

The high-level structure is much clearer and more compelling, however, in the Praeludium in g:

Praeludium in g, BuxWV 150

```
m.    16           28          37          49      52      54 58 61   64
      ┌────┐       ┌────┐       ┌────┐      ┌──┐   ┌──┐    ┌──────┐   ┌──┐
         S            A           S                                A
      S   A        S              A                           S
        A            A   S        A*               S***      A   S
                                     A   S**                       S
      i            i            i           v      VII     III iv i   i

              (* = in iv;  ** = in VII;  *** = in III)
```

All four of these fugues have simple subjects, without the significant profile or vitality typical of the canzona-inspired subjects of Weckmann's Fantasia and most of Buxtehude's subjects.[51] Moreover, only one of these fugues, that of the Praeludium in e, has a free ending which is anything more than a short extension. And this free ending is perhaps Buxtehude's most awkward one, built with metrically peculiar seven-beat phrases.

The kind of fugal plan ultimately employed by Buxtehude, then, departs considerably from that of his immediate predecessors. To be sure, Weckmann is clearly his most significant direct predecessor, and from him came the canzonalike subjects, several important models of modular fugal

First Fugal Section

construction (using a series of expositions rather than extra entries), and the free ending. All these things became integral parts of Buxtehude's fugal style. Buxtehude, however, increased the sense of order, system, and elegance of the north German organ fugue beyond any models provided by Scheidemann, Tunder, or Weckmann. Taking an essentially rambling technique, he brought it focus by transforming it into an architectural form built with modules of expositions. The precision of his plans reaches its peak in such fugues as those with the exposition carefully balanced by a second one, for example, the first fugues of the Praeludia in f♯, BuxWV 146, in g, BuxWV 149, and, lacking only the last entry, the Praeludium in d, BuxWV 140.[52] Several longer fugues, with more than two expositions, are also elegantly constructed, including those with also a few extra entries, as the first fugue of the Praeludium in D, BuxWV 139, and those consisting entirely of a series of expositions, as in the Praeludium in C, BuxWV 137.[53] Modularity is at its most impressive in the first fugue of the Praeludium in A, BuxWV 151. Its unusually rigorous use of a countersubject yields a modular effect at both the exposition and the midexposition levels:

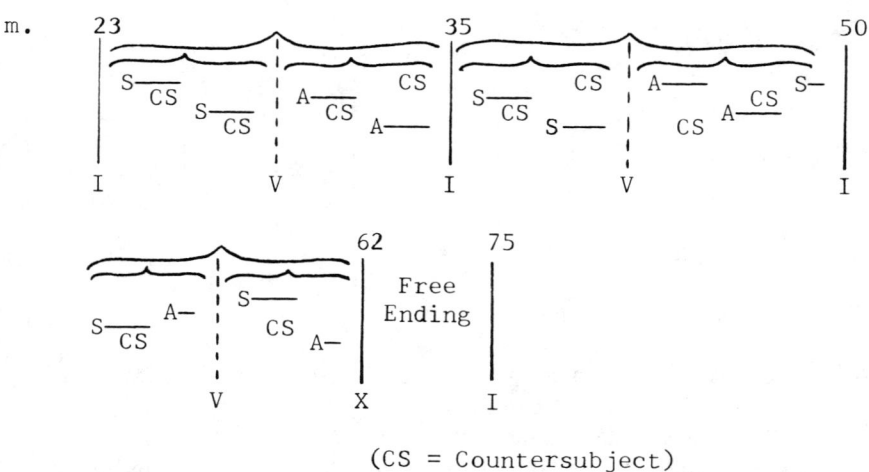

(CS = Countersubject)

Buxtehude also heightened the delineation between the first fugue and the following section. Among his predecessors, Tunder's praeludia usually flow as seamlessly as possible (by way of diminution of the subject) into the following section, but Weckmann's Fantasia, and indeed, the canzona style in general, provided important examples of a more forceful close of the first fugal section. Buxtehude's allegiance here clearly lay with Weckmann and the canzona tradition. More importantly, however, the use of a free ending also renders the fugue a fragment, for the fugue itself is broken off and not allowed to end by its own momentum. The effect of closure given by a free ending is sometimes arbitrary; a violent change of texture, unmotivated by the preceding fugal texture, may cast the close in doubt. The first fugues of the Praeludia in C, BuxWV 136, in A, BuxWV 151, and in a, BuxWV 153, most noticeably demonstrate this tendency. Even when the free ending is simply an elaboration of the penultimate dominant, as in the Praeludia in E, BuxWV 141, or in F, BuxWV 145, the close may seem forced. Ultimately, then, the lack of a fugally motivated close emphasizes the dependence of the fugue on the larger scheme of the praeludium: it is not permitted to develop into a complete form and overshadow other sections of the work. The independent/dependent status of the first fugal sections will be further investigated in connection with the praeludium as a whole in the final chapter.

8

The Remaining Sections

Style Analysis

While some praeludia stop after the first fugue, most contain other sections. These sections, which may be termed the remaining sections, can be relatively simple (with as few as one or more textural sections) or very complex (with many sections which form the greater portion of the composition).[1] They are the most unstable sections both texturally and harmonically.[2] The closed harmonic plans typical of the opening free section and the first fugue give way to a far greater use of open harmonic plans. While the remaining sections as a whole always lead ultimately to a final tonic cadence, their frequent use of a I-----V harmonic scheme clearly implies another section, I-----V[-----I], while the noticeably weak articulations often found between them reinforce closer connections. Further enhancing such interconnection is the often fragmentary nature of the remaining sections: it is here that fugatos and harmonically rich chordal passages, the shortest and most unstable sections, can be found.

The free sections after the first fugue include chordal, rhapsodic, figural, and ciacona textures; these textures have already been described.[3] However, when a praeludium ends with a free section (as opposed to a fugal one), the last section usually exhibits special uses of texture which are unparalleled elsewhere in the praeludium. These sections, which can be termed closing free sections, are aggregates of various free textures, often modular in construction, and usually, but not always, have a significant emphasis on the subdominant. Sometimes quite large, they may encompass what would otherwise be considered several sections of free textures. These closing free sections contain some of the most impressive gestures in the praeludia. The simplest of them are really nothing more than an expanded free ending of a fugue. The second fugue of the Praeludium in e, BuxWV 143, ends with a modular extension. Yet the extension does not cadence on the tonic. Other free textures follow, including a short chordal passage with an unexpected harmonic turn to the mediant and other dramatic gestures before a tonic pedal finally ends the work:

160 Remaining Sections

Praeludium in e, BuxWV 143

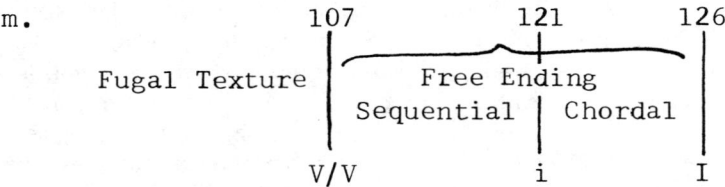

Such a variety of free textures after the last fugue is found on a larger scale in several other works. In the Toccata in d, BuxWV 155, the fugue closes with an unusually long and complex free ending of sequential (and thematically derived) material followed by a chordal passage which provides a strong tonic major cadence:

Toccata in d, BuxWV 155

```
m.                      107           121         126
        Fugal Texture  |   Free Ending   |
                       | Sequential | Chordal |
                           V/V          i          I
```

A "Final"[4] section follows, which consists entirely of an elaborate plagal cadence. Launched from the strong tonic major arrival of the free ending, the repeated V/iv–iv progressions suggest an ostinato, which eventually emerges as d–G:

Toccata in d, BuxWV 155

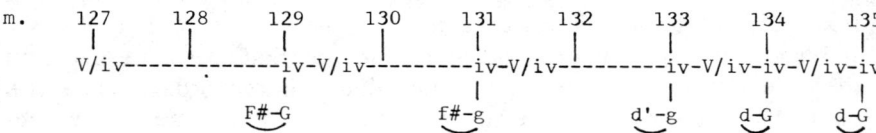

The tonic pedal which follows is joined to the preceding subdominant passage by a suspension, iv–I$_{4-3}^{6-5}$:

Toccata in d, BuxWV 155

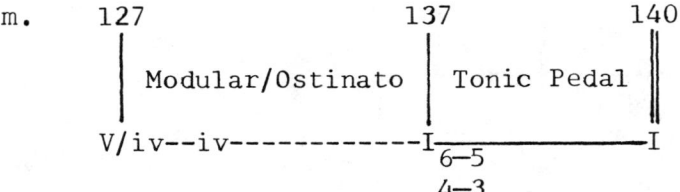

The closing free sections in a number of praeludia have an analogous emphasis on modular textures and subdominant harmony, and the term "Final" can usefully be applied to these as well. However, the Final sections of other works are not as independent as in the Toccata in d. The textural flexibility of the closing free sections allows gestures such as those contained in the Final section of the Toccata to be joined more closely to the preceding material.[5] The two largest closing free sections are found in the Praeludia in D, BuxWV 139, and in f♯, BuxWV 146. In both these works, additional free textures precede the subdominant/ostinato section (the Final). An even bigger complex of various free textures is the result:

Praeludium in D, BuxWV 139

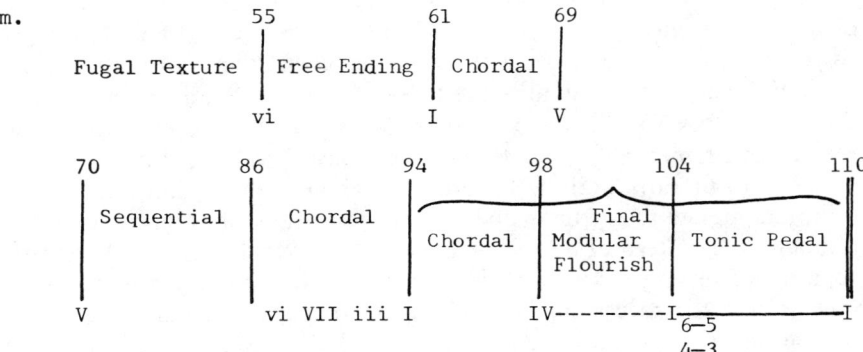

Praeludium in f♯, BuxWV 146

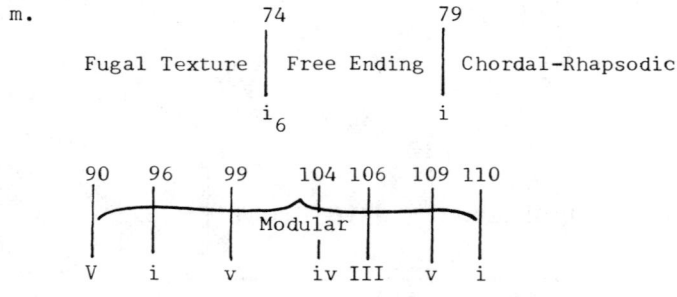

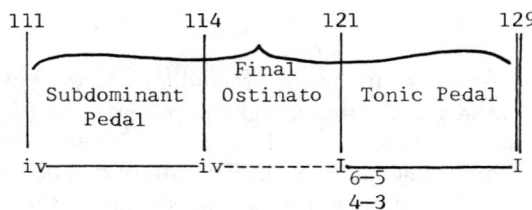

The textures of the closing free section of the Praeludium in f♯ are the most impressive of any praeludium. Modular texture in the more flexible style characteristic of the Final of the Praeludium in a, BuxWV 153, is incorporated into the dominant area preceding the I–IV–I motion. The result is even bolder and more dynamic than in the Praeludium in a, for these figures elaborate harmonic progressions charged with dominant rather than subdominant energy.[6]

The fugal sections after the first fugue also present new textures. While the first fugal section is always in common time, those following are generally in a different style: they are triple-time fugues, gigue fugues, or fugatos.[7] These fugues are also noticeably different in their construction from that observed in the common-time fugues.[8] Even when, as in the Praeludium in f♯, BuxWV 146, a second fugue is also in common time, its formal plan differs remarkably from that of the typical first one. While the entry plan of S (soprano)/A (alto)/S (tenor)/A (bass) is the most frequent, it does not predominate as is true of the first fugues. Many other plans are used, although the pattern of S/A/S/A is virtually never disturbed.[9] As in first fugues, answers are virtually always tonal;[10] a subdominant answer appears in a second (or succeeding) fugue only in the Praeambulum. Generally, second and third fugues are less modular in their overall plan than first ones; the reliance on a series of expositions is replaced in succeeding fugues by a greater use of extra entries and episodes. Such fugal devices as countersubjects and double counterpoint, however, can be found in these fugues as well as in the first ones; indeed, some of Buxtehude's most powerful examples of invertible counterpoint occur in second fugues.[11] Yet in the fugues in the remaining sections, the subjects are more likely after the first exposition to be reduced to fragments. Such a plan contrasts sharply with the constant use of subject/answer statements which generally dominate the entire duration of the first fugues. Finally, later fugues, especially if they actually come at the end of the praeludium, often contain free endings of far greater size than are found in any first fugue.

The triple-time fugue is more frequently found after the first fugue than any other type. Appearing in ten of the praeludia, examples range from the relatively short ones of the Praeambulum, BuxWV 158, or the Praeludium in a, BuxWV 152, to the grandiose chromatic fugue in the Praeludium in e, BuxWV 142, or the equally impressive *largo* fugue of the Praeludium in g, BuxWV 149. The second fugues of the Praeludium in a and the Praeambulum are very similar; their form, a series of two expositions, is strongly suggestive of the techniques encountered in most first fugues:

Praeludium in a, BuxWV 152

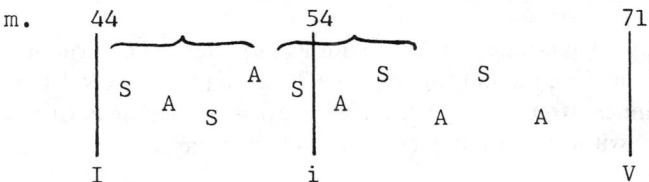

Praeambulum in a, BuxWV 158

(* = in III)

164   Remaining Sections

The second fugue of the Praeludium in g, BuxWV 150, approximates on a larger scale the modular construction typical of first fugues, but with atypical irregularities:

Praeludium in g, BuxWV 150

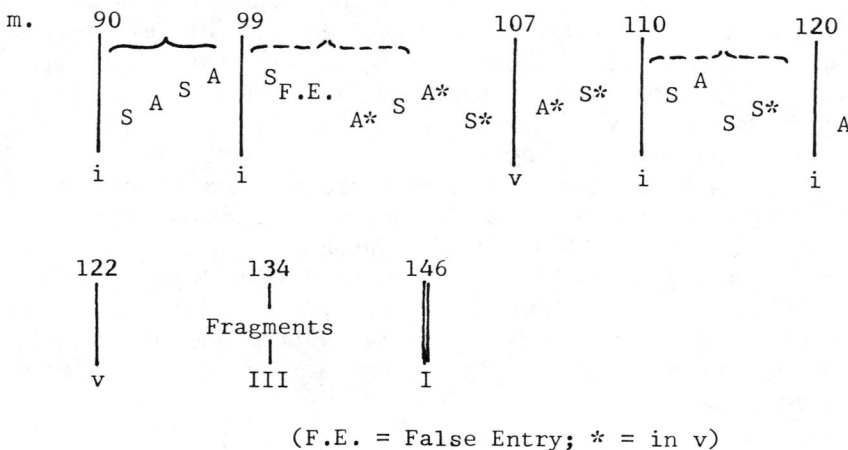

(F.E. = False Entry; * = in v)

Most of the large triple-time fugues are not as modular in construction as a typical first fugue. The second fugue of the Toccata in d, BuxWV 155, for example, continues after its exposition with extra entries in both the tonic and mediant without forming complete expositions in either key area:[12]

Toccata in d, BuxWV 155

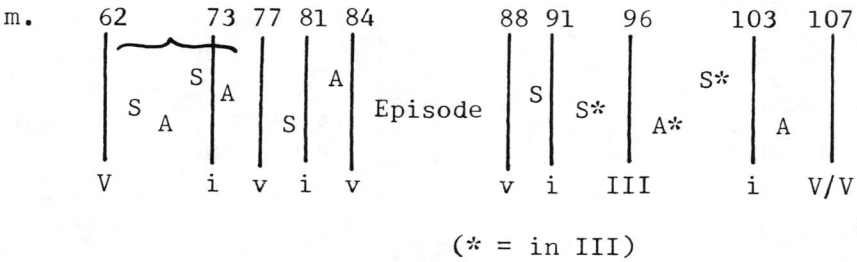

(* = in III)

Remaining Sections   165

The four fugues in common time which are found after the first fugue exhibit the same differences of form as do the triple-time fugues. The second fugue of the Toccata in F, BuxWV 156, for example, is a small-scale section, closely resembling a typical first fugue:

Toccata in F, BuxWV 156

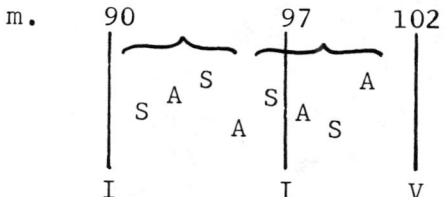

The fourth fugue of the Praeludium in E, BuxWV 141, and the second fugue of the Praeludium in A, BuxWV 151, both of which end their respective works, exhibit less rigorous constructions; they continue after the exposition with extra entries, and with several outside the tonic in each. The appearance of entries in the subdominant is symptomatic of their closing position:

Praeludium in E, BuxWV 141

```
m.     91              99       101                              110
       |    A      S   |   S*   |                                ||
       | S     S   A   |   S*   | S   S  Fragments/Free Ending   ||
       |        A      |        |                                ||
       I              IV        V                                 I
```

(* = in IV)

Praeludium in A, BuxWV 151

```
m.     75                                       87              92
       |          CS     S——   CS  S*——        | S——    CS**    ||
       |  S  CS A—CS                           |                ||
       |        A—                CS S——  CS*  | CS   S**——     ||
       I                                        V                I
```

(CS = Countersubject; * = in V; ** = in IV)

The second fugue of the Praeludium in f#, BuxWV 146, is a far bolder construction. It begins like a typical first fugue, but midway into the second exposition the third entry breaks off. The remainder of the section, some twenty-one measures, contains only one more relatively unobtrusive statement of the subject or answer. Episodic material, which develops a motif drawn from the subject, dominates the remainder of the fugue:[13]

Praeludium in f#, BuxWV 146

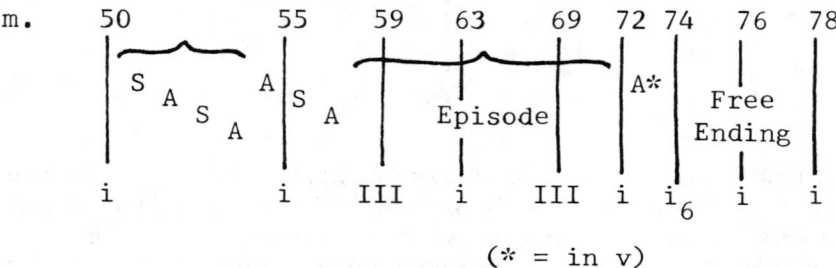

Gigue fugues are found in two of the praeludia, as the closing sections of the Praeludia in C, BuxWV 136, and in e, BuxWV 142. In the Praeludium in C, the subject or answer makes a few appearances after the exposition; episodes are used to fill out the form. The subject is later reduced to fragments, which are presented in stretto. During the large extension which follows, the thematic material of the subject is gradually eliminated from the texture:

Praeludium in C, BuxWV 136

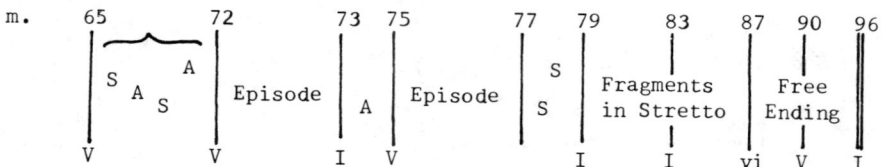

The Praeludium in e presents a similar case but with an altogether larger realization. A second exposition follows the first one, providing a larger base of stable fugal texture to balance an even larger passage in which the subject is treated in fragments. Again, a large extension follows. While it abandons the thematic material of the subject, the extension maintains the gigue character of the section:

Praeludium in e, BuxWV 142

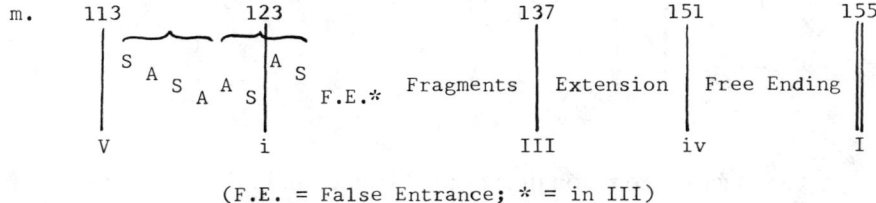

(F.E. = False Entrance; * = in III)

The fugatos found in the remaining sections never terminate a work; they are always intermediate sections, and often serve as a link between larger ones. Their size is often small and their form sometimes fragmentary; a few only hint at the procedures which so rigorously control the form of a typical fugal section. The gigue fugato of the Praeludium in E, BuxWV 141, stands closest of all to a typical fugue. It is a miniature fugue, $a3$ (a texture never found in real fugues); it only broadens to four-part writing during the extension:[14]

Praeludium in E, BuxWV 141

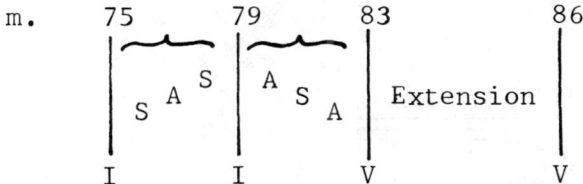

The *allegro* fugato of the Praeludium in C, BuxWV 136, also lies close to a typical fugue. However, the lack of codettas or other short interpolations in its constant succession of subjects and answers gives it the breathlessness typical of fugatos in the praeludia. Such a technique also creates a highly modular effect. Each measure contains a statement of the subject or answer and comes to rest on either the tonic or dominant:

168   Remaining Sections

Praeludium in C, BuxWV 136

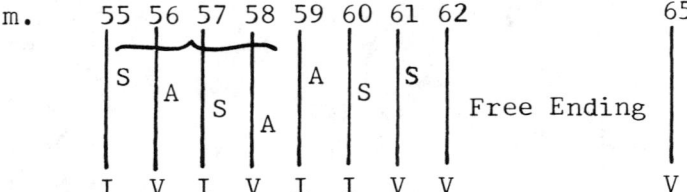

The fugato in common time of the Praeludium in E, BuxWV 141, only loosely resembles fugal procedure. While an exposition, with paired entries, is evident, its harmonic pattern is not a normal one:

Praeludium in E, BuxWV 141

The thematic material is almost immediately subjected to fragmentation and development. An entire subject or answer makes only one more appearance, as an extra entry directly following the exposition:

Praeludium in E, BuxWV 141

```
m.    59                              72              75
      |                               |               |
      | f#, b'    e''  f#''           | Fragments     | Free Ending
      |       b                       |               |
      |                               |               |
      V                               V/vi            I
```

(Entrances Indicated by Beginning Note)

The imitative section of the Praeludium in d, BuxWV 140, is even less like a typical fugato. While the successive entries of a fugue remain intact, the harmonic pattern is completely different: the circle of fifths, rather than the alternation of tonic and dominant, forms its structure:[15]

Praeludium in d, BuxWV 140

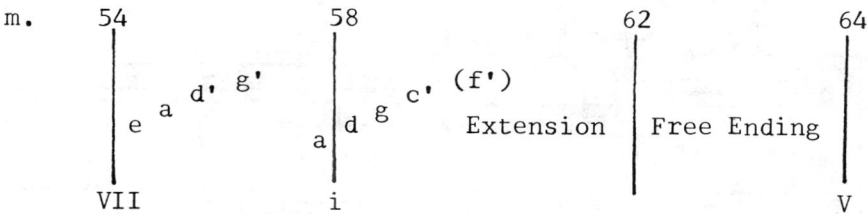

(Entrances Indicated by Beginning Note)

The free endings of the fugues and fugatos of the remaining sections are often far more elaborate than those typically found in a first fugue. The *allegro* fugato of the Praeludium in C, BuxWV 136, has a free ending which is more than one half as long as the fugal passage itself:

Praeludium in C, BuxWV 136

```
m.    55                    62              65
      |                     |               |
      | Fugal Texture       | Free Ending   |
      |                     |               |
      I                     V               V
```

The free ending also develops thematic material introduced in the fugato:

Praeludium in C, BuxWV 136

This procedure, unusual in first fugues, appears much more frequently in later ones.[16] In several of the large triple-time fugues and in the two gigue fugues, free endings are preceded (or replaced entirely) by sizeable extensions. During these passages the thematic material of the fugue is fragmented and developed without the formal rigor of fugal texture. Such a technique creates an even larger proportion of free (or not strictly fugal) texture in the section. The triple-time fugue which ends the Praeludium in g, BuxWV 150, is an example:

Praeludium in g, BuxWV 150

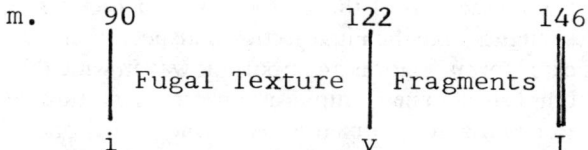

So, too, are the two large gigue fugues which close the Praeludia in C, BuxWV 136, and in e, BuxWV 142:

Praeludium in C, BuxWV 136

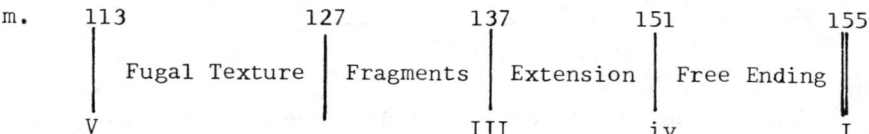

Praeludium in e, BuxWV 142

m.   113   127   137   151   155
       |Fugal Texture|Fragments|Extension|Free Ending|
       V   III   iv   I

The differences between the typical styles and forms of first and later fugues can be largely attributed to their different roles within the praeludium. The first fugue, typically a large, formally rigorous, and harmonically stable section, does not generally participate to a great degree in the build up and release of energy associated with the expressive climax. Fugues between the first and last in a work, however, are far more closely concerned with the climax. Their variable size, less stable harmonic schemes, and their often loose, if not fragmentary, formal plans, make them more flexible, which helps create the energy and excitement of the expressive climax.

The closing function of the large fugues which end several praeludia likewise dictates a very different style and formal structure than is found in first fugues. They have far more free texture and less fugal rigor than any first fugue. Occurring past the point of the expressive climax, they correspond to the subdominant Final sections of those praeludia which end with closing free sections. These fugues, like the Final sections, dispel rather than build energy; and their lack of formal rigor is an important way in which the release of energy is accomplished. Their emphasis on fragmentation of thematic material is not so much a developmental technique as it is one of liquidation. Not only the fugal form but the thematic material with which it is associated is gradually eliminated from the texture as the energy of the section, and the praeludium as a whole, is relaxed. Such endings provide an expansive rather than a summary close; in these fugues, there is no conflict between fugal momentum and the frame that contains it.

Final cadences can be either authentic or plagal. Slightly more than half of the works end with authentic cadences, especially those which have a fugue as their last section. Plagal cadences are associated with those works which have closing free sections, particularly those of the Final type.[17] As described above, the Final sections emphasize subdominant harmony; generally, however, a strong authentic cadence precedes the section:

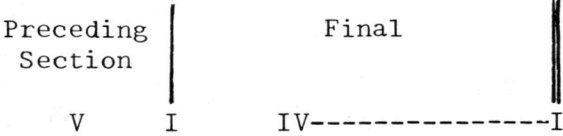

The coordination of the textural and harmonic plans in the remaining sections takes several forms. The simplest are those in which every section ends with a tonic cadence. The Praeludium in C, BuxWV 137, is an example. In this work, there are two textural sections after the first fugue and each is a relatively self-contained I-----I motion:

Praeludium in C, BuxWV 137

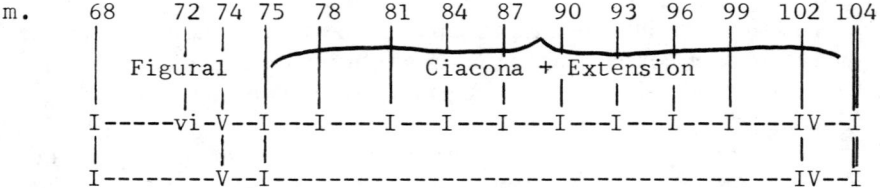

Or, more simply:

Praeludium in C, BuxWV 137

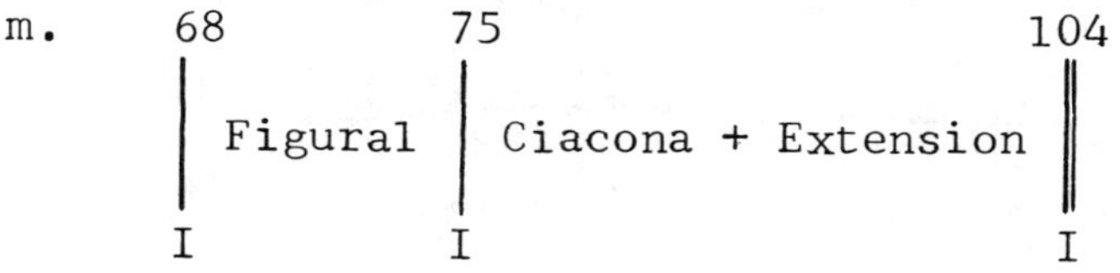

```
m.    68            75                      104
      |             |                       ‖
      | Figural     | Ciacona + Extension   ‖
      |             |                       ‖
      I             I                       I
```

The remaining sections of the Praeludium in a, BuxWV 153, also contain only one internal tonic pillar:

Praeludium in a, BuxWV 153

```
m.    67                         104       124
      |                          |         ‖
      | Triple-Time Fugue        | Final   ‖
      |                          |         ‖
      I                          I   iv    I
```

Most works, however, include at least one section after the first fugue which does not end with a tonic cadence. In these praeludia, several sections join to form one complete harmonic gesture. The Praeludium in C, BuxWV 136, is an example:

Praeludium in C, BuxWV 136

```
m.   55              62          65   70 72 73 75   79   83   87   90   96
     |               |           |    |  |  |  |   |    |    |    |    ‖
     | Fugato + Free Ending      |    | Gigue Fugue + Free Ending      ‖
     |               |           |    |  |  |  |   |    |    |    |    ‖
     I               V           V    I  V  I  V   I    I    vi   V    I
```

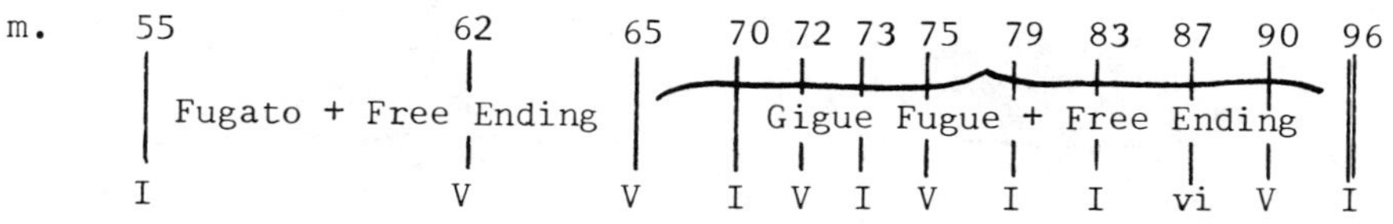

Or, more simply:

174   Remaining Sections

Praeludium in C, BuxWV 136

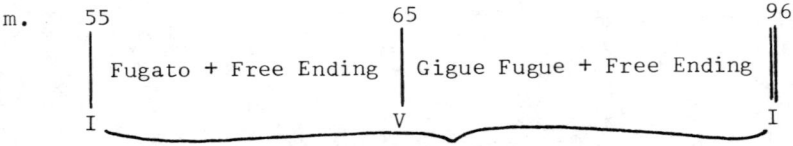

The Praeludium in e, BuxWV 142, has a similar plan, but with three textural sections and an expanded dominant area:

Praeludium in e, BuxWV 142

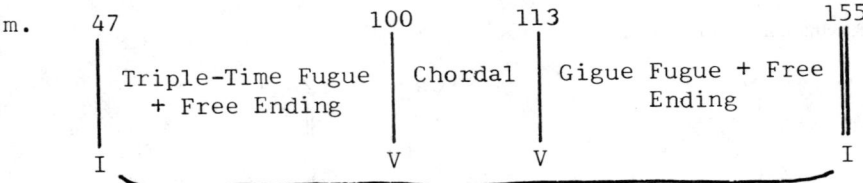

Three sections, but with two I-----I motions, are found in the Praeludium in g, BuxWV 150:

Praeludium in g, BuxWV 150

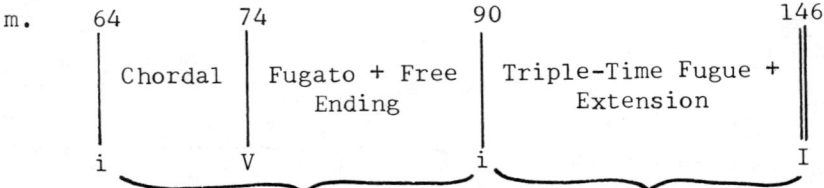

A similar plan, but built entirely of free textures, is found in the Praeludium in D, BuxWV 139:

Praeludium in D, BuxWV 139

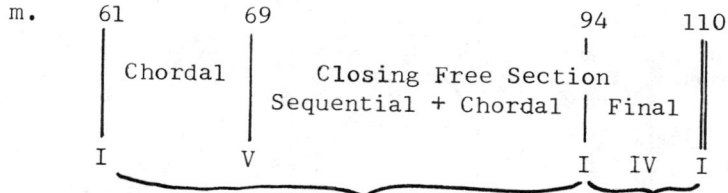

The Praeludium in d, BuxWV140, presents a more complex realization of the same overall I--(V)--I--(IV)--I plan:

Praeludium in d, BuxWV 140

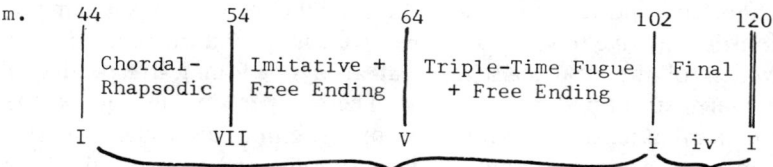

Two of the most complex plans, with three I-----I motions, are found in the Praeludia in f#, BuxWV 146, and in E, BuxWV 141. While in BuxWV 146 the second internal tonic pillar is not strongly articulated, in BuxWV 141, with its myriad of small sections, each tonic arrival is articulated by a new textural section:

Praeludium in f#, BuxWV 146

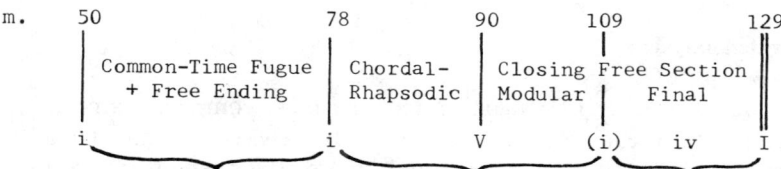

Praeludium in E, BuxWV 141

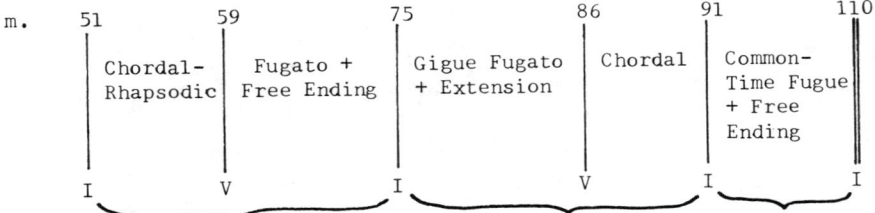

Thematic variation also plays an important role in the remaining sections. The thematic material introduced as the subject of the first fugue becomes the basis of the subsequent fugal and fugato subjects. Occasionally, other thematic material is also shared between the various sections.[18] Such processes, like the overall harmonic schemes, provide vital links between the sections, not only in the remaining sections, but throughout the praeludium as a whole.

Yet another important element in the overall coherence of the remaining sections is the drive towards an expressive climax and the relaxation of tension which follows.[19] Such a scheme can always be found, irrespective of the particular textural pattern employed. The two parts of the climax, the point of maximum tension and the point of resolution, are usually distributed between the penultimate and the last sections, and a powerful link is formed between them. Other preceding sections also contribute to the expressive climax by creating a drive towards it. The less stable and more intense sections sometimes found between the first fugue and the penultimate section are used to built momentum towards the point of climax.

Unlike in the first two sections, the great variety of textural, harmonic, and expressive shapes found in the remaining ones limits the elucidation of an archetypal form to its most basic elements: 1) alternations of free and fugal textures or, if the sections are all free, then various kinds of free textures are used; 2) a harmonic plan which, beginning after the typical tonic cadence of the first fugue, leads to the final tonic cadence of the work; 3) the development of thematic material from the first fugue; 4) the embodiment of the expressive climax and resolution of the work.

Structural Analysis

The sections after the first fugue present the most complex examples of synthesis and closure in the praeludia.[20] The relatively self-contained quality (as defined by background harmony and line) of the opening free section and the first fugue are not always found in the sections which follow.

Various of the remaining sections may join together to articulate a single background harmonic motion and fundamental line:

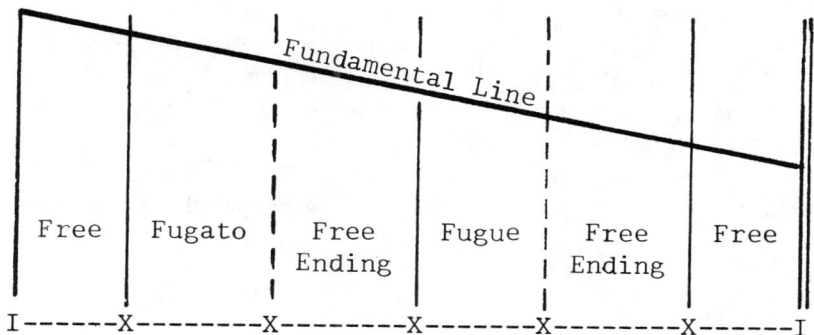

Or, the remaining sections may reiterate — or sometimes resolve — harmonic and linear motions begun in previous sections:[21]

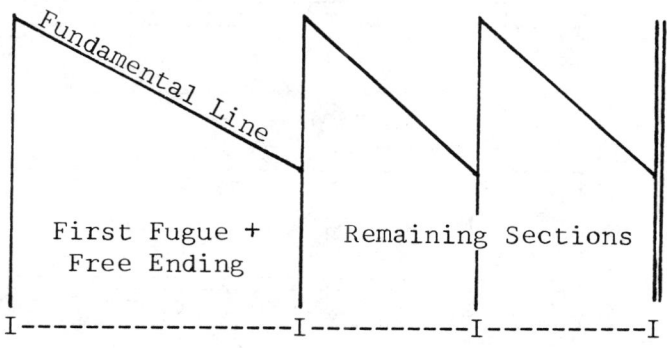

or

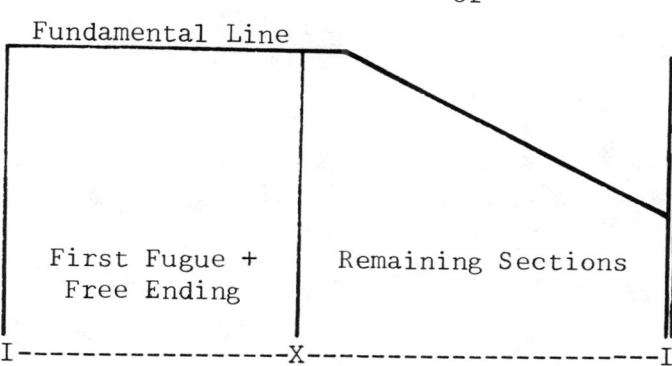

178   Remaining Sections

The great variety of forms is reflected in the equally great variety of structures. Yet, while individual works present unique solutions, several types can be delineated. In the Praeludium in C, BuxWV 137, the same line is repeated in both of the remaining sections. The figural section which follows the first fugue contains, as does the fugue which precedes it, a $\hat{5}$-$\hat{4}$-$\hat{3}$-$\hat{2}$-$\hat{1}$ (g″-f″-e″-d″-c″) line.[22] While the line is more strongly stated in the figural section than in the fugue, it is compromised in the figural section by chromatic coloration: $\hat{5}$-$\hat{4}$-$\flat\hat{3}$-$\hat{2}$-$\hat{1}$ (g″-f″-eb″-d″-c″). Noteworthy is the prolongation of $\hat{5}$ by a descending span, g″-f″-e″-d″-c″-b′-a′-g″, with a strong emphasis on the submediant, before the $\hat{5}$-$\hat{4}$-$\flat\hat{3}$-$\hat{2}$-$\hat{1}$ descent occurs:

Praeludium in C, BuxWV 137

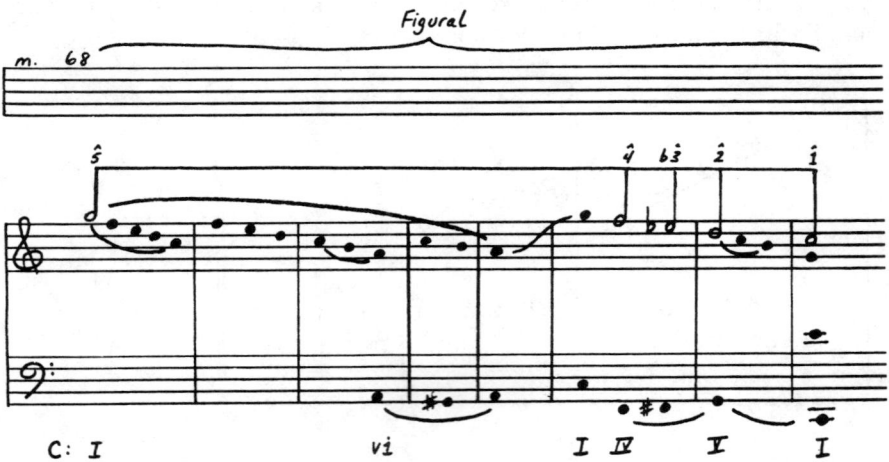

Although the ciacona which follows is more static, it nevertheless utilizes the same $\hat{5}$-$\hat{4}$-$\hat{3}$-$\hat{2}$-$\hat{1}$ line, but with $\natural\hat{3}$ instead of $\flat\hat{3}$. The $\hat{5}$ (g″) is established in the second statement of the ciacona:

Praeludium in C, BuxWV 137

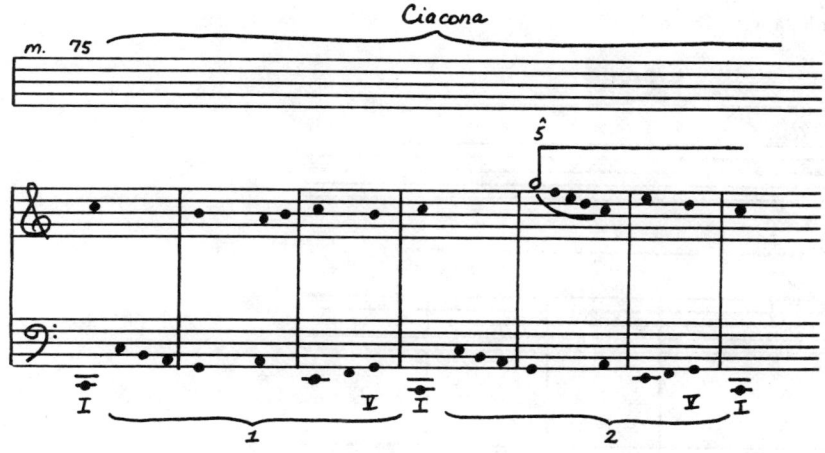

The $\hat{5}$ is prolonged until a descent is achieved in the seventh statement:

Praeludium in C, BuxWV 137

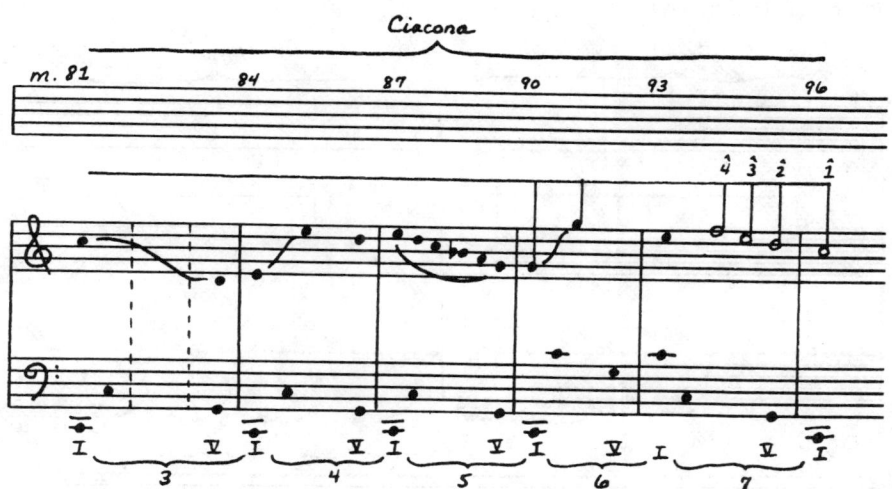

The eighth statement is like a coda:

Praeludium in C, BuxWV 137

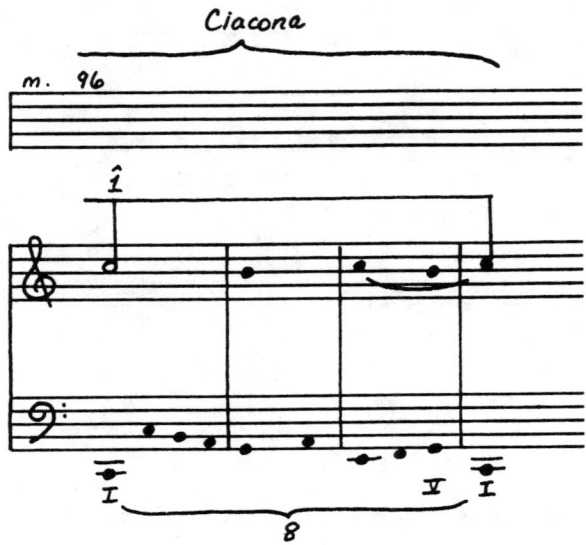

Both sections, then, establish $\hat{5}$ (g″) near the beginning of the section and prolong it until a rapid $\hat{4}$-$\hat{3}$-$\hat{2}$-$\hat{1}$ descent near the cadence:

Praeludium in C, BuxWV 137

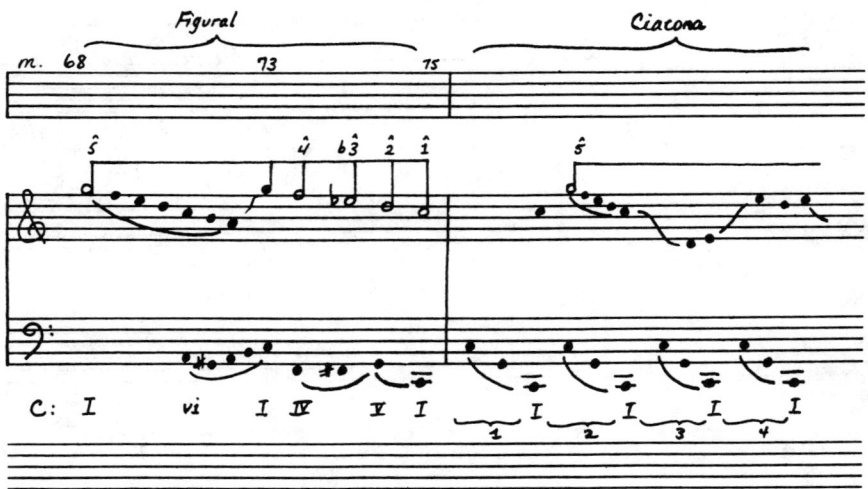

Remaining Sections 181

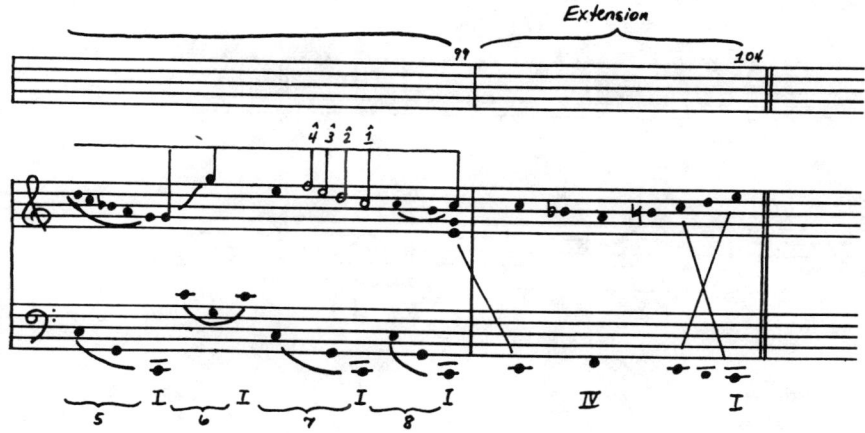

Further reduction leads, at higher levels, to the subordination of the $\hat{5}$-$\hat{4}$-♭$\hat{3}$-$\hat{2}$-$\hat{1}$ descent of the figural section to the succeeding and more normal $\hat{5}$-$\hat{4}$-♮$\hat{3}$-$\hat{2}$-$\hat{1}$ motion of the ciacona:

Praeludium in C, BuxWV 137

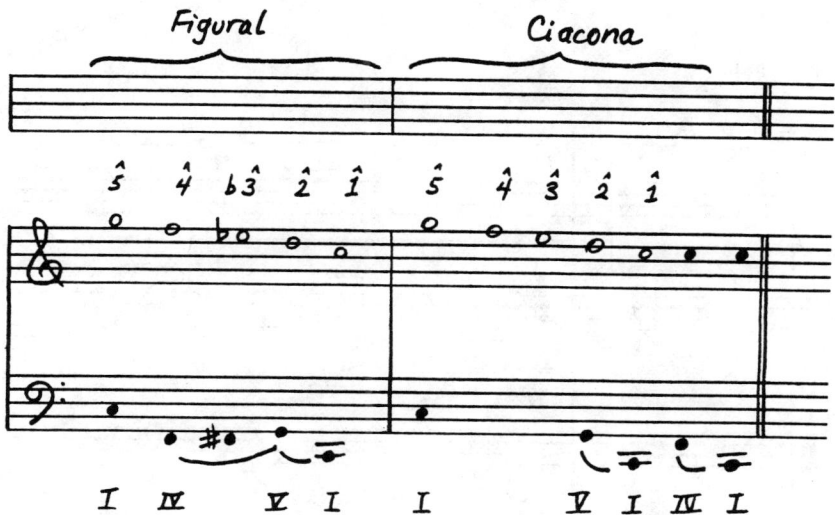

The remaining sections of the Praeludium in D, BuxWV 139, like those of the Praeludium in C, consist entirely of free textures. In the Praeludium in D, however, there are more sections: an *adagio* chordal section is followed by a closing free section which is an aggregate of a sequential section, another chordal section,[23] and lastly a Final section which stresses the subdominant before the tonic pedal to end the work. Linear coherence is achieved in a different way than in the Praeludium in C: after the fugue of the Praeludium in D, $\hat{1}$ (d″) serves as a pillar around which the sections are structured; established at the end of the fugue, it is prolonged throughout the following sections:[24]

Praeludium in D, BuxWV 139

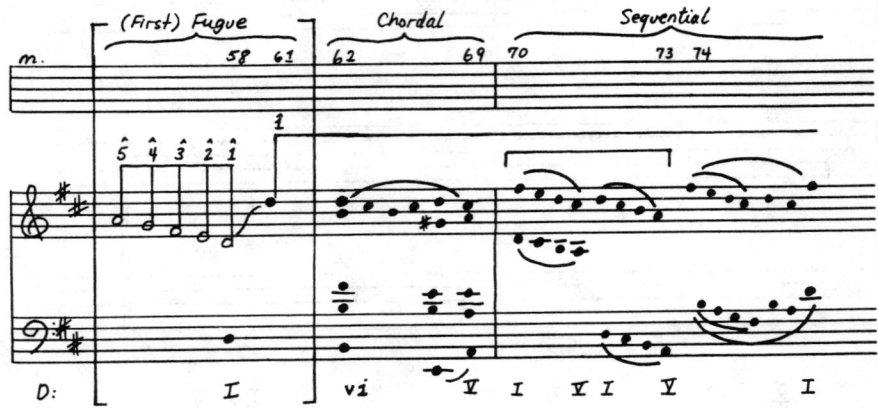

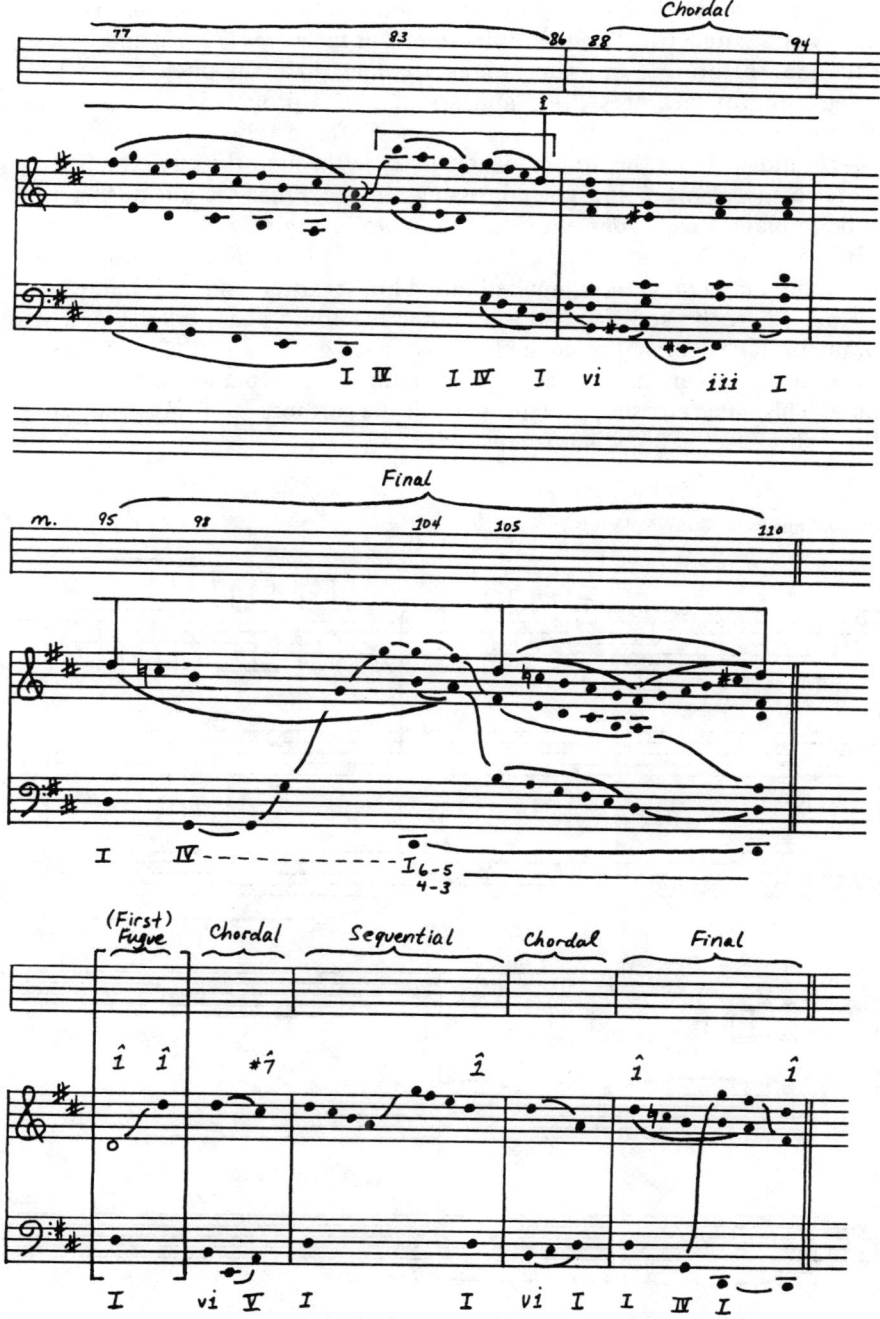

The sequential section, amid its profusion of middleground spans, has elements of a symmetrical structure. Its first four measures (70-73) and its last four (83-86) present the same phrase, but at different pitches: the I-V progression of measures 70-73 appears as a IV-I progression in measures 83-86. The passage in between these frames, after a false start in measures 74-76, moves from the dominant to the tonic through the circle of fifths. Noteworthy also are the voice crossings in the Final section during the subdominant area. A descent into a inner voice begins with the $\hat{1}$ in measure 95: d″-c♮″-b′-a′- (b-a-g-f♯-e-d). After $\mathrm{^6_{IV}}$ is reached, the bass of the subdominant area, G, is catapulted into a high register, and g″ is temporarily placed in the soprano. At this point the tonic pedal enters, and its dramatic $\mathrm{I^{6-5}_{4-3}}$ beginning is created. As soon as g″ falls to f♯″, the line is transferred into an inner voice, and d″ returns as the fundamental soprano note. This voice crossing explains why, at the surface, f♯″ is not connected through e″ to the d″ which follows:

Praeludium in D, BuxWV 139

Similar large subdominant areas can be found at the end of several other praeludia. In both the Praeludium in a, BuxWV 153, and the Toccata in d, BuxWV 155, complete octave descents encompass these sections. In the Toccata in d, as in the Praeludium in D, a transfer of register is prominent: $d''-c''-bb'-a'-g'-g''-f\#''-e''-d''$. And it is again used for a similar dramatic effect: IV–I$_{4-3}^{6-5}$, with the 4–3 suspension emphasized in a high register:

Toccata in d, BuxWV 155

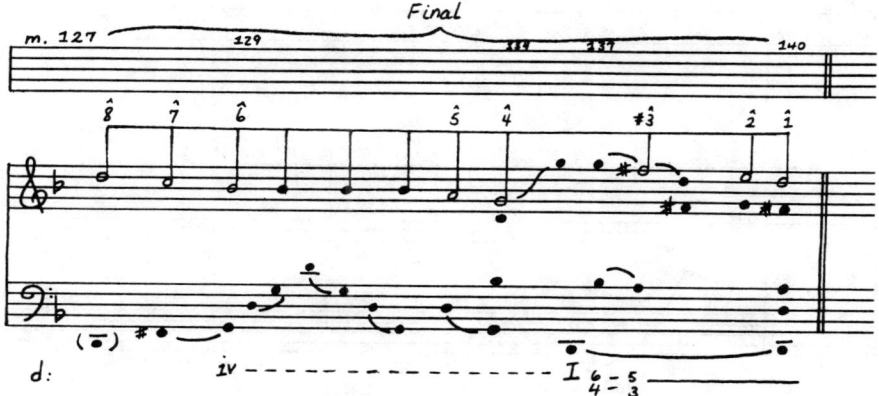

At a higher level, however, the entire Final is a prolongation of the arrival on $\hat{1}$ (d'') in the free ending of the second fugue which precedes it:

Toccata in d, BuxWV 155

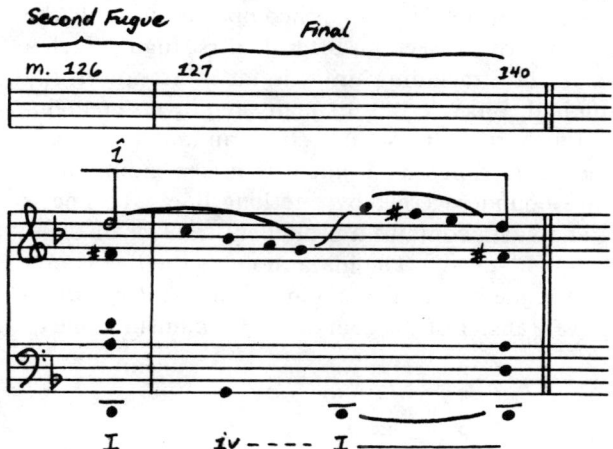

186   Remaining Sections

In the Praeludium in a, the climax of the preceding fugal section on a″ provides the starting point for the octave descent in the following free section:

Praeludium in a, BuxWV 153

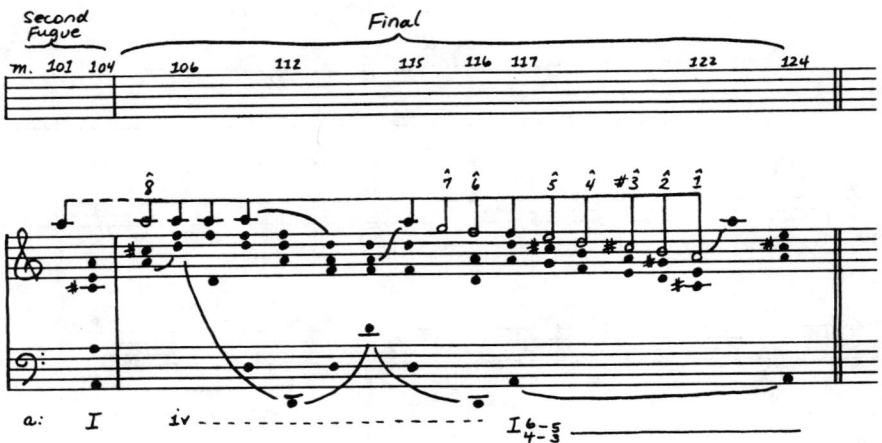

In several praeludia, such strong linear coherence, aided by the background harmonic progression which supports it, encompasses not only the last section of the work, but all of the sections after the first fugue. Such a structure, only suggested in the Praeludium in a, is far more powerfully realized in the Praeludium in d, BuxWV 140. Its many and diverse remaining sections—consisting of a chordal-rhapsodic section, an imitative quasi-fugato one with a free ending, a triple-time fugue with a free ending, and, lastly, a Final section—are bound together by one long line. The line is again an octave descent, and again contains a prominent transfer of register: d″-c″-b♮′-b♭′-a′-a″-g″-f″-e″-d″. The initial note of the line is prepared at the end of the first fugue in the same manner as in the Praeludium in D, with an upward octave transfer of the goal of the fundamental line of the fugue:[25]

Praeludium in D, BuxWV 139

Praeludium in d, BuxWV 140

The chromatic descent of the line, (8̂)-7̂-♮6̂-♭6̂-5̂, in the free ending of the quasi fugato concludes one of Buxtehude's most harmonically daring passages. The 5̂ is then transfered up an octave, establishing a new, more extreme register for the continuation of the line, 5̂-4̂-3̂, in the triple-time fugue which follows. The line is completed, 3̂-2̂-1̂, in the last section. The 1̂ is prolonged through the large subdominant area typical of a Final, in a way similar to the Praeludium in D and especially the Toccata in d:

Praeludium in d, BuxWV 140

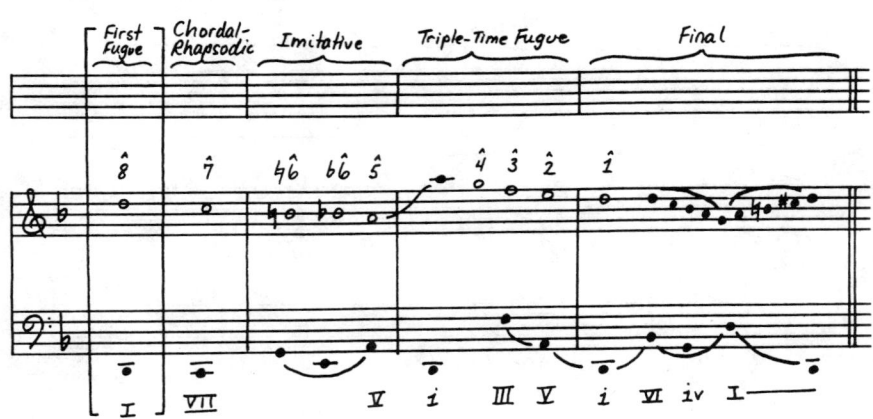

Some praeludia exhibit especially close structural links between the first fugue and the sections which follow. In the Praeludium in g, BuxWV 149, the first fugue ends with $\hat{\tilde{5}}$, and its free ending only prolongs that arrival.[26] The following *allegro* section (first basso continuo style texture followed by a modular passage), continues the line with a $\hat{4}$-$\hat{3}$-$\hat{2}$-$\hat{1}$ motion in much the same manner, but on a larger scale, as would a typical free ending. The form of the *allegro* also resembles a fugal free ending: its modular structure (measures 68–72 are repeated as measures 73–77 but with the voices rearranged), can be easily compared with the free ending of the triple-time fugue of the Praeludium in d, BuxWV 140. The second fugue begins a new line, which is again $\hat{8}$-$\hat{7}$-$\hat{6}$-$\hat{5}$-$\hat{4}$-$\hat{3}$-$\hat{2}$-$\hat{1}$; the ciaconalike closing free section which follows the second fugue prolongs the $\hat{\tilde{1}}$ arrival with a large subdominant area:[27]

Praeludium in g, BuxWV 149

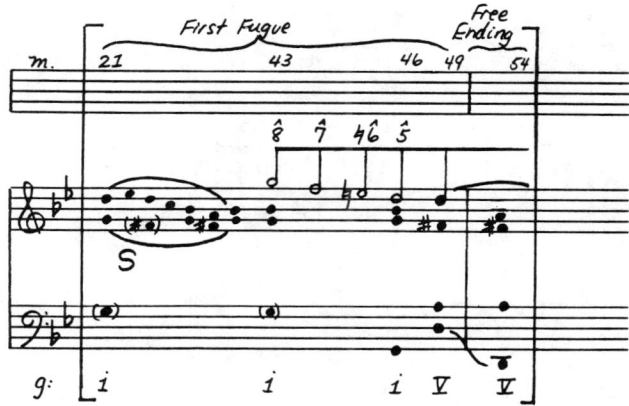

Allegro
55 67 68 72 73 77 78

Triple-Time Fugue
78 110 125 127 130 136

Closing Free Section (Ciacona)
142 145 148 151 155 159

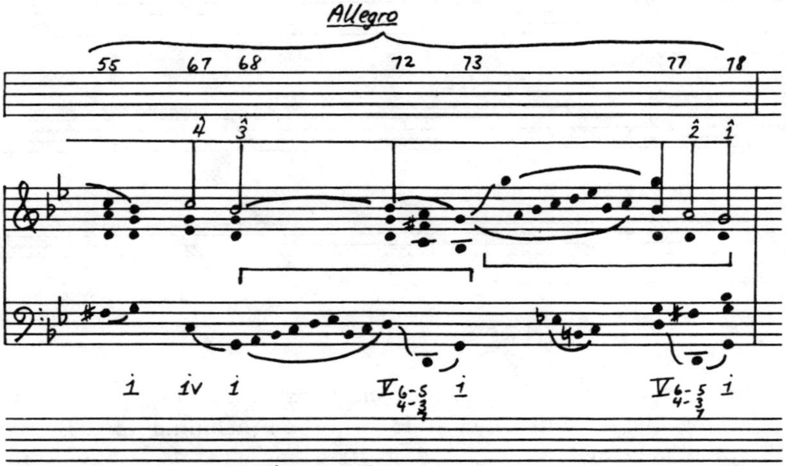

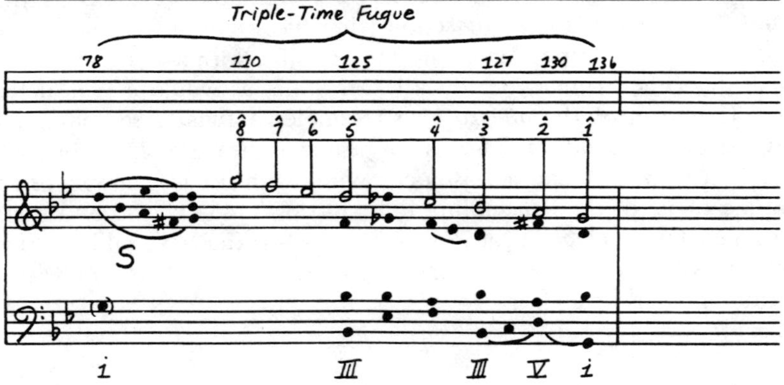

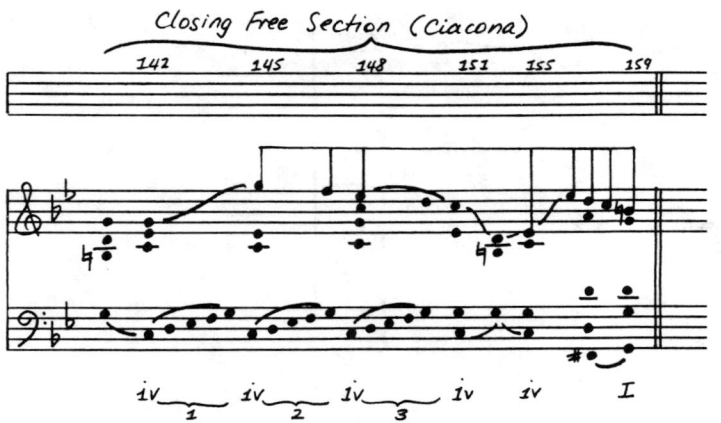

Remaining Sections

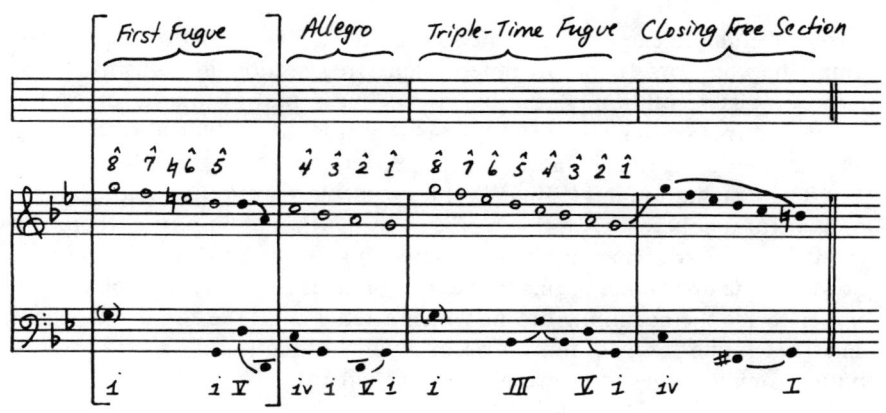

In the Praeludium in g, the typical scheme of fugue and free ending is expanded to include several free textures before the tonic arrival:

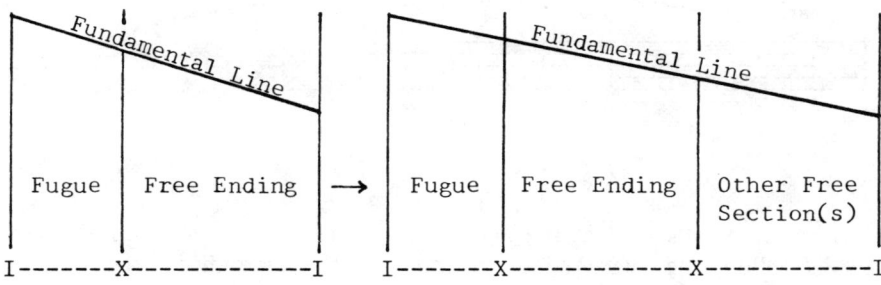

194 Remaining Sections

Such a technique can create ambiguous effects. The *allegro* of the Praeludium in g appears to be an independent free section in stylistic terms. However, its resolution of the harmonic/linear motion of the preceding fugue and free ending strongly suggests that it is, like a typical free ending whose function it fulfills, a dependent section.

The Praeludium in f♯, BuxWV 146, presents yet another bold example of structural coherence. In this work, as in the Praeludium in g, there is a significant linear connection with the first fugue. In the Praeludium in f♯, however, the line which begins in the first fugue is not quickly resolved, but rather forms the beginning of one which extends until the end of the work. The first fugue (*grave*), and the second which directly follows it (*vivace*), both strongly suggest an unresolved 5̂ at their cadences:

Praeludium in f♯, BuxWV 146

The 5̂ (c♯″) falls to 4̂ at the beginning of the chordal-rhapsodic section which follows the *vivace* fugue. The motion is first embodied in the opening flourish of the section as c♯″–f♯′–b:

Praeludium in f#, BuxWV 146

The descent to $\hat{4}$ is confirmed when it becomes firmly implanted as the fundamental soprano note of the section in its proper register (b'). It falls to $\hat{3}$ near the end of the section. A hurried continuation of that descent, a'–g#'–f#'–e#', ($\hat{3}$–$\hat{2}$–$\hat{1}$–$\hat{7}$), follows. Nevertheless, it does not prevent the strongly emphasized $\hat{3}$ an octave above (which occurs near the beginning of the closing free section) from being recognized as an octave transfer of a'. From this note, a long descent begins: a"–g#"–f#"–e"–d"–c#"–b'–a'–g#'–f#' ($\hat{3}$–$\hat{2}$–$\hat{1}$/$\hat{8}$–$\hat{7}$–$\hat{6}$–$\hat{5}$–$\hat{4}$–$\hat{3}$–$\hat{2}$–$\hat{1}$). The a" ($\hat{3}_I$) and e" ($\hat{7}_V$) are strongly supported by ostinatos, while g#" and f#" ($\hat{2}$–$\hat{1}$) are merely passing tones and do not suggest a conclusion to the overall $\hat{5}$–$\hat{4}$–$\hat{3}$–($\hat{2}$–$\hat{1}$) line begun in the fugal sections. After $\hat{7}_V$ (measure 103), the speed of the descent increases dramatically as the music swings from the dominant area (measures 99–103) to the following large subdominant area (measures 111–20) by way of an intermediary tonic: v–(iv–III–i–VI–V–i)–iv. During this passage, the V–i supports the concluding $\hat{2}$–$\hat{1}$ of the overall $\hat{5}$–$\hat{4}$–$\hat{3}$–$\hat{2}$–$\hat{1}$ line begun in the fugal sections. As in all of the other praeludia with large subdominant Final sections, the subdominant area of the Final here prolongs a tonic arrival ($\smash{^5_1}$). The octave descent which encompasses this section, is also typical:

```
f#"–e"–d"-------c#"–b'–a#'–g#'–f#'
(V/iv)–iv--I 6--5------------------
            4--3------------------
```

Praeludium in f#, BuxWV 146

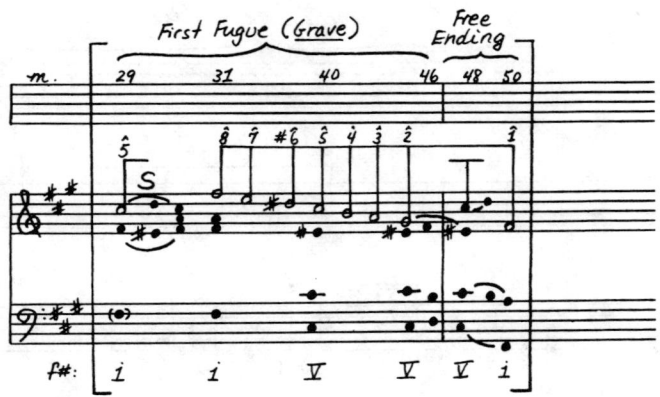

Closing Free Section
91
94
96
99
101
103
i i v v v

Final
105
107
109
110
111
121
125
129
2̂
1̂
iv III i V VI V i V i iv----I 6-5-6-5 4-3-4-3

First Fugue
Second Fugue
Chordal-Rhapsodic
Closing Free Section
5̂
4̂
3̂
2̂ 1̂
i i ii V i V i v i V i iv I

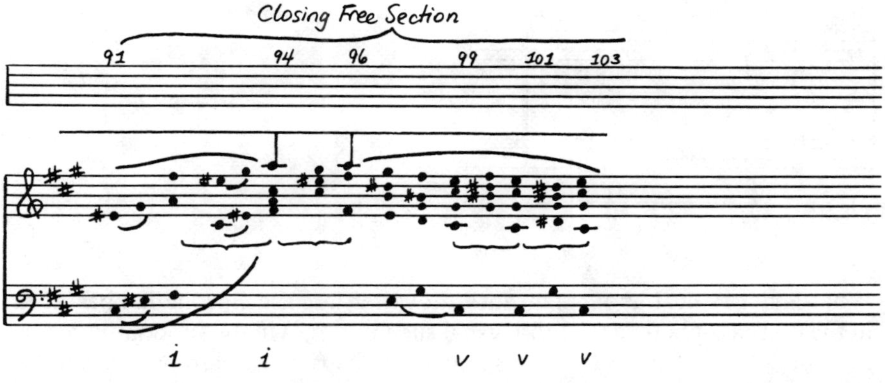

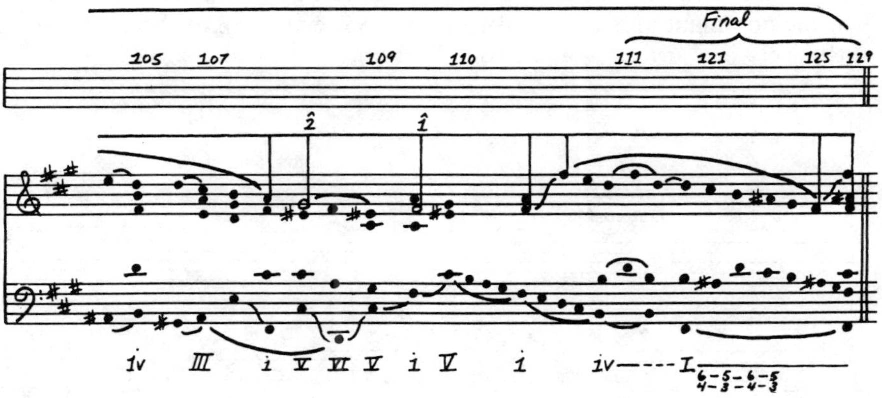

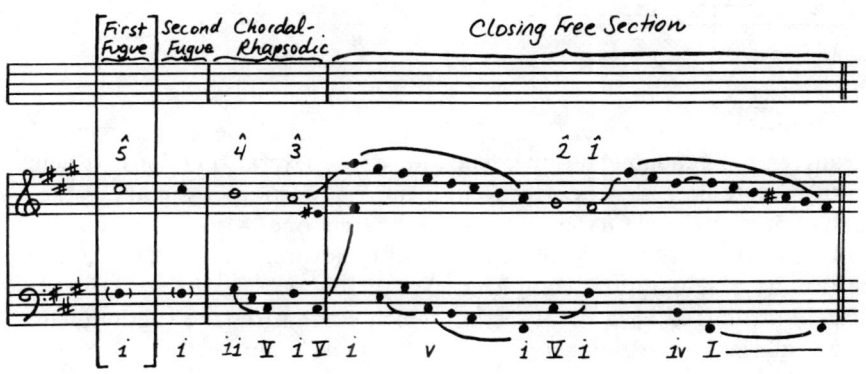

198   *Remaining Sections*

What is not typical about this work, however, are the ciaconalike passages in the dominant before the more usual such passages in the subdominant. In no other closing free section are so many and varied ostinato passages to be found. Buxtehude also provides a strong link between the descending line (a″–f#′) of the dominant area and the line of the subdominant area (f#″–f#′). The rapid descent of the first line after the extensively prolonged $\hat{7}\atop v$ of the dominant area allows us to hear a powerful link to the even more extensively prolonged $\hat{6}\atop iv$ of the following line:

Praeludium in f#, BuxWV 146

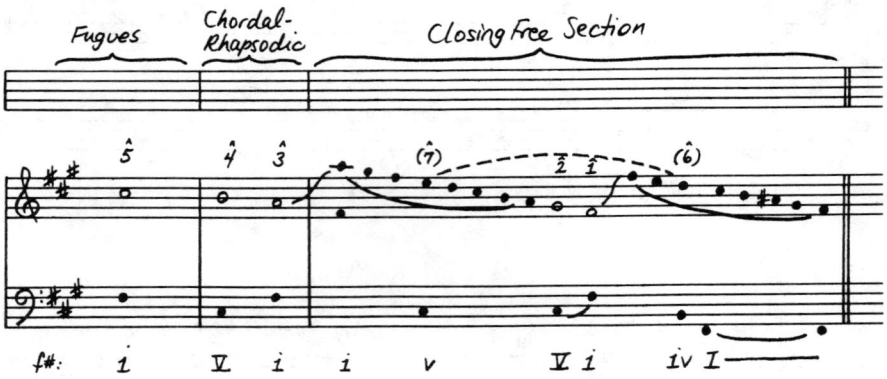

After the first fugue, then, synthesis and closure depend particularly strongly on a fundamental line. The line serves several functions. It helps justify nontonic cadences which close internal sections by making these arrivals just one goal on the way towards a larger one. Also, it is a powerful force drawing the music towards ultimate closure. Often the line ends before the praeludium is completed. When this occurs, the $\hat{1}$ arrival is usually prolonged by a Final section which emphasizes the subdominant. The result is the large plagal cadences which end many of the praeludia:

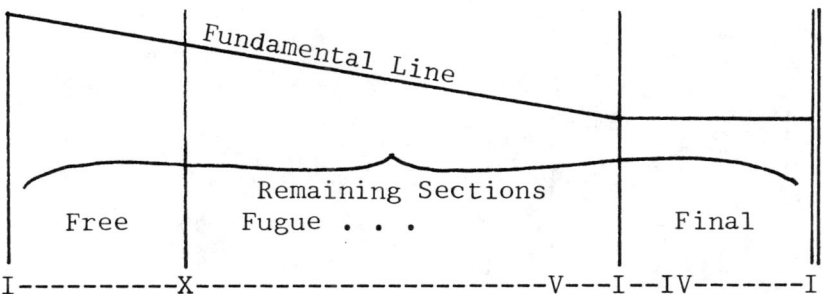

Such Final sections can thus be considered codas.[28]

Historical and Critical Evaluation

Several characteristics of the remaining sections can be found in the north German praeludia before Buxtehude.[29] While Scheidemann's praeambula usually end with a free section after the fugue (or imitative passages),[30] it is the works of Tunder that specifically foreshadow Buxtehude's techniques. Like Tunder's opening free sections, his closing free sections contain his most impressive moments, and stand closer to Buxtehude than his fugal sections do. For example, all four of Tunder's praeludia end with elaborate plagal cadences; Buxtehude's typical emphasis on the subdominant in closing free sections clearly derives from this north German practice. Tunder also anticipates Buxtehude's typical emphasis on the dominant of the subdominant in these passages. However, the ostinato figures which Buxtehude frequently uses to enliven his subdominant harmonic areas are only dimly perceivable in Tunder's praeludia.[31] As a link between the fugue and the closing free section, three of Tunder's four praeludia have quasi-free extensions based upon the diminution of the original subject.[32] Such an effect is most closely approximated by Buxtehude in the extensions which follow the second fugues of the Praeludium in e, BuxWV 143, and the Praeambulum in a, BuxWV 158. As these fugues are already based on lively triple-time transformations of originally less vivacious, common-time subjects, the diminution of their subjects is not as viable a procedure as it is for Tunder's stodgy, quarter-note subjects which have not seen triple-time derivations. However, the extensions of BuxWV 143 and 158 are modular in a way similar to the diminution passages of Tunder's praeludia; and, also like Tunder's, link directly into a closing free section or passage. Tunder's most elaborate complex of remaining sections is found in the Praeludium in g:[33]

200 Remaining Sections

Tunder: Praeludium in g

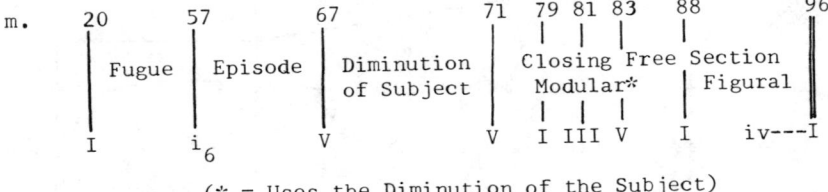

(* = Uses the Diminution of the Subject)

The remaining sections are linked by a fundamental line:

Tunder: Praeludium in g

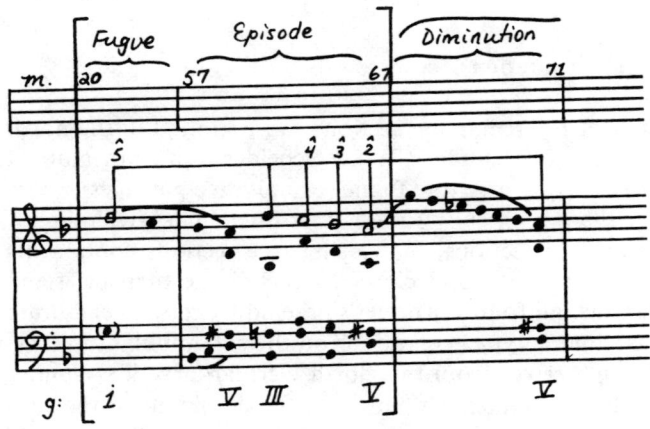

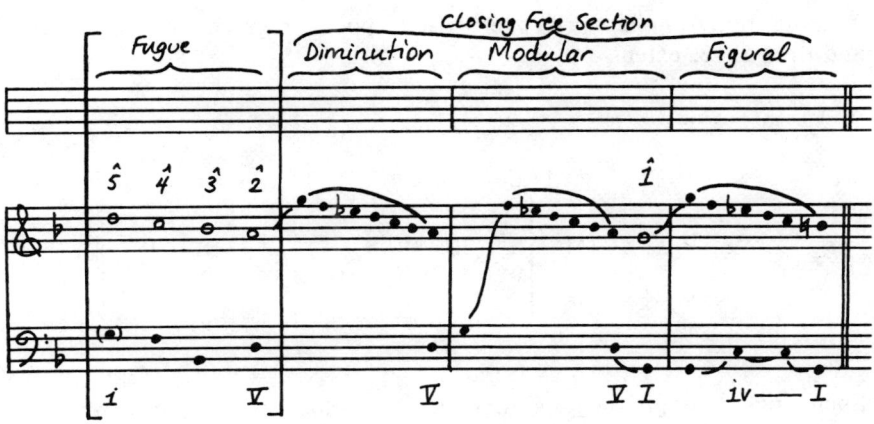

The linear coherence of this praeludium, however, is unusual for Tunder; his other praeludia have a weaker sense of overall line after the fugue.[34]

Weckmann's Fantasia, Fuga, and Praeambulum, all in d,[35] each have more than one fugal section. Their second fugues (and, in the Fuga, a third one as well) demonstrate several features typical of Buxtehude's second and third fugues.[36] In the Fantasia, for example, the second fugue is somewhat more wide-ranging harmonically than is the first fugue of that work.[37] Also suggestive of Buxtehude's practices is the irregular entry pattern of the second fugue of the Praeambulum. Such a plan as S (first tenor)/S (second tenor)/A (alto)/A (soprano)/A (bass) cannot be found in a first fugue of either Buxtehude or Weckmann, but is indicative of the looser fugal style sometimes found in Buxtehude's second (or third) fugues.

The transition from the last fugal section to the closing free section (or simply concluding free gesture in the Fuga and Praeambulum) is constructed differently in each of these works. In the Fuga, the fugal texture of the third fugue leads directly to a dominant pedal which forms the penultimate harmony of the work; over it first appear fragments of the subject, and then a free extension:

Weckmann: Fuga in d

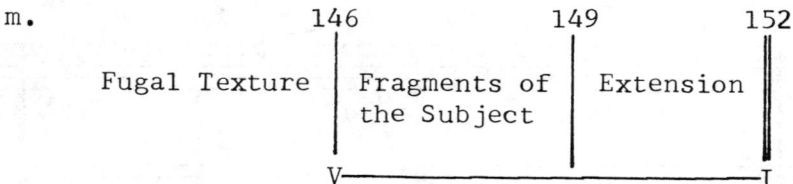

Such a plan strongly suggests Buxtehude's praeludia which end with a fugal section. In the Praeludium in C, BuxWV 136, the third fugal section (a gigue fugue) has a similarly extensive dominant harmonic area before the final tonic:

Praeludium in C, BuxWV 136

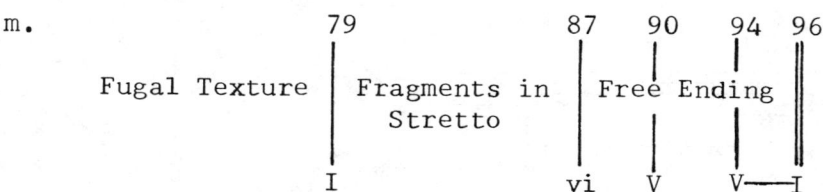

The Praeambulum ends with a penultimate subdominant harmonic area. The subdominant area does not begin with the change to free texture, however, but earlier, in the fugal texture:[38]

Weckmann: Praeambulum in d

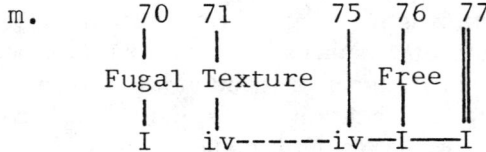

The Fantasia presents a more important example of a subdominant area as a penultimate harmony:

Weckmann: Fantasia in d

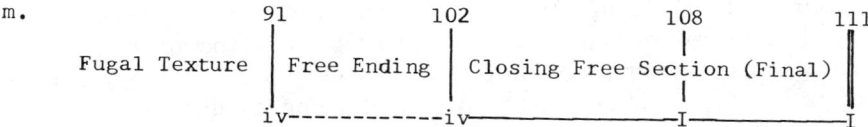

Created by both a free ending and a large part of the closing free section, it makes this prototypical Final section as bold as any of Tunder's closing free sections. And, together with the impressive subdominant passages which end Tunder's praeludia, it provides an important model for Buxtehude's notable subdominant passages in similar contexts.[39] The free ending of the second fugue contains some of Weckmann's most gesturally dramatic writing.[40] Indeed, the free endings of both fugues of this work are paradigmatic for Buxtehude in their highly contrasting textures.[41] The free ending of the second fugue, with its "dramatic rests,"[42] is a particularly individual gesture. It seems reflected, however, in a similar, but more rhythmically extreme passage (with even longer dramatic rests) in Buxtehude's Praeludium in e, BuxWV 143.[43] As a unit, the remaining sections of the Fantasia exhibit a rare degree of linear coherence for Weckmann's works:[44]

Weckmann: Fantasia in d

While Weckmann's toccatas occasionally reflect a similar degree of linear coherence as his Fantasia,[45] the most interesting models of a fundamental line in the many-sectioned toccata come not from north Germany but rather from Froberger. Buxtehude's practice of linking many sections together through both nontonic internal cadences and a long line, for example, in the Praeludia in d, BuxWV 140, and in f#, BuxWV 146, are most clearly foreshadowed in works such as Froberger's Toccata in d.[46] The Toccata strongly emphasizes the pattern of fugue and free ending, with each of its three fugal sections followed by a free ending in a distinctively different texture. Connecting the sections are linear links which, with the internal cadences on the dominant and the dominant of the dominant, help tie the work together:[47]

Froberger: Toccata in d

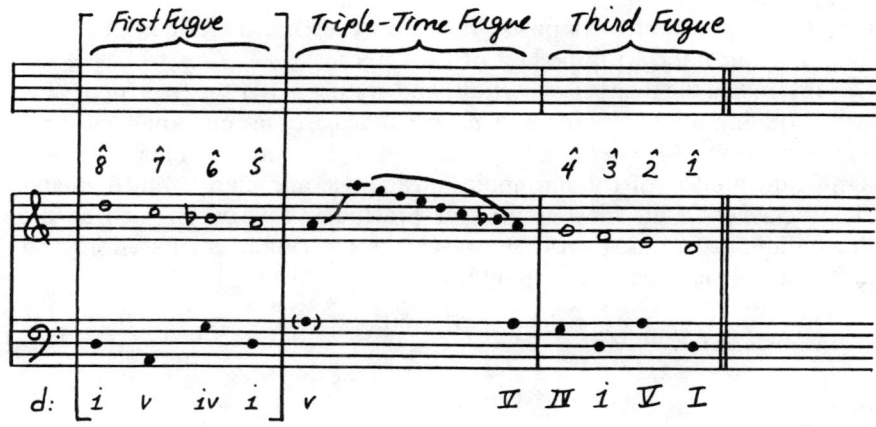

Buxtehude expanded the size and heightened the character of the remaining sections, and these innovations are crucial for the greater sense of climax and resolution with which he invested them. Only a rudimentary sense of climax can be found in Tunder's praeludia, and it is achieved largely through the successive acceleration of the rhythmic pulse: quarter notes in the fugue, eighths in the diminution section, and finally sixteenths in the closing free section. Froberger's toccatas have more sense of climax and drive, more sections, and are certainly more rhythmically sophisticated than are Tunder's praeludia. Weckmann provided the first, tentative examples of uniting these two styles: the Fantasia with its Italianate succession of thematically related fugues to which he added a north German subdominant closing section; and the Praeambulum, which incorporates a canzonalike triple-time fugue into an otherwise north German framework.[48] From among the welter of constituent parts possible in the remaining sections presented by these two traditions, Buxtehude created aggregates which in size, scope, and expressive power far surpass his north German predecessors, and can stand with the best of Froberger.

Increasing the number of sections and gestures after the first fugue also meant finding ways to control them; expanded size meant expanded techniques as well. And certainly it was Froberger who provided the most significant models of the harmonic/linear logic and clarity which Buxtehude achieves in his most impressive praeludia. In a work such as the Praeludium in E, BuxWV 141, however, the sheer number of sections and their relative shortness risk a jumbled effect:

Praeludium in E, BuxWV 141

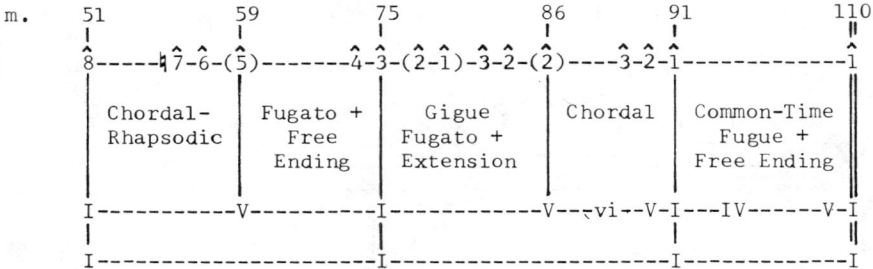

In this, Buxtehude's most extreme case of sectional proliferation after the first fugue, no one of the remaining sections can stand comparison to the large and elaborate first fugue. The remaining sections exhibit a potentially strong fundamental line which is given a somewhat weak realization: the cadence chords of several sections, particularly the chordal-rhapsodic one, obscure its progress. Other factors also contribute to a weakened sense of forward motion and climax. The two fugatos contribute excitement and tension but little real strength, as they are virtually without pedal parts. Moreover, the gigue fugato even suggests a relaxation from the previous peak of excitement in the first fugato and its free ending. Yet the *adagio* chordal section, in which the pedal returns, seems climactic for the work as a whole. Functioning like a free ending of the preceding fugato, it is too short to embody a strong sense of climax. Significantly, a fugue follows this arrival: the praeludium has not generated enough focused energy to warrant a Final section in which large amounts of tension could be diffused.[49] Nevertheless, as the fugue is the last section in the praeludium, the subdominant plays a larger than usual role.

The Praeludium in D, BuxWV 139, is another example in which the remaining sections are not joined linearly into a convincing synthesis:

Praeludium in D, BuxWV 139

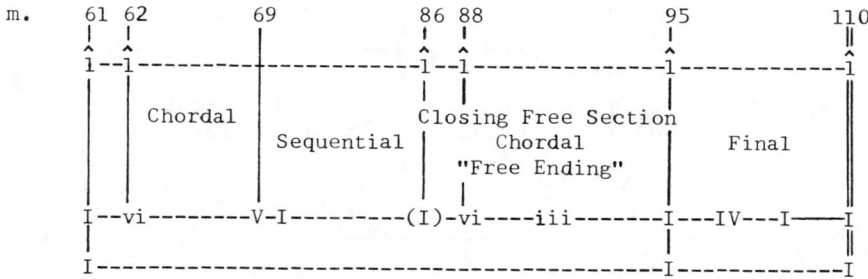

The sequential section and its chordal "free ending," however, build up more energy and momentum than the fugatos of the Praeludium in E. As a result, a subdominant Final is plausible, and provides a strong close.

Buxtehude's boldest creations in the remaining sections are found in those works in which the center of gravity of the work is unquestionably moved from the first fugue to the remaining sections themselves. The Praeludium in f♯, BuxWV 146, is an example. The first fugue (*grave*) is a miniature, paired with a larger and livelier second fugue (*vivace*). A large aggregate of free sections follows. The linear connection throughout these sections (including a chordal-rhapsodic one and ostinatos in both the dominant and then the subdominant) is very strong:

Praeludium in f♯, BuxWV 146

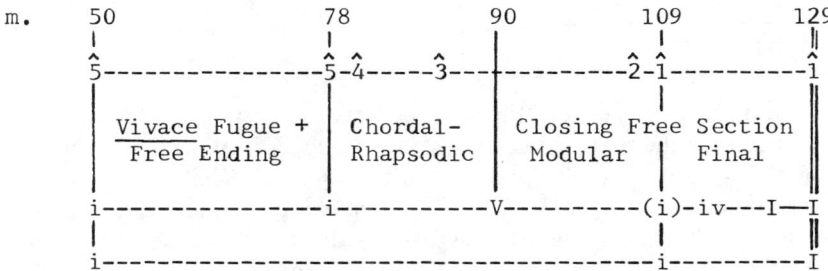

The Praeludium in d, BuxWV 140, balances both free and fugal textures in its strongly climactic remaining sections:

208 Remaining Sections

Praeludium in d, BuxWV 140

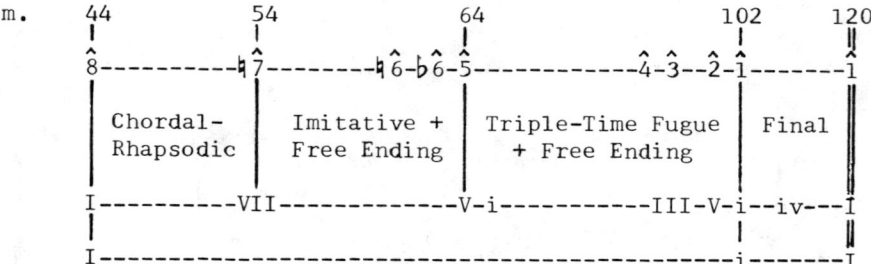

The impressive long line allows some of Buxtehude's most daring harmonic progressions to unite into a credible harmonic synthesis. It also provides both a strong sense of focus to the many sections and direction towards closure: its resolution is the impetus for an ostinato section in the subdominant to relax tension before the final cadence. In perhaps no other work can the center of gravity be so strongly felt as in the Praeludium in g, BuxWV 149. The second *largo* fugue, with its modern, expressive style, not only contrasts with, but clearly outweighs in power and expression the first fugue. Again, a closing free section (here approximating a ciacona) with subdominant harmony is penultimate to the final tonic:

Praeludium in g, BuxWV 149

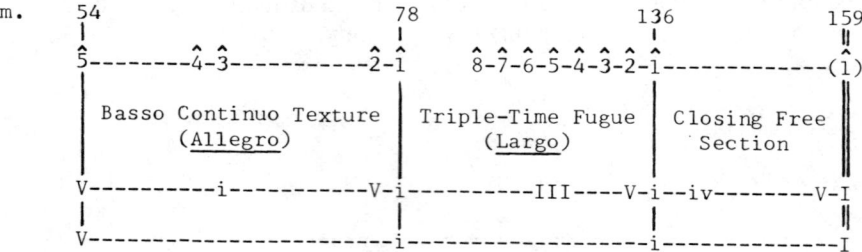

The linear links between the sections after the first fugue and, in some cases, including the first fugue itself, strongly suggest exploration of linear/harmonic coherence in the praeludium as a whole. While the first and second sections of the praeludia generally have a quasi-independent structural status, the remaining sections usually do not. Since they are more intimately involved in the creation and resolution of the climax, they are less stable, less poised, and more fragmentary then either the first or the second sections. And their close must function not just for themselves, but for the work as a whole. More than any other part, they demand consideration within the entire praeludium. In the following chapter, the linear/harmonic coherence of the whole praeludium is considered.

9

Coherence

Synthesis and Closure

The various sections of the praeludium as a whole are often joined in ways similar to those observed in the remaining sections:

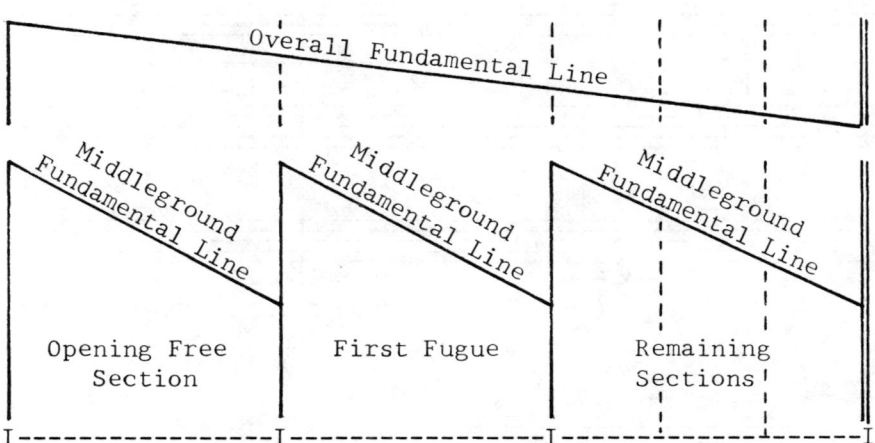

Considered in the context of the entire praeludium, the fundamental lines of the various sections and the harmonic progressions which support them are middleground structures. These are joined in various ways forming the larger structure which encompasses the entire praeludium. In some works, the middleground motions are more easily subsumed by an overriding motion, while in others they remain more staunchly independent of structural forces at the level of the whole praeludium.[1]

210   Coherence

When each of the middleground motions repeats the same line, links between them are easily made. The Praeludium in C, BuxWV 137, presents an example:

Praeludium in C, BuxWV 137

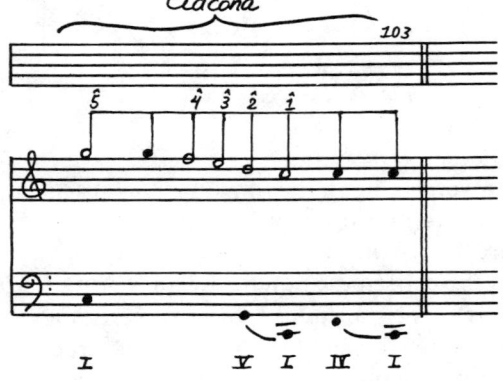

The fundamental line which spans the entire length of the Praeludium in C is an important factor in the overall synthesis of the composition. With its means of prolongation the middleground motions of the opening free section, the fugue, and the figural section, the descent in the last section becomes crucial, and so too does its harmonic support. At this highest level, a single $\genfrac{}{}{0pt}{}{\hat{5}\text{-}\hat{4}\text{-}\hat{3}\text{-}\hat{2}\text{-}\hat{1}}{\text{I-----V-I}}$ motion can be understood to be the background of the composition:

Praeludium in C, BuxWV 137

The reiteration of $\hat{5}$-$\hat{4}$-$\hat{3}$-$\hat{2}$-$\hat{1}$ (always at the same register) reinforces the sense that the sections belong together, established through thematic variation. It also suggests a $\hat{5}$------$\hat{4}$-$\hat{3}$-$\hat{2}$-$\hat{2}$-$\hat{1}$ line arching over the praeludium as a whole. The final descent becomes climactic for the work as a whole, especially as previous descents have been either weak (as in the fugue) or compromised by chromaticism (as in the figural section).[2] While the strength of this line is challenged by the several $\hat{1}$ closures, the repeated return to g″ soon after these arrivals argues for its vitality. Such an overall line, however, is static until near the end of the praeludium:

Coherence

[diagram: Fundamental Line spanning Opening Free Section, First Fugue, Remaining Sections — descending at the end]

These structures are frequently found in the middleground motions of the individual sections themselves, and their presence at various levels of the praeludia suggests that the lines are a typical aspect of the nature of structural coherence in these works. A line of this type, however, is not as strong as one which demonstrates movement spaced more evenly throughout a composition, for example:[3]

[diagram: Fundamental Line descending evenly across Opening Free Section, First Fugue, Remaining Sections]

This example points to the importance a particular pitch can have in overall coherence. The repeated return to the same note to begin similar motions is an important technique for building large-scale coherence. However, such a note is not always established in the opening section of a praeludium. Instead of the scheme observed in the preceding example,

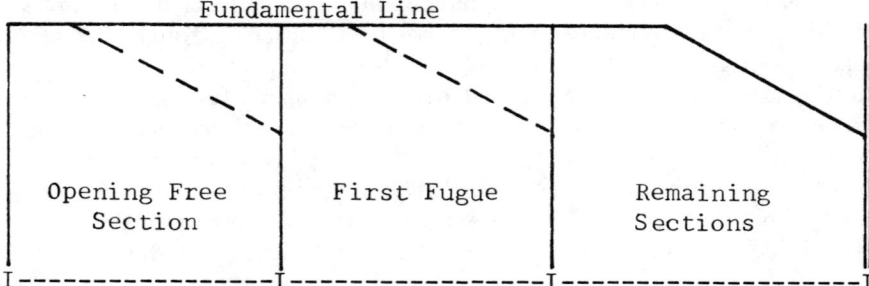

the opening free section may precede the establishment of an overall line:

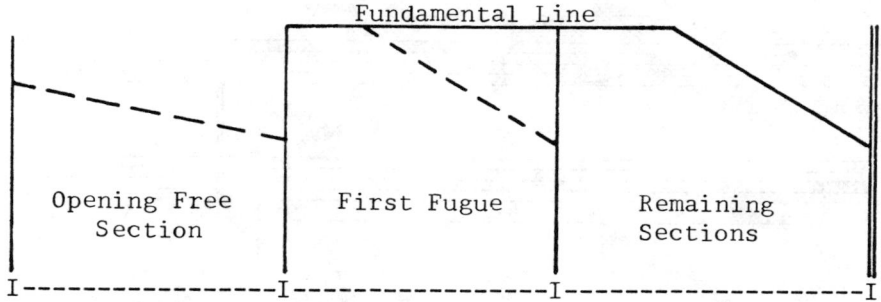

The Praeludium in C, BuxWV 136, is an example:

Praeludium in C, BuxWV 136

214   Coherence

The establishment of the fundamental line in the Praeludium in e, BuxWV 142, is delayed even further:

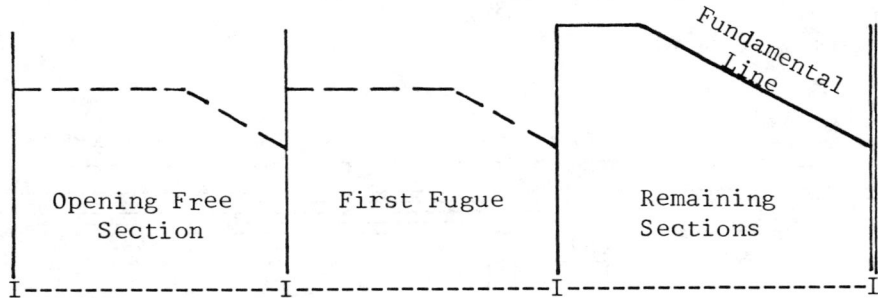

The importance of the beginning note of the line, e″, however, can be observed to grow in the first two sections. In the opening free section, it is only lightly stressed at the end, after the $^{\hat{4}-\hat{3}}_{V-I}$ cadence has occurred:

Praeludium in e, BuxWV 142

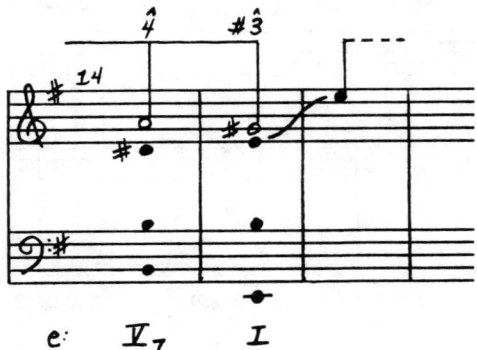

Although more important in the fugue which follows, e″ is abandoned near the end of that section. The cadence occurs at the octave below, $\genfrac{}{}{0pt}{}{\hat{4}-\hat{3}-\hat{2}-\hat{1}}{\text{V}\text{------}\text{I}}$ (a′–g′–f♯′–e′):

Praeludium in e, BuxWV 142

During the remaining sections, however, e″ becomes the initial note of a long line which leads to the end of the work:

Praeludium in e, BuxWV 142

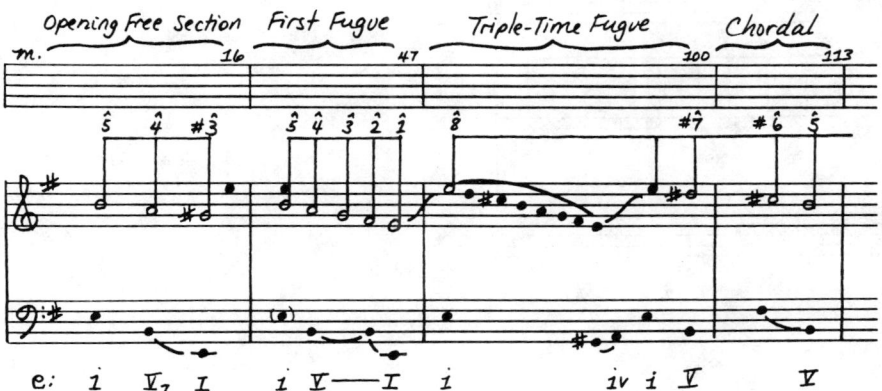

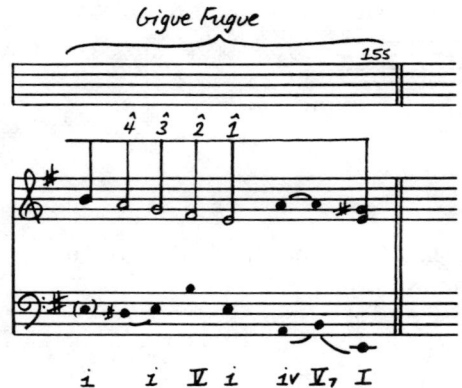

Coherence 217

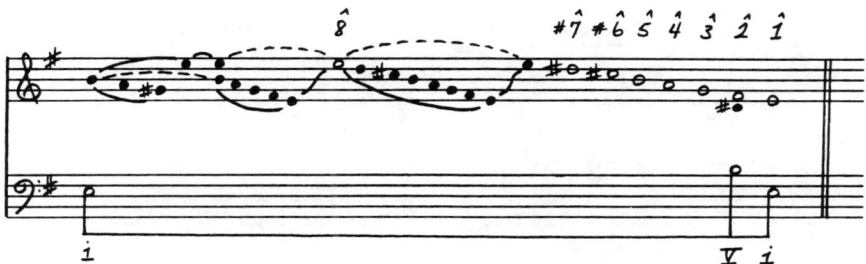

On the contrary, the crucial note of the first three sections of the Praeludium in f#, BuxWV 146, f#″, gives way to a line which begins with c#″ ($\hat{5}$) after the fugal sections. While c#″ is prepared during both fugal sections,[4] it is not until the chordal-rhapsodic section which follows them that the line which c#″ begins becomes the dominating linear force of the composition:

Praeludium in f#, BuxWV 146

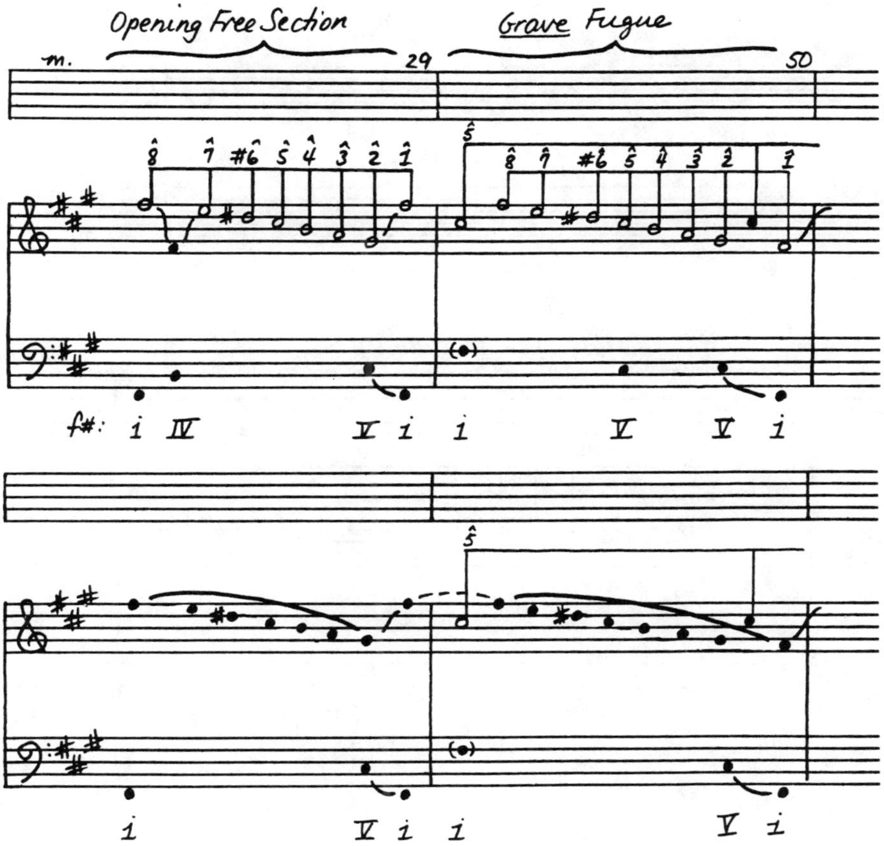

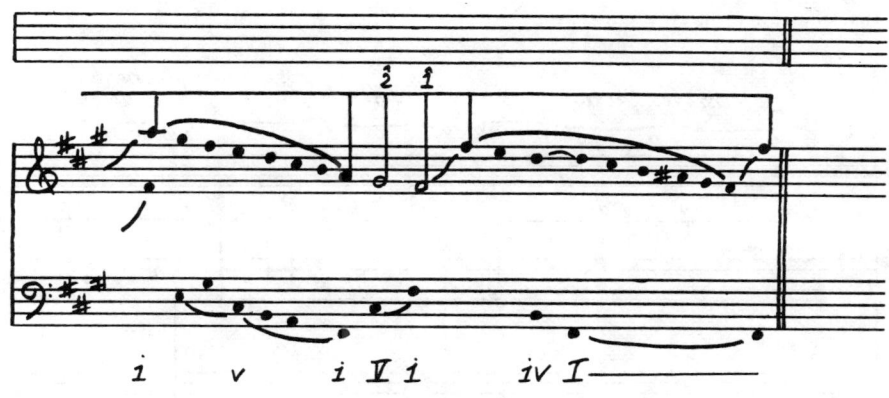

The fundamental lines of most praeludia remain within an octave range. The Praeludium in d, BuxWV 140, however, presents an interesting example of lines spanning two registers rather than one. The important fifth-span, a″-d′, in the opening free section returns in the triple-time fugue when an octave transfer catapults the $\hat{5}$-$\hat{4}$-$\hat{3}$-$\hat{2}$-$\hat{1}$ of an $\hat{8}$-$\hat{7}$-$\hat{6}$-$\hat{5}$-$\hat{4}$-$\hat{3}$-$\hat{2}$-$\hat{1}$ line (d″-d′) into a higher register; d″ instead of d′ is retained as the $\hat{1}$ at the close of the work:

Praeludium in d, BuxWV 140

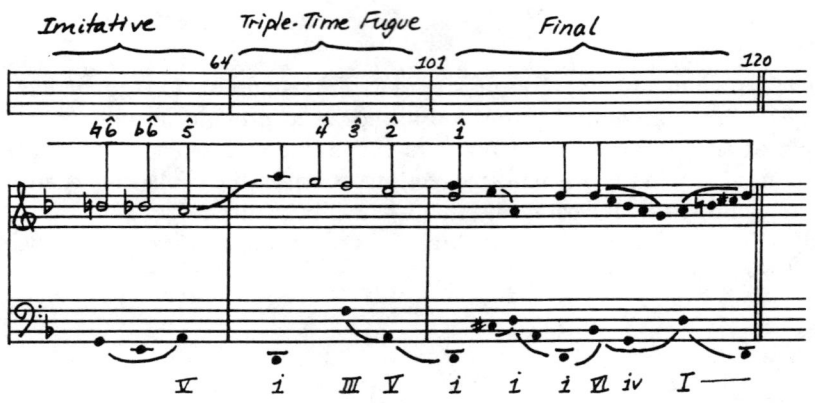

The synthesis of the various sections of the praeludium into a single, high-level structure also provides the praeludia with an overall drive towards closure. The main force of the closure, however, comes directly from the last middleground line and its harmonic support. Since previous motions (such as those in the opening free sections and the first fugue) by definition may reinforce — but do not preempt — the last linear motion and its harmonic support as the chief agents of closure, the last line becomes the climactic and conclusive one of the work. The most powerful drives towards closure are found in those works which have the most powerful lines in the remaining sections and, as a result, the most cogent high-level structure.[5]

Codas are often an important added element in strengthening closure. These Final sections prolong the $\hat{1}$ arrival which precedes them and provide yet one more $\hat{1}$ cadence.[6] But unlike previous arrivals, they are prepared by the subdominant. Unlike the dominant, the subdominant allows the uninterrupted prolongation of $\hat{1}$ at a high level: $\frac{\hat{2}-\hat{1}}{V-I} \ldots \frac{\hat{2}-\hat{1}}{V-I} \ldots \frac{\hat{2}-\hat{1}----\hat{1}}{V-I-IV-I}$. In a form so sectional as the praeludium such a distinctive harmonic/linear gesture as a Final section becomes, stylistically and structurally, an unambiguous indication of the finality of the cadence.[7]

Middleground and Background Form

The sectional form of the praeludium results in a series of strong middleground structures. These structures are the most powerful harmonic/linear forces of the praeludia, and unite at the highest level to form the somewhat more tenuous background motion of the composition. However, several aspects of their style can be noted. First, these motions are often static throughout most of the section. With the initial note prolonged far into the section, the actual descent becomes only a cadential gesture and not a span which actively encompasses the section which it closes. The result is sometimes weak counterpoint for the descent, as in the frequently encountered scheme in which the descent is presented over a dominant pedal:

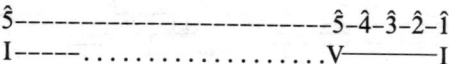

Such a structure not only hints at parallel motion at a high level, but also suggests that the resolution of the line is not final, for such a motion can be considered as a move into an inner voice:

Harmonically and contrapuntally, any of the following patterns would be stronger:[8]

$\hat{5}$--$\hat{4}$--$\hat{3}$--$\hat{2}$--$\hat{1}$ $\hat{5}$--$\hat{4}$--$\hat{3}$--$\hat{2}$--$\hat{1}$ $\hat{5}$--$\hat{4}$--$\hat{3}$--$\hat{2}$--$\hat{1}$
I-----I$_6$-V--I   I--II----V--I   I--IV----V--I

Even when the descent receives strong harmonic support, its compression in the last moments of the section weakens its overall effect.

Second, similar motions are frequently repeated as the fundamental lines of the various sections of a praeludium. Such a phenomenon is not simply the result of a limited number of possible fundamental lines, but more importantly of the process of thematic variation employed in the works. With several fugal sections based upon related thematic material, the shape of the fugal material itself becomes a chief reason for the similar backgrounds of the fugal sections of a given praeludium. The use of a similar series of expositions in such related fugues is also an important reason for their background congruence. However, similar lines are found in free sections as well. Clearly, the presence of similar "sectional backgrounds" reinforces the sense that the various sections of the praeludium belong together; successive waves of the same motion create one of the particular effects characteristic of the praeludium as opposed, for example, to the later prelude and fugue pair.

Finally, the number of these "sectional backgrounds" in a praeludium creates two basic structural forms. Two-part forms include those works which end after just a free and fugal section. Each section has a sectional background:

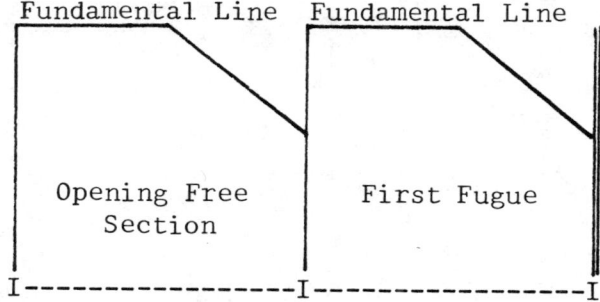

Most of the praeludia, however, have remaining sections, and typical of Buxtehude's style is the union of these sections into a single, sectional background motion, yielding a three-part form:

224 Coherence

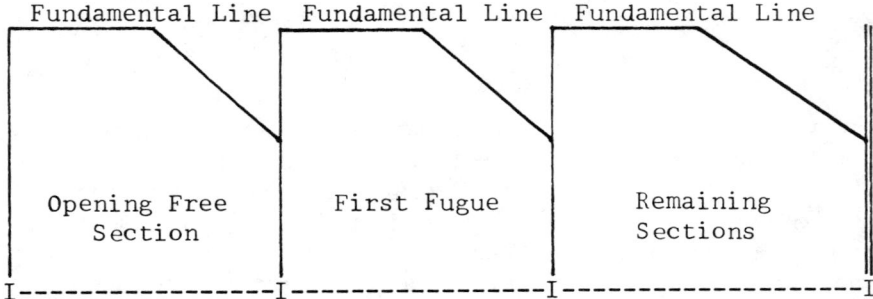

A Final section is sometimes added to three-part works. Such a section is a prolongation of the $\hat{1}$ arrival which ends the penultimate section. As it follows the establishment of the $\hat{1}$ of the fundamental line of the entire work, it is a true structural coda. It does not alter the three-part form, for its own sectional background is static:

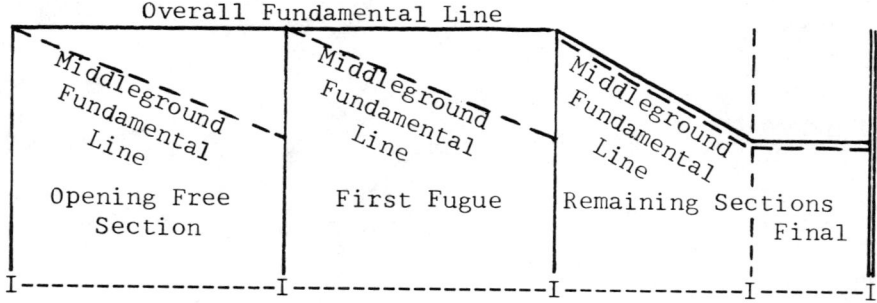

The synthesis of the sectional backgrounds, which are the middleground motions of the work as a whole, into an overall one-part form at the background level is more an additive than a synthetic process. Reflecting the frequent cadences and relatively open-ended form of the praeludium, synthesis of the sections into one large motion is relatively weak in comparison to the strength of the individual sectional motions. The background motion which results from the various middleground motions does so through the reinforcement of the last middleground descent rather than by the creation of an entirely new overall line out of the middleground motions. (Such a process, however, would create a stronger background.) Crucial to the relationship between the background and the middleground is the typical scheme in which each section of a work has similar descending lines. Such a structure makes possible the prolongation of the initial note of the lines over the course of the work:

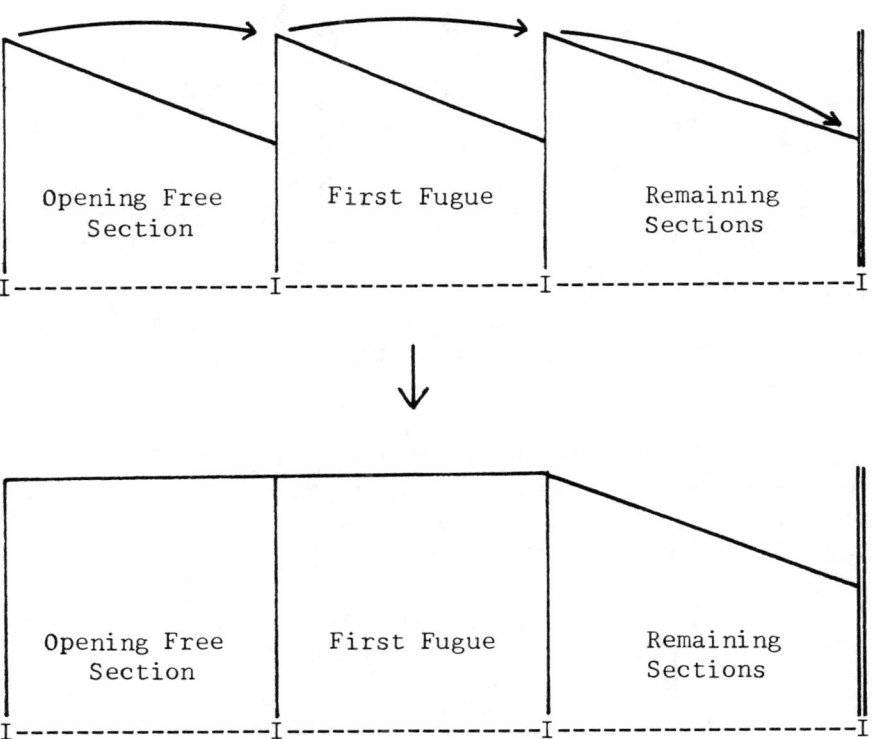

Structures in which the middleground motions of all the sections fit together into a single large line which descends over the entire course of the work are not found in the praeludia. The following scheme, for example, is not typical:

226 Coherence

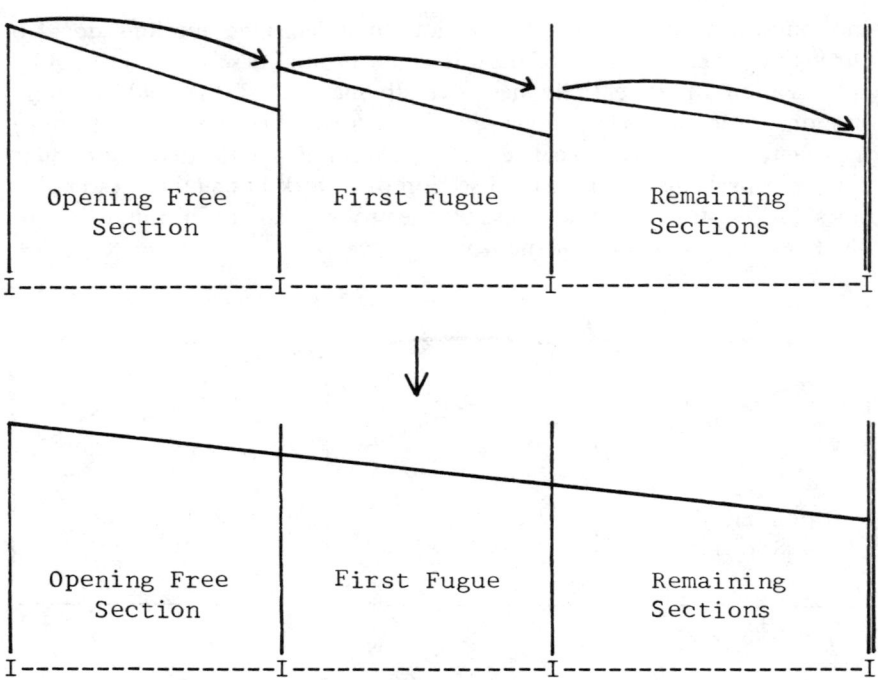

The way in which the background structure is created helps explain why praeludia can exhibit either a few or many sections: the middleground motions are joined in what is an essentially open-ended way. Any number of sections could conceivably be joined by this technique:

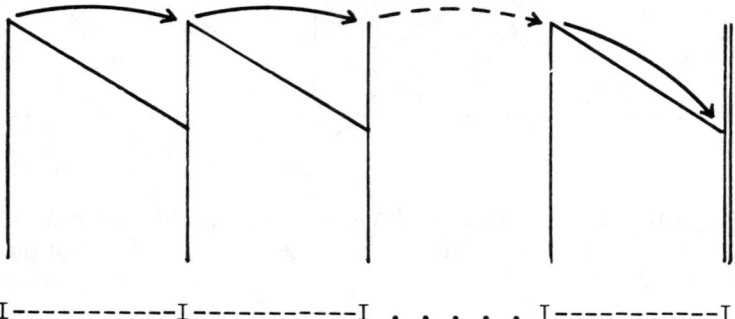

Historical and Critical Evaluation

The works of Tunder, Weckmann, and Froberger provide models of Buxtehude's techniques at the background level of structure as well as in foreground details.[9] Tunder's praeludia are examples of two-part form to which a coda is added. In the Praeludium in g,[10] the sectional background of the opening free section, $\hat{5}$–$\hat{4}$–$\hat{3}$–$\hat{2}$–$\hat{1}$, is repeated in the fugue. Following the $\hat{1}$ arrival, a coda which stresses the subdominant ensues. The background form of this work, then, is very similar to Buxtehude's typical plans:[11]

Tunder: Praeludium in g

228 Coherence

Weckmann's works also provide examples which anticipate Buxtehude's techniques. The Praeambulum in d,[12] for example, approximates three-part form. The opening free section, however, has a weak linear struc-

Coherence 229

ture centered on $\hat{5}$ (a'). The two fugal sections repeat similar lines ($\hat{3}$-$\hat{2}$-$\hat{1}$, f"-e"-d"), but they are hardly more than cadential gestures. Overall, the sense of line in this work is considerably weaker than in Buxtehude's praeludia:

Weckmann: Praeambulum in d

230 Coherence

The Fantasia in d,[13] however, provides an example of a longer, more vital line. Both the first and second fugues (there is no opening free section) have $\hat{5}$-$\hat{4}$-$\hat{3}$-$\hat{2}$-$\hat{1}$ lines (a"-d"). While $\hat{1}$ is established unusually early in the second fugue, the linear coherence of the work remains in evidence until the final cadence: the descent from d" continues into the closing free section, until finally #$\hat{3}$ is reached at the conclusion (d"-c"-bb'-a'-g'-f#'). Such large-scale linear connections are not only an important aspect of the coherence of this work, but also make the Fantasia an important model for Buxtehude:[14]

Weckmann: Fantasia in d

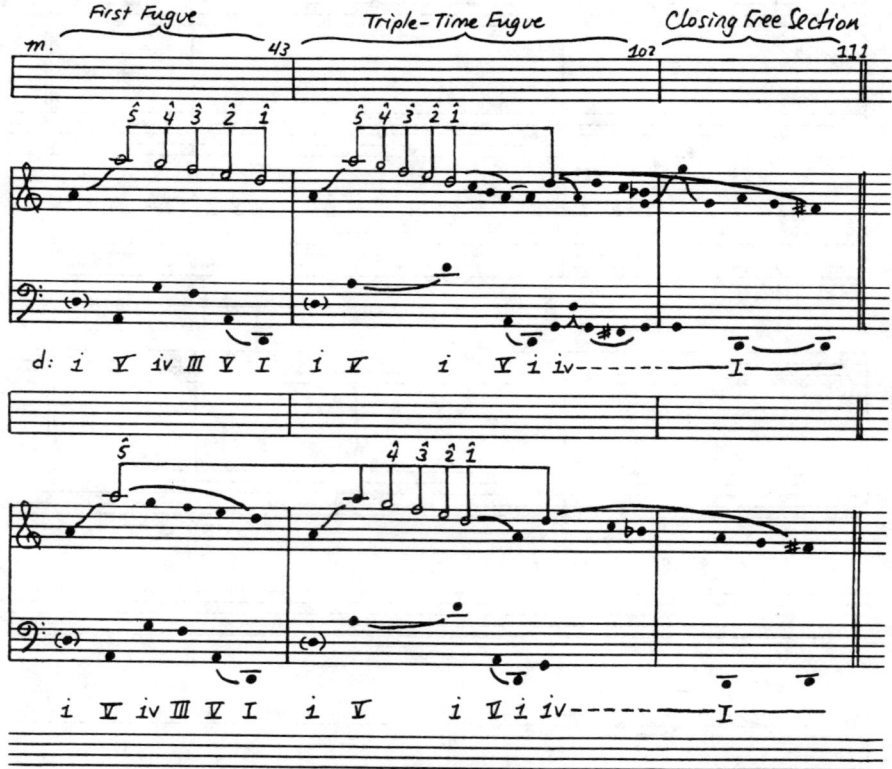

Coherence   231

The most remarkable examples of linear coherence come from Froberger. His Toccata in d[15] is a two-part work at the middleground level, but incorporates many textural sections. The $\hat{8}-\hat{7}-\natural\hat{6}-\hat{5}-\hat{4}-\hat{3}-\hat{2}-\hat{1}$ line of the opening free section is expanded into an even larger $\hat{8}-\hat{7}-(\flat)\hat{6}-\hat{5}-\hat{4}-\hat{3}-\hat{2}-\hat{1}$ line which encompasses the sections thereafter. Such a structure anticipates the manner in which Buxtehude creates overall synthesis in his praeludia:

Froberger: Toccata in d

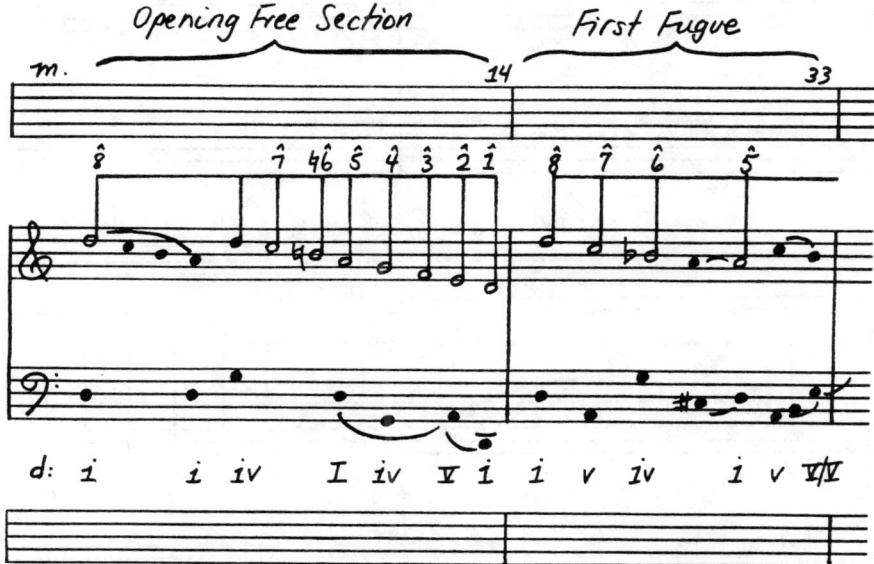

8̂ 7̂ 6̂ 5̂
i i iv I iv V i i v iv i
Triple-Time Fugue
Third Fugue
51
70
4̂ 3̂ 2̂ 1̂
v IV V iv V i IV i V I
4̂ 3̂ 2̂ 1̂
v iv V i IV i V I

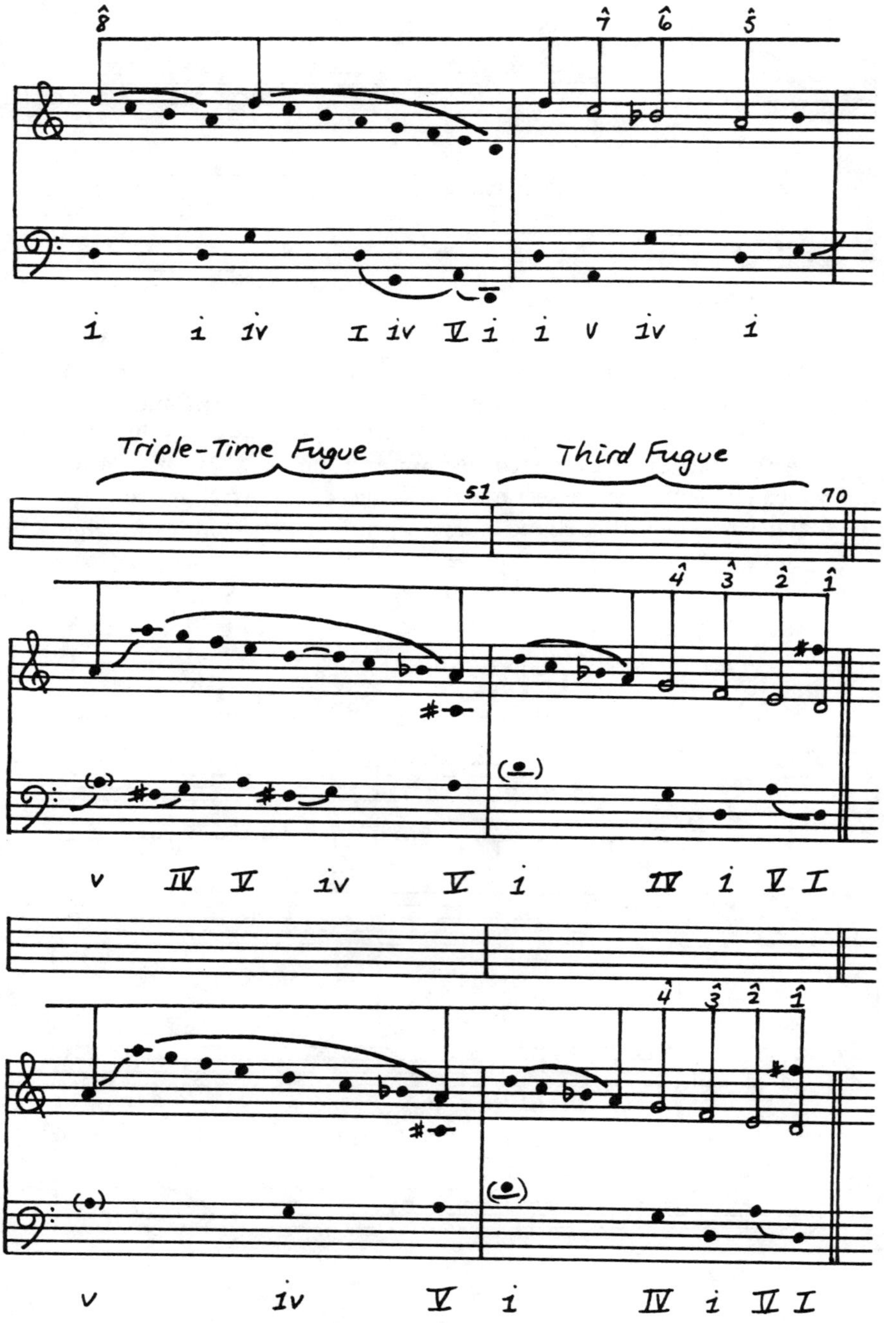

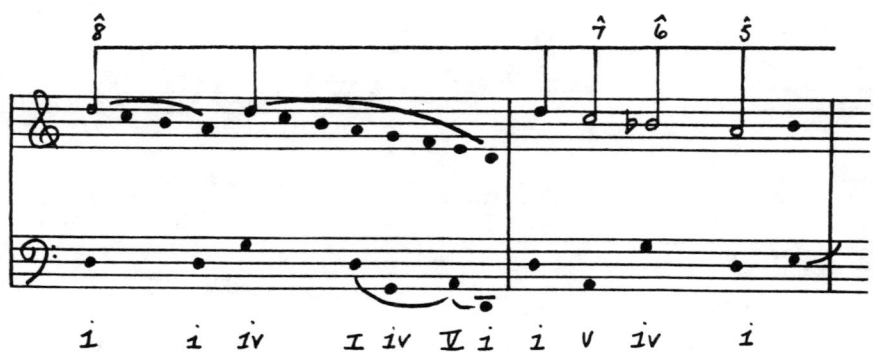

These works, as well as Buxtehude's praeludia, stand between the flat hierarchical structures of Renaissance music and the fully arched ones typical of tonal music in the eighteenth century.[16] The highest level of the praeludia do not contain the most powerful forces of coherence; rather, they lie in the backgrounds of the sections themselves, or in what is the middleground level of the work as a whole. It is, however, the presence of a viable—if not completely preeminent—background that helps keep the praeludium from disintegrating into completely separate sections.

The nature of the hierarchy helps explain not only the structure of the works but also their impact. The opening free section, structurally the most independent part of the work, is chiefly anticipatory in effect. Generally, the initial note of the fundamental line is introduced, and the descent of that line (which is to come in further sections) is foreshadowed. Indeed, the establishment of the tonic register of the work is often the chief structural function of the section. Sometimes, the initial note of the fundamental line of the work is not established until the first fugue (or, rarely, even later). In such cases, the introductory role of the opening free section is even clearer in the high-level structure. The first fugue is typically more closely knit to the rest of the work, although it, too, maintains some degree of structural independence in most praeludia. It usually has its own sectional background, often one which is more strongly constructed than that of the opening free section. Like that section, the background motion of the first fugue often foreshadows the definitive descent of the overall line which occurs in later sections.[17] Compared with the anticipatory opening free sections, the first fugue generally has considerably more stature within the praeludium. The remaining sections are the most interdependent, and are generally united through a single fundamental line. Taken together, they may outweigh either (or both) the opening section and the first fugue, not only in length but expressive effect. It is these sections which contain the final intensification of the expressive content of the work, its peak of tension and its resolution. Likewise, the fundamental line of the work, whose initial note is generally prolonged throughout the first two sections, is resolved through a descent to $\hat{1}$: the background motion of these sections becomes the conclusion of the overall motion of the work as a whole. The flexibility of the form of the praeludia with its various numbers of sections, however, means that the final closure must be particularly strong: it must ensure that the work actually ends, and not simply suggest the ending of yet another section. The codas, or Final sections, are an important structural device for this effect. While they may appear to be yet one more section in stylistic terms, they are structurally very different. With their emphasis on the subdominant as they prolong the preceding $\hat{1}$ arrival, they provide a distinctive closing gesture. For this reason, those praeludia which end with such sections exhibit some of the most convincing forms.

As the foregoing suggests, there is a palpable relationship between background structure and expressive shape. Generally the penultimate section, in which the maximum tension of the work is found, directly precedes the resolution of the fundamental line. The last section contains the resolution of the line as well as the resolution of tension:

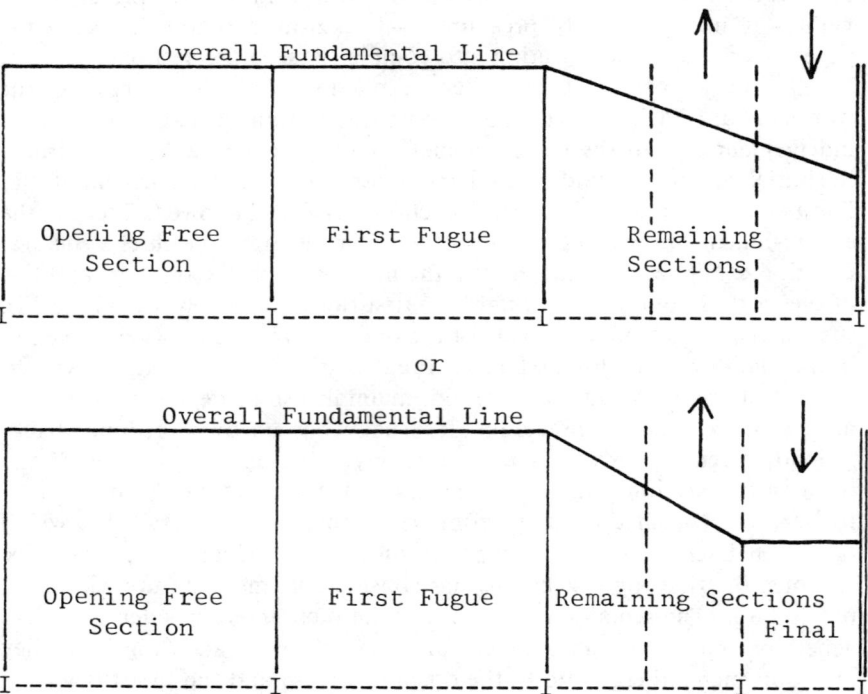

The relationship of these structures to a proposed chronology of the works is explored in the Conclusion.

Conclusion

Chronological Considerations

The Sources

Any attempt to order the praeludia in a chronological sequence must first take into consideration the manuscript sources which preserve them. No autographs of these works remain;[1] and many of the sources are not in tablature, as the autographs would doubtless have been. Indeed, some date from the eighteenth century, years after Buxtehude's death.[2] The most important are the Wenster Collection, the Lowell Mason Codex, Berlin 2681, and—with similar contents—the Wagener Manuscript and copies of it. Other important sources include the well-known Andreas-Bach-Buch, the Englehardt Collection, the Schmahls Tablature, one of the Möller Manuscripts, the Gotthold Manuscript, Berlin 30381, and finally the Grobe Tablature and one further Berlin manuscript, both of which are now lost.

The Wenster Collection[3] is in tablature, and of all the sources can be most directly linked with Buxtehude. The original source of the works by Buxtehude which it contains can be hypothesized as manuscripts, now lost, belonging to Gottlieb Klingenberg, who studied with Buxtehude before 1689. Klingenberg's student (or a student of his student, Michael Rohde), Gottfried Lindemann, was the copyist.[4] Writes Olivier Alain,

> Besides nine works of Buxtehude, the collection contains other works, mainly by Gottlieb Klingenberg and the latter's pupil Michael Rohde. The handwriting is mostly that of Gottfried Lindemann, likewise a pupil of Klingenberg, and organist in Karlshamn. Upon Lindemann's death, his successor, Christian Wenster, senior, inherited the collection. In the 1830s his grandson, Emanuel Wenster, presented the collection to the University.[5]

The works by Buxtehude in the collection can thus be dated before 1689. Powell, however, regards this hypothesis, advanced by Hedar, as "very shaky."[6]

The collection, nonetheless, can be considered one of the most reliable of the sources. For the three praeludia which are both included in Wenster and found in several other manuscripts, Wenster is regarded as the best source. Wenster was not known to either Spitta (first edition, 1875-76) or to Max Seiffert (who revised the Spitta edition in 1903, and issued a supplement to it in 1939). It was first used by Hedar for his edition (1952), and its use is one major reason why that edition superseded previous efforts.

The Lowell Mason Codex[7] is not in tablature. It is a large collection of harpsichord and organ works by many composers. Included are ten works by Buxtehude, most of which are not found in other sources.[8] Like Wenster, the manuscript has been dated: it carries the date 1688, and two of its contents are also dated.[9] Its purchase by Lowell Mason in 1852 brought it to the United States, and it was unknown to German scholars until 1904.[10] The Buxtehude praeludia which it contains were first published in the 1939 supplement to the Spitta edition edited by Max Seiffert. Recently, Snyder has suggested that it is probably the oldest of the major manuscripts which preserve the praeludia.[11]

Berlin 2681[12] contains an impressive group of nine praeludia. It dates from the beginning of the eighteenth century, and has been linked with C. P. E. Bach.[13] It was a major source for the Spitta edition. The Wagener Manuscript[14] contains the largest single group of praeludia of any of the manuscripts. Like Berlin 2681, it comes from the Bach circle: it was copied by Johann Friedrich Agricola, a pupil of J. S. Bach.[15] Later, the manuscript was owned by Wagener.[16] This manuscript and four copies of it in Berlin[17] all appear to date from the second half of the eighteenth century, significantly later than Berlin 2681. Several of these Berlin copies of Wagener were known to Spitta.

Berlin 2681 and the Wagener Manuscript have remarkably similar contents. Both sources transmit essentially the same group of praeludia, and do so in essentially the same order.[18] The Wagener Manuscript and its Berlin copies include one extra work, the Praeludium in f♯, BuxWV 146, to the group of nine praeludia in Berlin 2681.[19] Berlin 2681, however, includes five works for keyboard without pedal (BuxWV 163, 164, 168, 171, and 176) which are omitted in Wagener. The contents of Berlin 2681 and Wagener and their order are compared in table 3.

The remaining sources transmit no more than two of Buxtehude's praeludia in each collection. The Andreas-Bach-Buch[20] comes directly from the Bach circle[21] and includes works by not only Buxtehude, but some by Reincken, Pachelbel, J. S. Bach, and other composers. It was known by Spitta. The Englehardt Collection,[22] like Wenster which is also at Lund, is in tablature. Also like Wenster, it was unknown to Spitta and Seiffert, and was first used by Hedar for his edition. Two other manuscripts, also associated with Lowell Mason, contain keyboard works by Buxtehude.[23] These two sources were not known to either Seiffert in 1939, or to Hedar when

Table 3. The Berlin 2681 and Wagener Manuscripts

Berlin 2681		Wagener
		1. Magnificant primi toni, BuxWV 203
1. Praeludium in e, BuxWV 142	=	2. Praeludium in e, BuxWV 142
2. Praeludium in a, BuxWV 153	=	3. Praeludium in a, BuxWV 153
3. Praeludium in D, BuxWV 139	=	4. Praeludium in D, BuxWV 139
4. Praeludium in d, BuxWV 140	=	5. Praeludium in d, BuxWV 140
5. Praeludium in E, BuxWV 141	=	6. Praeludium in E, BuxWV 141
6. Canzonetta in G, BuxWV 171		
7. Praeludium in F, BuxWV 145	=	7. Praeludium in F, BuxWV 145
8. Fuga in B♭, BuxWV 176		
9. Praeludium in e, BuxWV 143	=	8. Praeludium in e, BuxWV 143
10. Canzona in d, BuxWV 168		
(11. by Buttstaed)		
12. Praeludium in g, BuxWV 163		
13. Toccata in F, BuxWV 156	=	9. Toccata in F, BuxWV 156
14. Toccata in G, BuxWV 164		
15. Praeludium in g, BuxWV 149	=	10. Praeludium in g, BuxWV 149
16. Nun lob, mein Seel, den Herren, BuxWV 213		
		11. Praeludium in f#, BuxWV 146

he prepared his edition of 1952, but were used for the Beckmann edition (1971).[24]

The Schmahls Tablature[25] and one of the Möller Manuscripts[26] present different versions of the same work, the Praeludium in A, BuxWV 151. The version in the Möller Manuscript, opening free section/first fugue + free ending/second fugue, can be considered a more authentic version than that of the Schmahls Tablature, which is: opening free section (greatly expanded with a passage in an untypical style)/first fugue + free ending.[27] Neither of these sources were known to Spitta; the Praeludium in A first appeared in the supplement to the Spitta edition of 1939, edited by Seiffert. There, however, Seiffert combined the two versions.[28] The work was more correctly printed in two versions by Hedar.[29] Beckmann relegates the Schmahls version to his appendix.[30] Nevertheless, the Schmahls version is significant because it carries a date: 1696. Beckmann, however, has questioned the authenticity of this version.[31]

The Gotthold Manuscript[32] and Berlin 30381[33] present praeludia found in other, larger collections (notably Berlin 2681 and Wagener). Finally, two sources, the Grobe Tablature[34] and a Berlin manuscript,[35] are now lost but were known to Spitta and were used for his edition. The Grobe Tablature, however, carried the date 1675, which gives a *terminus post quem non* for the one Buxtehude praeludium it contained. The sources and their contents are summarized in table 4.

The manuscripts, then, provide a general idea of a date beyond which many of the praeludia could not have been written. With dates of 1688 for the Lowell Mason Codex (LM 5056) and 1689 for the Wenster Manuscript, a *terminus post quem non* for half of the praeludia towards the end of the 1680s can be provided. With Berlin 2681 and the Wagener Manuscript, no such precision in dating is possible. However, the inclusion of one of the most impressive of the praeludia, the Praeludium in e, BuxWV 142, in all four of these major collections, and of the equally notable Praeludium in g, BuxWV 149, in Berlin, Wagener, and Wenster suggests that the praeludia of these two manuscripts do not have a significantly later origin. Riedel, however, has suggested 1683 as the date before which most if not all of Buxtehude's praeludia were composed. His argument is based in part on the Praeludium in g, BuxWV 148, which appears in the Grobe Tablature dated 1675. BuxWV 148, for Riedel, is as mature a work as any of the other praeludia, which suggests that Buxtehude was at the height of his powers in

Table 4. The Manuscripts and Their Contents

Manuscript	Beckmann Insignia[36]
Wenster Collection	C
Lowell Mason Codex	
LM 5056	A
LM 4838	H
Berlin 2681	D
Wagener Manuscript	E
Andreas-Bach-Buch	F
Englehardt Collection	G
Schmahls Tablature	B
Möller Manuscript	I
Gotthold Manuscript	J
Berlin 30381	K
Grobe Tablature	R
Berlin Ehemalige Bibliothek Manuscript	S

(*Table 4 continued*)

BuxWV	Hedar[37]	Title	Manuscript											
			C	A	H	D	E	F	G	B	I	J	K	R	S
136	2	Praeludium in C		*											
137	1	Praeludium in C						*							
138	...	Praeludium in C			*										
139	11	Praeludium in D	*			*	*		*						
140	19	Praeludium in d				*	*								
141	14	Praeludium in E				*	*								
142	9	Praeludium in e	*	*		*	*								
143	10	Praeludium in e				*	*						*		
144	16	Praeludium in F	*												
145	15	Praeludium in F				*	*						*		
146	13	Praeludium in f#					*								
147	7	Praeludium in G							*						
148	22	Praeludium in g		*									*		
149	24	Praeludium in g	*			*	*								
150	23	Praeludium in g						*							
151	12a	Praeludium in A									*				
151	12b	Praeludium in A								*					
152	6	Praeludium in a		*											
153	4	Praeludium in a				*	*								
154	21	Praeludium in B♭	*												
155	20	Toccata in d		*											
156	17	Toccata in F				*	*								
157	18	Toccata in F													*
158	5	Praeambulum in a		*											

the praeludia in the early 1670s. Moreover, the dates of the Lowell Mason Codex and the Wenster Collection do not necessarily mean, or even at all suggest, that the actual origin of the works which they contain was 1688/89.[38]

Little real evidence for dating specific works, however, is provided by the manuscripts. Only the Toccata in d, BuxWV 155, in the Lowell Mason Codex, and the (probably partially spurious) version of the Praeludium in A, BuxWV 151, in the Schmahls Tablature, carry specific dates, 1684 and 1696 respectively. These dates, appearing in conjunction with the titles of the works, can only be presumed to be dates of composition rather than dates of copying. Do the major manuscripts, however, contain different chronological layers of the praeludia? Clearly, Berlin 2681 and the Wagener Manuscript do not; they transmit a virtually identical group of praeludia. The one additional praeludium in Wagener, the Praeludium in f♯, BuxWV 146, might be a late addition to that collection.[39] The praeludia of the Wenster Collection can be grouped with those of Wagener and Berlin 2681, as three of its four praeludia with pedal parts (BuxWV 139, 142, and 149) appear in both of those manuscripts. Only the Praeludium in B♭, BuxWV 154, does not; it is, however, a fragment in Wenster. The Lowell Mason Codex, however, is virtually a completely different group of works; only BuxWV 142 appears both there and in the Berlin/Wagener/Wenster repertory. And only one other work, BuxWV 148, is not a unicum.[40] While the dates proposed for LM 5056 and Wenster are remarkably similar (1688 and 1689 respectively), their contents are not. This fact may be of considerable significance in attempting a chronology of the works.[41]

Previous Attempts at Chronology

The most elaborate—yet still rudimentary—chronology of the praeludia has been devised by Powell. Omitting those works which do not proceed beyond the first fugal section, his study encompasses the multifugal works from north Germany during the period 1650–1710.[42] Realizing that, clearly, any chronology of the praeludia will have to rely chiefly on analysis rather than source material, he outlines several stylistic features which can be considered early or late within this time span.[43] For the opening free section, salient features include the opening flourish (the bigger and bolder the flourish, especially when without the support of a pedal point, the later its origin), and the number of textures (several textures, rather than just one, also indicate a later origin). Fugal sections which emphasize entries on degrees other than the tonic or dominant, episodic material, modulation, stretto, and inversion are also seen as progressive. Pedal virtuosity also indicates a later origin. So, too, does the use of unusual keys, such as A, f♯, and E, which strain the bounds of unequal temperament. A bias towards modality, however, suggests an early origin. The use of tempo indications, such as *allegro, vivace,* and *grave,* are also regarded as indicating a later date of composition. Using these stylistic guidelines, he divides the multifugal praeludia into three categories: 1652–65 (early works, including BuxWV 140 and 152); 1660–80 (middle-period works, including BuxWV 136, 139, 143, 150, 156, and 158); and 1675–89 (late works, including BuxWV 137, 141, 142, 146, 148, 149, 151, 153, and 155).[44]

While many of these stylistic traits are unassailable as chronological guides, several are probably too general to be of much value, especially for a specific chronology.[45] Certainly the nature of the opening flourish and the complexity of the opening free section are important criteria in discerning a chronology. In fugal sections, devices such as modulation and inversion certainly indicate a mature style. Yet, certain elements of Buxtehude's fugal writing can be closely associated with the works of his immediate predecessors. These traits are probably more strongly indicative of an earlier, rather than a later, origin. The opening of a fugal section with the voices paired in stretto strongly suggests Scheidemann as does the use of subdominant answers; extra entries in various keys, and a lack of complete rigor as to the integrity of the fugal voices suggest Tunder; fugal writing *a*5 strongly recalls Weckmann. Buxtehude developed a distinctive style of fugal writing, one dependent on a series of expositions rather than extra entries. Generally devoid of many entries outside the original key, his tight, modular fugal sections are an important innovation in the north German praeludium.

Several other aspects of the works are helpful indicators of maturity. These include a number of additional stylistic traits. The sheer variety of textures within a work is an important guide, as is the way in which they are handled: textural virtuosity is an important element of the mature praeludium. Many figural styles are found in the praeludia, and some are definitely more modern than others (much the same can be said of the fugal styles). Moreover, certain textural idiosyncrasies can be discerned within specific groups of compositions, and these help reinforce a chronology. The harmonic style of the praeludia also varies widely; the most harmonically daring ones are almost certainly the most mature. The sophistication of the thematic variations is another important aspect, as are the power of expression and the sense of a convincing climax and resolution. Structural analysis also reveals added elements of sophistication and technical mastery which can be correlated with stylistic evidence. Indeed, it is only the conjunction of evidence in many areas—texture, harmony, thematic variation, form, structure, and expression—as well as source material, that most clearly points to the relative maturity of each praeludium. Finally, in addition to stylistic and structural analysis, a critical judgment is indispensable for a meaningful evaluation. Ultimately, the most crucial aspect of the stylistic and structural elements of the praeludia is their effect. The proposed chronology is summarized in table 5[46] and presented in detail in the following section.

A Proposed Chronology

A chronological survey of the Buxtehude praeludia can begin with the Praeambulum in a, BuxWV 158. For a variety of reasons, this work can be considered the earliest preserved praeludium by Buxtehude. The title is archaic, an evocation of Scheidemann, and it alone strongly suggests an early origin. A myriad of stylistic evidence, however, confirms this supposition. Its form (opening free section/common-time fugue/triple-time fugue, with brief free extensions after each fugue) lies close to the works of Tunder and Weckmann as does its short size (eighty-three measures).[47]

The opening free section begins with the most unadventurous flourish of any in the praeludia; and it begins on the downbeat of the first measure of the work, contrary to Buxtehude's usual practice of introducing the flourish as an upbeat to what follows. The figural texture after the flourish is the most wooden figural writing in all the praeludia. The pedal part, which moves entirely in wholes and halves and does not participate in the figural play, supports figures which are generally two beats long, rather than the usual quarter-note length. The harmonic language, not enriched by tonicization chains, drifts first to the mediant, and then to the subdominant as preparation for the cadence. At this point, a curiously unmotivated shift in texture to a chordal style announces the cadential gesture.

The first fugue has many archaic features. Its stodgy subject recalls those of Scheidemann and Tunder; its exposition in stretto pairs, however, specifically suggests the earlier composer.[48] The answer (real, not tonal, and in the subdominant) is also evocative of Scheidemann. So, too, is the fugal laxity: as in no other exposition of Buxtehude, when the third and fourth voices have entered, the first two drop out. The immediate continuation of the fugue by extra entries of the subject rather than by another exposition again suggests earlier fugal styles rather than Buxtehude's usual procedures. When another exposition does come, the entries are in stretto (and followed immediately by another exposition not featuring stretto). The remainder of the fugue is built with extra entries, including one in the subtonic. Buxtehude's typical overall modularity of form, built through a series of expositions, is not in evidence. As the section progresses, the gradual introduction of sixteenth-note motion represents an advance over both Scheidemann and Tunder. By the end of the section, however, the fugal texture grows awkwardly complex, and requires sudden and severe restraint for the close of the section. Such an ending is far removed from the Italianate free endings,

Table 5. Proposed Chronology

Early Works

BuxWV	Title	Stylistic and Structural Evidence for Dating
158	Praeambulum in a	Flourish (Simple); Form (Simple); Nonmodular Fugal Structure; Stretto Exposition; Subdominant Answer; Subject (Archaic); Textural Rounding; Thematic Variation (Simple); Title; Weak Fugal Writing
152	Praeludium in a	Form (Simple); Modality; Nonmodular Fugal Structure; Subdominant Answer; Subject (Archaic); Textural Rounding; Thematic Variation (Simple)

Relatively Early Works

150	Praeludium in g	Flourish (Simple); Subject (Archaic); Weak Fugal Writing (in 3/2 Fugue)
143	Praeludium in e	Closing Free Section (Small, without Subdominant Emphasis); Five-Part Fugal Writing; Form (Simple); Nonmodular Fugal Structure; Subject (Simple); Textural Rounding; Thematic Variation (Simple)
156	Toccata in F	Closing Free Section (without Subdominant Emphasis); Form (Jumbled); Nonmodular Fugal Structure; Textural Rounding
147	Praeludium in G	Subject (Simple); Textural Rounding

Middle Period Works

148	Praeludium in g	Flourish (Canonic); Modular Free Music; Nonmodular Fugal Structure (indicating Earlier Origin); Tempo Indication
153	Praeludium in a	Closing Free Section (with Subdominant Emphasis and Modularity); Development of Figural Motives; Flourish (Canonic); Modular Fugal Structure; Sophisticated Fugal Structure (Inversion and Modulation); Thematic Variation (Simple, indicating Earlier Origin)
151	Praeludium in A	Key (Unusual); Modular Fugal Structure; Tempo Indication
136	Praeludium in C	Flourish (Canonic); Modular Fugal Structure; Tempo Indication

(Table 5 continued)

BuxWV	Title	Stylistic and Structural Evidence for Dating
138	Praeludium in C	Ciacona-like Free Ending; Modular Fugal Structure
144	Praeludium in F	Flourish (Canonic); Modular Fugal Structure

Relatively Late Works

BuxWV	Title	Stylistic and Structural Evidence for Dating
139	Praeludium in D	Canonic Figuration; Closing Free Section (with Subdominant Emphasis and Modularity); Development of Figural Motives; Modular Fugal Structure; Tempo Indication; Thematic Sophistication
137	Praeludium in C	Canonic Figuration; Development of Figural Motives; Modular Free Music; Modular Fugal Structure; Tempo Indication; Thematic Sophistication; Virtuosity (including Pedal Solo Flourish); Weakened Articulation between Opening Free Section and First Fugue
145	Praeludium in F	Modular Fugal Structure; Opening Free Section (Unusually Large); Sophisticated Fugal Structure (Development of Thematic Material)
157	Toccata in F	Modular Free Music; Modular Fugal Structure; Thematic Sophistication
154	Praeludium in B♭ (Fragment)	Similarities to BuxWV 145 and 157

Late Period Works

BuxWV	Title	Stylistic and Structural Evidence for Dating
141	Praeludium in E	Canonic Figuration; Expressive Power; Key (Unusual); Linear Coherence; Modular Structures; Tempo Indications; Thematic Sophistication; Virtuosity
140	Praeludium in d	Canonic Figuration; Closing Free Section (with Subdominant Emphasis and Modularity); Expressive Power; Harmonic Boldness; Invertible Counterpoint; Linear Coherence; Modular Free and Fugal Structures; Small-Scale First Fugue; Thematic Sophistication; Virtuosity; Weakened Articulation between Opening Free Section and First Fugue

(Table 5 continued)

BuxWV	Title	Stylistic and Structural Evidence for Dating
155	Toccata in d	Closing Free Section (with Subdominant Emphasis and Modularity); Expressive Power; Flourish (Unusual); Invertible Counterpoint; Modular Free and Fugal Structures; Small-Scale First Fugue; Sophisticated Fugal Structure (Modulation); Virtuosity; Weakened Articulation between Opening Free Section and First Fugue
142	Praeludium in e	Development of Figural Motives; Expressive Power; Invertible Counterpoint; Linear Coherence; Modular Fugal Structure (3/2 Fugue); Nonmodular Fugal Structure (Common-Time Fugue, indicating Earlier Origin); Small-Scale First Fugue (in comparison to Second and Third Fugues); Sophisticated Fugal Structure (Modulation); Thematic Sophistication; Virtuosity
146	Praeludium in f#	Canonic Figuration; Closing Free Section (with Subdominant Emphasis and Modularity); Expressive Power; Key (Unusual); Linear Coherence; Modular Free and Fugal Structures; Small-Scale First Fugue; Tempo Indications; Thematic Sophistication; Virtuosity
149	Praeludium in g	Canonic Figuration; Closing Free Section (with Subdominant Emphasis and Modularity); Expressive Power; Flourish (Canonic); Invertible Counterpoint; Linear Coherence; Modular Free and Fugal Structures; Small-Scale First Fugue; Textural Modulation; Thematic Sophistication; Virtuosity; Weakened Articulation between Opening Free Section and First Fugue

inspired by the works of Froberger and Weckmann, which are found in many of the praeludia.

The second fugue, whose subject is a simple and unambiguous variation of the subject of the first fugue, is not a large section and does not stand comparison as a fugue with the first one.[49] The influence of Tunder and Weckmann is revealed in the choppy, blocklike construction of its later passages, the introduction of an ostinato, and its eventual drift towards the subdominant.[50] The tritone opposition of d and G♯ in the bass, however, clearly foreshadows Buxtehude's typical harmonic boldness at such junctures.[51] It introduces a small free ending, very simple in style, which recalls the figural texture and pedal points of the opening free section.[52]

The Praeludium in a, BuxWV 152, can be considered a companion piece to the Praeambulum. Both have a similar style and structure; and their size, shape, and expressive content are alike as well. Yet in many ways, the Praeludium seems to represent an advance over the Praeambulum — the latter appears more successful in only a few respects. While the title of the Praeludium is not archaic, its harmonic language is: the use of phrygian mode, rather than a clear major or minor tonality, sets it apart from the rest of the praeludia and strongly suggests an early origin. Its form (opening free section/common-time fugue/triple-time fugue, with a brief free extension after the second fugue) is virtually identical to that of the Praeambulum.

The opening free section is considerably bolder than that of the Praeambulum; and on this evidence alone, it seems reasonable to suggest that the work follows the Praeambulum chronologically. While the opening flourish still begins on the downbeat of the first measure, it is considerably more lively than that of the Praeambulum. A second flourish (a gesture comparable to measures 3–4 of the Praeambulum) is even more flamboyant. The figural texture which follows is altogether more flexible than in the Praeambulum, and the figures are based on a mixture of quarter-note and half-note lengths. The harmonic rhythm is correspondingly livelier, and the pedal part joins in the figural play. Unlike the lackluster opening of the Praeambulum, the rhapsody typical of Buxtehude's style here makes a strong appearance.[53]

The first fugue is considerably less like Scheidemann than its companion in the Praeambulum. The exposition does not employ stretto pairs, and there are no holes in the fugal texture. The answer, however, again lies in the subdominant and is again a real one. The section is shorter than that of the Praeambulum, but the second, triple-time fugue now more nearly balances the first, and commands equal respect as a fugal section.[54] The obvious transformation of the first fugal subject into the triple-time subject of the second fugue represents no advance over the Praeambulum; indeed, the triple-time subject of the Praeambulum is arguably more interesting. The free ending is also closely analogous to that of the Praeambulum. Its figural texture, as is true of the opening free section, is considerably more elaborate.[55] The resulting textural rounding of the whole is a strikingly similar procedure.

These two very similar works stand apart from the rest of the praeludia. They are surely the earliest examples of Buxtehude's praeludia, and lie close to the organ music of a generation before his own.[56] That they are both preserved as unica in the Lowell Mason Codex can be seen as yet another significant link between them. But as will be later shown, their presence there is not enough to suggest that all of Buxtehude's works in that manuscript are an early group of works.[57] The remainder of the praeludia do not present such clear stylistic clues for chronology. While a group of them can definitely be considered late, many fall in a transitional category and their chronology can only be more suggestively hypothesized. Therefore, in the remainder of the conclusion, the exact order in which the works are discussed is not meant to suggest a definitive chronological order, though reasons why the works can be considered to have originated in more or less that order will be presented.

The Praeludium in g, BuxWV 150, can be regarded as one of the earliest of the praeludia after the Praeambulum and the phrygian Praeludium. The form of the work (opening free section/common-time fugue/brief second free section/fugato/triple-time fugue) is somewhat larger than that of the earliest works, and results in a composition of one hundred and forty-six measures, actually one of the longest of the praeludia. The opening free section heralds the fugal preoccupation of this work: it is an imitative passage over a pedal point. Of rather short duration and limited expressive power, perhaps its most noteworthy features are its frames. The simple opening flourish, which begins on the downbeat of the first measure rather than on an upbeat, is far less exciting than that of the Praeludium in a. Indeed, it stands with that of the Praeambulum as one of the least adventurous. The cadential gesture of the section, which switches to chordal texture, also recalls a similar gesture in the Praeambulum.[58]

The fugal sections of BuxWV 150, however, are more sophisticated than any found in either BuxWV 158 or 152. The first fugue especially is a large conception, with a second exposition and numerous extra entries. The subject, however, is a relatively old-fashioned one. Though essentially a vocal idea, uninspired by the canzona tradition, it does represent a significant advance in expressivity over those of Scheidemann, Tunder, and the two earliest praeludia of Buxtehude. The answer is a tonal one, unlike those of the Praeambulum and the Praeludium in a; the use of a tonal rather than a real answer is a practice which is found in all the remaining praeludia.

Details of the fugal construction also mark it as a relatively early work, especially measures 37–54, in which the entries take the following form:

Praeludium in g, BuxWV 150

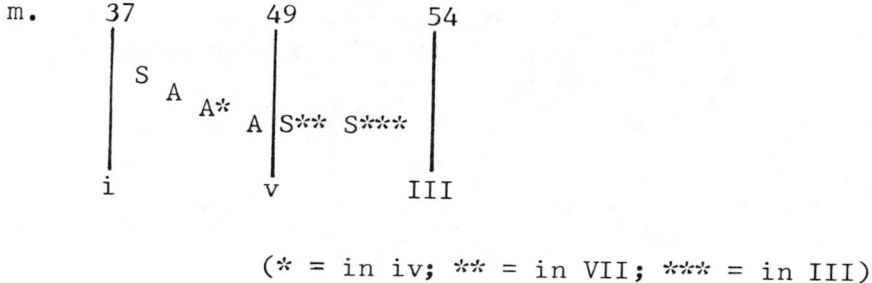

(* = in iv; ** = in VII; *** = in III)

Such a passage recalls Tunder, and is far removed from the modular clarity typical of Buxtehude. Also, with a countersubject having been recently introduced, the juncture between the first and the second exposition lacks Buxtehude's typical precision:

Praeludium in g, BuxWV 150

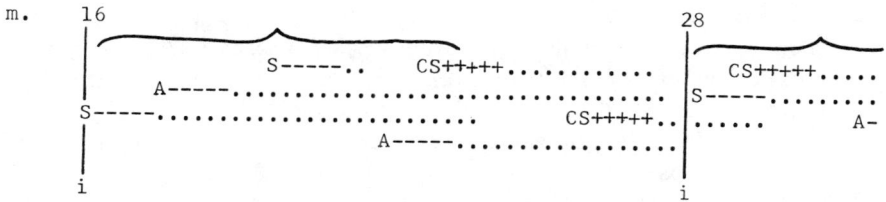

Also lacking in clarity is the fabric of the texture itself, for the counterpoint is dense and the contrapuntal effects are muddled. This is chiefly the result of a subject that is hardly more than a motive, and a countersubject which not only moves in the same rhythmic style and possesses a similar, essentially directionless, shape, but even begins with the same rhythmic gesture.

A second free section follows the first fugue. This brief chordal passage is at first a lightly decorated *a*4 progression, but after only a few measures switches to a more modular variety of chordal texture. The tonicizations of the submediant and the subdominant in the first phrase, and the tritones in the bass of the second, are some of the strongest harmonic gestures of the work.[59] While powerful in the context of early Buxtehude, such effects pale in comparison to the harmonic language of his mature praeludia. A fugato follows, whose subject is clearly derived from that of the first fugue. It is a strongly modular section, and this is especially true of the extension: repetitions of the subject are accompanied by a simple rhythmic figure with an ostinatolike tenacity. A large triple-time fugue follows. Such intermediate textures between two fugues appear in the center of a number of Buxtehude's praeludia;[60] this work contains what is probably the earliest preserved example:

Praeludium in g, BuxWV 150

```
m.                      64          69       74        85          90
                         |           |        |         |           |
          Common-Time       Chordal     Fugato + Modular    Triple-Time
          Fugue             |Modular    |        Extension  Fugue
                            |           |        |           |
              i       VI    iv    i     V        i           i
```

The highly changeable character of the textures, the modularity, the use of fugato, and especially the striving for intense and climactic expression all foreshadow Buxtehude's mature style. Yet, the failure to achieve a convincing climax, due at least in part to the lack of a large line spanning the complex of textures, suggests that this is indeed an early attempt at such a formal conception.

Characteristically for early Buxtehude, the triple-time fugue which ends the work uses a clearly derived variation of the first fugal subject. While the derivation of its subject is no more sophisticated than those of the Praeambulum or the Praeludium in a, its size (fifty-seven measures) dwarfs those of the two earlier works. Obviously an attempt at balancing the long and complex first fugue, such an expansive size is due to the large extension.[61] The metrical vagueness of the passage with which the extension begins is suggestive of an early origin.[62] The last measure contains a notational peculiarity—a meaningless change to common time for the final chord—which, if it originates with Buxtehude, would probably also point to an early origin.[63] Within the overall scheme of the work, however, the fugue is also significant because it represents a relaxation of tension vis à vis the preceding complex of textures. It is the first of several praeludia which conform to this expressive plan. The best examples are found in the Praeludia in C, BuxWV 136, and in e, BuxWV 142, which end with gigue fugues. The Praeludium in g also shares with them a tendency towards fugal saturation, and in this respect is matched only by the Praeludium in e, BuxWV 142. While neither BuxWV 150 nor 142 attains a balance between free and fugal textures, the Praeludium in g lacks the necessary intensity of character in the fugal sections (so admirably possessed by the Praeludium in e, BuxWV 142) to make such a plan really successful.

The Praeludium in e, BuxWV 143, can also be considered a relatively early work. Its form (opening free section/common-time fugue with free ending/triple-time fugue with free ending/closing free section) more nearly resembles the Praeludium in a and the Praeambulum than it does that of the Praeludium in g, BuxWV 150.[64] Yet several features, especially in the opening free section, show BuxWV 143 heightening the gestures of BuxWV 150. The opening free section is again imitative texture over a pedal point. However, in this work, the plan is more powerful: the opening flourish is a pedal solo, and it introduces a measure-long thematic idea which becomes the basis of the imitative passage over an ensuing pedal point. Unlike in the Praeludium in g, the pedal point does not dominate the entire section. It later drops out, allowing the appearance of a full exposition of the theme in fugato style (that is, without codettas). An ostinato passage, in an unwritten 3/4 meter, immediately follows; the texture of this passage strongly resembles the modular textures of the Praeludium in g.[65] The cadential gesture, which does not strongly reinstate common time, can be seen as a culmination of a gesture first observed in the Praeambulum, expanded in the Praeludium in g, and exaggerated in the Praeludium in e.[66]

The first fugue has a simple subject, but one which — unlike that of BuxWV 150 — begins to suggest the canzona-inspired subjects which dominate the praeludia. The answer (although a tonal one) tilts towards the subdominant, however, and thus recalls the Praeambulum and the Praeludium in a. The fugal texture is weaker than is typical of Buxtehude: the integrity of the voices is compromised far more often than is Buxtehude's usual practice. The unusual $a5$ texture is immediately reminiscent of Weckmann, and the continuation of the fugue with extra entries rather than further expositions recalls Tunder. The appearance of the subject in three key areas outside the tonic (in the subdominant, mediant, and dominant) as well as the preponderance of subject entries rather than a balance between subject and answer also recall his predecessor's techniques. The free ending of the first fugue is highly unusual: its modularity is strongly suggestive of Buxtehude's mature style, but its awkward seven-beat phrases are not. Neither is the conclusion of the fugue itself on the subdominant; that, too, hearkens back to Tunder:

Conclusion

Praeludium in e, BuxWV 143

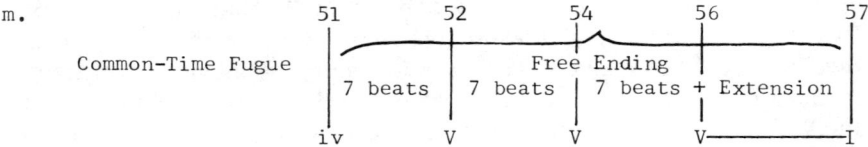

With its curious construction, this passage is probably the earliest preserved full-scale free ending in the praeludia.

The second fugue, like the first, is *a*5, and its vivacity recalls that of the second fugue of the Praeambulum. Again, a simple, straightforward transformation of the first fugue's subject yields a triple-time version for this section.

The closing free section which concludes the Praeludium, however, is unprecedented in BuxWV 158, 152, or 150. Here a large free section, longer and more powerful than a simple free ending to a second (or third) fugue, draws the work to a close. Gesturally, the section foreshadows Buxtehude's finest moments:[67]

Praeludium in e, BuxWV 143

```
m.                    87        93    96 98        107
     Triple-Time Fugue | Extension | Chordal | Tonic Pedal ||
                       V         V-III--V--I-----------I
```

It does not, however, stand comparison with them in terms of compositional finesse. The harmonic parenthesis of the mediant in the midst of dominant harmony makes a fine dramatic gesture but is an unusually arbitrary effect and lacks direction. The unusual punctuations which follow during the resumption of dominant harmony recall the close of the opening free section. This section is recalled even more in the passage which follows: figural play highly reminiscent of earlier in the opening free section appears over the tonic pedal point. The trend observed in BuxWV 158 and 152 towards the textural rounding of the work is in this Praeludium heightened considerably. Such a scheme, however, is not typical of Buxtehude's praeludia as a whole, and can be regarded as a fingerprint of his early style. Several details of the closing free section also suggest an early origin.[68] The unusual rhythmic idea, ♫, in measures 102-6, is also not typical of Buxtehude's praeludia. The lack of emphasis on the subdominant in the section, a prime characteristic of all his most impressive closing free sections, is also missing here. The section can be regarded as the oldest of the closing free sections, and as such is only suggestive of the expressive potential Buxtehude later drew from that section of the praeludium. The work is significant, like BuxWV 150, in that it demonstrates an expressive shape which would later serve for a number of the praeludia—considerably more praeludia than that of BuxWV 150 with its closing fugal section. But perhaps most important, the work demonstrates a significant advance over BuxWV 158, 152, and also 150 in its clear linear organization. Buxtehude's typical middleground forms are in evidence here,[69] in contrast to those other works which seem to evade significant long-range linear connections.

The Praeludium in e, unlike BuxWV 158, 152, or 150, belongs to a group of ten of the praeludia which are primarily preserved in the Wagener and Berlin 2681 groups of manuscripts.[70] These, the major sources of the praeludia, transmit virtually all of the most impressive of them; and the inclusion of BuxWV 143 in this group marks it as one of the more widely circulated works. It is surely the oldest of this prestigious group.

The Toccata in F, BuxWV 156, can be considered another relatively early work preserved in the Wagener/Berlin 2681 group of manuscripts. Spitta, who rarely questioned the high quality of the praeludia, observed that:

> The form of [this] great toccata in F Major . . . is at first sight very varied, but a regular fugue forms the germ which, in some degree, provides the material for the subjects which follow, in so far as they are compressed into intelligible forms, and do not ramble about in fantastic aimlessness.[71]

Beneath the surface of this large, jumbled work, however, can be detected the influence of both the Praeludia in g, BuxWV 150, and in e, BuxWV 143. From the former comes a large complex of free and imitative textures in the central core of the work between the two fugues; and from the Praeludium in e comes the closing free section. In both instances, the effects are considerably exaggerated in the Toccata—so greatly, in fact, that they indeed threaten to "ramble about in fantastic aimlessness." The form of the work (opening free section/common-time fugue/a complex of rhapsodic, imitative, and pedal point textures/another common-time fugue/closing free section) shows how the combined elements of BuxWV 150 and 143 could lead to a larger conception.

The opening free section, like those of BuxWV 150 and 143, is dependent on pedal points; the second, a dominant one, supports an imitative passage longer than the single pedal point of the opening free section of the

Praeludium in g. Its relaxed 12/8 rhythms are interrupted near the close by what is perhaps the single most curious passage in the praeludia: a jocular rhythmic effect, which seems incongruous following the calm of the preceding 12/8 passage.[72]

The first fugue betrays an early origin in its layout: a rare extra entry intervenes between the first and second exposition, and the second exposition is in stretto pairs. (The techniques of both stretto pairs and stretto for the second exposition have been observed in the Praeambulum.) The freedom of the voices necessitated by this technique is also unusual, as is the handling of the joint between the expositions:

Toccata in F, BuxWV 156

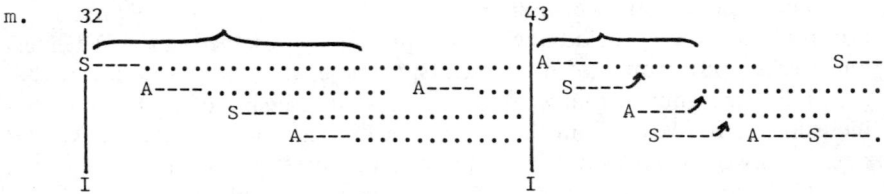

This plan is considerably removed from his typical interlocking expositions:

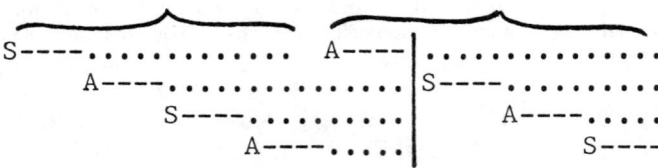

The string of entries in the bass after the stretto exposition is also strongly suggestive of the fugal techniques of Buxtehude's immediate predecessors, especially that of Tunder. The fugue ends with a dominant cadence, and what seems to be a free ending ensues. But an expected quick return to the tonic for a cadence is thwarted by the intervention of a complex of free and imitative textures in several harmonic areas. The tonic arrival is delayed some twenty-five measures. In what is one of the most improvisational passages in the praeludia, frequent and unpredictable changes of texture create an unusually capricious effect. The return of pedal points and 12/8 meter hint at but do not specifically recall passages from the opening free section. The harmonies reach past the submediant and subdominant towards the minor dominant and lead to an exceptionally colorful 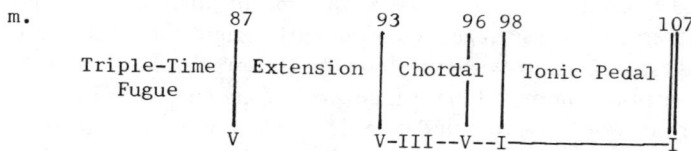 dominant pedal.

The second fugue, a miniature in comparison to the first, is untypically in common time. A rather sophisticated thematic variation lies behind its subject, however, and is one reason why this work can probably be dated after those such as BuxWV 150 and 143.

The closing free section is far grander in scope than that of the Praeludium in e:

Praeludium in e, BuxWV 143

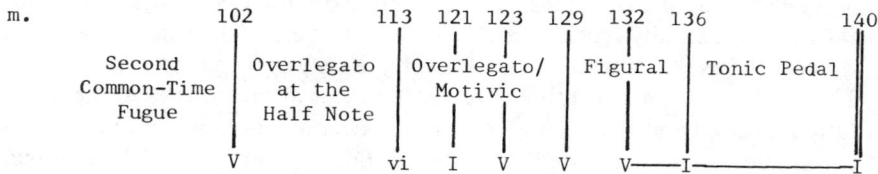

Toccata in F, BuxWV 156

```
m.              102         113  121 123  129 132 136        140
             Second      Overlegato  Overlegato/  Figural  Tonic Pedal
          Common-Time    at the      Motivic
             Fugue       Half Note
                V            vi    I    V    V——I————————I
```

However, as in the Praeludium in e, the characteristic emphasis on the subdominant found in most of Buxtehude's closing free sections is absent. Absent, too, are the typical ostinato textures Buxtehude generally associates with that part of the form. Again, as in the section between the fugues, rhapsodic improvisation holds sway. Some of the passages are more successful than others: in the first gesture, overlegato chords moving at the half note seem to move too slowly, even if ornamentations are added. The more rhapsodic passage which follows (and leads from the submediant to the dominant cadence in m. 123) is more powerful, but metrically curious.

Metrical irregularities are also present in the next passage.[73] Once again, a gesture towards textural rounding is in evidence, but its realization is more subtle than in the works previously described. When the dominant pedal enters in measure 132, the figural texture (sixteenth notes in parallel motion) suggests that of the first part of the opening free section.[74] The final flourish even seems purposefully reminiscent of the opening one.

Overall, the Toccata lacks a strong sense of line. The thread from the first fugue is all but lost during the central section, and the closing free section again lacks a strong line from the preceding fugue around which to organize its material and guide it towards closure. If the Praeludium in g, BuxWV 150, is Buxtehude's early high-water mark of fugal saturation, the Toccata is its counterpart in improvisational free textures.

Another group of praeludia can be assigned to a middle period in the chronology. The Praeludium in g, BuxWV 148, is one such work. While incorporating several features suggestive of an early origin, other elements of its style suggest a kinship with the bulk of the praeludia. The form (opening free section/common-time fugue with free ending/triple-time fugue with extension/ciacona) is a model of clarity; it combines the use of a large triple-time fugue similar to the one in the Praeludium in g, BuxWV 150, with an extensive free section to end the work as in the Toccata in F, BuxWV 156.

The opening free section in particular carries the traits of a mature style. The opening flourish is especially extravagant in comparison to those previously examined. It is also significantly more focused: it begins canonically and eventually reaches three-part texture before the tonic cadence to which it leads. Characteristic of Buxtehude's style, it begins off the beat. The pedal points which follow are shorter than in previous examples, and support varied and interesting figuration. After a pause on the dominant, a chromatic fugato, marked *allegro*, ensues. Both the intensity of the passage, and the tempo mark (presuming its originality) indicate an advance over previous such passages.

The first fugue suggests an advance over the previous fugal sections particularly in its subject, which is clearly derived from the canzona tradition; and its use of repeated notes is one of the most extreme examples of the technique in the praeludia. Several irregularities of the part writing, however, recall earlier works and also suggest a relatively early origin for this work.[75] The entry patterns lack Buxtehude's typical modular clarity: while a second exposition is suggested, its realization is obscured by the continuous counterpoint. Only one cadence intervenes between the beginning of the fugue and the free ending.

Praeludium in g, BuxWV 148

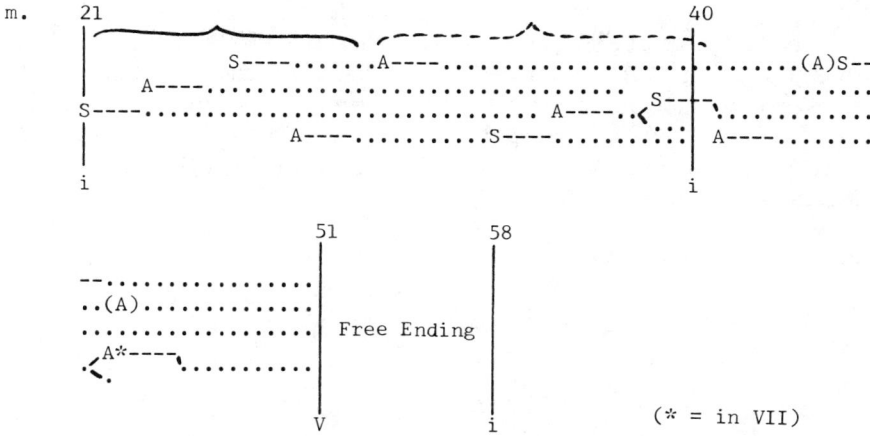

The final entry in the subtonic also recalls earlier works.[76] The free ending, perhaps echoing the simple contrapuntal style of the fugue, is an unusually modest passage with little elaboration to hide the chordal progressions. Its role as the cadential gesture of the fugue, however, could not be more clear: it completes a line from the fugue, which draws the section towards its tonic cadence:

Praeludium in g, BuxWV 148

258   Conclusion

Though the triple-time fugue is in many ways analogous to that of the Praeludium in g, BuxWV 150, the derivation of the fugal subject from the first common-time subject is far more subtle in BuxWV 148.[77] For this reason alone it can be strongly suspected that BuxWV 148 originated later than BuxWV 150. Furthermore, the triple-time section in BuxWV 148 shows considerably more control of fugal form. For example, in the second exposition in BuxWV 150 the first three entrances are in irregularly spaced stretto and two are outside the tonic. Together with the awkward spacing[78] it creates a scattered effect:

Praeludium in g, BuxWV 150

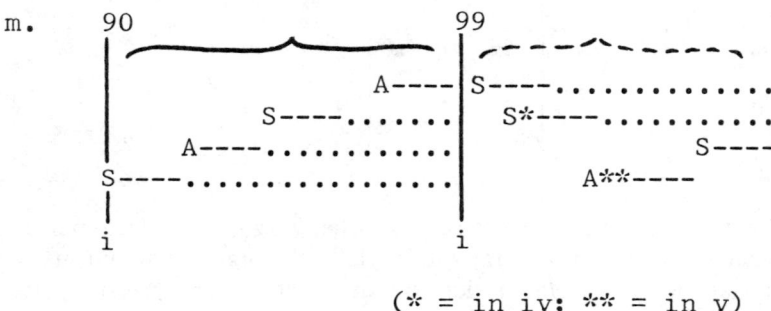

(* = in iv; ** = in v)

The opening plan of the triple-time fugue of BuxWV 148 shows no such problematic features:

Praeludium in g, BuxWV 148

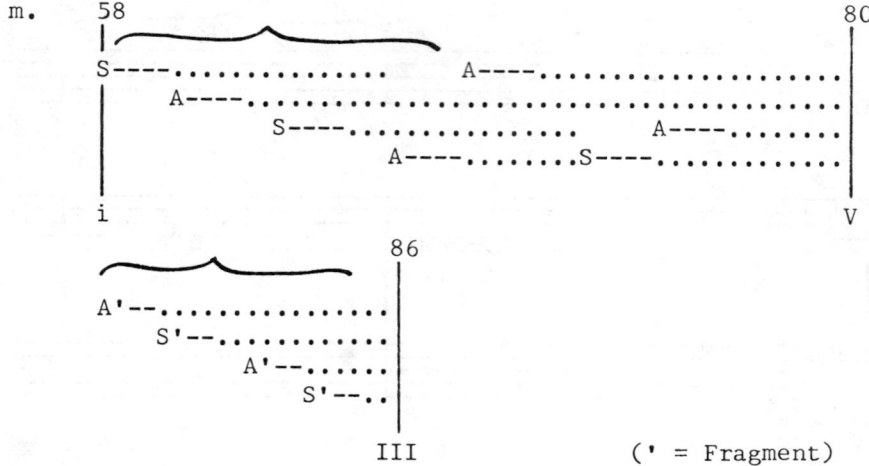

(' = Fragment)

An extensive dominant pedal prepares the entrance of the next section.[79]

The ciacona which ends the Praeludium, along with the opening free section, most strongly suggests a mature style. Unlike the closing free section of the Toccata in F, BuxWV 156, the ciacona features the ostinato textures which are typical of Buxtehude's closing free sections. Rarely, however, is a closing free section so completely dominated by a single texture. The form of this large section is particularly convincing: the theme alternates between the manuals and pedal part.[80] The figuration is also noteworthy: it is lively and intricate, and culminates in an appearance of a figure typically associated with Bach (and especially the *Orgelbüchlein*) rather than with Buxtehude.[81] However, the change of harmonic areas within the section from the tonic to the mediant and back again is not nearly as convincingly handled. The shift from the tonic to the mediant is particularly awkward.[82] The overall expressive scheme of the work is not as cogent as in many other praeludia. The large triple-time fugue, an example of which served as a closing section in BuxWV 150, here appears in an intermediate position between a fugue and a ciacona. As a result, the overall expressive shape of the work is less pronounced: other praeludia present sections in the middle of the form which more powerfully build towards a climax.

The Praeludium in g, BuxWV 148, has figured prominently in previous chronological investigations. Its relative maturity as it appeared in the Grobe Tablature which was dated 1675[83] can serve as a guide for the dating of other praeludia which have no such clue. Riedel, like Spitta before him, considers the work to be a fully mature example of Buxtehude's praeludia. The assumption leads to the view that many, if not most, of his other praeludia could have also originated before 1675. While the Praeludium does possess admirable features, particularly in the free sections, it lacks the distinctive stylistic traits which are characteristic of the most impressive, and presumably latest, praeludia. It should therefore not be regarded as their equal chronologically.[84]

The Praeludium in g, BuxWV 148, is the last piece in which fugal structure may be considered a significant determinant of chronology. (Several details of fugal style, however, will remain important.) After this work, the style of the free sections becomes more important as a criterion upon which chronological hypotheses can be based. The construction of such arguments, however, becomes increasingly tenuous. While a group of praeludia can be isolated which most probably are the final examples of Buxtehude's contributions to the genre, a significant number of works lie between those already discussed and his late style. These middle-period pieces—which works such as the Toccata in F, BuxWV 156, and the Praeludium in g, BuxWV 148, anticipate—cannot be securely ordered in a chronology. Significant aspects which suggest inclusion in this group, however, can be delineated. In this way, inferences (if not hypotheses) can be drawn about their chronology.[85]

A survey of the middle-period works can begin with the Praeludium in a, BuxWV 153. This work belongs to the Wagener/Berlin 2681 group of distinguished praeludia, and with it the world of Buxtehude's great organ praeludia is entered. The form of the work (opening free section/common-time fugue with a brief free ending/triple-time fugue/closing free section) is simple and remarkably close to that of the Praeludium in g, BuxWV 148. The canonic opening flourish as well strongly recalls that of BuxWV 148. The opening section has a new, more powerful figural style. A simple figure makes its first appearance immediately after the flourish and dominates the following ten measures; and its incomplete neighbor-note motions churn the music forward with a single-mindedness not previously observed. Towards the end of the passage it is developed (through fragmentation), and this clearly perceptible derivation is played off against the original figure.[86] The resulting crescendo of energy is then released over the following large dominant pedal using new figures.

The beginning of the first fugue also recalls the Praeludium in g, BuxWV 148, by its striking use of repeated notes in the subject. The fugue itself, however, is much more substantial than that found in BuxWV 148; and it illustrates Buxtehude's fugal form of successive expositions, which is found in virtually all the first fugues of the remaining works.[87] The scarcity of entrances outside the tonic is also typical of Buxtehude's mature fugal style, particularly in first fugues.[88] So, too, is the manner in which the joint between the first and second expositions is handled—i.e., with the first entry of the second exposition overlapping the cadence of the first exposition.

Praeludium in a, BuxWV 153

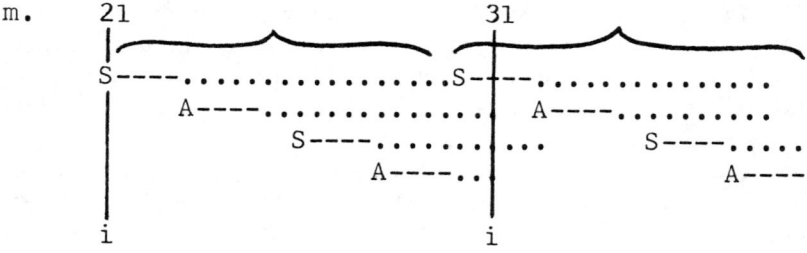

What is unique here, however, is that the second exposition presents the subject and answer in inversion. Setting off the second exposition through this technique is a novel interpretation of the typical plan, and strongly indicates that this is not the first of the fugues to employ a strongly modular format. While the briefness of the free ending might suggest an early origin, its dramatic realization (an abrupt halt of fugal texture and dramatic use of the pedal part) points to Buxtehude's mature style.

The triple-time fugue employs a subject which is obviously derived from the preceding fugue. The transformation is not as sophisticated as that in the Praeludium in g, BuxWV 148, but avoids blatancy through a derivation from the original answer rather than the subject. The section is a good illustration of several features which are typical of fugues in the remaining sections: the modular construction is treated significantly more loosely and there is a wider range of harmonic areas. The exposition in the mediant in the middle of this fugue is especially noteworthy; it is one of the largest such nontonic areas in any of the fugal sections.

The closing free section provides an impressive conclusion to the work, as it contains the subtle ostinatos and textural play which characterize Buxtehude's finest moments in these sections. The pronounced appearance of subdominant harmony also heralds his typical procedure. For a climactic idea, a gesture first heard as a development of the subject (in inversion) in the first fugue is recalled and amplified. The gesture itself may have been inspired by a similar one in Johann Adam Reincken's setting of "An Wasserflüssen Babylon."[89] The release of accumulated energy over a concluding tonic pedal, as well as the style of figuration which accomplishes it, are also highly characteristic of Buxtehude's mature style.

Another work containing many fine details but lacking the expressive power of the most impressive praeludia is the Praeludium in A, BuxWV 151. Unlike the Praeludium in a, it is preserved outside the large collections of Buxtehude's praeludia. Indeed, its sources present a puzzle, for two very different versions have been preserved:[90]

Möller Manuscript		*Schmahls Tablature*
Opening Free Section	=	Opening Free Section
		Additional Section
First Fugue + Free Ending	=	First Fugue + Free Ending
Second Fugue		

No other work survives in such radically different formal schemes.[91] The version in the Schmahls Tablature, due to its late date (1696) and the uncharacteristic style of the added section, can be regarded as spurious.[92] The opening free section common to both versions, however, is quite clearly in Buxtehude's style: it is full of exuberant rhapsody, and coalesces into a more strongly figural texture (with faster harmonic rhythm) towards the end of the section.

André Pirro, writing in 1913, made mention of this work as it was unknown to Spitta.[93] Like modern scholars, he strongly suspected the reading in the Schmahls Tablature. However, he went further and expressed doubts about the authenticity of virtually the entire composition. Such a view is curious, for the large first fugue is one of the most rigorous examples of Buxtehude's style of modular construction. Its uniqueness lies only in the fact that modularity is extended from the level of the exposition to that of the subexposition by the use of a countersubject. While the chordal progressions of the free ending ramble more than most (and led Pirro to question Buxtehude's authorship), the dramatic shift of texture from the fugue to the free ending is handled with Buxtehudian flair.[94]

The second fugue is also in common time and is unusually similar to the first fugue. The subject lies very close in shape, rhythm, and thematic substance to the original; and the prominent use of a countersubject is again featured. The result is a pair of fugues in virtually the same texture and style. The second fugue is significantly shorter than the first; indeed, the Praeludium in A (in the Möller version) is an extreme example of a praeludium with the balance of fugal sections tilted towards the first one. A similar but less extreme case can be observed in the Toccata in F, BuxWV 156.[95] A similar imbalance between the fugal sections can also be found in the Praeambulum, the Praeludium in a, BuxWV 152, and the Praeludia in e, BuxWV 143, in g, BuxWV 150, and in a, BuxWV 153. Such a relationship between the fugal sections is an important characteristic of early- and middle-period works. In spite of the sophistication of the internal construction of the fugal sections themselves, this particular kind of imbalance of their lengths is a strong reason for placing BuxWV 151 in the middle rather than the late period.

Another reason why this work should not be grouped with the most impressive praeludia is the lack of a strongly articulated drive towards a climax and resolution. The chordal passage of the free ending, rich in harmony through a tonicization chain, serves as the climax point. The second fugue seems to relax the tension, yet it sounds more like an afterthought than a well-calculated attempt to conclude the expressive plan of the praeludium.

The Praeludium in C, BuxWV 136, can be grouped with the middle-period works. It almost certainly antedates the great Praeludium in e, BuxWV 142: both works end with gigue fugues, but the conception is realized on a grander scale in BuxWV 142. Like other suggested middle-period praeludia, this Praeludium is in many ways a very sophisticated work but lacks the overall breadth and expressive power which can be considered one of the hallmarks of the late period. It is a work which stresses poise and balance rather than drama and pathos. While it survives as a unicum in the

Conclusion 263

Lowell Mason Codex, it fully deserves to stand with works such as the Praeludium in a, BuxWV 153, which are included in the group of distinguished praeludia preserved in the Wagener and Berlin manuscripts.

The form of the work (opening free section/common-time fugue with free ending/fugato with free ending/gigue fugue with free extension) is a model of balance. The proportions of the work are far more persuasive than those of the Praeludium in A. The weight of the work is still concentrated in the first fugue (another indication of middle period status), but the succeeding sections are not dwarfed by it.[96] The elegance of its layout is evident in the progression of new textures, which stand in contrast to the textural rounding observed in many of the early-period works.[97] The expressive shape of the work is typical: the fugato which begins the remaining sections drives hard towards a point of climax and culminates in a flurry of thirty-second notes in its free ending; and the gigue fugue effectively relaxes the accumulated tensions of the previous sections. The plan is reminiscent of the Praeludium in g, BuxWV 150, though such a shape is made to yield far more powerful results in several late-period works.

The opening free section carries several significant stylistic traits. The flourish, although more subdued than those of BuxWV 148 and 153, is also canonic. While the section is more modest than either of those two, it heralds the short but rigorously figural opening free section which can be found in several late-period works. Indeed, it is one of the most harmonically and linearly cogent of any opening free section, and shows Buxtehude in full control of figural technique. Tonicization chains play an important role in the section, and in the free ending of the first fugue. The emphasis on that technique is another strong indication of the work's mature origin.

The manipulation of thematic material can be compared with several other middle-period works. As in the Praeludium in a, BuxWV 153, the second fugal subject (that of the fugato) derives from the first fugue's answer rather than from its subject. (The subject of the gigue fugue, on the other hand, is a more obvious derivation.) The fugal sections stand close to those of the Praeludium in A, however, in their use of countersubjects. In the first fugue, a distinctive but curious and ultimately unconvincing syncopated figure serves as a countersubject. The work surpasses these two others, however, in the fugato. In what is a model of concentrated thematic development, the countersubject is derived from its subject, and is itself developed through fragmentation into an ostinato figure which appears in the free ending. With this kind of sophisticated thematic treatment, Buxtehude's most mature style is announced.

Signs of Buxtehude's late style also appear in the Praeludium in D, BuxWV 139. Like the Praeludium in a, BuxWV 153, it survives in the Wagener and Berlin 2681 collections of the great praeludia. Unlike most of

264   Conclusion

them, however, the Praeludium in D also appears in other manuscripts, including the Wenster Collection. Indeed, from its unusually frequent appearance in manuscripts, it appears likely that it was one of the most popular and widely circulated of Buxtehude's praeludia.

The form of the work (opening free section/common-time fugue with an elaborate free ending/chordal passage/closing free section) includes only one fugal section. (This is the first such work discussed in this survey.) Compensating for the omission of a second fugal section is a multifaceted closing free section of a scope and expressive power challenged only by that of the Toccata in F, BuxWV 156. The outgoing, expansive style of the work begins immediately with the opening flourish. Generating a fine sweep of energy, it establishes the unusually cheerful spirit which dominates the work. The figural language of the section, like that of the Praeludium in a, BuxWV 153, includes developmental procedures:

Praeludium in D, BuxWV 139

Conclusion 265

The fugue, built on a lively repeated note theme, is a particularly convincing example of Buxtehude's modular form. There are three expositions before extra entries begin:

Praeludium in D, BuxWV 139

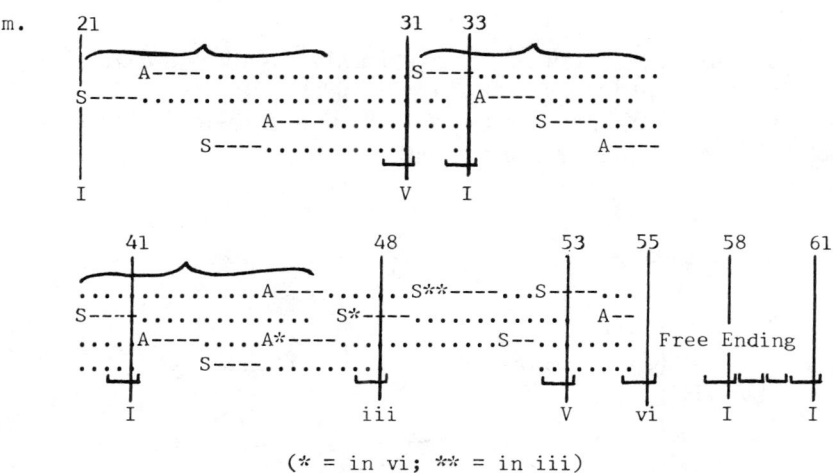

(* = in vi; ** = in iii)

The modular scheme is reinforced by a figure in the bass at all the cadences (indicated as ⌊⌋ above). Appearing almost unnoticed in the opening free section, it becomes an important element of the structure of the fugal section. It also plays a prominent role in the free ending: first, at the tonic cadence midway through the passage; and in the second part, where it becomes a virtual ostinato:

Praeludium in D, BuxWV 139

The closing free section is also modular, but in a way different from that of the fugue. Its three sections (sequential/chordal tonicization chain/ Final) and the preceding chordal *adagio*[98] show Buxtehude juxtaposing blocks of four and eight measure units:

Praeludium in D, BuxWV 139

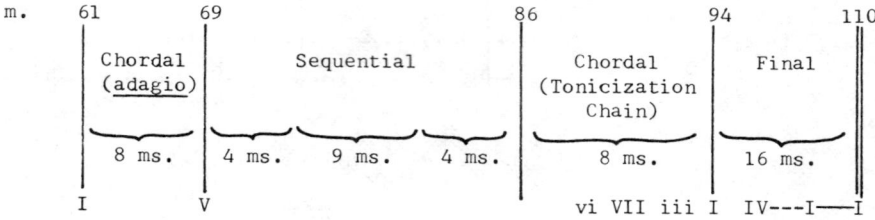

The chordal *adagio* and the tonicization chain, both eight measures long, frame the first half of the section. Between them lies the sequential section, and it is also constructed with frames (parallel passages of four measures each). In many ways, the sequential section is best understood as a substitute, in free texture, for a second fugal section. With its intense and breathless energy, it functions much like a fugato within the expressive scheme of the work. The tonicization chain which follows is not only strikingly similar to the free ending of the first fugue of the Praeludium in C, BuxWV 136, but is approached in the same manner of dramatic juxtaposition. It serves as the climax of the work. The Final section is an example of Buxtehude at his most expansive. Overall, it is simply a IV---I$_{4-3}^{6-5}$ progression with Buxtehude's favorite dramatic suspension linking the subdominant to the concluding tonic. The gesture is here handled with a great deal more flair than in the Praeludium in a, BuxWV 153; and the juxtaposition of extreme registers (g″ and D) anticipates examples found in works in a more clearly defined late style. Even though the strength of the linear coherence is not on a par with Buxtehude's greatest praeludia, in expressive power it exceeds the Praeludia in a, BuxWV 153, in A, BuxWV 151, and in C, BuxWV 136. Despite the fact that the sequential passage was most probably modeled on a similar passage from a work by Weckmann,[99] it can (like BuxWV 136) be considered a work of full maturity.

The Praeludium in C, BuxWV 137, another lighthearted work, stands close to the Praeludium in D. It is preserved in the Andreas-Bach-Buch along with the Praeludium in g, BuxWV 150, and for that reason might also be suspected to be an early work. However, the Andreas-Bach-Buch also preserves the three great ground bass pieces of Buxtehude, at least two of which (the Ciacona in e, BuxWV 160, and the Passacaglia in d, BuxWV 161) are without doubt works of Buxtehude's maturity. Stylistic evidence suggests the origin of the Praeludium to be close to that of the Passacaglia and the Ciacona.[100]

The form of the work (opening free section/common-time fugue with a brief free ending/figural/ciacona with extension) again contains only one fugue plus several free sections after it. The opening free section is one of the largest and most impressive Buxtehude conceived. Its opening pedal solo alone is enough to suggest a mature origin.[101] The rhapsody of the opening flourish gives way to an imitative passage, whose heavy reliance on sequence recalls similar passages in Scheidemann and Tunder.[102] Rhapsodic texture then resumes with motives similar to those which preceded the imitative passage. The texture (one active line supported by punctuating chords) which soon emerges is a significant one;[103] and similar textures reappear in many of the late period works. Almost immediately, however, the texture begins to develop a more strongly figural character with the help of some masterful manipulations of the motives:

Praeludium in C, BuxWV 137

The figural texture which soon evolves is quite reminiscent of that of the Praeludium in D.[104] Overall, the opening free section is one of the most impressive of all such sections in scope and expressive power. And unlike all but a few, it contains the germ of the first fugal subject.[105]

The fugue is the most doggedly modular of any in the praeludia. It is entirely (except for one final extra entry) a series of expositions, with no episodes and virtually no codettas. It also shares the procedure found in the Praeludium in D in that a motive reinforces the modular structure.[106] While in the Praeludium in D the motive is a simple bass motion, in the Praeludium in C it is the actual cadential figure of the subject itself.[107] The subject of BuxWV 137 ends with untypical cadential force; and its subsequent appearances (at regular intervals due to the reliance on expositions) creates a modular effect at the level of the entry patterns. Whereas in the Praeludium in D the motive occurred at the important cadence points (spaced irregularly throughout the section), in the Praeludium in C the motive gives the fugal section a modularity nearly equal to that of a ciacona. Although structurally not identical to a ciacona, the result is clearly akin to the regularly repeating cadences of ostinato textures. This fugue, more than any other, incorporates Buxtehude's evident fondness for ostinato structure.[108]

The figural section — like the fugue — employs thematic material from the opening free section, and its stress on the submediant also recalls that section. The canonic flourish with which it begins is closely analogous to a flourish in the Final section of the Praeludium in D.[109] It leads to harmonies which are strikingly rich, and seem especially so after the unusually bland fugal section. The section is the most intense of any save the impressive rhapsodic passages in the opening free section. As such, it serves as the expressive climax of the work.

Conclusion

The ciacona, marked *presto*, which ends the work suggests comparison with that of the Praeludium in g, BuxWV 148.[110] While the ciacona in BuxWV 148 has a grander conception, is denser and more intricate, and modulates to another harmonic area, the ciacona of BuxWV 137 features an important advance: its theme is derived from the preceding fugal subject. Indeed, it is the density of the thematic web in the Praeludium in C which is perhaps its most notable feature. Very few of the praeludia achieve such a powerful integration of the various sections through thematic interconnection.

The five two-part praeludia which have only an opening free section, a single fugal section, and no remaining sections do not evidence many traits of Buxtehude's early period. But these works, the Praeludia in C, BuxWV 138, in F, BuxWV 144 and 145, in G, BuxWV 147, and the Toccata in F, BuxWV 157, do not all suggest an origin in Buxtehude's most mature phase. Their form alone, in spite of its anticipation of the prelude and fugue pair of J. S. Bach (among others), does not warrant the conclusion that they are the final phase of Buxtehude's development of the praeludium. Neither were they all, apparently, widely circulated: all but one are unica, and are not in the Wagener and Berlin 2681 collections.[111]

Probably the earliest of these works is the Praeludium in G, BuxWV 147, a unicum in the Englehardt Collection. The overall shape of the opening free section has similarities to that of the Praeludium in C, BuxWV 137: an opening pedal solo, rhapsodic texture, an imitative passage, and, finally, the return of rhapsodic and figural texture. The section here, however, is not comparable in either expressive power or cogent thematic development. Several other features indicate a less than mature origin. The conclusion of the opening pedal solo presents an awkward moment rare in Buxtehude's praeludia.[112] Only after a second pedal solo do the manual parts begin the main body of the section.[113] And only the final passage, in a more figural style and with its move to the submediant, achieves any real sense of breadth or power.

The subject of the fugue is an unusual theme, built entirely with quarter notes. The section is singularly devoid of the rhythmic vitality derived from eighths and sixteenths which characterizes Buxtehude's fugal style. The form of the section, however, carries his distinctive mark: it is a series of overlapping expositions. In the second exposition a countersubject is introduced, but it is so similar in style to the subject that, as in the first fugue of the Praeludium in g, BuxWV 150, its effect is not particularly strong. The third exposition is in stretto, and that also has precedents in other early-period works. The section moves to the subdominant for the cadence which ends the fugal texture. A similar harmonic scheme— observed in the first fugue of the Praeludium in e, BuxWV 143, but found elsewhere — can be regarded as yet another mark of a relatively early style.[114] The concluding free ending is simple in style; an *a2* flourish, it lacks the canonic construction typical of those found in middle period works. A final clue to its origin is a subtle hint of rounding: the last bit of flourish in the penultimate measure seems to echo the opening pedal solo.[115] Such an effort at rounding the work, whether through texture or motive, is a feature which can be associated with the early-period works.

The Praeludium in C, BuxWV 138, was recently discovered in the Lowell Mason Collection. The origin of this work can be considered to postdate that of the Praeludium in G. The flourish of the opening free section is unusually expansive — on the scale of that of the Praeludium in D — although it lacks the same tight, modular organization and sequential control. The section soon coalesces around pedal points which are adorned by a shimmering haze of figuration. In an unusual move, the cadence of the section is repeated, echolike, without a pedal part. A somewhat similar gesture can be found in the free ending of the fugue of the Praeludium in D. Also like that work, the entrance of the fugal subject on the fifth degree is highlighted by an ornamental sharped fourth degree in the previous cadence.

The fugue has several indications of a relatively mature origin. It begins with a modular format of two overlapping expositions. However, midway into what appears to be a third exposition, a countersubject makes an unexpected appearance:

Praeludium in C, BuxWV 138

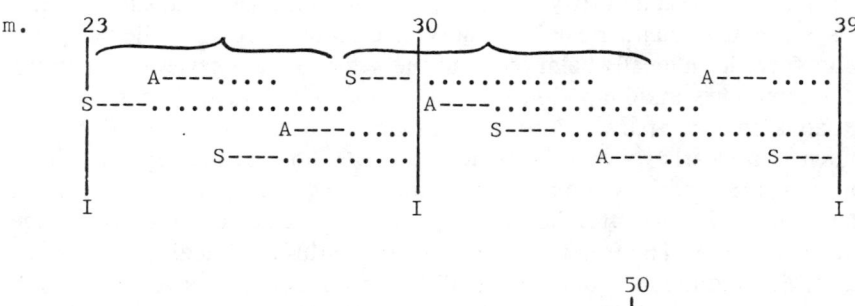

A similar effect of the entrance of a countersubject (signaling a fresh start, rather than simply greater contrapuntal density) can be found in several other praeludia. This example is the least successful, and is probably also the earliest.[116]

The most impressive passage of this still largely neglected work is the free ending of the fugue. A freely constructed ostinato passage, it is built upon a two-measure theme (x + y).[117] The eight measures of the passage take an unexpected form, x y y x y y y y, in which no two measures are identical; and there is much cleverness in the way thematic ideas are treated. A sixteenth-note figure originally found in the answer and developed in the preceding episode is the basis of the figuration in the first x measure. The second y measure sounds like an echo of the first y because the pedal part drops out, but is not actually the same music. The following x and y correspond to the first x and y, but the upper parts are inverted. The following measure is a pedal solo; the next is another echo of the first y, again without a pedal part. The last measure is cadential. The result is an intricate plan which embodies both the clever logic and the sense of improvisational freedom which characterizes Buxtehude's finest moments. Such is particularly true of closing free sections of which this passage is reminiscent. A pedal flourish[118] then leads to a more conventional closing gesture: a tonicization chain rich in figural overlay which recalls the free ending of the first fugue of the Praeludium in C, BuxWV 136. Without much doubt, then, this Praeludium can be considered a mature work.

The Praeludium in F, BuxWV 144, is a unicum in the Lowell Mason Codex. With only fifty-four measures, it is virtually a miniature alongside the many praeludia which exceed one hundred measures and sometimes reach one hundred and fifty or more. Yet there is no reason to suppose that it is a fragment. Neither can it be considered an early work, as the two parts of its form seem ideally balanced, and the work contains several indications of Buxtehude's middle-period style. The opening flourish is canonic and expands to three-part writing and finally to a four-part chord for its cadence; it clearly follows the same pattern as those of the Praeludia in g, BuxWV 148, and in a, BuxWV 153. And again, like the Praeludium in a, the flourish resumes after the cadence and leads to a genuine figural passage the second time. The frequent parallel thirds in this section also recall those in the Praeludium in a, but in general the section does not have the strength of figural logic and development found in BuxWV 153. The fugue has a lively subject which stands close to that of the Praeludium in C, BuxWV 138. Its form is also typical of Buxtehude's middle period: two overlapping expositions are followed by extra entries, some in the dominant; and it ends with fragments of the subject in stretto. Unlike the strettos in previous examples, in this Praeludium they fulfill a special role as a substitute for a free ending—and make a climactic gesture in doing so. While BuxWV 144 cannot be considered one of the composer's most powerful or expressive creations, it is completely successful as a small-scale work. Its origin would seem to lie alongside those of the larger middle-period praeludia.

Though a work on the scale of the grandest praeludia,[119] the Praeludium in F, BuxWV 145, demonstrates virtually the same proportion of free and fugal music as does the miniature Praeludium in F, BuxWV 144. The opening free section is tripartite: figural texture in common time, a 12/8 section with hints of imitation, and a concluding passage of ostinatos and a pedal point. The three-part scheme recalls the opening free sections of the Toccata in F, BuxWV 156, and the Praeludium in C, BuxWV 137. With its thirty-nine measures, however, BuxWV 145 has the longest of any such section in the praeludia, one which dwarfs most all others, which often are not even half as long. The first passage is almost more rhapsodic than figural, and is held together by a series of whole-note pedal points. The harmonies of the section, lacking a strong figural language to propel them forward, drift rather aimlessly. It is not until the harmonic rhythm quickens to dotted quarter notes at the 12/8 passage that the music coalesces and begins to make a powerful impression. In this passage and the next, the mastery of the work becomes evident. The 12/8 passage contains powerful harmonies cogently directed, and the flowing eighth-note figuration forms powerful crosscurrents above the marching bass in dotted quarters. The switch back to common time is deftly handled: the eighths of 12/8 time naturally accelerate into sixteenth-note motion and the dotted quarters continue unabated as quarters, now forming ostinato patterns. Finally, shimmering figuration like that observed in the Praeludium in C, BuxWV 138, decorates the penultimate dominant pedal.

The fugue is the most spacious and expansive of any in the praeludia: no other fugal section comes close to its eighty-four measure length. The unusually long subject is largely responsible for the size of the section: and the subject's cheery character and repetitiveness call to mind Bach's Fugue in D, BWV 532. There are only two expositions, but these have an unusual developmental power: the subject is frequently fragmented and eventually churned through several different key areas. This, too, recalls Bach's Fugue in D, and it is with good reason that Spitta considered this work a predecessor of Bach's great organ fugues.[120] Of all the two-part works, this is the only one contained in the Wagener and Berlin 2681 manuscripts, copies of which are known to have been in the possession of Bach's circle. This fully mature work can be placed alongside the most impressive of the multifugal praeludia, for it achieves a balance, poise, and effect comparable to theirs.

While it avoids the drama and pathos of the great minor mode praeludia, it exemplifies the cheerful, buoyant world of the great major mode works, such as the Praeludia in C, BuxWV 137, and in D, BuxWV 139.

The Toccata in F, BuxWV 157, is another mature example of the opening free section/single fugue form. Preserved in only one manuscript (which is now lost) outside the main body of the praeludia, it has nevertheless been in print since before the time of Spitta.[121] The opening free section, like that of the Praeludium in C, BuxWV 137, presents a sophisticated example of the pattern which moves from rhapsodic to figural texture over the course of the section. The figure which appears in the midst of flourishes in measure 15 becomes a transitional motive between the rhapsody of the opening and the strongly figural music which begins around measure 25. Its five-part texture and spacing are also significant anticipations of the figural passage. Even the decoration of the alto in measure 16 later becomes thematic. What is really special about this opening free section, however, is its modularity. More than any other first section, it is constructed in blocks of measures, generally two measure groups which sometimes form four measure phrases. Such a tendency, noticed in the closing free section of the Praeludium in D, BuxWV 139, is rare outside of ciacona sections. The effect is enhanced even more if Beckmann's suggestions for the revision of the text of measures 3, 15, and 17 in his edition are adopted.[122] Not reflected in the reading in his edition, they apparently were afterthoughts (but remain sound suggestions). In particular the curious thirty-second note flourish of measure 17 should be corrected (as he suggests) to become two measures of sixteenth-notes following the pattern of measures 13–14, for they form part of a module which is the repetition of the preceding four measures up a third (measures 13–16 and measures 17–19).

The subject of the fugue recalls the thematic material of several other praeludia and seems distilled from the subject of the Praeludium in F, BuxWV 145. In addition, figures from other mature praeludia also appear, including the prominent figure from the fugue of the Praeludium in D, BuxWV 139. The countersubject shares a cadential figure with the subject of the Praeludium in C, BuxWV 137, as well as BuxWV 139:

Toccata in F, BuxWV 157

Praeludium in F, BuxWV 145

Praeludium in D, BuxWV 139

Toccata in F, BuxWV 157

Praeludium in C, BuxWV 137

Praeludium in D, BuxWV 139

But most significant of all is how these elements have been carefully prepared in the opening free section. The Toccata in F presents one of the most sophisticated cases of thematic anticipations of a fugue subject in the praeludia. The fugue itself is a model of Buxtehude's modular construction at its best: after two expositions, a new counterpoint is introduced in the third and provides just the intensification needed at that point in the form. The final passages after the third exposition are some of Buxtehude's most impressive. Using motives from the subject and its countersubject, a large sequential structure is built. Its symmetrical construction surpasses that of the closing free section of the Praeludium in D, and draws the work to a powerful close. Without doubt, this work can be placed alongside the best of the multifugal praeludia, and can also be considered a product of Buxtehude's mature phase of praeludium composition.

The Praeludium in B♭, BuxWV 154, of which only a fragment of the opening free section survives, seems most closely connected in spirit and thematic material to works such as the Praeludium in F, BuxWV 145, and the Toccata in F, BuxWV 157.[123] The cadential gesture which appears three times during the course of its opening eighteen measures recalls several characteristics of the Toccata in F; certainly the opening figure recalls the subject of the Praeludium in F. What remains shares the expansive, outgoing character of the opening free section of the Toccata in F. The fragment does not coalesce into figural textures, but that would have probably occurred in what followed. Judging from the scope of what is left, it would have been a large-scale opening free section, and perhaps a large-scale work as well. The repetition of transposed blocks of material in the opening free section also suggests comparison with the Toccata in F and indicates that it, too, may have made further use of sequential constructions of which only hints remain. For these reasons, it seems reasonable to consider the fragment to be of a mature origin.

The remaining multifugal praeludia all demonstrate elements of a late style. The Praeludium in E, BuxWV 141, ranks with the Praeludia in C, BuxWV 137, and in D, BuxWV 139, and the Toccata in F, BuxWV 157, as the best of the major mode works. However, more than the others, it strives towards a more profound expression. While hardly as intense or poignant as the great minor mode works, it reaches beyond the predominantly light-hearted mood of BuxWV 137, 139, and 157 to find a power and drama which is consistent with its major mode optimism. Instrumental in this achievement are its unusually rich harmonies and textures. Several other aspects of the work suggest a late origin. Powell singles out the use of tempo markings (*presto, adagio*, and *allegro* all appear), the opening flourish with its thirty-second and sixty-fourth notes, the virtuosic use of the pedals, and its key (an unusual one which strains the bounds of unequal temperament).[124] The form is also unusually complex (opening free section/ common-time fugue with a brief free ending/chordal-rhapsodic/fugato with a free ending/gigue fugato with a free extension/chordal/common-time fugue with a free ending). But complex forms have been observed in early works, particularly in the Toccata in F, BuxWV 156. The Praeludium in E shares with that work the tendency towards a proliferation of many small sections and gestures after the first fugue. However, it is the coherence with which they are made convincing here that suggests, as much as anything else, a completely mature origin for BuxWV 141.

The opening free section, like that of the Praeludium in C, BuxWV 136, is rich in detail despite its very modest length. The opening flourish is unusually flashy, and the texture modulates from rhapsodic to figural effortlessly. The quasi-canonic figuration in measure 6 is a significant detail: similar passagework appears in three other late-period works:[125]

Praeludium in E, BuxWV 141

The following melody-and-accompaniment rhapsodic style is also significant. It can be associated with the late style as well.[126]

The first fugue is the largest of the four imitative sections. As in virtually all the early- and middle-period multifugal works, the first fugal section surpasses the others in size and fugal rigor. Its form is a familiar one: two overlapping expositions are followed by several extra entries. Also familiar is the figure in the counterpoint during the second and third entrances — a figure which also appears prominently in the fugues of

278   Conclusion

BuxWV 137, 139, and 157.[127] While playing a small role in this section, it reappears at several important junctures later in the work. Although hardly a novel motive, its presence in these three works nevertheless reinforces their kinship. The cadential passage is a subtle recall of the corresponding measures of the opening free section; and the sudden burst of thirty-second note figuration which recalls the extravagant passagework of the opening free section reinforces this unusual relationship.

Yet another imaginative link occurs between the end of the fugal section and the following free section. The ornamental raised fourth degree of the cadence of the fugue (measure 50), as well as the figure in which it is embedded, is heard again as a pedal solo immediately after the cadence and effects a move to the dominant. This gesture is the most sophisticated treatment of this type of cadence in the praeludia.[128] The passage itself is also noteworthy. While based on whole-note harmonic motion, it is so highly decorated in the characteristic thirty-second note motion of this work that its rhapsodic character almost gives way to figural texture. In spite of the fact that its harmonic rhythm is too slow to support true figural music, its ornamentation is so dense that the strongly motivic overlay of the figural style is approximated. The following *presto* is Buxtehude's most freely constructed imitative section. It pushes forward through rich harmonic progressions (a rising tonicization chain) only to be dramatically cut off with a statement of the figure heard in the first fugue:

Praeludium in E, BuxWV 141

A "con discretione" flourish which follows heightens the dramatic effect and brings the section to a tonic cadence. Another brief and unusual fugato then ensues, cast in the 12/8 meter and flowing style of a gigue. It too has a dramatic concluding gesture, paralleling that of the *presto*. After a free extension and a pause on the dominant, a short but powerfully expressive chordal *adagio* leads to a tonic arrival.[129] Yet another touch of sophistication is the graceful elision of the cadence of the *adagio* with the beginning of the final *allegro* fugal section. While the *allegro* fugue is a more substantial section than either of the two preceding ones, it is still significantly shorter than the first fugue. A move to the subdominant (measure 99), rare in a fugue, suggests that it is indeed the final section and recalls the subdominant drift typical of closing free sections. A move to the submediant sees the return of the figure from the first fugue via the end of the *presto* to become the cadential figure of the free ending. The free ending is a significant one, a fine example of the kind of modular structures which can be taken as a sign of the late period. The final seven measures of the work take the following form:

Praeludium in E, BuxWV 141

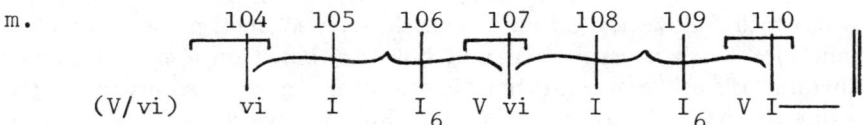

Measures 104-6 and 107-9 are, except for the smallest of details, identical.[130]

The many sophisticated and subtle aspects of this work argue strongly for a fully mature origin. In addition, the thematic derivations of the fugal subjects are particularly refined, and are suggestive rather than blatant.[131] Other thematic links provided by free floating figures reinforce thematic unity. Also helping to unify the work is the octave descent which can be traced from the chordal-rhapsodic section through the two imitative sections to the beginning of the last *allegro* fugue.[132] The line and the expressive shape of the work are closely coordinated: the remaining sections move towards a climax point in the *adagio*, with resolution following in the *allegro* fugue. The plan, however, is not as forcefully realized as in several other praeludia. The tonic arrival which concludes the *presto* and its "con discretione" flourish provides an anticipatory climax point from which the gigue seems to recoil.[133] The effect of the climax point of the entire remaining sections in the *adagio* is weakened, and the sense of an expressive sweep from the first fugue through the imitative sections to the last section is correspondingly reduced.

Conclusion

The Praeludium in d, BuxWV 140, like the Praeludium in E, is a member of the group of praeludia which is found in the Wagener and the Berlin 2681 manuscripts, and appears only in those collections. It, too, can be considered a fully mature work;[134] and with it the world of the great, late period minor mode praeludia is entered. Many of the characteristics which distinguish the Praeludium in E can also be observed in this work. These include complex and strongly climactic remaining sections, significant linear coherence, subtle thematic derivations,[135] free floating motives unrelated to the fugal subjects, sophisticated formal articulations, modular structures, and an accent on virtuosity. The form (opening free section/common-time fugue with a free ending/chordal-rhapsodic/imitative with a free ending/triple-time fugue with a free ending/closing free section) is virtually as complex as that of the Praeludium in E, though the remaining sections here are somewhat fewer but more substantial. Just as important is a better balance between the fugal sections: in the Praeludium in d, the first fugue does not so strongly overshadow the following ones as it does in the Praeludium in E.

The opening free section is a particularly striking one; the figural texture which follows the opening flourish is based upon a figure which is much longer than usual. It is not, however, based on a slow harmonic rhythm. More like a real theme than a stock figure, it seems to suggest string writing, and anticipates the Vivaldi-like motivic work found in Bach:

Praeludium in d, BuxWV 140

Bach: Prelude in G, BWV 541[136]

Conclusion   281

It gives the section a powerful, modern sound; but predictably, its development does not take the same form as is found in Bach's Prelude in G. Rather, its successive appearances suggest a fugal exposition. Other thematic ideas add to the grandeur of the conception: the section is twice punctuated by a powerful half cadence amid the sweep of descending scalar passagework. The section exceeds virtually all other opening free sections as a portentous beginning; its tightly wrought, cogent shape only barely contains the intensity of its expression.

The joint between the opening free section and the fugue is a particularly sophisticated one. The fugal subject is anticipated at the close of the opening free section; and the rare feminine cadence which ends that section further softens the articulation between the sections. The fugue itself has a typical construction of two overlapping expositions plus several extra entries. What is special, however, is the counterpoint. A particularly expressive countersubject contrasts sharply with the subject; and the invertibility of the two considerably increases the expressive potential. Invertible counterpoint can be found in a number of both early and later works. In the early works, however, the countersubjects are similar to the subjects and the results, while sometimes clever, are generally bland and inexpressive.

The chordal-rhapsodic section, like that following the first fugue in the Praeludium in E, is based on a tonicization chain. The elaboration of the harmonies is more purely rhapsodic than in the Praeludium in E, and the effect is correspondingly more dramatic: powerful juxtapositions and dislocations of register are held together by the force of a cogent harmonic progression. The cadence of the section on the subtonic is highly unusual, and is evidence of the special harmonic daring of the work. The imitative section which follows, again like the corresponding section in the Praeludium in E (the *presto*), is not a typical fugato. The plan in the Praeludium in d, however, is more highly structured: each voice enters a fourth higher than the previous one, swinging the music through the circle of fifths. The process is repeated, like a second exposition, but over a grandly descending stepwise bass in eighth notes. The motion strongly recalls similar gestures in the opening free section.[137] This passage is harmonically an extraordinary one, for in no other passage in the praeludia do the harmonies dare to move so far from the tonic. The triple-time fugue mimics the first one in the use of what is virtually the same countersubject, again to good effect in invertible counterpoint. The free ending recalls that of the last fugue of the Praeludium in E with its modular structure. Here, however, instead of exact repetition, the outer voices are inverted.[138]

The closing free section is seamlessly joined to the preceding fugue. The increase in figuration from the quarter-note motion (which dominates the free ending) through eighths to sixteenths before the tonic cadence (which

282 *Conclusion*

marks the articulation point) softens the joint and creates a single sweep of energy from the fugue to the closing free section. Enhancing the sense of unity is the derivation from the subject of the imitative section of the opening of the pedal flourish with which the closing free section begins. The subject, in turn, recalls the motive of the opening free section as well as the first fugue. The end of the triple-time fugue and the beginning of the closing free section marks the expressive climax of the work.[139] From then on, the music moves into the resolution phase of the expressive scheme. The typical move towards the subdominant at this point in the form is presented with some masterful manipulations of texture: the eighth-note chords which punctuate the pedal solo next appear as support for figuration in the soprano (and in doing so suggest a free modular structure).[140] Similar textures in the opening free section of the Praeludium in E are also evoked.[141] The chords then lengthen into quarters and halves and finally into dotted quarters as the subdominant area is entered. All the while, beautifully constructed passagework drives the music forward. The quasi-canonic figuration, a mannerism of the late style which was also observed in the opening free section of the Praeludium in E, then makes a fine effect over an ostinato. Its essentially static nature makes it particularly appropriate for this moment in the form: as do other figurative patterns in the praeludia, it creates more of a haze of sound than real motion.[142] With it, the tension of the work is spun out and the energy of the passage relaxes into eighths as the subdominant falls back to the tonic for the final plagal cadence.

The expressive plan of the Praeludium in d is especially convincing. It is paradigmatic of the praeludia with a closing free section and the result of Buxtehude's extensive efforts at perfecting the dramatic sweep possible in the praeludium. In no way can such an achievement be understood as an early effort. Neither can the linear control exercised (particularly in the remaining sections) be taken as anything other than Buxtehude at the height of his powers.[143] This admirable work can stand as an equal beside the great praeludia which are currently more often performed.

The Toccata in d, BuxWV 155, is the only multifugal praeludium not preserved in the Wagener and Berlin 2681 manuscripts for which a late origin can be strongly suspected. In its only source, the Lowell Mason Codex, it is dated 1684; such a date can be considered a relatively late one in the chronology of the praeludia.[144] While some of its aspects suggest a kinship with the earlier Toccata in F, BuxWV 156, it shares with the Praeludia in E and in d, as well as with the three remaining works discussed below, distinctive characteristics of the late period. The form (opening free section/common-time fugue with a free ending/chordal/triple-time fugue with a large free ending/closing free section) is less complex than either of those of the Praeludia in E or in d. Most noteworthy, however, is the concentration of fugal weight in the second fugue. This pattern can also be observed in the three remaining works (BuxWV 142, 146, and 149).

The opening free section, like that of the Praeludium in d, is an unusual and striking one. An emphasis on virtuosity is apparent from the beginning. The typical shape of flourish/rhapsodic/figural is hardly discernable. The opening flourish is a series of short repeated gestures rather than a single long one; but the arrival on the tonic some six measures after the beginning of the piece is easily recognized as the usual structural pillar which occurs at that moment in the form. The rhapsodic music which follows is some of the most impressive ever conceived by Buxtehude. The alternation of broken chords and thirty-second note passagework recalls one of the most effective passages of the Toccata in F, BuxWV 156.[145] The passage leads to a strong dominant cadence, after which a fugato ensues. With entrances at the space of only one quarter note, it generates considerable momentum. Its free ending is another example of the two-part modular type also found in the Praeludia in E and in d, as well as in several other late-period works.[146] Most importantly, however, the thematic material is clearly the source of the two following fugal subjects. And, as Lena Jacobson has recently pointed out, the fugato subject is foreshadowed in the opening motive of the work.[147] The fugato uses a more complex version of the idea than does the first fugue. The result is a reversal of the usual process of thematic derivation: the first fugal subject sounds like a distillation of the preceding fugato subject. The relationship provides a strong, yet subtle, link between the opening free section and the first fugue. A similar attempt to soften that formal articulation has already been observed in several other works, most notably in the Praeludium in d. The technique employed in the Toccata in d, however, is by far the most powerful one.

The first fugue is a section of only modest length, not nearly as extensive as most first fugues. While the first fugue of the Praeludium in d seems small in comparison to that of the Praeludium in E, the first fugue of the Toccata in d is even shorter than that of the Praeludium in d.[148] Like the first fugue of the Praeludium in d, the section relies heavily on an invertible countersubject of contrasting profile. The free ending, like moments in the opening free section, bears an uncanny resemblance to a passage from the Toccata in F, BuxWV 156. In this case, the parallel passages are both from the free ending of the first fugue.[149] Like the free ending of the Toccata in F, it does not lead to a tonic cadence; rather, it soon leads to a dominant cadence. While the term Toccata cannot be taken to denote a special form of the praeludium, the similarity of these two passages, when taken with the similarities noted above and the use of the Toccata name in both works, suggests that Buxtehude had the Toccata in F in mind when the Toccata in d was written. There are, however, very few other similarities between these works which most probably originated in different periods in the chronology of the praeludia.[150]

As in both the Praeludia in E and in d, a chordal-rhapsodic passage follows the first fugue. While in the Toccata it is more purely chordal than in the other two, the formal similarity is yet one more link between this group of works. The passage, like the preceding free ending, also cadences on the dominant. With two articulation points on the dominant, it presents the most advanced harmonic scheme of these three works at the midway point in the form:[151]

Praeludium in E, BuxWV 141

m.		50		59	
	First Fugue + Free Ending		Chordal-Rhapsodic		Fugato
		I		V	

Praeludium in d, BuxWV 140

m.		44		54	
	First Fugue + Free Ending		Chordal-Rhapsodic		Imitative
		I		VII	

Toccata in d, BuxWV 155

m.		53		62	
	First Fugue + Free Ending		Chordal		Triple-Time Fugue
		V		V	

The second fugue is built on an obvious transformation of the first fugal subject. But the blatancy of earlier triple-time derivations is avoided by an unexpected rhythmic twist: |♩♩|♩♩| instead of a swinging |♩♩|♩♩| to replace the rhythm of the pitch series originally presented in quarter notes: |♪(♩)♩♩♩|. Another prominent countersubject, used invertibly to good effect, is featured. Modular structures appear even before the free ending. Measures 97–102 and 103–7, which immediately precede the free ending, are parallel passages built around statements of the answer in the bass, first in the mediant and then in the tonic. The effect is reinforced not only by similar counterpoint, but above all by the cadence of the first of the two phrases. Its preparation (indeed a curious measure to find in fugal texture) appears also at the end of the second phrase as a half cadence.[152] The following free ending is extremely large, and yet another example of two-part modular structure.[153] A motivic idea derived from the countersubject of the preceding fugue is spun-out in sequence in the soprano. It is supported by punctuating chords in the first phrase, and then—with the motive and its chords inverted—appears in the bass in the second phrase. The texture of this passage strongly recalls textures following the free ending of the final fugue in the Praeludium in d.[154] The next five measures provide a strong tonic major cadence. Interestingly, the penultimate measure of this passage echoes the curious cadence at the end of the two phrases of the first set of modular phrases.[155]

The closing free section (labeled "Final") is paradigmatic of that special type of closing free section which emphasizes the subdominant; and the typical ostinatos are also present. Both the ostinato figure and the passage-work recall the Praeludium in d.[156] The section here, however, is far more free-standing—it is not approached through the sophisticated textural modulation of the Praeludium in d. Rather, its approach and commencement are comparable to the corresponding moment in the Praeludium in a, BuxWV 153. The dramatic juxtaposition of the penultimate subdominant and final tonic areas also resembles that work; and it bears even greater resemblance to the (probably later) Praeludium in D, BuxWV 139.[157]

The expressive plan of the work is rather different from that of the Praeludium in d, and is quite different from that of the Praeludium in E. In the Toccata, there is a greater sense of sweep past the first fugue (reduced in size) into the remaining sections. This is achieved through the close of the first fugue, its free ending, and the chordal section, which are all on the dominant rather than on the tonic. Instead of a jumble of small sections after the first fugue, a style especially noticeable in the Praeludium in E, the Toccata manifests fewer but larger sections. The biggest fugue of the work, the large triple-time fugue, generates a great amount of energy and drive towards the climax, which occurs at the end of the fugal texture of that section. An unusually large series of textures follow for the relaxation of the climax, including the large modular free ending and the subsequent Final with its ostinatos and subdominant harmony. The turn to triplets (with the return of common time) at the concluding tonic pedal provides yet another means of relaxation of the accumulated tension of the work.[158]

The Praeludium in e, BuxWV 142, has been recognized since the time of Spitta's first analysis as "one of his [Buxtehude's] greatest organ compositions...."[159] It may well have been so recognized in Buxtehude's own day as well, for it is the only one which can be found in all the major sources of the praeludia. The form (opening free section/common-time fugue with a brief free ending/triple-time fugue with a very brief free ending/chordal/ gigue fugue with a long free extension) demonstrates its fugal bias. Like the Praeludium in d and the Toccata in the same key, the work shifts its emphasis away from the first fugue and into the remaining sections. As in the Toccata in d, the second fugue is the core of the work; but while the Toccata contains a clear balance between free and fugal textures, the Praeludium in e (like several before it) is weighted noticeably in the direction of fugal texture. It is thus appropriate that the second fugue of this work is one of Buxtehude's most impressive fugal creations, one comparable in expressive power only to the second, *largo*, fugue of the Praeludium in g, BuxWV 149, discussed below. Several factors other than the big second fugue also indicate a relatively late origin. These include the work's large size (one hundred fifty-five measures), the modern chromatic style of the second fugue, the sophisticated thematic treatment,[160] the strongly climactic expression, and the high virtuosity required for its performance.

The opening free section can be considered the most sophisticated example of the entirely figural type. While comparable in several ways to that of the Praeludium in C, BuxWV 136 (in size, exclusive reliance on figural texture, tonicization chains, and in the appearance of a short, one-measure flourish), the thematic material of the flourish in the Praeludium in e is the basis of that of the entire section. Instead of the usual ABC . . . flow of figural motives, here a pattern closer to A'A''A''' . . . is found.[161]

The first fugue is based on a lively, canzonalike subject, though its form lacks the clearly modular structure of most of Buxtehude's fugues. It seems to begin in the typical manner but the expected overlapping of expositions is untypical in several ways: the first entrance after the opening exposition occurs before the last one of the first exposition is completed, creating an oddly placed stretto effect; the expected articulation at the second entrance after the first exposition does not materialize until midway through the third entrance; and when the cadence does come, it is untypically on the subdominant:

Praeludium in e, BuxWV 142

m.   17   27
    |S----..............   A----......|..   S*----
    | A----...... S----.......... |S'----..........
    | S----..............A   +--..............
    | A----.............. | S----....
    i   iv

(' = Distorted; * = in v)

Conclusion   287

The entries directly after the first exposition are not clearly grouped to form a second one; and the continuation of the fugue is a maze of added entries, some distorted, most fragmented, and a few outside the tonic. Surely part of the seeming disorder is due to the subject itself. It contains quarters, eighths, and sixteenths, but not in an accelerating order.

A further rhythmic twist in this subject is its beginning on the downbeat of the measure. (Buxtehude's subjects virtually always begin on an upbeat, or at least on a weak beat.)[162] The bias towards the subdominant (in both the subject and the answer, but at different places) is unusual, and it seems to affect the ease of the harmonic flow. The approach to the free ending through extensions of both parts of the subject (in different voices) is a masterful touch:

Praeludium in e, BuxWV 142

The free ending itself is particularly brief, and its sudden turn to chordal texture is reminiscent of several cadential gestures in opening free sections.[163] However, the chordal texture here is not unmotivated: the eighth-note chords clearly derive both their rhythm and chromaticism directly from the subject.[164]

If the first fugue seems to be a rather weak one for a late-period work, the second fugue is one of Buxtehude's strongest. The impressive chromatic subject which moves mostly in quarter notes seems inspired by the eighth-note chromatic motion in the first subject. It results in some of Buxtehude's richest harmonic writing. The passage has no precedent in the organ music of his north German predecessors, but derives from the modern style of dissonance treatment practiced in vocal music, and especially operatic works.[165] A particularly rigorous contrapuntal style is evident from the beginning. The countersubject which accompanies the subject in the opening exposition and for several extra entries thereafter is closely related to the subject:[166]

Praeludium in e, BuxWV 142

A second countersubject in flowing eighth-note motion is introduced thereafter. The introduction of a countersubject after the section is already underway has already been observed in several other works. The example here is by far the most convincing: not only is the countersubject strongly contrasting, but unlike the analogous gesture in the Toccata in F, BuxWV 157, it is also given sufficient time to develop its expressive potential alongside the original subject. While it is used invertibly, the real contrapuntal interest comes from the use of the subject in inversion, which was foreshadowed by the original countersubject used in the opening exposition. The chromatically descending and ascending (when inverted) quarters of the subject pitted against the eighth-note flow of the countersubject and its derivatives create some of the most notable contrapuntal passages in the praeludia. Statements of both the answer and the subject in inversion in the bass, plus extreme registers in the soprano (first b″ and finally c‴), provide a climax. A very brief free ending brings the section to a half cadence. The elegance of the part writing, the cogent flow of the harmonies, and the finely calculated drive towards the climax all contribute towards making this intensely expressive section one of the summits of Buxtehude's art.[167]

The following chordal passage tries very hard to maintain the fever pitch of excitement generated by the closing passages of the preceding fugue, though it only barely succeeds. Despite its rich harmonic language, its decorative style is irregular, varying from highly elaborate written-out trills to virtually bald half-note chordal progressions.[168] The harmonic drift is also unsure. From the dominant half cadence of the fugue, the initial move is to the subdominant. The swing from the dominant through the tonic to the subdominant is largely accomplished by the one-measure flourish which introduces the section:

Praeludium in e, BuxWV 142

From the subdominant, the section winds its way to the tonic and finally beyond to the dominant for its close. Even though a line from the d#″ of the cadence of the second fugue to the b′ of the opening of the next fugue helps direct the course of the section, its chromatic vacillations give the passage a wandering effect. The chordal passage in the Toccata in d, for example, also lies between two dominant pillars. The direction of its line is clearer, and as a result, its effect more cogent:

Praeludium in e, BuxWV 142

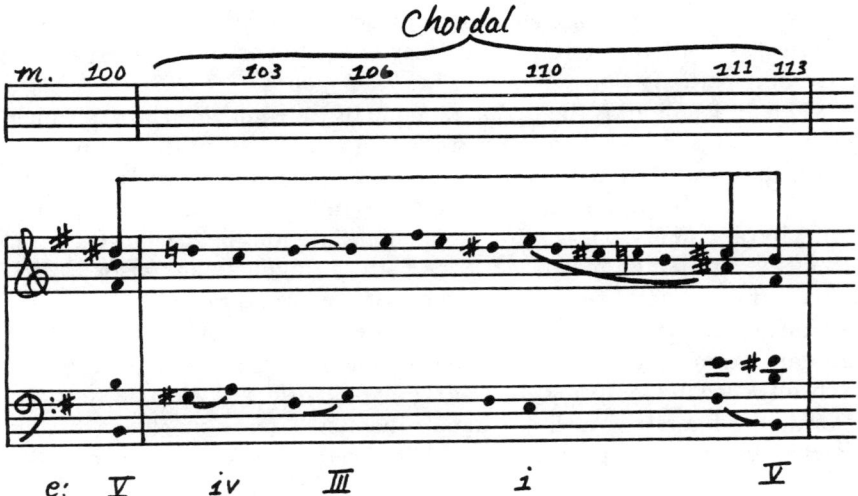

Toccata in d, BuxWV 155

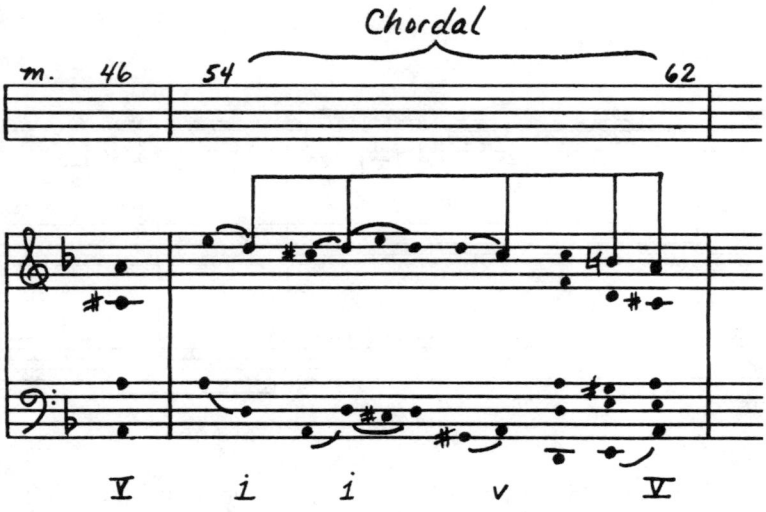

The last section, the gigue fugue, is an unusually spacious section, and far exceeds the scope of the gigue fugue of the Praeludium in C, BuxWV 136. Two overlapping expositions are followed by a large extension, first using fragments of the subject and finally freely invented material. The section eventually drifts towards the subdominant, symptomatic of its final position in the form. A short free ending in common time leads the music back through the dominant to the tonic major cadence. The Lombardic rhythms in the penultimate measure provide a final capricious touch; and the effect is somewhat bizarre when they are juxtaposed with the flowing long/short patterns which dominate the 12/8 gigue.

This Praeludium is the major example of the multifugal works which end with a fugal rather than a free section. As with most of the late praeludia which end with a free section, the center of gravity of the work is shifted from the first fugue into the remaining sections. And like those works, strong linear connections within the remaining sections help achieve a sense of unity, even though in this work the pattern of climax and resolution is not coordinated with it — as it is in most of the great praeludia which end with a free section. The tensions accumulated in the second fugue and the chordal section which mark the climax of the work are, however, as effectively dispelled in the closing gigue as they would be in a closing free section. Indeed, the impressive second fugue generates a sense of climax hardly matched in any other praeludium. While several sections (particularly the first fugue and the chordal section) are definitely not on a par with the second fugue, the overall effect of the work is still a tremendously impressive one. Even though several aspects of Buxtehude's late-period style are not presented here (such as modular structures, quasi-canonic figuration, and rhapsodic passagework with punctuating chords), these are associated specifically with free textures, and this work is dominated by fugues. The strong character of the three fugues in this work parallels the most impressive achievements in the free textures of the other great praeludia, and suggests that this work should be ranked alongside them.

The Praeludium in f♯, BuxWV 146, is yet another of the praeludia preserved alongside those of the Wagener and Berlin 2681 group (though it appears only in the Wagener Manuscript). Both its omission in Berlin 2681 and its location in the Wagener Manuscript following the others suggest the possibility of a particularly late origin. Many aspects of its style can also be associated with the other late-period works, in particular the Praeludium in d, BuxWV 140. A counterpart to the Praeludium in e (with its impressive fugal textures), the Praeludium in f♯ has what are easily the most notable free textures of any of the praeludia. The form of the Praeludium in f♯ (opening free section/common-time *grave* fugue with free ending/common-time *vivace* fugue with free ending/chordal-rhapsodic/a very large closing free section) shows how free textures command the most music here. The fugues, however, are not without interest: they are both finely wrought, and show a kinship with those of the Toccata in d. As in that work, the first fugue is reduced in size and the second fugue assumes added importance. Like other late-period works, the Praeludium in f♯ also has a sophisticated web of thematic connections. Motives other than those which stem from the fugal subjects play particularly important roles. The use of tempo marks (*grave* and *vivace*) can, like those of the Praeludium in E, be taken to signify a relatively late origin.[169] Like the other great works from the Wagener and Berlin 2681 manuscripts, an emphasis on virtuosity is also apparent. Finally, the key of the work challenges the bounds of unequal temperament, also suggesting a late origin.

The opening free section is an unusual one. Evading figural texture entirely, it is in two parts: a flourish plus arpeggiations over a tonic pedal point, and then a bold chordal progression in unadorned quarter notes. Quasi-canonic figuration, of the type observed in the Praeludia in E and in d, appears in the first passage.[170] The striking harmonies of the second part announce the exaggerated expression which will characterize the work.

The first fugue is comparable in many ways to the first fugue of the Toccata in d. Not only do the subjects have a similar outline, but their forms (two expositions with a rigorous use of a countersubject) are also similar:

292 Conclusion

Toccata in d, BuxWV 155

Praeludium in f♯, BuxWV 146

Toccata in d, BuxWV 155

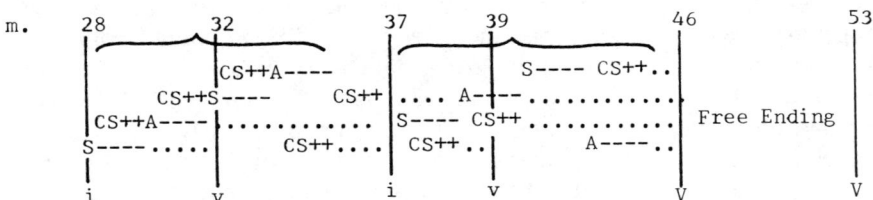

Praeludium in f♯, BUXWv 146

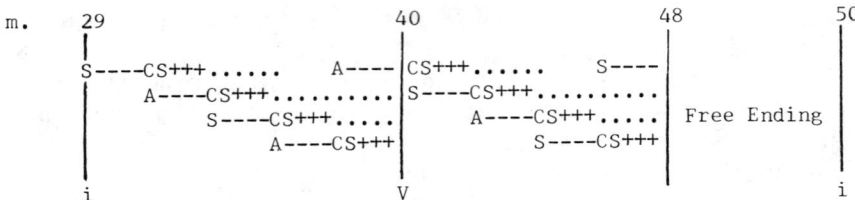

Marked *grave*, the character of the first fugue of the Praeludium in f♯ is even more severe than that of the Toccata in d. These fugues are worlds apart from the lively canzonalike ones of such works as the Praeludium in

F, BuxWV 145, the Toccata in F, BuxWV 157, and the Praeludium in E. While a tone of severity can be distinguished in the first fugue of the Praeludium in d, it is with the Toccata in d and especially the Praeludium in f♯ that this particular conception becomes striking.[171] The free ending of the first fugue is another fine example of a modular structure.[172]

The second fugue, while remaining in common time, carries a new tempo mark, *vivace*. The transformation of the first fugal subject into a lively common-time version rather than a triple-time subject yields one of Buxtehude's most curious subjects. It seems even harder to handle than that of the first fugue of the Praeludium in e, BuxWV 142. Abandoned midway through the second exposition, it appears thereafter mostly as fragments. Indeed, the remainder of the fugue is the freest common-time fugal section found in the praeludia. Typical of second fugues, the harmonic movement is noticeably more wide-ranging than that of the first fugue. The move to the mediant, first tentative (measures 58–60) but then secure (measures 67–69) recalls a similar move in the second fugue of the Praeludium in a, BuxWV 153. However, the laxity of fugal rigor here allows a new thematic idea to be introduced. While not deriving from the fugal subjects, nor acting as a countersubject, the new quarternote bass theme is nevertheless prepared in the preceding passages of the second fugue.[173] A motive which does derive from the second fugal subject becomes closely associated with the new bass theme:

Praeludium in f♯, BuxWV 146

294   Conclusion

These thematic ideas together dominate the modular free ending.[174] And together, they will be even more significant in the closing free section.

The chordal-rhapsodic section which follows is the most impressive such section conceived by Buxtehude. It is even more flamboyant and harmonically daring than those in works such as the Praeludia in E and in d. In no other such section does Buxtehude so strain the confines of unequal temperament. Yet the part writing, notably in measures 85-90, is especially elegant: rhapsodic language has not ever carried such expressive weight or evoked such pathos in the praeludia.

The closing free section begins with a freely constructed ciacona using the bass theme introduced in the *vivace* fugue accompanied by the motive which was associated with it there. After two statements in the tonic, a modulating passage leads to another two in the dominant. The second statement of the theme in the dominant is transferred to the pedal part as a solo.[175] As the music swings back from the dominant towards the tonic, the development of the thematic material yields powerful results: the 𝄾 𝅘𝅥𝅯𝅘𝅥𝅯 motive is tossed between the manuals and the pedal part, and immediately thereafter a free diminution of the ciacona theme appears.[176] The harmonic goal, however, is not the tonic but the subdominant. This move, the typical gesture of the closing free section, has elements which recall those of several praeludia. The ciacona theme in diminution suggests similar ostinato figures from the Praeludium in a, BuxWV 153.[177] The simpler ostinato figures which follow are virtually identical to those in the Praeludium in d and the Toccata in the same key.[178] The tonic pedal enters dramatically, iv–I$_{6-5}^{4-3}$, as in the Praeludia in a, BuxWV 153, and in D, BuxWV 139, and the Toccata in d. The relaxation over the final pedal strongly recalls the corresponding passage in the Praeludium in a. As a compendium of Buxtehude's best techniques in the closing free section, this section's indebtedness to what can almost surely be taken to be its predecessors can be seen. Moreover, the expansion of the scheme to include a preceding dominant area is unprecedented in those examples. The great length of the section led Spitta to question its aesthetic effect.[179] The effect, however, needs to be understood in relationship to several factors of the work, including the extreme expression of the preceding chordal-rhapsodic section (which prepares the unusually large climax at the beginning of the last section) and also the long line which spans the closing free section.[180] Of extraordinary length, the descending line from a″ to f#′ is not only a structural justification for the size of the section but is also an important aspect of the sweep of motion and energy which flows through the section as it recoils from the climax. Surpassing its models, the section wrings every last ounce of energy out of the expressive plan before the arrival of the final cadence.

There can be no question that the Praeludium in f♯ should be grouped with the most impressive of the praeludia, especially the Praeludium and the Toccata in d. Not only does it share numerous characteristics with those works, but it is also at the very least their equal in expressive power. While almost as biased towards free textures as the Praeludium in e is to fugal ones, the Praeludium in f♯ with its extravagant chordal-rhapsodic and closing free sections ranks with the Praeludium in e and its chromatic fugue at the height of Buxtehude's achievement.

The Praeludium in g, BuxWV 149, can in many ways be considered the most accomplished of the praeludia. Appearing with the great praeludia in the Wagener and Berlin 2681 collections, it can also be found in the Wenster collection along with the Praeludia in D and in e. This apparently widely circulated work exhibits a quintessential balance between free and fugal textures (opening free section, actually a ciacona/common-time fugue with a free ending/*allegro* free section in first basso continuo style and then modular/triple-time *largo* fugue/closing free section resembling a ciacona). The most notable feature of the work, however, is the thematic process; in what is virtually a *grundgestalt* procedure, the ciacona theme of the opening free section is the basis of the thematic material in all the following sections:[181]

Praeludium in g, BuxWV 149

Several aspects of the style and structure of the Praeludium in g also suggest a late origin, including the shift in fugal weight from the first to the second fugue, the use of modularly organized free passages, sophisticated linear links, tempo indications (*allegro* and *largo*), an accent on virtuosity, and a powerfully expressive content.

The opening free section is the only one in the praeludia which is a ciacona. That form, with its repeated bass theme, creates an unusually strong emphasis on thematic content; indeed, in no other opening free section is thematic material so stressed. The figuration in the first measure is thematically unrelated to that which commences in the second measure, and thus corresponds to the typical flourish. However, its surging sixteenth-note triplets join seamlessly to the following figuration which is also a constant stream of the same rhythmic values. The canon beginning in the second measure also recalls canonic constructions in opening flourishes;[182] yet it also suggests the style of quasi-canonic figuration found throughout the late-period works.[183] The figuration creates an immense sweep of energy, uninterrupted even in the seventh measure when the ciacona theme makes its first dramatic entry. The last complete statement of the ciacona, with an inverted pedal point in the manuals, bears a strong resemblance in not only the bass theme but the pedal point to the free ending of the *vivace* fugue of the Praeludium in f♯. A final, abbreviated statement of the theme is unaccompanied and makes an epigrammatic effect. It functions, however, as a textural modulation: suddenly the texture becomes similar to the opening of a fugue. It is strongly implied that the thematic material of the fugue which follows immediately should derive from it.[184]

The first fugue, like those of the Toccata in d and the Praeludium in f♯, is a subdued, severe section. And—also like the first fugues of those two works, and that of the Praeludium in d—it is a beautifully constructed pair of expositions. The free ending, however, leads to a dominant rather than to a tonic cadence.

The *allegro* free section which follows the first fugue is closely linked to the preceding section; and it is the *allegro*, rather than the fugue's free ending, which provides the tonic cadence expected at the end of the fugue. As such, the *allegro* functions as a second free ending. A similar ambiguity between a fugal free ending and a following free section can be found, on a smaller scale, in the Praeludium in E:

Praeludium in E, BuxWV 141

```
m.     75              83           86             91
       |               |            |              |
       Gigue Fugato + Extension   Chordal Adagio   Common-Time Allegro
       |               |            |              Fugue
       |               |            |              |
       I               V            V              I
```

Praeludium in g, BuxWV 149

```
m.     21              49           54             78
       |               |            |              |
       Common-Time Fugue + Free Ending   Basso Continuo   Triple-Time
       |               |            Style Allegro   Largo Fugue
       |               |            |              |
       i               V            V              i
```

The scheme is more elaborate in BuxWV 149, for the *allegro* section is really a complex of several passages. The first, in basso continuo style, ends with a tentative (plagal) cadence on the tonic; the following two passages, modularly organized, are strongly cadential. Like the modular free ending in the Praeludium in d, the outer parts are inverted in the second passage. Arching over the entire section is a descending line originating in the preceding fugue. Both a powerful link between the two sections and a persuasive force in the *allegro* itself,[185] it is one of the most structurally sophisticated and cogently realized linear constructions in the praeludia.

The *largo* fugue, featuring a subtly derived triple-time version of the first subject, stands alongside the chromatic fugue of the Praeludium in e as Buxtehude's most impressive fugal section in the praeludia. The most stately, even elegaic of Buxtehude's fugues, it has a bold harmonic style and finely-wrought counterpoint.[186] The countersubject makes effective appearances both in the bass and soprano, and with the subject creates the climactic moments of the section. Through a masterfully constructed series of pitch peaks, c''' is eventually reached.[187] The final statement of the subject in the subdominant (the only statement outside the tonic) provides a link to the closing free section. The transition alone, one of Buxtehude's most deft textural modulations, marks the work as one of his best.[188] The closing free section is a virtual ciacona (appearing exclusively in the subdominant) and corresponds to similar structures in the closing free sections of such works as the Toccata in d and the Praeludium in the same key. It is even more integrated into the praeludium than that of the Praeludium in d: the theme, the inverted pedal points, and cadential figures all recall both the ciacona in the opening free section and the modular passages of the *allegro* in the center of the work. As in those works with similar ostinato free endings, and in particular the Praeludium in d, the return to the tonic is postponed until the virtual end of the work.[189]

The linear coherence of the Praeludium is one of the most cogent of any in the praeludia, and its expressivity also ranks it with Buxteude's finest. The web of thematic connections yields a sense of unity unmatched by any other praeludium, while the rise to a climax and subsequent relaxation of tension is masterfully calculated.[190] It does not seem unreasonable, then, to consider this work the *chef d'oeuvre* of the praeludia.

The bulk of the mature works, then, are preserved in the Wagener and Berlin 2681 manuscripts. The Buxtehude praeludia which they contain, however, cannot all be considered to date from that period: two works, BuxWV 143 and 156, seem out of place in the company of the great praeludia, and probably have a significantly earlier origin. The Lowell Mason Codex, on the contrary, appears to be more heavily weighted with earlier works. Not only is it the only source for the two earliest ones, BuxWV 158 and 152, but the other Buxtehude praeludia it contains seem to stem mostly from the middle period. Only BuxWV 142 and 155 can be considered to belong in the ranks of the greatest praeludia. The Wenster Collection, of much smaller size, preserves what appears to be a chronologically fairly consistent group of praeludia whose likely origins are relatively late. The Andreas-Bach-Buch, however, again presents a more varied picture: the two praeludia it contains most probably stem from different chronological periods. The majority of the manuscripts which are important sources for only one or two works do not contain later period praeludia; those works remain concentrated in the Wagener and Berlin 2681 group or else appear in Wenster or the Lowell Mason Codex.[191]

With so little manuscript evidence, actual dates of the praeludia can only be suggested with caution. The early works may have originated as early as the 1650s; the group of relatively early works more probably from the 1660s. With the Praeludium in g, BuxWV 148, known to have been composed before 1675, middle period works like it can probably be assigned an origin in the late 1660s and 1670s. Relatively late works may also stem from the decade of the 1670s. The date of 1684 given to the Toccata in d, BuxWV 155, in the Lowell Mason Codex suggests that the late period works may have originated as late as the first part of that decade.[192]

Even if the manuscripts present a mixed picture, the overall stylistic evolution of the praeludia is still clear. Starting with the works of Tunder and Weckmann as models, their style and content are mimicked in such works as the Praeambulum in a, BuxWV 158, and the Praeludium in a, BuxWV 152. But virtually all others move beyond these works in structural sophistication and expressive content. The influence of the works of Froberger and those of Weckmann in the Italianate style mark a decisive turning point. Buxtehude's own distinctive style is a composite of techniques derived from these composers and elements mastered from the north German style. Already seen in what can be considered relatively early works (such as the Praeludium in e, BuxWV 143, and the Toccata in F, BuxWV 156), an impressive series of compositions which establish Buxtehude's typical procedures follows. These presumably middle-period works include the Praeludia in g, BuxWV 148, in a, BuxWV 153, and two in C, BuxWV 136 and 138. An additional group, all in the major mode and each possessing only one fugal section, contain similar thematic elements and structural characteristics. These works, the Praeludia in C, BuxWV 137, in D, BuxWV 139, in F, BuxWV 145, and the Toccata in F, BuxWV 157, seem to build on the achievements of the middle-period works. A final group of works, including the Praeludia in E, BuxWV 141, in d, BuxWV 140, the Toccata in d, BuxWV 155, and the Praeludia in e, BuxWV 142, in f#, BuxWV 146, and in g, BuxWV 149, demonstrate complete control of multifugal forms. Their accent is on virtuosity, but not just that of the performer. Compositional virtuosity is marked by the creation of increasingly elaborate thematic connections, elegant counterpoint, cogent linear control, and strongly climactic expression. In what may be the last praeludia, the traditional commanding position of the first fugue gives way as a shift in fugal weight from the first to the second fugue redefines the overall shape of the praeludium. These great climactic fugal sections, including the chromatic fugue of the Praeludium in e, BuxWV 142, and the *largo* fugue of the Praeludium in g, BuxWV 149, stand beside the impressive free textures of works such as the Preludium in f#, BuxWV 146, at the summit of Buxtehude's art.

Notes

Introduction

1. Philipp Spitta, ed., *Dietrich Buxtehudes Orgelkompositionen*, 2 vols. (Leipzig: Breitkopf & Härtel, 1875-76). The publication history of the praeludia is discussed further in the first section of the Conclusion.

2. Philipp Spitta, *Johann Sebastian Bach*, 2 vols. (Leipzig: Breitkopf & Härtel, 1873-80). Trans. Clara Bell and J. A. Fuller-Maitland, 3 vols. (London: Novello & Co., 1889; reprint ed., New York: Dover Publications, 1951). See pp. 261-76 (pp. 267-79 in the translation) for his discussion of the praeludia.

3. Philipp Spitta, ed., *Dietrich Buxtehudes Orgelkompositionen*. 2 vols. Leipzig: Breitkopf & Härtel, 1875-76; *Dietrich Buxtehudes Werke für Orgel*. Revised by Max Seiffert. 2 vols. Leipzig: Breitkopf & Härtel, 1903-4; *Ergänzungsband*. Edited by Max Seiffert. Leipzig: Breitkopf & Härtel, 1939; *Dietrich Buxtehude: Orgelwerke*. Preface by Walter Kraft. 4 vols. Wiesbaden: Breitkopf & Härtel, 1952; reprint ed., New York: Edwin F. Kalmus, n.d.

4. Josef Hedar, ed., *Dietrich Buxtehude: Sämtliche Orgelwerke*, 4 vols. (Copenhagen: Wilhelm Hansen, 1952).

5. Josef Hedar, *Dietrich Buxtehudes Orgelwerke* (Stockholm: Nordiska Musikförlaget, 1951; Frankfurt: Wilhelmiana Musikverlag, 1951).

6. The most important being the Wenster and Englehardt Collections at the University of Lund.

7. The Spitta edition, however, is not without value. It presents variant readings that were suppressed by Hedar but which have a certain legitimacy of their own. It is also the only source for two of the praeludia whose manuscripts have been lost. Spitta had access to several other manuscripts lost during World War II, but the contents of these are also preserved in other sources.

8. Klaus Beckmann, ed., *Dietrich Buxtehude: Sämtliche Orgelwerke*, 2 vols. (Wiesbaden: Breitkopf & Härtel, 1971). For a review, see that by Jon Gillock in *Notes: The Quarterly Journal of the Music Library Association* XXXII (December, 1975), pp. 374-77. A concordance of the various editions can be found in the Introduction of this study.

9. For an explanation of his methodology, see the *Einleitung* and *Kritischer Bericht* of his edition; also his "Textkritische Uberlegungen zu Buxtehudes Orgelwerken," *Musik und Kirche* XXXVIII (May-June, 1968), pp. 106-13.

10. The Wenster and Englehardt Collections at the University of Lund are the most important sources which are still in tablature. They contain ten pieces, six of which are unica. The sources are discussed in detail in the first section of the Conclusion.

11. Reflecting the two greatest weaknesses of organ tablature, the errors often concern register and pitches. The letter names a, c, and e are especially easy to confuse in tablature, while the letter names b, d, f, g, and h are usually more distinctive and less likely to be misread. The degree of vagueness that may have existed in Buxtehude's autographs (or whatever manuscripts from which these sources derive), can be, of course, only a matter of speculation.

12. Beckmann has also edited the organ music of Franz Tunder, Johann Adam Reincken, Nicolaus Bruhns, Vincent Lübeck, and other composers following these text-critical methods.

13. Willi Apel, *The History of Keyboard Music to 1700*, trans. and rev. Hans Tischler (Bloomington: Indiana University Press, 1972), p. 610.

14. Richard Crocker, *A History of Musical Style* (New York: McGraw-Hill, 1966), p. 292.

15. Donald Jay Grout, *A History of Western Music*, rev. ed. (New York: W. W. Norton & Co., 1973), p. 375.

16. The details of Bach's visit to Lübeck are too well known to warrant repetition here.

17. The degree of revelation varies from work to work. Beckmann may well be credited with literally saving the Toccata in d, BuxWV 155; the reading in the Hedar version reflects its unusually corrupt state in the Lowell Mason Codex. The Toccata in F, BuxWV 156, is also peculiar enough in its details in previous editions as to discourage performance. But in such cases we no longer have to argue that idiosyncracy rather than clumsiness is responsible for the overall impression of *bizarrerie* at the local level.

18. One further work, the Praeludium in B♭, BuxWV 154, is a fragment.

19. Georg Karstädt, ed., *Thematisch-systematisches Verzeichnis der musikalischen Werke von Dietrich Buxtehude* (Wiesbaden: Breitkopf & Härtel, 1974).

20. Spitta, ed., *Dietrich Buxtehudes Orgelkompositionen*; Spitta, ed., *Dietrich Buxtehudes Werke für Orgel*.

21. Philipp Spitta, ed., *Dietrich Buxtehude: Orgelwerke*, rev. Max Seiffert, with a Preface by Walter Kraft, 4 vols. (Wiesbaden: Breitkopf & Härtel, 1952; reprint ed., New York: Edwin F. Kalmus, n.d.).

22. Hedar, ed., *Dietrich Buxtehude: Sämtliche Orgelwerke*.

23. Beckmann, ed., *Dietrich Buxtehude: Sämtliche Orgelwerke*.

24. Added in Seiffert, ed., *Ergänzungsband*.

25. There are two versions. Seiffert (in 1939) conflated the two; that reading appears in the Spitta-Seiffert-Kraft edition as well. Hedar and Beckmann present the versions separately.

26. A fragment.

27. Karstädt, ed., *Thematisch-systematisches Verzeichnis*.

28. Praeludium, or the related term Preludio, is the name by which these works are generally called in the manuscripts. In place of the plural *praeludien*, used, for example, by Beckman, *praeludia* has been prefered. The latter term can also be found in the current

literature; see Kerala J. Snyder, "Buxtehude's Organ Music: Drama without Words," *The Musical Times* CXX (June, 1979), pp. 517-21.

29. Some scholars have prefered toccata as the generic title; for example, Hedar, Apel, and Powell. See chapter 1.

30. One chorale partita, in the form of a dance suite, also survives; it is probably for harpsichord or clavichord rather than organ. A fragment of another chorale setting also survives.

31. There are four such works, two praeludia and two toccatas. The use of pedals in the praeludia as a whole is not nearly as clear in most of the manuscripts as it would appear to be from the editions. However, these four works have still been omitted from this study.

32. These include four canzonas, five canzonettas, and three fugas.

33. These stylistic categories, however, are here substantially refined.

34. Felix Salzer, *Structural Hearing: Tonal Coherence in Music*, 2 vols. (New York: Charles Boni, 1952; reprint ed., New York: Dover Publications, 1962), vol. 1, p. 23.

35. Such an avenue has been used, for example, by Ursula Kirkendale, "The Source for Bach's *Musical Offering*," *Journal of the American Musicological Society* XXXIII (Spring, 1980), pp. 88-141.

36. Lena Jacobson, "Musical Rhetoric in Buxtehude's Free Organ Works," *The Organ Yearbook* XIII (1982), pp. 60-79.

37. "Buxtehude and His Contemporaries: Pushing the Limits of Meantone," a conference held at Wellesley College under the auspices of The Westfield Center for Early Keyboard Studies, June, 1984.

38. Kenneth George Powell, "The North German Organ Toccata (1650-1710)" (D.M.A. dissertation, University of Illinois, 1969), p. 101.

Chapter 1

1. It is also a baroque view, to the extent that *stylus fantasticus*, *stylus motecticus*, etc., can be considered texture-oriented classifications. See Friedrich Wilhelm Riedel, *Quellenkundliche Beiträge zur Geschichte der Musik für Tasteninstrumente in der 2. Hälfte des 17. Jahrhunderts*, Schriften des Landesinstituts für Musikforschung, Kiel, vol. 10 (Kassel: Bärenreiter-Verlag, 1960), pp 23-26.

2. Willi Apel, *The History of Keyboard Music to 1700*, trans. and rev. Hans Tischler (Bloomington: Indiana University Press, 1972), p. 613.

3. Following Apel, *History of Keyboard Music*; Donald J. Grout, *A History of Western Music*, rev. ed. (New York: W. W. Norton & Co., 1973); Crocker, *A History of Musical Style* (New York: McGraw-Hill, 1966); and Kenneth George Powell, "The North German Organ Toccata (1650-1710)," (D.M.A. dissertation, University of Illinois, 1969) who all follow Hedar, *Dietrich Buxtehudes Orgelwerke* (Stockholm: Nordiska Musikförlaget, 1951; Frankfurt: Wilhemiana Musikverlag, 1951).

4. Grout, *History of Western Music*, p. 376.

5. Hedar, *Dietrich Buxtehudes Orgelwerke*, pp. 148-51. Hedar includes one other important stylistic feature, the use of variation in the derivation of succeeding fugal subjects,

Notes for Chapter 1

into his method of classification. (Thematic variation is discussed in chapter 4 of this study.)

6. In Hedar's words, "Die Grenze zwischen ihnen in mehreren Fällen schwer zu ziehen sein mag." Ibid., p. 148.

7. BuxWV 144, which Hedar places in his second group, and BuxWV 139, which he places in his third, could both be understood as belonging in the first group.

8. Apel, *History of Keyboard Music*, p. 613.

9. Ibid.

10. Powell, "North German Organ Toccata." Powell's thesis surveys a large part of the north German repertory, not just the works of Buxtehude.

11. Ibid., p. 28.

12. Ibid. See his table 5, pp. 29-31.

13. Ibid., p. 62.

14. In the present study, fugatos are considered as a subgroup of fugal sections and not as interludes.

15. Less common types of elaboration include arpeggiation and overlegato articulation. Overlegato articulation is closely associated with arpeggiation, the important difference being that in the overlegato style a note of the chord is held as the other notes of the chord are added one by one or repeated. The resulting accumulation of sound is especially effective on the organ. The difference in articulation between simple and overlegato arpeggiation has been made clearer recently through the work of Harald Vogel.

16. Mm. 48-50. The last fugue of BuxWV 141 ends with a similar repetition, beginning in m. 104, which also hinges on the submediant.

17. Mm. 74-78. The eighth-note rests in all the parts between the repetitions suggest the possibility of changing registration, perhaps for an echo effect.

18. See, for example, Buxtehude's sequential *tour de force* beginning in m. 108 of BuxWV 155 (following the Beckmann edition).

19. Apel, *History of Keyboard Music*, pp. 614-15.

20. See BuxWV 140, mm. 112-16. Further examples can be found in BuxWV 155, mm. 132-35, and in BuxWV 146, mm. 119-20. In the concluding passage of the opening section of BuxWV 143, a similar but slightly more complex figure, g-d#-e, is repeated four times, then three times more, centered on the dominant, e-A#-B (mm. 16-21).

21. The other two are found in BuxWV 137, where the ciacona is the last section, and in BuxWV 149, where it is the opening section.

22. The section begins at m. 113. Apel has suggested that mm. 115-16 are missing what would be the second statement of the ground bass theme; see his *History of Keyboard Music*, p. 615, fig. 654. It should be noted that the first statement of the theme, in mm. 113-14, appears unaccompanied, an effect which Bach employed to begin the Passacaglia in c, BWV 582. That idea is occasionally credited to Bach as the three entirely ground bass pieces of Buxtehude (BuxWV 159, 160, and 161) begin immediately with accompanimental figures.

23. Following Hedar and Powell.

Notes for Chapter 1   305

24. See. p. 10.

25. See table 5 in Powell, "North German Organ Toccata," pp. 29-31 (for Buxtehude's works, pp. 29-30), which gives a breakdown of these works in a similar fashion, but without distinguishing between varieties of free and fugal texture.

26. The opening flourish has also been called the *passaggio*, following Johann Mattheson in *Der vollkommene Capellmeister* (Hamburg: 1739; reprint ed., Kassel: Bärenreiter, 1954). For quotation of the passage, see George B. Stauffer, *The Organ Preludes of Johann Sebastian Bach*, Studies in Musicology, no. 27 (Ann Arbor: U.M.I. Research Press, 1980), p. 186.

27. The structural role of the opening flourish is discussed in chapter 6.

28. Other reasons for this grouping, including harmony, expression, and middleground structure are discussed in chapters 2, 5, and 8, respectively.

29. The coordination of textural form and harmony will be discussed in chapter 2.

30. See, for example, BuxWV 139, mm. 86-87.

31. See, for example, BuxWV 136, mm. 61-62.

32. See especially mm. 138-39. Snyder has also pointed to this transition, noting how "the second fugure melts seamlessly into the final homophonic section." [Kerala J. Snyder, "Buxtehude's Organ Music: Drama without Words," *The Musical Tones* CXX (June, 1979), p. 519.]

33. See, for example, BuxWV 151, mm. 61-62.

34. See Werner Breig, ed., *Heinrich Scheidemann: Orgelwerke*, 3 vols. (Kassel: Bärenreiter, 1971), vol. 3. See also Werner Breig, *Die Orgelwerke von Heinrich Scheidemann*, Beihefte zum Archiv für Musikwissenschaft, vol. 3 (Wiesbaden: Franz Steiner Velag, 1967). The works list (WV) established by Breig is used here.

35. Johann Mattheson, *Grundelage einer Ehren-Pforte* (Hamburg: 1740). Ed. Max Schneider (Berlin: Kommissions-Verlag von L. Liepmannssohn, 1910; reprint ed., Kassel: Bärenreiter-Verlag, 1969), s.v. "Weckmann."

36. See particularly BuxWV 137, mm. 12-22.

37. See Klaus Beckmann, ed., *Franz Tunder: Sämtliche Orgelwerke* (Wiesbaden: Breitkopf & Härtel, 1974).

38. Ibid., #5.

39. See Max Seiffert, ed., *Matthias Weckmann: 14 Präludien, Fugen und Toccaten*, Organum, Fourth series, no. 3 (Cologne: Kistner & Siegel & Co., n.d.).

40. For the details of Weckmann's association with Froberger, see Apel, *History of Keyboard Music*, p. 598.

41. The close connections between Buxtehude and Weckmann have been described in Kerla J. Snyder, "Dietrich Buxtehude's Studies in Learned Counterpoint," *Journal of the American Musicological Society* XXXIII (Fall, 1980), pp. 560-63.

42. Apel, *History of Keyboard Music*, p. 602.

43. Ibid.

44. Seiffert, ed., *Weckmann: 14 Präludien*, #12.

45. G. B. Sharp has pointed to the ending of the Toccata in e (Seiffert, ed., *Weckmann: 14 Präludien*, #11) as anticipatory of Buxtehude's style. See his "Matthias Weckmann: 1619-74," *The Musical Times* CXV (December, 1974), p. 1040.

46. Pointed out by Hedar, *Dietrich Buxtehudes Orgelwerke*, p. 185. See Weckmann's Toccata in d (Seiffert, ed., *Weckmann: 14 Präludien*, #9), beginning at m. 21.

47. Weckmann's authorship of all but one of the six toccatas and all five of the canzonas attributed to him by Seiffert has recently been questioned. These works are preserved in the Lüneburg Tablatures, KN 147. See Bärbel Roth, "Zur Echtheitsfrage der Matthias Weckmann zugeschriebenen Klavierwerke ohne Cantus firmus," *Acta Musicologica* XXXVI (January-March, 1964), pp. 31-36. Even though they are preserved anonymously in KN 147, Apel considers them to be authentic. See Apel, *History of Keyboard Music*, p. 809, note 42. Whether or not these works are actually by Weckmann, they provide important examples of free keyboard music immediately before Buxtehude. For the purposes of this study, they will be referred to as Weckmann's works. Weckmann's authorship of the Toccata in d (Seiffert, ed., *Weckmann: 14 Präludien*, #9), whose relationship with BuxWV 139 has been noted above, has not been questioned. That work is preserved in KN 207.

48. For a summary of the free organ works of Scheidemann, see the Preface to Breig, ed., *Scheidemann: Orgelwerke*, vol. 3.

49. Breig, ed., *Scheidemann: Orgelwerke*, vol. 3, #8. Like most of Scheidemann's praeambula, this one is preserved in the Lüneburg Tablatures, KN 207. It can also be found in Uppsala Ms. 408. The work can be considered more progressive than most due to its large size (58 mm.), clarity of formal articulation, and the unusual liveliness of its imitative section.

50. They are preserved in the Lüneburg Tablatures, KN 207.

51. Beckmann, ed., *Tunder: Orgelwerke*, #1. In the second part of the fugal section, the subject appears in diminution.

52. Ibid., #2.

53. Ibid., #3. In the second part of the fugal section, the subject appears in diminution.

54. Ibid., #4. The imitative passage in the fugal section is an episode; the subject appears in diminution within a modular texture in the closing free section.

55. Seiffert, ed., *Weckmann: 14 Präludien*, #1, #2, and #3 respectively. The Fantasia is preserved in the Lüneburg Tablatures, KN 209, and the Praeambulum in KN 207. The Fuga is found in the organ tablature, II.2.51, of the Leipzig Stadtbibliothek.

56. See John R. Shannon, *Organ Literature of the Seventeenth Century: A Study of its Styles* (Raleigh: Sunbury, 1978), p. 219.

57. The preserved canzonas of Scheidemann and Tunder are small-scale works in comparison to Weckmann's Fuga. Only this one is on a par with the praeludium in size and use of the pedals.

58. This technique will be discussed in chapter 4.

59. This is achieved primarily through nontonic sectional articulations; see chapter 2.

60. See Max Seiffert, ed., *Anonymi der norddeutschen Schule: 6 Praeludien und Fugen*, Organum, Fourth series, no. 10 (Cologne: Kistner & Siegel & Co., n.d.), #4 and #5. Both of these works are found in KN 207.

61. Seiffert, ed., *Anonymi*, #4. Seiffert suggests that this work is by Weckmann. See the Preface to Seiffert, ed., *Anonymi*. Hedar has suggested Tunder or Böhm. See Hedar, *Dietrich Buxtehudes Orgelwerke*, pp. 137-38. The various conjectures as to authorship are summarized in the Preface of Beckmann, ed., *Tunder: Orgelwerke*.

62. Seiffert, ed., *Anonymi*, #5. Seiffert suggests this work is by Tunder. See the Preface to Seiffert, ed., *Anonymi*. The extremely close relationship between the opening free section of this work and that of the Praeambulum of Weckmann would indicate that Weckmann is a more likely candidate.

63. Apel, *History of Keyboard Music*, p. 602.

64. Seiffert, ed., *Weckmann: 14 Präludien*, #9.

65. The modeling relationship between these two works as regards the sequential passages has already been pointed out. See p. 21.

66. Seiffert, ed., *Weckmann: 14 Präludien*, #13.

67. Hedar points out that the subject and answer are in canon at the fifth, which he compares to a similar case in Scheidemann's Praeambulum in d, WV 35. (*Dietrich Buxtehudes Orgelwerke*, p. 171.)

68. In BuxWV 158, see the passage beginning at m. 78; in BuxWV 152, that beginning at m. 71.

69. The chronology of the praeludia is discussed in detail in the Conclusion.

70. This work is matched in this regard only by the Praeludium in e, the so-called Great, by Buxtehude's student, Nicolaus Bruhns. See Klaus Beckmann, ed., *Nicolaus Bruhns: Sämtliche Orgelwerke* (Wiesbaden: Breitkopf & Härtel, 1972), #1.

71. See, for example, BuxWV 136.

72. This aspect of BuxWV 140 is discussed in the Conclusion.

Chapter 2

1. For discussion of seventeenth-century harmony see: Delbert M. Beswick, "The Problem of Tonality in 17th Century Music" (Ph.D. dissertation, University of North Carolina, 1951); Robert W. Wienpahl, "The Emergence of Tonality" (Ph.D. dissertation, University of California at Los Angeles, 1953); and Carl Dahlhaus, *Untersuchungen über die Entstehung der harmonischen Tonalität*, Saarbrücker Studien zur Musikwissenschaft, vol. 2 (Kassel: Bärenreiter, 1968).

2. Willi Apel, *The History of Keyboard Music to 1700*, trans. and rev. Hans Tischler (Bloomington: Indiana University Press, 1972), pp. 614-15.

3. Kenneth George Powell, "The North German Organ Toccata (1650-1710)," (D.M.A. dissertation, University of Illinois, 1969), pp. 44-45.

4. John R. Shannon, *Organ Literature of the Seventeenth Century: A Study of its Styles* (Raleigh: Sunbury, 1978), p. 226. A short example from BuxWV 153 (wrongly labeled Praeambulum in A—it is the Praeludium in a), follows with Roman numerals and inversions indicated.

5. Occasionally an entire passage or section is chromatic; this is a special effect, created by the use of a chromatic subject or subject in a fugue or fugato.

Notes for Chapter 2

6. See Powell, "North German Organ Toccata," pp.44-46.

7. This cadential decoration was employed by other north German organists, especially Tunder. See his setting of "Jesus Christus, unser Heiland," the conclusion of versus 3. (Beckmann, ed., *Tunder: Orgelwerke*, #11.)

8. BuxWV 136, 138, 139 (twice), 141, 142, and 153.

9. See BuxWV 138 and 139. In BuxWV 139, the 5-♯4-5 is used as the beginning of the fugue subject. In BuxWV 142, the 4-♯4-5 of the cadence of the opening free section is echoed at the end of the subject of the first fugue.

10. Schenker called such areas a "Stufe," usually translated as "scale-step." See Heinrich Schenker, *Harmony*, ed. and annotated Oswald Jonas, trans. Elisabeth Mann Borgese (Chicago: University of Chicago Press, 1954; reprint ed., Cambridge: MIT Press, 1973).

11. Dominant pedals are most frequently used to end the opening free section; they are less frequently found at the end of fugal sections.

12. Most dominant pedals are two mm. long. For larger examples see BuxWV 145, mm. 34-38, and BuxWV 138, mm. 16-20. The dominant pedal point in BuxWV 156, mm. 86-88, is not the longest, but has the most highly elaborate prolongational devices.

13. See especially BuxWV 146, mm. 27-28 (e♯'-e♯"), and BuxWV 145, mm. 34-38 (a"-a').

14. Similar but larger examples can be found in BuxWV 156, mm. 133-40, and BuxWV 157, mm. 85-91.

15. Following the Beckmann edition. The Hedar and Spitta-Seiffert editions, which more closely follow the manuscript, the Lowell Mason Codex (Yale University, LM 5056), conclude the flourish on g'. However, this manuscript, the only source for the Toccata, is one of the most garbled of all the sources in its reading of this work, and Beckmann's version can be prefered. Another example of the same g"-D juxtaposition can be found in BuxWV 139, mm. 103-4.

16. This type of closing tonic pedal, $(IV--)I^{6-5}_{4-3}$, is the basis for the large pedal points which close BuxWV 139, 146, and 153. The dramatic effect is greatest in BuxWV 139, which, like BuxWV 155, juxtaposes g" and D to begin the tonic pedal; however, in the former, the winding down from this dramatic/registral highpoint is much more extensive.

17. See BuxWV 143, 146, 148, 150, and 156. As was noted in chapter 1, the pedal point is not the usual way Buxtehude constructs an opening free section.

18. The closest approximation of a genuine subdominant pedal occurs at the opening of the subdominant area in BuxWV 146, mm. 111-13. Other notable examples can be found in BuxWV 139, mm. 95-103, BuxWV 146, mm. 111-20, BuxWV 149, mm. 142-55, and BuxWV 155, mm. 127-36.

19. See the example from BuxWV 140, above, where the repeated progression is really only an oscillation between a chord and its dominant.

20. See chapter 7 for a detailed discussion of the first fugues; chapter 8 for those in the remaining sections. Only rarely are subdominant answers employed or implied. The first fugal section of BuxWV 143 answers its subject (E-D-D♯-E) with a tonal answer that tilts strongly towards the subdominant (B-G-G♯-A). The only true subdominant answers, however, are found in both the fugal sections of BuxWV 158, and the first fugue of BuxWV 152.

21. Other fugues continue in a similar manner, but with an added entry or two in other keys. The most frequent choices for nontonic entries are the dominant and the mediant. Entries of the subject or answer can also be found in the subdominant; the submediant and the subtonic are far less frequently used.

22. The largest exposition outside the tonic occurs in BuxWV 153, in III; smaller expositions consisting of only three entries are found in BuxWV 150, in V, and BuxWV 152, in III and IV, and BuxWV 155, in III.

23. The four exceptions are BuxWV 149, 155, 156, and 158. BuxWV 152, while best understood as phrygian on a, begins and ends with E-major harmonies; the cadence of its first fugue on A-major thus gives the impression that it, too, ends the first fugue with a nontonic cadence. The modal harmonic scheme of this work, however, suggests it be omitted from such considerations.

24. See also BuxWV 138, 144, 145, 147, 151, 153, and 157. See chapter 1 for key to diagrams.

25. See also BuxWV 139, 143, 148, and 150.

26. See the second section of chapter 1 for a more complete discussion of Buxtehude's immediate predecessors.

27. See especially the opening free section of his Praeludium in g (Beckmann, ed., *Tunder: Orgelwerke*, #2), in which V/iv is made to carry a great deal of expressive weight. The large role given iv in the opening free section by Tunder was abandoned by Buxtehude.

28. Seiffert, ed., *Weckmann: 14 Präludien*, #3.

29. Seiffert, ed., *Anonymi*, #5.

30. See, for example, Weckmann's Toccata in e, mm. 22-27 (Seiffert, ed., *Weckmann: 14 Präludien*, #11). While Weckmann introduced canzona-style fugue subjects into the praeludium (most noticeably in his Praeambulum in d), he did not incorporate the tonicization chains also characteristic of the Italian style into the praeludium.

31. The praeludium tradition here includes also those works entitled praeambulum (Scheidemann and Weckmann), while the toccata tradition includes those works in the Froberger style (most notably Weckmann).

32. The degree to which these sections can be considered codas is considered in chapters 8 and 9.

33. See Weckmann's Fantasia in d, mm. 91-102 of which anticipate the actual subdominant pedal of mm. 103-7. See also the anonymous Praeludium in G, beginning in m. 103, for a similar construction (Seiffert, ed., *Weckmann: Präludien*, #1, and Seiffert, ed., *Anonymi*, #4, respectively).

34. See especially mm. 57-60 of the Tunder Praeludium (Beckmann, ed., *Tunder: Orgelwerke*, #2) and ms. 111-16 of BuxWV 140.

35. While Weckmann's Fantasia in d anticipates in its figuration the ending of BuxWV 155, Buxtehude places Weckmann's subdominant figuration over a tonic pedal. Compare the passage beginning at m. 103 of the Fantasia with that beginning at m. 137 in BuxWV 155.

36. See BuxWV 165.

37. See the anonymous Praeludium in F, which employs an unusual number of pedal points in its opening free section, including a large dominant pedal to prepare the cadence.

Large-scale pedal points can be found in the opening free sections of BuxWV 143, 146, 150, and 156.

38. See Scheidemann's Praeambula WV 30, 33, 35, 36, 40, and 73 for examples of a tonic cadence for the opening section; see WV 31, 32, 34, and 39 for dominant cadences. The Praeambulum in e, WV 38, which, significantly, begins with an E-major chord, cadences on IV; the other praeambula evade a clear cadence to mark the end of the opening section and the beginning of the next one.

39. See, for example, the Praeambula WV 30, 34, and 36.

40. The latter can be understood as a heightening of the subdominant. See his Praeludia in F and g (Beckmann, ed., *Tunder: Orgelwerke*, #1 and #2, respectively) for cadences on IV; and in g (Ibid., #3 and #4) for cadences on V/IV. The dominant of the subdominant is, of course, the tonic major chord; however, these articulations take place in a context which suggests these chords are elaborations of IV.

41. See diagrams of these works in chapter 1.

42. See diagrams of these works in chapter 1. Probably because the Praeludium in F has only one fugue, Seiffert suggested Tunder as its composer; the opening free section, however, strongly suggests Weckmann's Praeambulum in d. See note 62 in chapter 1.

43. See chapter 1 for a more complete discussion of these genres.

44. Seiffert, ed., *Weckmann: 14 Präludien*, #11.

45. The use of a dominant cadence at this point in the form in BuxWV 149, 155, 156, and 158, was discussed earlier in this chapter. (See note 23.)

46. This was also an important innovation for the later development of the "prelude and fugue," in which each section is not only comparable in structural stability (that is, both are tonally closed, I-----I), but are structurally independent. The degree of structural independence achieved by Buxtehude in the sections of his praeludia is explored in Part II.

47. Further support for this argument through structural analysis is presented in Part II.

Chapter 3

1. A useful distinction between rhythm and meter is that given in Andrew Imbrie, "Metrical Ambiguity in Beethoven," in *Beethoven Studies*, ed. Alan Tyson (New York: W. W. Norton & Co., 1973), p. 53; "Rhythm is the patterning or proportional arrangement of sounds and silences with respect to their durations, while meter is the measurement of the distances between points in time."

2. This is chiefly due to the fact that the change of meter in these works is closely associated with thematic variation, a twin process inherited by Buxtehude from the variation canzonas of Frescobaldi, Froberger, and Weckmann. See the next section of this chapter and also chapter 4.

3. On the relationship of rhythm and tonal motion see Robert P. Morgan, "The Theory and Analysis of Tonal Rhythm," *The Musical Quarterly* LXIV (October, 1978), pp. 435-73.

4. The Passacaglia in d, BuxWV 161, handles changes of key in a more convincing way and its overall structure is considerably more elegant.

5. Only two works provide an exception: BuxWV 136, which ends in 12/8, and BuxWV 153, which turns from common time to 3/4 several measures before the final cadence. In BuxWV 150, the last measure—which contains only the last chord of the work—changes from 3/2 to common time. This notational peculiarity has no actual musical significance. It does indicate, however, that Buxtehude's habit of ending in common time was strong enough to lead to notational curiosities.

6. See BuxWV 142, 148, 149, 150, and 152 for 3/2 fugues; BuxWV 140 and 143 have 3/4 fugues, as does BuxWV 155 (following the Beckmann edition, in which the 3/4 is editorial). Fugues in 6/4 appear in BuxWV 153 and 158.

7. See in particular BuxWV 142, mm. 98–100, and BuxWV 149, mm. 154–55.

8. Harald Vogel has suggested the use of proportional relationships between these two meters.

9. See the 12/8 passages in the opening free section of BuxWV 145, and the 12/8 passages in the opening and second free sections of BuxWV 156. See also Kenneth George Powell, "The North German Organ Toccata (1650–1710)," (D.M.A. dissertation, University of Illinois 1969) p. 73.

10. See the first fugue of BuxWV 149, for the use of ₵. In the Beckmann edition, ₵ is repeated for the following *allegro*. Surely this is a misprint; Hedar gives C for the *allegro*. The two instances of 2/4 and 6/8 indicate only half measures of C and 12/8 respectively. (BuxWV 162, for manuals without pedal, however, has an extensive passage in 6/8.)

11. Hedar attempts to bar the passage in strict common time, while Beckmann, trying the same thing, departs even farther from the manuscript. The problem, of course, is that the music is not strongly metrical. The quality of the manuscript reading in the Lowell Mason Codex (Yale University, LM 5056), its only source, deteriorates badly towards the end. The manuscript is discussed in more detail in the Conclusion. The opening page of the Toccata in the Lowell Mason Codex has been reproduced in Paul Henry Lang, "Buxtehude: Complete Organ Works," *The Musical Quarterly* XLV (July, 1959), facing p. 418.

12. See, for example, BuxWV 137, in which the first eleven measures evade a clear articulation of common time. The barrings are as arbitrary as those of BuxWV 155. Only with the imitative passage beginning in m. 12 does the meter in BuxWV 137 become really clear.

13. BuxWV 143 presents two examples: mm. 16–20, notated in common time, are really in 3/4; mm. 51–56, also notated in common time, move in seven-beat phrases.

14. In the words of Edward T. Cone, "On some level this metric principle . . . must give way to a more organic rhythmic principle that supports the melodic and harmonic shape of the phrase and justifies its acceptance as a formal unit." *Musical Form and Musical Performance* (New York: W. W. Norton & Co., 1968), p. 26. Andrew Imbrie has challenged this view in "Metrical Ambiguity in Beethoven," *Beethoven Studies*; ed. Alan Tyson (New York: W. W. Norton & Co., 1973) pp. 52–53. Imbrie suggests that meter can be flexible at higher levels and still be meter.

15. In music of later styles, especially the classical style, metrical hierarchies are apt to penetrate much higher into the structure of a work.

16. A ciacona is one such example.

17. See the opening free section of BuxWV 142, especially mm. 8-12.
18. Note the change of figuration at m. 105, the measure after the pedal's entrance. This suggests the beginning of a metrical group.
19. See the second section of chapter 1 for a more complete discussion of Buxtehude's immediate predecessors.
20. See chapter 4. Also see Powell, "North German Organ Toccata," pp. 84-85.
21. Werner Breig, ed., *Heinrich Scheidemann: Orgelwerke* (Kassel: Bärenreiter, 1971) vol. 3, #18. Of the two canzonas of Scheidemann, the one in G, WV 74, does not have a triple-time section, but it also appears in a variant reading under the title of Fantasia, which is generically a more apt description. See chapter 1 for key to diagrams.
22. Klaus Beckmann, ed., *Franz Tunder: Sämtliche Orgelwerke*, 2 vols (Weisbaden: Breitkopf & Härtel, 1971), #6.
23. Max Seiffert, ed., *Matthias Weckmann: 14 Präludien, Fugen, und Toccaten*, Organum, Fourth series, no. 3 (Cologne: Kistner & Siegel & Co., n.d.), #4-#8.
24. Ibid., #1-#3, respectively. See chapter 1 for a more complete discussion of these works and their stylistic traits. A similar example can be found in the anonymous Praeludium in G (Seiffert, ed., *Anonymi*, #4). (See the illustration on page 24.)
25. Seiffert, ed., *Weckmann: 14 Präludien*, #9-#14.
26. Ibid., #10.
27. Ibid., #13.
28. Ibid., #11.
29. Breig, ed., *Scheidemann: Orgelwerke*, vol. 3, #7.
30. Beckmann, ed., *Tunder, Orgelwerke*, #4.
31. Breig, ed., *Scheidemann: Orgelwerke*, vol. 3, #6.
32. Beckmann, ed., *Tunder: Orgelwerke*, #3.
33. The opening of the anonymous Praeludium in F (Seiffert, ed., *Anonymi*, #5), is very similar. It has phrases of fifteen, seven, ten, and fourteen measures.
34. Seiffert, ed., *Weckmann: 14 Präludien*, #11.
35. Beckmann, ed., *Tunder: Orgelwerke*, #3.
36. Ibid., #4.
37. Ibid., #1.
38. See BuxWV 137, illustrated above.
39. Edward T. Cone, *Musical Form and Musical Performance* (New York: W. W. Norton & Co., 1968), pp. 59-62.

Chapter 4

1. Isolated examples also occur in the works of Scheidemann and Tunder. See the third section of this chapter.
2. Willi Apel, *The History of Keyboard Music to 1700*, trans. and rev. Hans Tischler (Bloomington: Indiana University Press, 1972), p. 615. Josef Hedar's analyses are found

in his *Dietrich Buxtehudes Orgelwerke* (Stockholm: Nordiska Musikförlaget, 1951; Frankfurt: Wilhemiana Musikverlag, 1951). Hans-Jacob Pauly agrees with Hedar. See his *Die Fude in den Orgelwerken Dietrich Buxtehudes*, Kölner Beiträge zur Musikforschung, vol. 31 (Regensburg: Gustav Bosse Verlag, 1964), p. 144. See also Kenneth George Powell, "The North German Organ Toccata 1650–1710" (D.M.A. dissertation, University of Illinois, 1969), p. 42.

3. Powell, "North German Organ Toccata," pp. 36–44.

4. Especially BuxWV 141, 142, 146, 148, 151, and 156. For some of these, Powell admits that "a possibility of thematic variation exists." (Ibid., p. 42).

5. See Powell, "North German Organ Toccata," p. 53, Example 10. His comments on this example, on pp. 42–44, are as follows: "Example 10 gives four fugue subjects randomly chosen from all the minor fugue subjects, transposed into g minor. One has to admit that there is as much relationship between all four of these subjects as there is between the two subjects in example 11 which are from the same toccata, and which Pauly cites as an example of thematic variation. [Pauly, *Die Fuge in den Orgelwerken Dietrich Buxtehudes*, pp. 144–45.] These examples show that we should not assume an intentional thematic relationship between two fugue subjects unless the relationship is an obvious one."

6. Ibid., p. 55.

7. See John R. Shannon, *Organ Literature of the Seventeenth Century: A Study of its Styles* (Raleigh: Sunbury, 1978), p. 220.

8. Ibid.

9. Apel, *History of Keyboard Music*, p. 602. The numbering of Weckmann's works is that of Seiffert, ed., *Weckmann: 14 Präludien*.

10. Apel, *History of Keyboard Music*, p. 615.

11. Though they are hardly the "wretched scraps" of Harvey Grace's characterization. See Harvey Grace, *The Organ Works of Bach* (London: Novello & Co., 1922), p. 17. (See Powell, "North German Organ Toccata," p. 54.)

12. See the second section of chapter 1.

13. The D-B♭ which opens the second subject (and replaces the opening G-D of the first subject) can be understood to derive from the D-(C)-B♭ of the first subject which appears as the opening idea of the *allegro* section which follows the first fugue. See the second section of this chapter.

14. There is hardly a fugal section in any of Buxtehude's praeludia with less reliance on its actual subject than this one. The second fugal section, however, contributes several important new motives to the work. See the second section of this chapter.

15. It is also plausibly related to the 1-3-1 pattern in the imitative passage of the opening free section which is also in 12/8.

16. The unusual factor here is that the fugato passage in the opening free section has in it the thematic material from which the remaining fugal subjects are derived.

17. Two of his multifugal works for keyboard without pedal parts, however, seem to avoid thematic variation. They are BuxWV 163 and 176.

18. As was discussed in chapter 2, the use of a cadence decorated with the sharped fourth degree to end the opening free section usually influences the coming fugal subject. In

BuxWV 141, a similar kind of influence was noted between the first fugue and the following free section. Such techniques, however, are a minor means of estabishing thematic links between sections.

19. See chapter 1 for key to diagrams.
20. M. 15 reflects a change recommended by Beckmann: e″ for c″ in the first tenor, beats 1-2 (see the *Nachtrag* to vol. 1 of his edition). Stauffer has suggested a link between the opening free section and the fugal subjects of BuxWV 142. (*Organ Preludes of Bach*, pp. 128-29). The thematic relationship between the opening motive of BuxWV 155 and the fugal subjects of that work has been noted in Lena Jacobson, "Musical Rhetoric in Buxtehude's Free Organ Words," *The Organ Yearbook* XIII (1982), p. 64.
21. This same figure also links the opening free section and the first fugue in both BuxWV 137 and 139. In BuxWV 137, the figure first appears at the cadence of the opening free section (m. 35); it is then made the cadential figure of the fugal subject. In BuxWV 139, it appears again in the cadence of the opening free section (m. 20) and in the fugal subject which follows.
22. In the closing free section see through m. 103. The quarter-note bass line in diminution (in eighth-note motion) also plays a large role beginning in m. 108, and particularly in mm. 114-18.
23. See mm. 13-19 in the opening free section; clearly heard as a development of that passage is the return of descending scalar motion in eighth notes in the imitative section, especially mm. 58-60.
24. The Spitta edition gives G as the second as well as the first note of the ciacona theme: G-G-c-d-e♭-c-d. Hedar and Beckmann give G-B♭-c . . . The ciacona has been the subject of several text studies; see Alfred Dürr, "Noch ein Buxtehude-Problem," *Musik and Kirche* XXVI (May-June, 1956), pp. 122-24, and Klaus Beckmann, "Textkritische Uberlegungen zu Buxtehudes Orgelwerken," *Musik und Kirche* XXXVIII (May-June, 1968), pp. 106-13.
25. The cut-time signature for the *allegro* in the Beckmann edition is surely a misprint; Hedar and other editions give common time.
26. So too does the inverted b♭' pedal point. See the last variation of the ciacona in the opening free section and mm. 68-73 of the *allegro*.
27. See the second section of chapter 1 for a more complete discussion of Buxtehude's immediate predecessors. See chapter 3 for a discussion of triple-time sections. (Only the free works are under consideration here; thematic variation is also an aspect of works based on chorales.) Simple diminution, the most elementary kind of thematic variation, appears in several free works of this repertory. See the Praeambulum by Jacob Praetorius (1586-1651) in Max Seiffert, ed., *Orgel-Meister I*, Organum, Fourth series, no. 2 (Lippstadt: Kistner & Siegel & Co., n.d.), #3. (This example is mentioned by Powell, "North German Organ Toccata," p. 82.) Similar techniques can be observed in Tunder's Praeludium in g (Klaus Beckmann, ed., *Franz Tunder: Samtliche Orgelwerke* (Wiesbaden: Breitkopf & Härtel, 1974), #4. Buxtehude avoided such a simple approach to thematic variation in his praeludia.
28. Werner Breig, ed., *Heinrich Scheidemann: Orgelwerke*, vol. 3 (Kassel: Bärenreiter, 1971), #18.
29. A third fugal section follows, with a subject which begins with a rhythmic pattern and also a triadic figure similar to the first subject.

30. Beckmann, ed., *Tunder: Orgelwerke*, #6.
31. Seiffert, ed., *Weckmann: 14 Präludien*, #3.
32. Ibid., #1.
33. Ibid., #2.
34. Max Seiffert, ed., *Anonymi der norddeutschen Schule: 6 Praeludien und Fugen*, Organum, Fourth series, no. 10 (Cologne: Kistner & Siegel & Co., n.d.), #4.
35. See Powell, "North German Organ Toccata," pp. 82-84.
36. Seiffert, ed., *Weckmann: 14 Präludien*, #10 and #11, respectively.
37. Ibid., #7; its thematic material closely resembles that of the Toccata in d discussed above.
38. See especially BuxWV 169 and 175. Neither of these, however, has a middle section in triple time.
39. Seiffert, ed., *Weckmann: 14 Präludien*, #6.
40. Mentioned by Shannon, *Organ Literature of the Seventeenth Century*, p. 220.
41. Seiffert, ed., *Weckmann: 14 Präludien*, #4.
42. Such an idea was used, but with more logic and rigor, in BuxWV 170. In his work, the second subject derives from the first part of the original subject, and the third subject from the second part.
43. Ibid., #8.
44. If these works really are by Weckmann, they would establish him as an even more important figure in the development of Buxtehude's style.
45. Seiffert, ed., *Anonymi*, #5.
46. BuxWV 141 is used as an example of Buxtehude's thematic derivation by Donald J. Grout in *A History of Westen Music*, rev. ed. (New York: W. W. Norton & Co., 1973), p. 377. This example was doubtlessly chosen because the work also appears in Archibald T. Davison and Willi Apel, ed., *Historical Anthology of Music*, 2 vols. (Cambridge: Harvard University Press, 1950), vol. 2, pp. 99-101. While it is hardly a typical example of Buxtehude's use of thematic derivation, it is one of his most sophisticated.
47. Such thematic connections are rare in the praeludium even after Buxtehude. An example is the Praeludium in E by Vincent Lübeck. See Klaus Beckmann, ed., *Vincent Lübeck: Sämtliche Orgelwerke* (Wiesbaden: Breitkopf & Härtel, 1973), #4. The fugal subject is suggested in the *adagio* passage in the opening free section, but the result is far less cogent or powerful than in BuxWV 149.

Chapter 5

1. Donald J. Grout, *A History of Western Music*, rev. ed. (New York: W. W. Norton & Co., 1973), p. 376.
2. The flourish of sixteenth notes in m. 101 occurs because of registral manipulations of the fundamental line of the work. See chapter 8.
3. See chapters 1 and 4 for keys to diagrams.

4. The overall harmonic stasis of the closing free section (the tonic arrival in m. 102 is prolonged through subdominant harmony until the final cadence) will be discussed further along with other examples of its type in chapter 8. The relationship of the point of climax to the harmonic/contrapuntal structure of the work at middleground and background levels is discussed in chapter 9.

5. See also BuxWV 143, 149, 153, 155, and 156.

6. Lesser arrivals on the tonic occur in mm. 92 and 94. These are not convincing as a point of resolution because of their approach, E♯-F♯, rather than C♯-F♯, and also because of their uncertain metrical placement at higher levels. It is only the arrival in m. 96 which is approached by descent of a fifth in the bass and is a strong downbeat at higher levels. For another example of both the point of maximum tension and the point of resolution contained in free textures, see the closing free section of BuxWV 139.

7. BuxWV 138, 144, 145, 147, and 157.

8. BuxWV 144 is unusual in that it does not have a free ending to its fugue. The final measures of the fugue, beginning at the stretto passage (m. 47), are climactic, but lack the strong sense of tension and resolution that can be found in most of the larger works.

9. A similar pattern can be discerned in BuxWV 136, which also ends with a gigue fugue.

10. See footnote 23 in chapter 2 for exceptions.

11. This is true not only in the chordal-rhapsodic sections, but also in the fugal sections as well. BuxWV 142, with its chromatic fugue and following free section, can serve as an example of both.

12. This is most noticeable in works which either have three or more subject transformations, such as BuxWV 150, or develop their thematic material in both free and fugal sections, such as BuxWV 149.

13. BuxWV 137 and 148.

14. See, for example, BuxWV 153, mm. 117-21.

15. BuxWV 136 and BuxWV 142.

16. For example, BuxWV 155.

17. For example, BuxWV 141.

18. For example, BuxWV 146.

19. See the second section of chapter 1 for a more complete discussion of Buxtehude's immediate predecessors.

20. See the second sections of chapters 1 and 2 for discussion of the form of Scheidemann's praeambula.

21. A model for Tunder's procedure can be found in Scheidemann's Praeambulum in d, WV 34 (Werner Breig, ed., *Heinrich Scheidemann: Orgelwerke* [Kassel: Bärenreiter, 1971], vol. 3, #6). It is probably the best known of Scheidemann's praeambula at least in part because of its unusually cogent expressive form.

22. Klaus Beckmann, ed., *Franz Tunder: Sämtliche Orgelwerke* (Wiesbaden: Breitkopf & Härtel, 1974), #3.

23. Max Seiffert, ed., *Matthias Weckmann: 14 Präludien, Fugen und Toccaten*, Organum, Fourth Series, no. 3 (Cologne: Kistner & Siegel & Co., n.d.), #1, #2, and #3, respectively.
24. See especially those in the Fantasia and the Praeambulum.
25. The Fuga is indeed a large canzona. See the second section of chapter 1.
26. See the Toccatas in d and e. Seiffert, ed., *Weckmann: 14 Präludien*, #9 and #12, respectively.
27. Max Seiffert, ed., *Anonymi der norddeutschen Schule: 6 Praeludien und Fugen*, Organum, Fourth Series, no. 10 (Cologne: Kistner & Siegel & Co., n.d.), #4.
28. See the second section of chapter 1; see also the Conclusion.
29. In both cases a" is eventually attained.
30. Works such as BuxWV 139, 140, 146, 149, 155, and 156 provide the best examples.

Chapter 6

1. See chapters 1 and 2.
2. These types of opening sections are summarized in chapter 1.
3. Many other opening sections are closely analogous to that of BuxWV 136, including those in BuxWV 139, 140, 141, 142, 144, 152, and 158. Also analogous are those which are not figural but have only one texture, such as BuxWV 149 and 150.
4. Similar works include BuxWV 147 and 157. The former work, however, has a harmonic scheme with a greater emphasis on the dominant: the cadence which is equivalent to that in m. 11 of BuxWV 137 is on the dominant. A somewhat similar construction can be found in BuxWV 146. The first passage, a tonic pedal, is anticipatory to the second passage, in chordal texture, in which real harmonic motion occurs.
5. Figural texture depends on a relatively fast harmonic rhythm; as the harmonic rhythm slows (generally past the half-note value), figural texture disintegrates into the more rhapsodic texture characteristic of pedal points. (See chapter 1).
6. Similar cadential patterns can be found in BuxWV 136, 142, 147, and 157.
7. Similar constructions can be found in BuxWV 138, 144, 145, 146, and 156. A somewhat similar case can be found in BuxWV 148, in which the pedal is implied underneath a flourish.
8. Such a practice is contrary to the close of every other opening section in which the penultimate dominant is enhanced by V/V.
9. See the discussion of BuxWV 140 in the Conclusion.
10. See, for example, the first eleven measures of BuxWV 137.
11. BuxWV 141 is a typical example.
12. See chapter 4.
13. See Charles Rosen, "Art Has Its Reasons," *The New York Review of Books*, June 17, 1971, especially p. 33, concerning the cadential aspects of high-level structure.
14. See particularly the works of Heinrich Schenker, especially *Der Freie Satz*, Neue musikalische Theorien und Phantasien, vol. 3 (Vienna: Universal Edition, 1935). This work

is also available as *Free Composition*, New Musical Theories and Fantasies, vol. 3, trans. and ed. Ernst Oster (New York: Longman, 1979).

15. Its entirely figural texture and single large harmonic gesture are discussed in the first section of this chapter.

16. The background reduction is unusual: the large dominant pedal which dominates much of the section contains not only the $\hat{2}$ of the fundamental line, but also the $\hat{5}$–$\hat{4}$–$\hat{3}$ as well. The opening tonic area ascends to $\hat{3}$ rather than descends to $\hat{2}$, and is thus essentially anticipatory. (A more normal archetype would be $\hat{5}$–$\hat{4}$–$\hat{3}$–$\hat{2}$–$\hat{1}$.)

17. The $\hat{6}$ in this case is ♯$\hat{6}$ (d♯″) rather than ♮$\hat{6}$ (d♮″).

18. See the opening section of BuxWV 146 illustrated above.

19. See the opening section of BuxWV 156 illustrated above.

20. See chapters 7, 8, and 9.

21. See the second section of chapter 1 for a more complete discussion of Buxtehude's immediate predecessors.

22. Beckmann, ed., *Tunder: Orgelwerke*, #1.

23. All are much larger in size than the opening free sections of Tunder's more important north German predecessor, Scheidemann. Tunder's sections also have a richer harmonic language and a greater array of textures. Most notably, rhapsodic texture is added to the basically chordal texture of Scheidemann, but in no particular pattern.

24. Beckmann, ed., *Tunder: Orgelwerke*, #2.

25. Seiffert, ed., *Weckmann: 14 Präludien*, #3.

26. The opening free section of the anonymous Praeludium in F (Seiffert, ed., *Anonymi*, #5) is remarkably similar in this respect.

27. Guido Adler, ed., *Johann Jacob Froberger: Werke für Orgel und Klavier*, 3 vols., Denkmäler der Tonkunst in Osterreich, vols. 8, 13, and 21 (Vienna: Artaria & Co., 1897-1903), vol. 1, #2.

28. Ibid., #19.

29. See chapter 1.

30. See chapter 9.

Chapter 7

1. The occasional use of fugato passages in the opening free section is discussed in chapter 6.

2. See note 23 in chapter 2 for exceptions.

3. Various aspects of these fugues have already been discussed in Part I of this study.

4. See Kenneth George Powell, "The North German Organ Toccata, 1650-1710," (D.M.A. dissertation, University of Illinois, 1969), pp. 54-60, for a brief overview of the stylistic aspects of Buxtehude's fugal writing. A more complete treatment can be found in Hans-Jacob Pauly, *Die Fuge in den Orgelwerken Dietrich Buxtehudes*, Kölner Beiträge zur Musikforschung, vol. 31 (Regensburg: Gustav Bosse Verlag, 1964).

5. Exceptions occur in BuxWV 136, 138, 139, 148, 150, 151, and 155.

6. See BuxWV 136, 151, and 155.
7. See especially BuxWV 140 and 155.
8. BuxWV 136, 139, 150, 151, 153, and 156.
9. BuxWV 137, 142, 143, 144, and 147.
10. BuxWV 138, 140, 142, 145, 146, 148, 149, 155, and 157. (BuxWV 152 and 158 have subdominant answers.)
11. See all but BuxWV 156 in note 8.
12. See all but BuxWV 147 and 149 in notes 9 and 10.
13. See also BuxWV 136, 150, 151, and 155.
14. See also BuxWV 138, 139, 141, 143, 149, 152, 153, 156, and 158. BuxWV #148 presents several extra entries before reaching a tonic cadence.
15. All but two of the first fugues have a second exposition; only BuxWV 143 and 152 continue with extra entries.
16. The scarcity of episodes and entrances of the subject or answer outside the tonic is surely related to the alternation of free and fugal sections within the praeludium; as Kerala J. Snyder has remarked, "There is very little episodic material or real modulation [in the fugues], these functions being fulfilled by the free sections between the fugues." "Dietrich Buxtehude," *The New Grove Dictionary of Music and Musicians*, 6th ed., ed., Stanley Sadie (London: Macmillan Publishers, 1980), vol. 3, p. 530.
17. See BuxWV 141, 146, 147, 149, 156, and 157. The typical entry pattern of the first exposition, S (soprano)/A (alto)/S (tenor)/A (bass), is the second most frequent plan for the second exposition; see BuxWV 138, 139, 153, and 158.
18. Only a few fugues close with the second exposition; see BuxWV 145, 149, and 155. In BuxWV 146, a single extra entry is added to the second exposition before the fugue ends.
19. In BuxWV 157, the third exposition is highlighted by new counterpoints in a faster rhythm (sixteenth-note motion). Other works with a third exposition are BuxWV 137, 138 (which adds a new countersubject for the third one), 139, 151, 153, and 158.
20. See also BuxWV 136, 140, 142, 144, 148, and 156. In all but the first, entries of the subject and/or answer occur outside the tonic. An entire exposition outside the tonic does not occur in the first fugues; however, a rare example can be found in the second fugue of BuxWV 153. See chapter 8.
21. For entries in III see BuxWV 139, 142, and 150; for IV, 142, 143, and 150; for V, 140, 142, 143, 144, and 153; for VI, 138, 139, and 156; for VII, 148, 150, and 158.
22. The trill D-C-D-C . . . D decorates the root of dominant harmony with the lower neighbor note.
23. This is a typical procedure of all the fugues in the praeludia.
24. See BuxWV 151, mm. 61-62. See also BuxWV 136 and 138.
25. For another example of a short extension type of free ending, see BuxWV 158.
26. Only two fugues achieve harmonic closure without a free ending. The fugue of BuxWV 144 ends with a stretto passage based upon fragments of its subject. The unusually long first fugue of BuxWV 150 closes with an impressive fourth exposition in which a rare use of double pedal technique adds finality.

27. See note 23 in chapter 2.

28. Stretto is rarely found in the praeludia, especially in the first fugues. Other examples can be found in BuxWV 147, 156, and 158.

29. See the second section of chapter 6.

30. See the first section of this chapter.

31. A fugue could also end with a half cadence after the conclusion of a fundamental line, for example: $\hat{5}$-$\hat{4}$-$\hat{3}$-$\hat{2}$-$\hat{7}$ / I---V-I-V. Such a scheme is not found in the first fugues, and is not characteristic of the praeludia. It is approximated most closely in the tripe-time fugue of BuxWV 142. See chapter 8.

32. The extension of fundamental lines and their harmonic support outside the first fugal section into the following sections anticipates techniques typical of the sections after the first fugue. See chapter 8.

33. See the second section of chapter 1 for a more complete discussion of Buxtehude's immediate predecessors.

34. See, for example, Scheidemann's Praeambulum in d, WV 36 (Werner Breig, ed., *Heinrich Scheidemann: Orgelwerke* [Kassel: Bärenreiter, 1971], vol. 3, #8), which has entries in not only i and v, but VII, and iv as well.

35. See chapter 4.

36. See Scheidemann's Praeambula WV 35, 36, 38, 40, 41, and his Fuga in d, WV 42.

37. Klaus Beckmann, ed., *Franz Tunder: Sämtliche Orgelwerke* (Wiesbaden: Breitkopf und Härtel, 1974), #2.

38. Ibid., #3.

39. See chapter 4.

40. Max Seiffert, ed., *Matthias Weckmann: 14 Präludien, Fugen und Toccaten*, Organum, Fourth series, no. 3 (Cologne: Kistner & Siegel & Co., n.d.), #3.

41. Ibid., # 1 and #2, respectively.

42. John R. Shannon, *Organ Literature of the Seventeenth Century: A Study of its Styles* (Raleigh: Sunbury, 1978), p. 219.

43. Compare the change from fugal texture to episodic texture in m. 40 of the Fuga with the change in mm. 54-55 of the Praeludium. See chapter 1 for the previously mentioned relationship.

44. Compare mm. 40-41 of the Fantasia with mm. 45-46 of the Praeludium.

45. See, for example, his Toccata in d, mm. 27 and 42; also his Canzona in C, m. 27 (Guido Adler, ed., *Johann Jacob Froberger: Werke für Orgel und Klavier* [Vienna: Artaria & Co., 1897-1903], vol. 1, #19 and #5, respectively). See also the Canzon Dopo il Post Comune from the *Messa delli Apostoli* in Frescobaldi's *Fiori Musicali* of 1635; each of the three fugal sections has an elaborate free ending. See Pierre Pidoux, ed., *Girolamo Frescobaldi: Orgel- und Klavier Werke*, 5 vols. (Kassel: Bärenreiter, 1954), vol. 5, pp. 46-48.

46. Similar free endings can also be found in Weckmann's canzonas, such as at the end of the first fugal sections of those in c and d (Seiffert, ed., *Weckmann: 14 Präludien*, #6 and #7, respectively); the latter includes an interesting indication of a tempo change to

adagio for the free ending. Such indications are strongly suggested in some of Buxtehude's free endings, although they rarely carry such special indications. (The "*con discretione*" at the end of the *presto* fugato of BuxWV 141 is an example.) Tempo indications in general are not often employed in the praeludia.

47. See Josef Hedar, *Dietrich Buxtehudes Orgelwerke* (Stockholm: Nordiska Musikförlaget, 1951; Frankfurt: Wilhelmiana Musikverlag, 1951), p. 171. He emphasizes the similarity in its canonic construction to works of Scheidemann.

48. BuxWV 152, while it does not employ archaic entry pairs, does not even match BuxWV 158 in its formal logic after the exposition. Extra entries in various keys fill out the form.

49. Fugal writing *a*5 is particularly evocative of Weckmann, who employed it in the first fugues of his Fantasia and Praeambulum. It can be found also in the anonymous Praeludium in F (Seiffert, ed., *Anonymi*, #5); its presence there is yet one more reason why Weckmann seems its likely composer. While this work has also been attributed to Tunder, that composer never used *a*5 writing in the fugal sections of his praeludia. Buxtehude's fugues are virtually always *a*4. See note 62 in chapter 1 for discussion of the attribution of the Praeludium in F.

50. The subject of BuxWV 143 also has a peculiar list towards the subdominant which is not typical of Buxtehude's fugue subjects.

51. These fugues also have the restricted use of the pedals typical of Tunder and Weckmann. In most of Buxtehude's fugues, and indeed, in his praeludia as a whole, the pedal part is far more active than in his north German predecessors; Buxtehude made sixteenth-note motion in the pedal part a typical rather than extraordinary feature of his works. As Snyder has remarked, "Buxtehude's fugures can indeed be considered the first body of such works to be really idiomatically conceived for the organ; . . ." ("Dietrich Buxtehude," p. 530).

52. Buxtehude's techniques strongly influenced north German organ music in the following generation; see especially the first fugue of the Praeludium in e, the so-called Great, of Nicolaus Bruhns (Klaus Beckmann, ed., *Nicolaus Bruhns: Sämtliche Orgelwerke* [Wiesbaden: Breitkopf & Härtel, 1972], #1), which is clearly modeled on these works.

53. Only one extra entry occurs in the fugue; it follows the last (fourth) exposition.

Chapter 8

1. See chapter 1.
2. See chapter 2.
3. See especially chapter 1. See also chapters 2 and 3.
4. The term "Final" appears in the only manuscript which preserves this work, the Lowell Mason Codex (Yale University, LM 5056). The reading of the Toccata is unusually faulty, and the usage of "Final" may not be authentic. A Final can also be considered a coda. See chapter 9.
5. The closing free sections of BuxWV 140 and 153 are examples.
6. See mm. 99–103.
7. Fifteen of the praeludia have two or more fugal sections. Triple-time fugues (in 3/2, 3/4, or 6/4) are found in BuxWV 140, 142, 143, 148, 149, 150, 152, 153, 155, and 158;

fugatos or similar imitative passages in 136, 140, 141 (2), and 150; common-time fugues in 141, 146, 151, and 156; gigue fugues in 136 and 142.

8. See chapter 7.

9. An S/A/A/S entry plan is used in the second fugue of BuxWV 151; the first fugato of BuxWV 141, the fugato of BuxWV 150, and the imitative section of BuxWV 140 are irregular. See below.

10. The second fugues of BuxWV 152 and 158 use real answers.

11. See particularly the triple-time fugues of BuxWV 140, 149, and 155.

12. A similarly nonmodular form can be found in the second fugue of BuxWV 143. This unusual $a5$ fugue also contains nontonic entries, in the subdominant and dominant.

13. The extensive area in III is comparable to that in the second fugue of BuxWV 153. In that work, however, the III area is an exposition rather than an episode.

14. Significantly, however, the pedal is never employed. Pedal parts are virtually always reserved for real fugues.

15. The placement and effect of this passage within the Praeludium, however, justifies its classification as a fugato.

16. A similarly developmental free ending is found on a far larger scale in the second fugue of BuxWV 155. (M. 108, the beginning of the free ending, is derived from the countersubject.) Again, the free ending itself is about half the length of the fugal passage.

17. BuxWV 147 is a rare example of a praeludium which ends with a fugal section and a plagal cadence; its first (and only) fugal section ends on the subdominant, from which point the free ending moves to the tonic.

18. Thematic variation is discussed in chapter 4.

19. The expressive shapes characteristic of the praeludia and especially of the remaining sections are discussed in chapter 5.

20. See the second sections of chapters 6 and 7.

21. Structural links between the opening free section, the first fugue, and the remaining sections will be explored in chapter 9.

22. The same $\hat{5}$-$\hat{4}$-$\hat{3}$-$\hat{2}$-$\hat{1}$ motion is also found in the opening free section. The role of this motion in the overall coherence of the Praeludium is discussed in chapter 9.

23. The second chordal section strongly resembles a free ending of a fugue. Its approach, by a dramatic interruption and radical change of texture and harmonic rhythm, is analogous to several fugal free endings. See especially the free endings of BuxWV 137 and 151.

24. See chapter 7. The important role of d'' in the opening free section of this work is discussed in chapter 6.

25. See chapter 7 for graphs of these fugues.

26. See chapter 7.

27. The ciacona passage contains harmonic and linear motions comparable to the large IV areas which close BuxWV 139, 140, 153, and 155.

28. See chapter 9.

29. See the second section of chapter 1 for a more complete discussion of Buxtehude's immediate predecessors.

30. See, for example, the Praeambulum in d, WV 34 (Werner Breig, ed., *Heinrich Scheidemann: Orgelwerke* [Kassel: Bärenreiter, 1971], vol. 3, #6), which even includes a significant move to the subdominant as the penultimate harmonic area (before the final tonic). This section is also progressive in another way: unlike the previous ones which are dominated by eighth-note motion, it is set apart from them by its prevailing sixteenth-note rhythms. A similar scheme can be found in all four of Tunder's praeludia, though Tunder employs more sixteenth-note motion in the opening free sections than does Scheidemann. The pattern can also be observed in several of Buxtehude's praeludia, such as BuxWV 140. In it the section preceding the last free section, a triple-time fugue which moves in quarters and eighths, contrasts with the closing section which is dominated by sixteenths.

31. See, for example, the Praeludium in g (Klaus Beckmann, ed., *Franz Tunder: Sämtliche Orgelwerke* [Wiesbaden: Breitkopf & Härtel, 1974], #4), discussed below. The G-d-G figure (i-V-i) of m. 79, which appears also as B♭-f-B♭ in m. 81, d-a-d in m. 83, and again as G-d-G in m. 88, also appears, finally in the subdominant, as G-c-G (V/iv-iv-V/iv) in m. 90. Similar ostinato figures appear in the subdominant areas of Buxtehude's praeludia, but more firmly grounded in the subdominant (iv-V/iv-iv), such as G-d-G in both BuxWV 140 and 155, and B-f♯-B in BuxWV 146.

32. See Beckmann, ed., *Tunder: Orgelwerke*, #1, #3, and #4; #2 has no free ending or extension of its fugue before the closing free section.

33. Ibid., #4.

34. A very similar structure can be found in the anonymous Praeludium in G (Max Seiffert, ed., *Anonymi der norddeutschen Schule: 6 Praeludien und Fugen*, Organum, Fourth Series, no. 10 [Cologne: Kistner & Siegel & Co., n.d.], #4).

35. Max Seiffert, ed., *Matthias Weckmann: 14 Präludien, Fugen und Toccaten*, Organum, Fourth Series, no. 3 (Cologen: Kistner & Siegel & Co., n.d.), #1, #2, and #3, respectively.

36. Weckmann's influence on Buxtehude's fugal style is discussed in chapter 7 in reference to the first fugues of their works.

37. The dotted-note motive, first introduced as a countersubject in m. 57 (in the second exposition) later comes to dominate the section during both entries and episodes. Such a procedure is symptomatic of a less rigid approach to fugal writing in second (or third) fugues.

38. As in some of Buxtehude's free endings, not only does the texture change, but the meter as well (from 3/2 to ₵).

39. See chapter 2, note 35, for its similarities to the Final of BuxWV 155.

40. See in particular mm. 96-102.

41. The first free ending's sudden switch to figural texture can be compared to several such moments in Buxtehude's praeludia. See chapter 7.

42. Willi Apel, *The History of Keyboard Music to 1700*, trans. & rev. Hans Tischler (Bloomington: Indiana University Press, 1972), p. 602.

43. See the passage beginning in m. 95.

44. The Fantasia is comparable in this regard to the Praeludium in g of Tunder analysed above.

45. See, for example, the Toccata in d (Seiffert, ed., *Weckmann: 14 Präludien*, #10). In this work, the second, triple-time fugue is linked to the free section which ends the work by a line from f″ to a′ (f″-e″-d″-c#″-d″-c♮″-b′-b♭′-a′) in mm. 25-38.

46. Guido, Adler, ed., *Johann Jacob Froberger: Werke fur Orgel und Klavier* (Vienna: Artaria & Co., 1897-1903), vol. 1, #19. See chapter 6 for an analysis of the opening free section of this work.

47. The role of nontonic internal cadences in building the form of these works and their use by Weckmann and Tunder is discussed in chapter 2.

48. The anonymous Praeludium in G (Seiffert, ed., *Anonymi*, #4), presents another, larger example of the innovations found in Weckmann's Praeambulum.

49. Thematically as well, the Praeludium does not make a strong impression. The thread of thematic variations which runs through the four fugal sections is extremely tentative. See chapter 4.

Chapter 9

1. The overall coherence of the praeludium is reinforced by several other factors, including the use of thematic variation, rhythmic acceleration and variation, and the drive towards an expressive climax and its resolution. See chapters 3, 4, and 5.

2. The remaining sections of BuxWV 137, as well as other sections from other works discussed in this chapter, are analysed in greater detail in chapters 6, 7, and 8.

3. Examples similar to BuxWV 137 can be found in many other works. BuxWV 145 has only two sections; they share similar lines ($\hat{5}$-$\hat{4}$-$\hat{3}$-$\hat{2}$-$\hat{1}$, c″-f′). BuxWV 156 also relies on $\hat{5}$-$\hat{4}$-$\hat{3}$-$\hat{2}$-$\hat{1}$ lines but uses more complex prolongations.

4. The subjects of both fugues stress c#″; in addition, that note is left unresolved at the close of both. See chapter 8.

5. See BuxWV 136, 137, 140, 142, 143, 146, 148, and 149.

6. Codas also provide for the relaxation of tension after the point of resolution. See chapter 5.

7. See BuxWV 139, 140, 146, the extension of BuxWV 137, and the closing free section (resembling a ciacona) of BuxWV 149.

8. See Heinrich Schenker, *Der Freie Satz* (Vienna: Universal Edition, 1935), Anhang, fig. 16.

9. See the second section of chapter 1 for a more complete discussion of Buxtehude's immediate predecessors.

10. Klaus Beckmann, ed., *Franz Tunder: Sämtliche Orgelwerke* (Wiesbaden: Breitkopf und Härtel, 1974), #4.

11. Buxtehude usually employs codas in three-part rather than two-part forms. BuxWV 147, however, is an example of a two-part work with a subdominant extension (but not an entire Final section) as the free ending of a fugue.

12. Max Seiffert, ed., *Matthias Weckmann: 14 Präludien, Fugen und Toccaten*, Organum, Fourth series, no. 3 (Cologne: Kistner & Siegel & Co., n.d.), #3.

13. Ibid., #1.
14. Note especially the powerful line after the $\dot{|}$ which runs throughout the subdominant-oriented coda. A similar example in Buxtehude's praeludia can be found in BuxWV 149 in the closing free section where a similar 8-#3 line is employed (g″-b♮′).
15. Adler, ed., *Froberger: Werke*, vol. 1, #19.
16. See Leonard Meyer, *Music, The Arts, and Ideas: Patterns and Predictions in Twentieth-Century Culture* (Chicago: University of Chicago Press, 1967), p. 311, for a discussion of flat and arched hierarchies and their relationship to music history.
17. In praeludia which have only two sections, the descent embodied in the fugue becomes that of the fundamental line of the work.

Conclusion

1. Nor were any of these works published by Buxtehude. Many first appeared in print in the nineteenth century in the Spitta edition (1875-76). Most others were not published until Max Seiffert edited a supplement to the Spitta edition in 1939. See the Introduction.
2. For discussion of the sources see the *Kritischer Bericht* in Klaus Beckmann, ed., *Dietrich Buxtehude: Sämtliche Orgelwerke* (Wiesbaden: Breitkopf & Härtel, 1971), vol. 1. His *Quellenverzeichnis* which appears there is summarized in table 3; his insignia for the sources have been included in table 3 for convenience. See also the *Bemerkungen zu den Quellen* of his edition (vol. 1, pp. 207-7). The sources are also discussed by Josef Hedar (both in *Dietrich Buxtehudes Orgelwerke* [Stockholm: Nordiska Musikförlaget, 1951; Frankfurt: Wilhelmiana Musikverlag, 1951], pp. 12-17, and in the Prefaces of the volumes of his edition). See also Friedrich Wilhelm Riedel, *Quellenkundliche Beiträge* (Kassel: Bärenreiter-Verlag, 1960), and Kenneth George Powell, "The North German Organ Toccata, 1650-1710" (D.M.A. dissertation, University of Illinois, 1969); however, Powell does not discuss sources for works which end after the first fugal section. For a discussion of the problems of source transmission from tablature to modern notation see the Introduction of this study and references listed there.
3. Lund. Universitetsbibliotek Handskriftsavdelningen Sammlung Wenster. It preserves BuxWV 139, 142, 149, and 154, the last of which is a fragment and preserved only in Wenster. (It also contains, and is the only source for, BuxWV 162, 167, 169, 170, and 173.)
4. Powell reports that "His name appears in the manuscripts along with the dates ranging from May 1713 to April 1714." ("North German Organ Toccata," p. 22.)
5. Olivier Alain, "The Organ Works of Dietrich Buxtehude," trans. Herman Adler, accompanying *The Complete Organ Works of Dietrich Buxtehude* (New York: Musical Heritage Society Records), OR 309-15, p. 3. This quotation summarized Hedar's argument presented in *Dietrich Buxtehudes Orgelwerke*, pp. 12-13.
6. Powell, "North German Organ Toccata," p. 22.
7. New Haven, Yale University, LM 5056 (Codex E.B. 1688). It preserves BuxWV 136, 142, 144, 148, 152, 155, and 158. All these works have reliable texts except the Toccata, which beginning especially with the second fugue, is garbled. A transcription by Beckmann of the actual state of the manuscript at that point can be found as *Anhang* 2 (vol. 1) of his edition.

8. BuxWV 136, 144, 152, 155, and 158 are unica. The manuscript also contains three other keyboard works by Buxtehude, and is the only source for them as well: BuxWV 166, 175, and a curious Sonata in d, which is transcribed by Beckmann in the *Nachtrag* to vol. 1 (*Anhang* 4), found at the end of vol. 2 of his edition.

9. Buxtehude's Toccata in d, BuxWV 155, is dated 1684; Jacob Bölsche's Praeambulum in E is dated 1683. The Bölsche Praeambulum, along with a Fuga by Peter Heidorn, also from LM 5056, has been edited in Friedrich Wilhelm Riedel, ed., *Jacob Bölsche: Praeambulum; Peter Heidorn: Fuga*, Die Orgel, Fourth series, no. 4 (Lippstadt: Kistner & Siegel & Co., 1957). The manuscript carries the inscription "E.B. 1688" from which both Hedar and Riedel derive their conclusions. Both authors provide a history of the manuscript, which can be traced back to 1776. (After several owners, it was sold from the estate of J. C. H. Rinck to Lowell Mason. After Mason's death, it was given to Yale University.) See Josef Hedar, *Dietrich Buxtehudes Orgelwerke*, pp. 15-17, and Riedel, *Quellenkundliche Beiträge*, pp. 104-5. Snyder feels that the date of the Codex is less secure, and that it was probably not copied before 1688.

10. See Riedel, *Quellenkundliche Beiträge*, p. 101.

11. Kerala J. Snyder, "Dietrich Buxtehude," *Grove 6*, ed. Stanley Sadie (London: Macmillan Publishers, 1980), vol. 3, p. 532. Some reasons why this may well be true are discussed in the third section of the Conclusion.

12. Berlin. Preussischer Kulturbesitz, Musikabteilung Mus. ms. 2681. It preserves BuxWV 139, 140, 141, 142, 143, 145, 149, 153, and 156. All of these works are preserved elsewhere, most notably in a group of manuscripts in Brussels and Berlin (see below). It also contains several other works by Buxtehude for keyboard without pedal, including BuxWV 163, 164, 168, 171, 176, and 213.

13. See Riedel, *Quellenkundliche Beiträge*, p. 79.

14. Brussels. Bibliothèque du Conservatoire Royal de Musique U 26659/Wagener. It preserves BuxWV 139, 140, 141, 142, 143, 145, 146, 149, 153, and 156. All of these works are preserved in other manuscripts (chiefly Berlin 2681) except BuxWV 146 which is found only in the Wagener Manuscript and copies of it in Berlin. (Wagener itself, however, is the only source for BuxWV 203.)

15. See Snyder, "Buxtehude's Organ Music," p. 521. She considers it possible that this manuscript "transmits a tradition that Bach had received directly from Buxtehude." She also points out its notational peculiarity of rendering all the pedal parts in red ink.

16. See the Preface by Max Seiffert to the Spitta editon of 1903.

17. The Berlin copies also derive from the Bach circle: Berlin. Deutsche Staatsbibliothek, Musikabteilung Mus. ms. Am. 462 and 430 (which are linked to Kirnberger), and Berlin. Staatsbibliothek Preussischer Kulturbesitz, Musikabteilung Mus. ms. 2683 and 2681/1. These manuscripts, along with Wagener, also transmit two works by Nicolaus Bruhns, a student of Buxtehude. Yet another Berlin manuscript, Bibliothek der ehemaligen Hochschule für Musikerziehung und Kirchenmusik Ms. 1476, has been linked with this group by Riedel (*Quellenkundliche Beiträge*, p. 197) and Powell ("North German Organ Toccata," p. 13). Beckmann, however, groups it with Berlin 2681 rather than the Wagener Manuscript. Associated like the Wagener Manuscript with Agricola, it is now lost.

18. Spitta, who knew Berlin 2681 and some of the Berlin copies of the Wagener Manuscript, hypothesized a common ancestor, now lost. See the Preface of his edition (not in the 1952 reissue); see also Riedel, *Quellenkundliche Beiträge*, p. 197. Snyder also holds this

Notes for Conclusion 327

view. She suggests that the hypothesized manuscript contained not only praeludia, but canzonas as well. As Berlin 2681 contains more of the canzonas than Wagener, she feels Berlin 2681 probably stands closer to that original manuscript than do the others. See "Dietrich Buxtehude," p. 532.

19. This might suggest a late origin for BuxWV 146. See the third section of the Conclusion.

20. Leipzig. Musikbibliothek der Stadt Leipzig. Ms. III.8.4. It preserves BuxWV 137 and 150, as well as 159–61, 174, as well as a fragmentary chorale prelude. For all but BuxWV 159, the Andreas-Bach-Buch is the only source.

21. Powell writes, "This is a manuscript which was in the possession of Andreas Bach, a nephew of J. S. Bach, in 1754. It was probably copied by Bernard Bach, brother of Andreas, while he studied with his uncle in Weimar from 1715–1717." ("North German Organ Toccata," p. 13).

22. Lund. Universitetsbibliotek Handskriftsavdelningen Sammlung Englehardt Nr. 216. It is the only source for BuxWV 147; it also preserves two vocal works by Buxtehude.

23. New Haven. Yale University, LM 4838 and LM 4983. LM 4838 contains BuxWV 138, and is its only source. (LM 4983 contains BuxWV 164 and 172, the latter of which is also an unicum.)

24. BuxWV 138, from LM 4838, was first published in Dietrich Kilian, ed., *Dietrich Buxtehude: Präludium und Fuge C-Dur* (Berlin: Verlag Merseburger, 1963). BuxWV 164, from LM 4983, was already known from other sources; BuxWV 172 was first published in the Beckmann edition (1971).

25. Berlin. Deutsche Staatsbibliothek, Musikabteilung Mus. ms. 40295. Until recently this manuscript was lost. (However, photocopies remained.) Snyder has informed the present author that the manuscript has been located in Cracow. This source preserves BuxWV 139 and 151. According to Riedel (*Quellenkundliche Beiträge*, p. 200), it dates from the beginning of the eighteenth century.

26. Berlin. Staatsbibliothek Preussischer Kulturbesitz, Musikabteilung Ms. ms. 40644. It preserves BuxWV 151 and 165. Writes Powell, "This is one of the so-called Möller manuscripts which can be traced back to J. G. Walther. It dates from the first half of the eighteenth century. . . ." ("North German Organ Toccata," p. 14.) (It is also a source for works by Bruhns and Böhm.)

27. The Schmahls version ends inconclusively; the notation suggests the second fugue has simply been left out. See the Hedar edition, vol. 2, #12b; also the Beckmann edition, vol. 1, *Anhang* 1.

28. It appears in that conflation in the reissue of 1952, vol. 2, #21.

29. The Möller version is vol. 2, #12a; the Schmahls version is #12b.

30. Vol. 1, *Anhang* 1.

31. See the *Einleitung* in his edition, vol. 1, p. vii. Beckmann terms Seiffert's conflation of the two versions "unglückliche;" he further quotes Pauly, *Fuge in den Orgelwerken Dietrich Buxtehudes*, p. 192, on the unlikelihood of the authenticity of the added passage in the Schmahls version.

32. Köningsberg. Universitätsbibliothek Sammlung Gotthold 14214(12), now lost. It preserved BuxWV 143. A photocopy remains, however, of this source which was available

Notes for Conclusion

to Spitta in the original. Riedel dates it from the first half of the eighteenth century. (*Quellenkundliche Beiträge*, p. 199.)

33. Berlin. Staatsbibliothek Preussischer Kulturbesitz, Musikabteilung Mus. ms. 30381, No. 3. It preserves BuxWV 145.

34. Höngeda bei Mühlhausen/Thüringen. Tablaturbuch von Georg Grobe 1675. Now lost. It was preserved in a copy belonging to A. G. Ritter, which is also now lost. It preserved BuxWV 148.

35. Berlin. Ehemalige Bibliothek des Königlich-akademischen Instituts für Kirchenmusik. Now lost. It preserved BuxWV 157, and was its only source. Besides appearing in the Spitta edition, BuxWV 157 was printed in 1839 by Commers, most probably from this lost manuscript. (See the *Kritischer Bericht* in the Beckmann edition, vol. 1, p. 205.).

36. See the *Kritischer Bericht* in Beckmann, ed., *Buxtehude: Orgelwerke*, vol. 1, pp. 203-5.

37. Josef Hedar, ed., *Dietrich Buxtehude: Sämtliche Orgelwerke* (Copenhagen: Wilhelm Hansen, 1952), vol. 2.

38. Riedel, *Quellenkundliche Beiträge*, p. 207; the passage is translated in Powell, "North German Organ Toccata," p. 25. The validity of Riedel's judgment of BuxWV 148 will be discussed later in the Conclusion. Riedel also suggests that the presence of BuxWV 142 in the Lowell Mason Codex, which has a middle German origin similar to the 1675 Tablature, and that work's further appearance in Berlin and Wagener, may mean an earlier origin for that work, and the others as well, than is suggested by the dates of LM 5056 or Wenster. Further, both Riedel (*Quellenkundliche Beiträge*, p. 104), and Hedar (*Dietrich Buxtehudes Orgelwerke*, p. 16), suggest that LM 5056 was compiled between 1673 and 1688, which lends support to an earlier cut-off date. Powell, however, maintains that 1688/9 is a more reasonable assumption ("North German Organ Toccata," p. 101). He also points to several other relevant factors. First, Nicolaus Bruhns, Buxtehude's pupil until 1687, also composed praeludia similar to Buxtehude's. For Powell, "It is possible to assume that Buxtehude [in 1687] was actively or at least had been recently composing music in this form." (Ibid., p. 99.) He continues, however, pointing out that this is not necessarily true. Second, he calls attention to the fact "that organ playing in north Germany seemed to be falling into disfavor in the last quarter of the seventeenth century." (Ibid., p. 103.) However, as Powell suggests, this argues for an earlier *terminus post quem non*.

39. See below. Note also its position in Wagener (see table 3).

40. BuxWV 148 also appears in the Grobe Tablature (dated 1675), but not in any of the other three major manuscripts.

41. See below.

42. See chapter 1 for a critique of his study. His chronology includes works by Reincken, Weckmann, Kneller, Werckmeister, Böhm, Bruhns, Lübeck, and an anonymous composer (author of the Praeludium in G, Seiffert, ed., *Anonymi*, #4), as well as works by Buxtehude, including some for keyboard without pedal omitted in this study.

43. See Powell, "North German Organ Toccata," pp. 99-105.

44. Ibid., p.102, tables 6 and 7. Reasons for these designations are also detailed.

45. Powell himself suggests as much: "These influences, which must be tentative in themselves, are certainly not enough evidence to develop a specific chronology." (Ibid.,

p. 101.) In several instances, however, the results are not only tentative but suspect, especially as regards BuxWV 140 and 158. See below.

46. The order in which the works appear in the table is not always meant to indicate a precise order of compostion. In only a few cases can such relationships be assumed with any confidence. Reasons why the works are presented in this order, as well as evidence which might suggest a somewhat different scheme, are presented in the text which follows ("A Proposed Chronology"). Table 5 does not include such evidence as that provided by manuscripts, nor does it detail critical evaluations; such observations as the relative awkwardness or finesse of various passages or works is presented in the text. Also, traits which link only a few of the works have usually not been included—these are also presented in the text.

    Several chronological guides presented by Powell ("North German Organ Toccata," pp.99-102) have been incorporated into table 5. These include the use of keys such as E, f#, and A (in BuxWV 141, 146, and 151, respectively), which can be considered a mark of a mature phase of composition; the virtuosic use of the pedals (subsumed under the general heading of virtuosity in table 5); the use of such techniques as inversion, modulation, episodes, stretto, and entries outside the key in fugal sections (although, as previously remarked, some of these traits may not indicate maturity as Powell suggests); the presence and complexity of the opening flourish (in table 5, several types are delineated, moving beyond the classifications established by Powell); the use of modality (particularly in BuxWV 152), which indicates an early origin; and the use of tempo indications (such as *allegro*, etc.), which probably indicate a later origin. His use of the "one-part" opening section as a guide to chronology has been abandoned here—far too many opening free sections in several textures and sections are grouped in this category to make it a useful one. His suggestion of virtuosity in BuxWV 148 has also been eliminated. (Powell provides specific reasons for the chronological period of only those works he labels early or late; his middle-period works are not so delineated.)

47. Weckmann's Praeambulum in d (Max Seiffert, ed., *Matthias Weckmann: 14 Präludien, Fugen und Toccaten*, Organum, Fourth series, no. 3 [Cologne: Kistner & Siegel & Co., n.d.], #3), his only organ work with an opening free section, is seventy-seven measures long. Tunder's four praeludia are seventy-three, sixty-four, sixty-nine, and ninety-six measures long (following the order in Beckmann, ed., *Tunder: Orgelwerke*).

48. See Hedar, *Dietrich Buxtehudes Orgelwerke*, p. 171.

49. Both these style features suggest Weckmann; see, for example, his Praeambulum in d.

50. See also the anonymous Praeludium in G (Seiffert, ed., *Anonymi*, #4).

51. See mm. 77-78.

52. A similar textural rounding can be found in Weckmann's Praeambulum in d.

53. Indeed, the opening of this work is cited by Richard Crocker, *A History of Musical Style* (New York: McGraw-Hill, 1966), p. 293, as typical of Buxtehude's style.

54. The two fugues of the Praeambulum are forty-three and eighteen measures, respectively; those of the Praeludium a more balanced twenty-seven and twenty-eight. The triple-time fugue of the Praeludium is notated in 3/2, a more frequently used meter in the praeludia than the 6/4 of the Praeambulum.

55. See chapter 1, note 68.

56. While Powell considers the Praeludium to be an early work, his classification of the Praeambulum as a middle-period work is untenable. ("North German Organ Toccata," p. 104.)

57. See the first and third sections of the Conclusion.

58. The gesture is more deftly handled in the Praeludium; the chordal texture is prepared in m. 11, and the bass states the theme of the section.

59. See mm. 65-71. Tritone opposition in the bass was also observed in the Praeambulum (mm. 77-78).

60. See especially BuxWV 136, 140, 141, and 156.

61. Beginning in m. 122.

62. See especially mm. 122-34.

63. While virtually all of the praeludia return to the common time with which they begin, they characteristically do so because they end with common-time musical ideas.

64. The size of BuxWV 143 (one hundred and seven measures) is also more nearly comparable to those of BuxWV 158 (eighty-three measures) and BuxWV 152 (seventy-seven measures).

65. Compare the extension of the fugato of BuxWV 150 (especially mm. 80-87) and the modular passage in the opening free section of BuxWV 143 (especially mm. 13-20).

66. Compare BuxWV 158, mm. 14-16; BuxWV 150, mm. 13-16; and BuxWV 143, mm. 21-23.

67. See particularly mm. 93-99.

68. See especially the curiously abandoned d♮ in m. 98. This note is particularly bothersome as it is a seventh in the prevailing tonic harmony. Its resolution is suggested, but only weakly, in m. 100.

69. For example, the closing free section resolves a long line established in the previous section.

70. See the first section of the Conclusion. BuxWV 158 and 152 are unica in the Lowell Mason Codex; BuxWV 150 is an unicum in the Andreas-Bach-Buch. There is no reason to believe that all of Buxtehude's praeludia survive, and early ones are surely the least likely to have been preserved. It would seem reasonable to assume that other praeludia were written at the time of BuxWV 158, 152, 150, and 143 but have not survived, judging from the stylistic gap between BuxWV 158 and 152 on the one hand, and works such as 150 and 143 on the other.

71. Philipp Spitta, *Johann Sebastian Bach*, trans. Clara Bell and J. A. Fuller-Maitland (London: Novello & Co., 1889; rpt. ed., New York: Dover Publications, 1951), vol. 1, p. 278. His continuation obscures the question of the effect of this work: "More cannot be demanded of a form which can at most be agreable and pleasing, though it is fully justified when the higher claims of art are not set aside for it. The toccatas of Buxtehude are naturally immensely superior to those of older masters—such as Froberger—in variety, genius, and effectiveness, and especially in the use of the pedal, as has been remarked before with regard to his productions in general." Spitta's remarks in this work written in the 1870s are still the most extended critical treatment of the praeludia and were intended to popularize the works. He is at times unnecessarily effusive; for

example, he unqualifyingly praises BuxWV 143, concluding that "Beethoven himself could hardly have done it differently." (Ibid., p. 274.)

72. See the passage beginning in m. 24. Beckmann has suggested some appealing revisions of the text of this passage as it appears in his edition. See the *Hinweis* preceding the second part of vol. 1 of his edition.

73. Mm. 103-12 are an awkward passage in overlegato style in eighth notes (rather than the usual sixteenth); as a result the passage seems to move in slow motion (and surely needs improvised ornamentation). The main thematic material of the remainder of the work, an idea using the more normal overlegato in sixteenth notes, first appears in m. 116 and leads the music from the submediant back to the tonic. When it reappears beginning in m. 123, its problematic metrical placements (beginning on beat two of m. 123 but on beat one of m. 125) suggest improvisational rhapsody. Similar metrical ambiguities can also be found in mm. 114 (beats three and four) and 115 (beats two and three). Mm. 114-20 in particular have been obviously corrupted by transmission in tablature and are significantly altered by Beckmann.

74. Compare especially mm. 8 and 134.

75. See particularly mm. 44-45, in which the alto entrance occurs after a pause with counterpoint rather than a subject or answer and in the soprano, a false entrance of the answer immediately precedes a true entrance of the subject. The integrity of the four-part texture is loosely handled in m. 40, in which five voices are suggested (but not realized). Five voices actually occur momentarily in m. 47. The counterpoint is unusually accompanimental, explicable in part as a response to the extremely bouncy subject. Vincent Lübeck, in his Praeludium in d, adopts the same solution with a strikingly similar subject (see Klaus Beckmann, ed., *Vincent Lübeck: Sämtliche Orgelwerke* [Wiesbaden: Breitkopf & Härtel, 1973], #3).

76. In the first fugue of BuxWV 158, the only entry outside the tonic is in VII; in the first fugue of BuxWV 150, entries occur outside the tonic in III, iv, and VII.

77. The repeated-note subject of BuxWV 148 presents a more challenging problem for variation than the more conventional (that is, Tunderian) first subject of BuxWV 150. Weckmann, however, provides examples of triple-time transformations of common-time repeated-note subjects. See for example, the Canzon in c (Seiffert, ed., *Weckmann: 14 Präludien*, #6). Weckmann's transformations, however, preserve the repeated-note trait; in BuxWV 148, Buxtehude alters it more substantially by substituting neighbor notes instead. See chapter 4.

78. In mm. 100-101, the soprano and alto are usually only a third apart while the bass lies nearly two octaves below (the tenor is silent). Similar spacing problems afflict the section again in mm. 115-17. The situation is turned to better effect in the extension (beginning with m. 122).

79. Spitta discovered in this passage a subtle thematic link to the chromatic fugato of the opening free section. His remarks on the thematic links in this work, however, are particularly curious. For example, he denies a relationship between the fugato subject and that of the first fugue (in spite of the fact that D-B♭ is central to both); why the second subject (and especially the pedal part in mm. 104-6) should be related to the fugato but not the first subject is not at all clear. The pedal part in mm. 104-6 seems to prepare the coming ciacona theme (first stated alone in the pedal part, mm. 113-14) as much as anything else. Two of his observations, however, are worth stressing: the "unwieldly" nature of the first fugue and the sense of the ciacona theme as "the off-

spring, as it were, of the development of the whole." As for the second remark, however, such a relationship is difficult to establish tangibly. (Spitta, *Bach*, trans. Bell and Fuller-Maitland, vol. 1, p. 279.)

80. Unlike in BuxWV 137, the theme of the ciacona is not directly related to the preceding thematic material. However, Spitta has speculated on its relationship nonetheless. See note 79.

81. See especially the tenor part in mm. 133-34.

82. See mm. 124-25. Modulations in ground bass forms are much more elegantly realized in BuxWV 161. There, short modulatory passages are provided between the statements of the theme in various harmonic areas. For that reason, BuxWV 161 might be considered a more mature work.

83. See the first part of the Conclusion. The work also appears in the Lowell Mason Codex.

84. Style traits which can be associated with fully mature praeludia are discussed below.

85. Most of the works Powell assigns ("North German Organ Toccata," p. 102) by default to a middle period (that is, neither early nor late), have here been placed in a relatively early category. Powell suggests that only two of the works by Buxtehude he surveyed can be considered early (in a chronology of Buxtehude's works, not in a chronology of the north German praeludium as a whole). One of these works, BuxWV 140, cannot be considered early at all; the other, BuxWV 152, has been considered early here. His middle-period works consist of BuxWV 136, 139, 143, 150, 156, and 158. (Perhaps BuxWV 148 should also be added to that list: he considers it to be a late work, but its presence in a manuscript—the Grobe Tablature—dated 1675 indicates it must overlap with his middle period.) Of these works, BuxWV 143, 150, 156, and especially 158 have been considered here as relatively early or early compositions. Thus in the present study, Powell's early and most of his middle period works are considered relatively early; the middle period here combines some of his own middle-period works plus a few he considers to be a part of the late period.

86. The 4-5-2-3 figure and its derivations first heard in m. 5 becomes 2-3-2-3 in mm. 13-14 above 4-5-2-3 and its derivations in the bass.

87. Such a plan is not presented here with the thoroughness found in some other works, for example, BuxWV 137. The first fugue of BuxWV 142, however, is an exception and does not have a strongly modular plan.

88. There is only one entry outside the tonic (a subject in v, mm. 40-42). Contrary to Powell's suggestion ("North German organ Toccata," p. 100), entries outside the tonic cannot automatically be taken as a mark of Buxtenude's late style; in fact, quite the opposite seems to be the case, particularly in reference to first fugues.

89. Snyder has pointed out the close connections between Buxtehude and Reincken. See particularly "Dietrich Buxtehude's Studies in Learned Counterpoint," pp. 561-63. For Reincken's "An Wasserflüssen Babylon" see Klaus Beckmann, ed., *Joh. Adam Reincken: Sämtliche Orgelwerke* (Wiesbaden: Breitkopf & Härtel, 1974), #1. Compare mm. 57-58 of BuxWV 153 with mm. 111-12 and mm. 158-60 of Reincken's chorale setting.

90. See the first section of the Conclusion.

91. Various details of the work differ in the two versions; however, those variants are far less surprising.

92. The additional section is in an unusual, quasi-imitative style. Its part writing, as Pirro pointed out, is far below Buxtehude's standards. The constant sixteenth-note pulse and motoric style reminiscent of string writing are also uncharacteristic of Buxtehude's organ works. It is, however, thematically linked to the end of the opening free section common to both versions.

93. André Pirro, *Dietrich Buxtehude* (Paris: Librairie Fischbacher, 1913), pp. 461–62. Overall, Pirro abdicated responsibility for surveying the organ works in view of Spitta's extensive treatment of 1873.

94. One of the problems of the free ending is that, apparently, Buxtehude began to notate decorations for the chordal progressions, but ceased to include them for the entire passage. The use of a tempo indication, *adagio*, for the free ending, however, points to a mature origin for the work.

95. The difference in size between the first and second fugues of BuxWV 151 (thirty-nine vs. eighteen measures) is more extreme than that of BuxWV 156 (twenty-four vs. thirteen measures).

96. The work consists of thirteen, thirty-two + nine, seven + four, and twenty-one + ten measures, corresponding to the opening free section and the three fugal sections with their free endings.

97. Only the free extension of the gigue fugue does not employ a new texture but continues in the style of the preceding fugal section.

98. The use of a tempo indication is another indication of a mature origin.

99. See chapter 1, p. 21.

100. Indeed, the Praeludium in C lies closer to those works in the manuscript than to the Praeludium in g.

101. Powell considers pedal virtuosity to be a sign of a late origin. ("North German Organ Toccata," p. 100.)

102. See, for example, the Praeambulum in d, WV 34 (Werner Breig, ed., *Heinrich Scheidemann: Orgelwerke* [Kassel: Bärenreiter, 1971], vol. 3, #6); the Praeludium in g of Tunder (Beckmann, ed., *Tunder: Orgelwerke*, #2) has a similar sequential passage at a similar juncture in the form.

103. See the passage beginning in m. 26.

104. Compare BuxWV 137, mm. 30–31, with BuxWV 139, mm. 13–14.

105. See chapter 4.

106. In both works, the motive is anticipated in the final cadence of the opening free section, and returns in the free ending to close the fugue as a whole.

107. The eighth/eighth/dotted eighth/sixteenth rhythmic pattern of the subject's cadence is anticipated in the cadence of the opening free section. BuxWV 139 evidences the same pattern in its subject, which is also anticipated at the cadence of its opening free section.

108. This may in part explain the unusually thin contrapuntal texture of the section.

109. Compare BuxWV 137, mm. 68–69, with BuxWV 139, mm. 101–2. Canonic flourishes which begin a work have been observed in BuxWV 136, 148, and 153.

110. The use of a tempo indication also suggests a mature origin.

111. Only BuxWV 145 is contained in the Wagener and Berlin 2681 group.
112. See m. 4. Improvised passagework seems suggested here. The flourish in m. 5 may be only the suggested conclusion for a larger, improvised one.
113. Such a syntax of gestures can also be found, for example, in the opening free sections of BuxWV 137, 144, and 153. In these examples, however, the thematic logic is more convincing.
114. So, too, is the arrival at a cadence point at the juncture between the fugue and the free ending; middle- and late-period works generally avoid an actual cadence at that point.
115. Compare beats three and four of m. 1 with beats three and four of m. 70. A similar gesture was also observed, handled in an almost identical way, in BuxWV 156.
116. See especially the second fugue of BuxWV 142.
117. See mm. 56–63.
118. The gesture is surprisingly similar to one in Bach's Toccata, Adagio, and Fugue in C, BWV 564, mm. 132–33 of the Fugue.
119. With a total of one hundred and twenty-seven measures, it is as large as many of the praeludia with two or more fugal sections. Its proportion of free and fugal music (thirty-nine out of one hundred and twenty-seven measures) is within a single percentage point of the balance of the two sections in the other Praeludium in F (seventeen out of fifty-four measures).
120. Spitta, *Bach*, trans. Bell and Fuller-Maitland, vol. 1, pp. 277-78.
121. See note 35 of the Conclusion.
122. See the *Nachtrag* to vol. 1 of the Beckmann edition which appears at the end of vol. 2 (p. 164). See also the *Hinweis* which appears at the beginning of the second half of vol. 1 in the practical edition (that is, the edition lacking full critical commentary).
123. See *Anhang* 3 of vol. 1 of the Beckmann edition. It also appears in the Hedar edition, vol. 2, pp. 120–21; Hedar has provided a summary conclusion to the section.
124. See Powell, "North German Organ Toccata," pp. 99–102.
125. See BuxWV 140, 146, and 149, discussed below. Similar examples can also be found in somewhat different contexts in BuxWV 137, m. 68, and BuxWV 139, mm. 101-2.
126. See BuxWV 140 and 155, discussed below. See also BuxWV 137, mm. 23–28, discussed above.
127. Compare the dotted figure in m. 16 of BuxWV 141 with the dotted figures (noted on pp. 274–75 above) in BuxWV 137, 139, and 157.
128. See chapter 2, p. 32.
129. A somewhat similar kind of double free ending can be found closing the fugue of BuxWV 139.
130. Similar examples can be found in BuxWV 140, 146, and 149, all discussed below.
131. See chapter 4, pp. 71–72.
132. See chapter 8, p. 206.
133. The gigue fugues of BuxWV 136 and 142 both recoil from the major climax point of their respective works.

134. Powell's supposition ("North German Organ Toccata," pp. 99-105) that the work is an early one because of the pedal point underneath the opening flourish and the one-part form of the opening free section cannot be maintained in view of the myriad of other features which point to a late origin.
135. See chapter 4, p. 80.
136. The most recent study of the Bach organ preludes suggests that the prelude in G, BWV 541, is a work of Bach's later years in Weimar. See George B. Stauffer, *The Organ Preludes of Johann Sebastian Bach*, Studies in Musicology, no. 27 (Ann Arbor, Michigan: U.M.I. Research Press, 1980), p. 14.
137. The descending bass line of mm. 59-61 recalls similar motions in mm. 4-5 (hidden in sixteenth-note figuration), mm. 13-15, and mm. 16-19.
138. Compare mm. 91-95 and 95-99.
139. M. 102. See chapter 5 for a detailed description of the climax.
140. Mm. 102-4 and 105-7.
141. See mm. 6-8 of BuxWV 141.
141. The parallel passage in BuxWV 146, discussed below, makes a similar use of this figuration.
143. See chapter 8.
144. See the first section of the Conclusion. Snyder believes that the date of 1684 can probably be accepted as the date of composition of BuxWV 155.
145. Compare the passage beginning in m. 65 of BuxWV 156 with that beginning in m. 13 of BuxWV 155.
146. M. 25 (beat three) to m. 26 (beat three); m. 26 (beat four) to m. 28 (beat one).
147. Jacobson, "Musical Rhetoric in Buxtehude's Free Organ Works," p. 64.
148. The first fugue of BuxWV 141 is thirty-eight measures long; that of BuxWV 140, twenty-five measures, and that of BuxWV 155, twenty-six measures long. However, the free ending of the first fugue of BuxWV 155 is seven measures, while that of BuxWV 140 is only three, so the actual length of fugal texture is shortest in BuxWV 155 (seventeen measures). Only BuxWV 146, discussed below, has so short a first fugue.
149. Compare the passage beginning in m. 55 of BuxWV 156 with the passage beginning in m. 47 of BuxWV 155.
150. A similar case could be made for BuxWV 150 and 140, particularly regarding the fugato section of BuxWV 150 and the imitative section of BuxWV 140 and their unusual openings.
151. The cadence of the chordal-rhapsodic section of BuxWV 140 on VII can be considered a heightening of the dominant cadence found in BuxWV 141. The use of two nontonic cadences in BuxWV 155 can be considered a further heightening.
152. Compare mm. 101-2 and 106-7.
153. Mm. 108-14 parallel mm. 115-21.
154. Compare the passage beginning at m. 102 in BuxWV 140 with the passage beginning in m. 115 in BuxWV 155. BuxWV 137 and 141 also have textures of this sort in their opening free sections.

155. Compare mm. 102-3 and 125-26.
156. Compare mm. 107-8 and 112-13 of BuxWV 140 with mm. 128-29 and 132-33 of BuxWV 155, respectively.
157. The iv–I$^{6-5}_{4-3}$ is most dramatically handled in BuxWV 139 and 155; both works juxtapose g" and D.
158. The three works discussed below all have an unusually large amount of music following the climax point, in particular BuxWV 146.
159. Spitta, *Bach*, trans. Bell and Fuller-Maitland, vol. 1, p. 268. He accords this work pride of place by both discussing it first in his survey and giving it the most extended treatment. He may have been influenced in this choice by the fact that the work appears first in Berlin 2681 and is the first praeludium to appear in Wagener, of which Spitta knew copies.
160. See chapter 4, pp. 70-71. Spitta (Ibid., p. 269) also details the manner of the thematic variations.
161. See chapter 6, pp. 113-14. Developmental procedures in figural style have already been observed in BuxWV 153. The example in BuxWV 142, however, is more thorough and leads to a figurally unified section. Stauffer (*Organ Preludes of Bach*, pp. 127-28) suggests further thematic links between the opening free section and the fugue subjects.
162. Only BuxWV 158 has a first fugue subject which also begins on the downbeat of the measure. Two other works, BuxWV 136 and 148, have first subjects which begin on the third beat. None of these fugues are particularly impressive; Buxtehude seems considerably more at ease when handling subjects which begin with an upbeat pattern.
163. See particularly BuxWV 158, 150, and 143.
164. See chapter 7, p. 137.
165. See Snyder, "Buxtehude's Organ Music," p. 519.
166. Snyder points out that it resembles the subject in retrograde. (Ibid.)
167. Harald Vogel has suggested that the first part of the second fugue, which is playable in meantone, may well be older than the second part, which is not playable in meantone. If this is true, the first fugue, whose archaic features are noted above, may have originated with the first part of the second fugue.
168. It is this section for which Spitta coined the term "organ recitative," (*Bach*, trans. Bell and Fuller-Maitland, vol. 1, p. 270; "Orgel-Recitative" in the original 1873 edition, p. 264). It has been used by other scholars, notably Hedar, to describe these chordal-rhapsodic passages.
169. See also BuxWV 149, discussed below.
170. See m. 6.
171. BuxWV 149, the only remaining work to be discussed, is another example of this development.
172. Mm. 48 and 49. See chapter 1, p. 11.
173. See mm. 57-59, 61-63, and 67-69.
174. Mm. 74-76 and 76-78.
175. Mm. 99-100 and 101-2. A similar technique can be observed in BuxWV 153.

176. M. 108 (beat three).
177. See m. 113 of BuxWV 153; mm. 114-17 of BuxWV 146.
178. See mm. 132-35 of BuxWV 155, mm. 112-16 of BuxWV 140, and mm. 119-20 of BuxWV 146.
179. See Spitta, *Bach*, trans. Bell and Fuller-Maitland, vol. 1, pp. 276-77.
180. See chapter 8, pp. 194-98.
181. See chapter 4, pp. 80-83, for a more complete presentation of the thematic relationships of BuxWV 149.
182. See BuxWV 136, 144, 148, and 153. The effect is similar in BuxWV 140 as well.
183. See BuxWV 140, 141, and 146, discussed above.
184. Imaginative downgrading of the articulation between the opening free section and the first fugue can be observed in not only BuxWV 149, but BuxWV 137, 140, and 155 as well. It can be taken as another aspect of the late style.
185. See chapter 8, pp. 191-93.
186. Snyder holds similar views of this remarkable fugue. See "Buxtehude's Organ Music," p. 519. Harald Vogel has pointed out that, like the second part of the chromatic fugue of BuxWV 142, the *largo* fugue is not playable in meantone.
187. M. 131. The note, c''', is the highest generally attainable on the instrument of the day. Interestingly enough, the Praeludium also calls for low C♯, which was often left out on those instruments.
188. Mm. 138-41.
189. Snyder feels this sort of gesture "provides dramatic tension." ("Buxtehude's Organ Music," p. 519.)
190. The magical transition passage between the fugue and the ciacona is largely responsible for the finely modulated sense of movement between the point of climax and the subsequent relaxation of tension.
191. This observation is a further indication that the controversial Praeludium in g, BuxWV 148, which is preserved in the Lowell Mason Codex (which contains mostly early- and middle-period works) and in the Grobe Tablature (in which it was the only Buxtehude praeludium) is most probably not a late-period work.
192. All of Buxtehude's surviving praeludia can be assumed to date from before the end of the 1680s. See the first section of the Conclusion.

Bibliography

Musical Editions Cited

Adler, Guido, ed. *Johann Jacob Froberger: Werke für Orgel und Klavier.* 3 vols. Denkmäler der Tonkunst in Osterreich. Vols. 8, 13, and 21. Vienna: Artaria & Co., 1897-1903, vol. 1.

Beckmann, Klaus, ed. *Dietrich Buxtehude: Sämtliche Orgelwerke.* 2 vols. Wiesbaden: Breitkopf & Härtel, 1971.

―――, ed. *Franz Tunder: Sämtliche Orgelwerke.* Wiesbaden: Breitkopf & Härtel, 1974.

―――, ed. *Joh. Adam Reincken: Sämtliche Orgelwerke.* Wiesbaden: Breitkopf & Härtel, 1974.

―――, ed. *Nicolaus Bruhns: Sämtliche Orgelwerke.* Wiesbaden: Breitkopf & Härtel, 1972.

―――, ed. *Vincent Lübeck: Sämtliche Orgelwerke.* Wiesbaden: Breitkopf & Härtel, 1973.

Breig, Werner, ed. *Heinrich Scheidemann: Orgelwerke.* 3 vols. Kassel: Bärenreiter, 1971, vol. 3.

Davison, Archibalt T., and Apel, Willi, ed. *Historical Anthology of Music.* 2 vols. Cambridge: Harvard University Press, 1950, vol. 2.

Hedar, Josef, ed. *Dietrich Buxtehude: Sämtliche Orgelwerke.* 4 vols. Copenhagen: Wilhelm Hansen, 1952.

Kilian, Dietrich, ed. *Dietrich Buxtehude: Präludium und Fuge C-Dur.* Berlin: Verlag Merseburger, 1963.

Pidoux, Pierre, ed. *Girolamo Frescobaldi: Orgel- und Klavier Werke.* 5 vols. Kassel: Bärenreiter, 1954, vol. 5.

Riedel, Friedrich Wilhelm, ed. *Jacob Bölsche: Praeambulum; Peter Heidorn: Fuga.* Die Orgel. Fourth series, no. 4. Lippstadt: Kistner & Siegel & Co., 1957.

Seiffert, Max, ed. *Anonymi der norddeutschen Schule: 6 Praeludien und Fugen.* Organum. Fourth series, no. 10. Cologne: Kistner & Siegel & Co., n.d.

―――, ed. *Matthias Weckmann: 14 Präludien, Fugen und Toccaten.* Organum. Fourth series, no. 3. Cologne: Kistner & Siegel & Co., n.d.

―――, ed. *Orgel-Meister I.* Organum. Fourth series, no. 2. Lippstadt: Kistner & Siegel & Co., n.d.

Spitta, Philipp, ed. *Dietrich Buxtehudes Orgelkompositionen.* 2 vols. Leipzig: Breitkopf & Härtel, 1875-76.

―――. *Dietrich Buxtehudes Werke für Orgel.* Revised by Max Seiffert. 2 vols. Leipzig: Breitkopf & Härtel, 1903-4.

―――. *Ergänzungsband.* Edited by Max Seiffert. Leipzig: Breitkopf & Härtel, 1939.

―――. *Dietrich Buxtehude: Orgelwerke.* Preface by Walter Kraft. 4 vols. Wiesbaden: Breitkopf & Härtel, 1952; reprint ed., New York: Edwin F. Kalmus, n.d.

Selected Bibliography of Buxtehude's Praeludia

Alain, Olivier. "The Organ Works of Dietrich Buxtehude." Translated by Herman Adler. Accompanying *The Complete Organ Works of Dietrich Buxtehude*. New York: Musical Heritage Society Records, OR 309-15.

Apel, Willi. *The History of Keyboard Music to 1700*. Translated and revised by Hans Tischler. Bloomington: Indiana University Press, 1972.

Arnold, Richard Corliss. *Organ Literature: A Comprehensive Survey*. Metuchen, N.J.: The Scarecrow Press, 1973.

Beckmann, Klaus. "Ein anderer Buxtehude?: Zur umstrittenen Textfrage bei Buxtehudes Orgelwerken." *Der Kirchenmusiker* XXXV (January-February and March-April, 1984), pp. 1-12 and 48-59.

_____. "Textkritische Uberlegungen zu Buxtehudes Orgelwerken." *Musik und Kirche* XXXVIII (May-June, 1968), pp. 106-13.

Blume, Friedrich. "Dietrich Buxtehude." *Die Musik in Geschichte und Gegenwart*. Edited by Friedrich Blume. Kassel: Bärenreiter-Verlag, 1952, vol. 2, cols. 548-71.

Bradshaw, Murray C. "Pre-Bach Organ Toccatas: Form, Style, And Registration." *The Diapason* LXIV (March, 1972), pp. 26-28.

Buszin, Walter. "Dietrich Buxtehude (1637-1707) on the Tercentenary of his Birth." *The Musical Quarterly* XXIII (October, 1937), pp. 465-90.

"Buxtehude and His Contemporaries: Pushing the Limits of Meantone." Conference held at Wellesley College under the auspices of The Westfield Center for Early Keyboard Studies (June, 1984).

Dufourcq, Norbert. *J. S. Bach: Le Maître de l'Orgue*. Paris: Librairie Floury, 1948.

Dürr, Alfred. "Noch ein Buxtehude-Problem." *Musik und Kirche* XXVI (May-June, 1956), pp. 122-24.

Frotscher, Gotthold. *Geschichte des Orgelspiels*. 2 vols. Berlin: Verlag Merseburger, 1935; reprint ed., 1959.

Gillock, Jon. " 'Dietrich Buxtehude: Sämtliche Orgelwerke.' Ed. by Klaus Beckmann." *Notes: The Quarterly Journal of the Music Library Association* XXXII (December, 1975), pp. 374-77.

Grusnick, Bruno. "Dietrich Buxtehude." *Musik und Kirche* VII (January-February and March-April, 1935), pp. 22-28 and 58-65.

Hambraeus, Bengt. "Praeludium – Fuga – Toccata – Ciacona. Ein Studie kring några Formproblem i Buxtehudes Orgelmusik." *Svensk Tidskrift for Musikforskning* XXXIX (1957), pp. 89-113.

Hedar, Josef. *Dietrich Buxtehudes Orgelwerke*. Stockholm: Nordiska Musikförlaget, 1951; Frankfurt: Wilhelmiana Musikverlag, 1951.

Hering, Hans. "Das Tokkatische." *Die Musikforschung* VII (1954), no. 3, pp. 277-94.

Jacobson, Lena. "Musical Rhetoric in Buxtehude's Free Organ Works." *The Organ Yearbook* XIII (1982), pp. 60-79.

Karstädt, Georg. "Richtiges und Zweifelhaftes in Leben und Werk Dietrich Buxtehudes." *Musik und Kirche* XLIX (July-August, 1979), pp. 163-70.

_____, ed. *Thematisch-systematisches Verzeichnis der musikalischen Werke von Dietrich Buxtehude*. Wiesbaden: Breitkopf & Härtel, 1974.

Keller, Hermann. "Zwischen Sweelinck und Bach: Die Blütezeit der norddeutschen Orgelmusik." *Musica* XI (May, 1957), pp. 261-64.

Krummacher, Friedhelm. "Orgel- und Vokalmusik im Oeuvre norddeutscher Organisten um Buxtehude." *Dansk Åarbog for Musikforskning* 1966-67, pp. 63-90.

———. "Stylus phantasticus und phantastische Musik Kompositorische Verfahren in Toccaten von Frescobaldi und Buxtehude." *Schütz-Jahrbuch* II (1980), pp. 7–77.

Lang, Paul Henry. "Buxtehude: Complete Organ Works." *The Musical Quarterly* XLV (July, 1959), pp. 418–25.

Moe, Lawrence. Notes accompanying *Buxtehude [Organ Music]*. Wellesley, Mass.: Cambridge Records, CRS 2515.

Montillet, William. "L'Œuvre d'Orgue de Dietrich Buxtehude." *La Revue Musicale* XVIII (February–March, 1937), pp. 109–11.

Moser, Hans Joachim. *Dietrich Buxtehude, der Mann und sein Werk*. Berlin: Merseburger, 1957.

Pauly, Hans-Jacob. *Die Fuge in den Orgelwerken Dietrich Buxtehudes*. Kölner Beiträge zur Musikforschung, vol. 31. Regensburg: Gustav Bosse Verlag, 1964.

Pirro, André. *Dietrich Buxtehude*. Paris: Librairie Fischbacher, 1913.

———. "L'Art des Organistes." *Encyclopédie de la Musique et Dictionnaire du Conservatoire*. 2 parts, 11 vols. Paris: Librairie Delagrave, 1925, part 2, vol. 2, pp. 1181–374.

Powell, Kenneth George. "An Analysis of the North German Organ Toccata." *The Diapason* LXII (April, 1971), pp. 27–29.

———. "The North German Organ Toccata (1650–1710)." D.M.A. dissertation, University of Illinois, 1969.

Riedel, Friedrich Wilhelm. *Quellenkundliche Beiträge zur Geschichte der Musik für Tasteninstrumente in der 2 Hälfte des 17. Jahrhunderts*. Schriften des Landesinstituts für Musikforschung, Kiel. Vol. 10. Kassel: Bärenreiter-Verlag, 1960.

Shannon, John R. *Organ Literature of the Seventeenth century: A Study of its Styles*. Raleigh: Sunbury, 1978.

Snyder, Kerala J. "Buxtehude's Organ Music: Drama without Words." *The Musical Times* CXX (June, 1979), pp. 517–21.

———. "Dietrich Buxtehude." *The New Grove Dictionary of Music and Musicians*. 6th ed. Edited by Stanley Sadie. London: Macmillan Publishers, 1980, vol. 3, pp. 526–37.

———. "Dietrich Buxtehude's Studies in Learned Counterpoint." *Journal of the American Musicological Society* XXXIII (Fall, 1980), pp. 544–64.

Spitta, Philipp. *Johann Sebastian Bach*. 2 vols. Leipzig: Breitkopf & Härtel, 1873–80. Translated by Clara Bell and J. A. Fuller-Maitland. 3 vols. London: Novello & Co., 1889; reprint ed., New York: Dover Publications, 1951.

Stahl, Wilhelm. *Dietrich Buxtehude*. Kassel: Bärenreiter-Verlag, 1937; reprint ed., 1952.

Viderø, Finn. "Buxtehude-Probleme." *Musik und Kirche* XXV (September–October, 1955), pp. 231–38.

———. "Nogle Buxtehude-Problemer." *Dansk Musiktidsskrift* XII (April, 1937), pp. 74–82.

Wenk, Arthur. "The Organ Prelude and Fugue before Bach." *Music: The A.G.O. & R.C.C.O. Magazine* X (June, 1976), pp. 31–33.

Other Works Cited

Beswick, Delbert M. "The Problem of Tonality in 17th Century Music." Ph.D. dissertation, University of North Carolina, 1951.

Breig, Werner. *Die Orgelwerke von Heinrich Scheidemann*. Beihefte zum Archiv für Musikwissenschaft. Vol. 3. Wiesbaden: Franz Steiner Verlag, 1967.

Cone, Edward T. *Musical Form and Musical Performance*. New York: W. W. Norton & Co., 1968.

Crocker, Richard. *A History of Musical Style*. New York: McGraw-Hill, 1966.

Dahlhaus, Carl. *Untersuchungen über die Entstehung der harmonischen Tonalität.* Saarbrücker Studien zur Musikwissenschaft. Vol. 2. Kassel: Bärenreiter, 1968.
Grace, Harvey. *The Organ Works of Bach.* London: Novello & Co., 1922.
Grout, Donald Jay. *A History of Western Music.* Rev. ed. New York: W. W. Norton & Co., 1973.
Imbrie, Andrew. "Metrical Ambiguity in Beethoven." In *Beethoven Studies.* Edited by Alan Tyson. New York: W. W. Norton & Co., 1973, pp. 45–66.
Kirkendale, Ursula. "The Source for Bach's *Musical Offering.*" *Journal of the American Musicological Society* XXXIII (Spring, 1980), pp. 88–141.
Mattheson, Johann. *Der vollkommene Capellmeister.* Hamburg: 1739; reprint ed., Kassel: Bärenreiter, 1954.
_____. *Grundlage einer Ehren-Pforte.* Hamburg: 1740. Edited by Max Schneider. Berlin: Kommissions-Verlag von L. Liepmannssohn, 1910; reprint ed., Kassel: Bärenreiter-Verlag, 1969.
Meyer, Leonard B. *Music, the Arts, and Ideas: Patterns and Predictions in Twentieth-Century Culture.* Chicago: University of Chicago Press, 1967.
Morgan, Robert P. "The Theory and Analysis of Tonal Rhythm." *The Musical Quarterly* LXIV (October, 1978), pp. 435–73.
Rosen, Charles. "Art Has Its Reasons." *The New York Review of Books*, June 17, 1971, pp. 32–38.
Roth, Bärbel. "Zur Echtheitsfrage der Matthais Weckmann zugeschriebenen Klavierwerke ohne Cantus firmus." *Acta Musicologica* XXXVI (January–March, 1964), pp. 31–36.
Salzer, Felix. *Structural Hearing: Tonal Coherence in Music.* 2 vols. New York: Charles Boni, 1952; reprint ed., New York: Dover Publications, 1962.
Schenker, Heinrich. *Der Freie Satz.* Neue musikalische Theorien und Phantasien. Vol. 3. Vienna: Universal Edition, 1935. *Free Composition.* New Musical Theories and Fantasies. Vol. 3. Translated and edited by Ernst Oster. New York: Longman, 1979.
_____. *Harmony.* Edited and annotated by Oswald Jonas, translated by Elisabeth Mann Borgese. Chicago: University of Chicago Press, 1954; reprint ed., Cambridge: MIT Press, 1973.
Sharp, G. B. "Matthias Weckmann, 1619–74." *The Musical times* CXV (December, 1974), pp. 1039–41.
Stauffer, George B. *The Organ Preludes of Johann Sebastian Bach.* Studies in Musicology, no. 27. Ann Arbor: U.M.I. Research Press, 1980.
Wienpahl, Robert W. "The Emergence of Tonality." Ph.D. dissertation, University of California at Los Angeles, 1953.

Index

Agricola, Johann Friedrich, 236, 326n17
Alain, Olivier, 235
Andreas-Bach-Buch. *See* Leipzig, Musikbibliothek der Stadt Leipzig, Ms. III.8.4
Anonymous
　individual works:
　　Praeludium in G (Seiffert, ed., #4), 24-25, 45-46, 85-91, 101-3, 309n33, 311n24, 323n34, 324n48
　　Praeludium in F (Seiffert, ed., #5), 24-25, 43, 45, 90, 309n37, 310n42, 312n33, 318n26, 321n49, 329n42
Apel, Willi, 9-10, 11, 31, 63-65, 303n29, 304n22, 306n47
archetypal form. *See* form, archetypal
autographs, hypothesized, 1, 233, 302n11, 326n18. *See also* tablatures

Bach, Carl Philipp Emanuel, 236
Bach, Johann Sebastian, 2, 61, 64, 236, 259, 270, 273, 302n16, 304n22, 335n136
　individual works:
　　Orgelbüchlein, 259
　　Fugue in D, BWV 532, 273
　　Prelude in G, BWV 541, 281, 335n136
　　Toccata, Adagio and Fugue in C, BWV 564, 334n118
　　Passacaglia in c, BWV 582, 304n22
Beckmann, Klaus, 1-2, 238, 273, 274, 302n12, 302nn12, 17, 25, 28, 308n15, 311n11, 314n20, 325n7, 326nn8, 17, 327n31, 331nn72, 73
Berlin
　Bibliothek der ehemaligen Hochschule für Musikerziehung und Kirchenmusik Ms. 1476, 326n17
　Deutsche Staatsbibliothek, Musikabteilung:
　　Mus. ms. 40295 (Schmahls Tablature), 233, 238, 241, 261-62, 327nn25, 27, 29, 31
　Mus. ms. Am. 430, 326n17
　Mus. ms. Am. 462, 326n17
　Ehemalige Bibliothek des Königlich-akademischen Instituts für Kirchenmusik, 233, 238, 328n35
　Staatsbibliothek Preussischer Kulturbesitz, Musikabteilung:
　　Mus. ms. 2681, 233-41, 253, 260, 262-65, 270, 273, 280, 282, 291, 295, 298, 326nn12, 14, 17, 18, 328n38, 334n111, 336n159
　　Mus. ms. 2681/1, 326n17
　　Mus. ms. 2683, 326n17
　　Mus. ms. 30381, No. 3, 233, 238, 328n33
　　Mus. ms. 40644 (Möller Manuscript), 233, 236-38, 260-61, 327nn26, 29
Böhm, Georg, 2, 307n61, 328n42
Bölsche, Jacob
　individual works:
　　Praeludium in E, 326n9
Breig, Werner, 365n34
Bruhns, Nicolaus, 302n12, 326n17, 328nn38.42
　individual works:
　　Praeludium in e (Great), 307n70, 321n52
Brussels
　Bibliothèque du Conservatoire de Musique: U 26659/Wagener, 233-41, 253, 262-65, 270, 273, 280, 282, 291, 295, 298, 326nn14, 17, 18, 328nn38, 39, 334n111
Buxtehude, Dietrich. *See also* autographs, hypothesized; editions; form; praeludium; sources; tablatures
　individual works:
　　Praeludium in C, BuxWV 136
　　　main discussion, 262-65
　　　reductions, 33, 38-39, 115-18, 213-14
　　　mentioned, 39, 42, 51, 54, 68, 87, 91, 109-10, 115-18, 127, 153, 157, 166-71, 173-74, 202, 213-14, 242, 251, 267, 272, 277, 286, 290, 299,

305n31, 307n71, 308n8, 311n5, 316nn9, 15, 317nn3, 6, 318n5, 319nn5, 6, 8, 13, 14, 20, 24, 320n44, 321n7, 325nn5, 7, 326n8, 330n60, 332n85, 333n109, 334n133, 336n162, 337n182

Praeludium in C, BuxWV 137
  main discussion, 267-69
  reductions, 178-81, 210-11
  mentioned, 41, 48, 52, 54, 73-74, 91-92, 104, 110-12, 131-36, 156, 172, 173, 178-82, 210-11, 242, 270, 273, 274-78, 299, 304n21, 305n36, 311n12, 312n38, 314n21, 316n13, 317n10, 319nn8, 9, 14, 19, 320n43, 322nn22, 23, 324nn2, 3, 5, 7, 327n20, 332nn80, 87, 333nn100, 104, 109, 334n113, 125, 126, 127, 335n154, 337n184

Praeludium in C, BuxWV 138
  main discussion, 271-72
  mentioned, 12, 96, 137-38, 270, 272-73, 299, 308nn8, 9, 12, 309, 316, 317, 318, 319nn10, 17, 19, 21, 24, 327nn23, 24

Praeludium in D, BuxWV 139
  main discussion, 263-67
  reductions, 119, 141-45, 182-84, 186-87
  mentioned, 21, 25, 26-27, 47, 55, 62, 101-2, 118-19, 124, 135, 141-45, 153, 156, 161, 174-75, 182-87, 206-7, 241-42, 269-70, 271, 274-78, 285, 294-95, 299, 304n7, 305n30, 308nn4, 9, 16, 18, 309n25, 314n21, 316n6, 317nn30, 3, 318n5, 319nn17, 19, 21, 322n27, 324nn6, 7, 325n3, 326nn12, 14, 327n25, 332n85, 333nn104, 107, 109, 334nn125, 127, 129, 336n157

Praeludium in d, BuxWV 140
  main discussion, 280-83
  reductions, 38, 147, 186, 188-91, 219-21
  mentioned, 28-29, 36, 42, 43, 51, 69, 79-80, 91, 94-96, 99, 103, 112, 127, 146-47, 156, 169, 175, 186, 188-91, 204, 207-8, 219-21, 242, 283-86, 291-95, 296-98, 299, 304n20, 307n72, 308n19, 309n34, 311n6, 317nn30, 3, 9, 319nn7, 10, 21, 321nn5, 7, 322nn9, 11, 15, 27, 323nn 30, 31, 324nn5, 7, 326nn12, 14, 328n45, 330n60, 332n85, 334nn125, 126, 130, 335nn148, 150, 151, 336n156, 337nn178, 182, 183, 184

Praeludium in E, BuxWV 141
  main discussion, 276-80
  mentioned, 32, 47, 71, 77, 89, 96, 111, 134, 157, 165-68, 175, 206-7, 242, 280-84, 285, 291-94, 296-97, 299, 304n16, 308n8, 313nn4, 18, 315n46, 316n17, 317nn3, 11, 319nn 14, 17, 320n46, 321n7, 322n9, 324n48, 326nn12, 14, 330n60, 334n127, 335nn141, 148, 154

Praeludium in e, BuxWV 142
  main discussion, 285-91
  reduction, 288-90
  mentioned, 28, 37, 42, 47, 70-71, 87, 91, 96, 104-5, 113, 127, 137, 163, 166-67, 171, 174, 238, 241-42, 251, 262, 282-83, 288-90, 293-95, 298, 299, 308n8, 311nn6, 7, 17, 312n17, 313n4, 314n20, 316nn11, 15, 317nn3, 6, 319nn 9, 10, 20, 21, 320n31, 321n7, 324n5, 325n7, 326nn12, 14, 332n87, 334nn116, 133, 336n161, 337nn183, 186

Praeludium in e, BuxWV 143
  main discussion, 251-53
  mentioned, 66, 155, 159-60, 199, 203, 242, 253-55, 262, 270, 298-99, 304n20, 308nn17, 20, 309nn25, 37, 311nn6, 13, 319nn9, 14, 15, 21, 321nn50, 7, 322n12, 324n5, 326nn12, 14, 327n32, 330nn64, 65, 66, 70, 71, 322n85, 336n163

Praeludium in F, BuxWV 144
  main discussion, 272-73
  mentioned, 27-28, 138, 148, 270, 303n7, 309n24, 316nn7, 8, 317nn3, 7, 319nn9, 20, 21, 26, 325nn7, 8, 334nn111, 119, 337n182

Praeludium in F, BuxWV 145
  main discussion, 273-75
  reduction, 35
  mentioned, 27-28, 35, 47, 149, 157, 270, 274-76, 293, 299, 308nn12, 13, 309n24, 311n9, 316n7, 317n7, 319nn10, 18, 324n3, 326nn12, 14, 328n33, 333n111

Praeludium in f#, BuxWV 146
  main discussion, 291-95
  reductions, 122, 194-98, 217-21
  mentioned, 11, 48, 51-52, 62, 67, 78-79, 96, 104, 122, 127, 132, 136, 156, 161-62, 166, 175, 194-98, 204, 207, 217-19, 236, 241, 242, 283, 296-97, 299, 304n20, 308nn13, 16, 17, 18, 309n37, 313n4, 316n18, 317nn30, 4, 7, 319nn10, 17, 18, 323n31, 324nn5, 7, 326n14, 327n19, 334nn125, 130, 335nn142, 148, 336n158, 337nn177, 178, 183

Index   345

Praeludium in G, BuxWV 147
  main discussion, 270-71
  mentioned, 131, 134, 270, 309n24,
    316n7, 317nn4, 6, 319nn9, 17,
    320n28, 322n17, 324n11, 327n22
Praeludium in g, BuxWV 148
  main discussion, 256-59
  reduction, 257
  mentioned, 13, 50, 66, 238-42, 260-61,
    270, 272, 299, 308n17, 309n25,
    311n6, 313n4, 316n13, 317n7,
    318n5, 319nn10, 14, 20, 21, 321n7,
    324n5, 325n7, 328nn34, 38, 40,
    329n46, 331n77, 322n85, 333n109,
    336n162, 337nn182, 191
Praeludium in g, BuxWV 149
  main discussion, 295-98
  reductions, 149-50, 191-94
  mentioned, 12, 15, 28, 50, 67, 80-81, 91,
    127, 149-50, 153-56, 163, 191-95,
    208, 238-42, 283, 286, 299, 304n21,
    308n8, 309n23, 310n45, 311nn6, 7,
    10, 315n47, 316n12, 317nn30, 3,
    319nn10, 14, 17, 18, 321n7, 322n11,
    324nn5, 7, 325nn14, 3, 326nn12,
    14, 334nn125, 130, 336nn169, 171,
    337nn181, 184, 187
Praeludium in g, BuxWV 150
  main discussion, 248-51
  reduction, 123
  mentioned, 27, 69, 91, 122-23, 136, 155,
    164, 170-71, 174, 242, 251-56, 258-
    59, 262-63, 267, 270, 308n17,
    309nn22, 25, 37, 310nn5, 6,
    316n12, 317n3, 318n5, 319nn8, 13,
    21, 26, 321n7, 322n9, 327n20,
    330nn65, 66, 70, 331n77, 332n85,
    333n100, 335n159, 336n163
Praeludium in A, BuxWV 151
  main discussion, 261-63
  mentioned, 67-68, 156-57, 165, 238-41,
    242, 263, 267, 305n33, 309n24,
    313n4, 318n5, 319nn8, 13, 19, 24,
    321n7, 322nn9, 23, 327nn25, 26,
    333n95
Praeludium in a, BuxWV 152
  main discussion, 244, 247-48
  mentioned, 26, 27-28, 65-66, 103, 130,
    163, 248-53, 262, 298-99, 307n68,
    308n20, 309nn22, 23, 311n6, 317n3,
    319nn10, 14, 15, 321nn48, 7, 322n10,
    325n7, 326n8, 329n54, 330nn56, 58,
    64, 70, 332n85
Praeludium in a, BuxWV 153
  main discussion, 260-61
  reduction, 186
  mentioned, 11, 48, 66, 111, 127, 133,
    157, 162, 173, 185-86, 242, 262-67,
    272, 285, 293-94, 299, 307n4,
    308nn8, 16, 309nn22, 24, 311nn5,
    6, 316n14, 319n14, 319nn8, 14, 17,
    19, 20, 21, 321nn5, 7, 322nn13, 27,
    326nn12, 14, 332n89, 333n109,
    334n113, 336nn161, 175, 337nn177,
    182
Praeludium in B♭, BuxWV 154
  main discussion, 276
  mentioned, 241, 302n18, 325n3
Toccata in d, BuxWV 155
  main discussion, 282-85
  reductions, 35, 185, 290
  mentioned, 35, 53, 62, 70, 127-28, 160,
    164, 185, 241, 242, 286, 290, 291-
    92, 294-95, 297-99, 302n17,
    304nn18, 20, 308nn15, 16, 18,
    309nn22, 23, 35, 310n45, 311nn6,
    11, 12, 314n20, 316n16, 317n30,
    318n5, 319nn6, 7, 10, 13, 18,
    321nn4, 7, 322nn11, 16, 27,
    323nn31, 39, 325n7, 326nn8, 9,
    334n126, 335nn144, 145, 148, 149,
    151, 154, 336nn156, 157, 337nn178, 184
Toccata in F, BuxWV 156
  main discussion, 253-56
  reduction, 121
  mentioned, 29, 48, 69-70, 120-21, 132-
    33, 165, 242, 259, 262, 264, 272-73,
    276-77, 282-84, 298-99, 302n17,
    308nn12, 14, 17, 309nn23, 27,
    310n45, 311n9, 313n4, 317nn30, 7,
    319nn8, 14, 17, 20, 21, 320n28,
    321n7, 325n3, 326nn12, 14, 330n60,
    332n85, 333n95, 334n115,
    335nn145, 149
Toccata in F, BuxWV 157
  main discussion, 273-76
  mentioned, 28, 74-75, 133-34, 137, 270,
    276-78, 287-88, 291-93, 299,
    308n14, 309n24, 316n7, 317nn4, 6,
    319nn10, 17, 19, 328n35, 334n127
Praeambulum in a, BuxWV 158
  main discussion, 243-47
  mentioned, 25-26, 65, 103, 130, 154,
    163, 199, 242, 247-54, 262, 298-99,
    307n68, 308n20, 309n23, 310n45,
    311n6, 317n3, 319nn10, 14, 17, 19,
    21, 25, 320n28, 321nn48, 7, 322n10,
    325n7, 326n8, 328n45, 329n54,
    330nn56, 59, 64, 66, 70, 331n76,
    332n85, 336nn162, 163
Ciacona in c, BuxWV 159, 4, 304n22,
  327n20
Ciacona in e, BuxWV 160, 4, 267, 304n22,
  327n20

Passacaglia in d, BuxWV 161, 4, 267, 304n22, 308n4, 327n20, 332n82
Praeludium in G, BuxWV 162, 325n3
Praeludium in g, BuxWV 163, 237, 313n17, 326n12
Toccata in G, BuxWV 164, 237, 326n12, 327nn23, 24
Toccata in G, BuxWV 165, 309n36, 327n26
Canzona in C, BuxWV 166, 326n8
Canzonetta in C, BuxWV 167, 325n3
Canzona in d, BuxWV 168, 237, 326n12
Canzonetta in e, BuxWV 169, 315n38, 325n3
Canzona in G, BuxWV 170, 315n42, 325n3
Canzonetta in G, BuxWV 171, 237, 326n12
Canzonetta in G, BuxWV 172, 327nn23, 24
Canzona in g, BuxWV 173, 325n3
Fuga in C, BuxWV 174, 327n20
Fuga in G, BuxWV 175, 315n38, 326n8
Fuga in B$_b$, BuxWV 176, 237, 313n17, 326n12
Magnificat primi toni, BuxWV 203, 326n14
Nun lob, mein Seel, den Herren, BuxWV 213, 326n12
Sonata in d, 326n8

canzona, as a genre, 23-25, 56-57, 63, 84, 152, 155-56, 248, 251, 256, 309n30, 310n2
climax, defined, 94
closure, defined, 115
Cone, Edward T., 61, 311n14

editions, 1-2, 236-38, 273-76, 301n7, 308n15, 311n10, 314nn20, 24, 25, 325n1, 334n123
Englehardt Collection. *See* Lund, Universitetsbibliotek, Handskriftsavdelningen Sammlung Engelhardt Nr. 216

figural style, defined, 10-11
"Final" section, defined, 160-62
flourish, opening. *See* opening flourish
form
  archetypal:
    entire praeludium, 10, 14, 40-41, 46-47, 53, 72-73, 94, 100, 209-13, 223-26, 233-34
    first fugue, 130, 139-40
    opening free section, 109-11, 112-13, 118
    remaining sections, 172, 176, 198-99

hierarchical, 14, 22, 29, 40, 46, 233
three-part, 41, 46, 223-25, 324n11
two-part, 223, 270, 273-74, 324n11
Frescobaldi, Girolamo, 2, 20-23, 61, 63, 311n2
  individual works:
    Canzon Dopo il Post Comune, 320n45
Froberger, Johann Jacob, 2, 20-21, 43-44, 57, 61, 63, 86, 125-26, 154, 204-6, 227-32, 247, 299, 305n40, 309n31, 310n2
  individual works:
    Toccata in d (Adler, ed., vol. 1, #2), 125-26
    Canzona in C (Adler, ed., vol. 1, #5), 320n45
    Toccata in d (Adler, ed., vol. 1, #19)
    reductions, 125-26, 204, 231-33
    mentioned, 125-26, 204-5, 231-33, 320n45
fugato, defined, 13

Gotthold Manuscript. *See* Königsberg, Universitätsbibliothek Sammlung Gotthold 14314(12)
Grace, Harvey, 313n11
Grobe Tablature. *See* Höngeda bei Mühlhausen/Thüringen, Tabulaturbuch von Georg Grobe 1675
Grout, Donald Jay, 9, 315n46
grundgestalt, 79, 295

Handel, George Frederick, 61
Hedar, Josef, 1, 4, 9-11, 233-38, 301n7, 302n25, 303nn29, 5, 304nn7, 23, 307nn61, 67, 311n11, 312n2, 325n5, 326n9, 334n123, 336n168
Heidorn, Peter
  individual works:
    Fuga, 326n9
hierarchical form. *See* form, hierarchical
Höngeda bei Mühlhausen/Thüringen Tabulaturbuch von Georg Grobe 1675, 233, 238, 259, 328nn34, 38, 40, 332n85, 337n191
hypothesized sources. *See* autographs

Imbrie, Andrew, 310n1, 311n14

Jacobson, Lena, 5, 283

keys, original, hypothesized, 5
Klingenberg, Gottlieb, 233
Kneller, Andreas, 328n42
Königsberg
  Universitätsbibliothek:
    Sammlung Gotthold 14314 (12), 233, 238, 327n32

Praeambulum in d, WV 31, 310n38
Praeambulum in d, WV 32, 310n38
Praeambulum in d, WV 33, 310n38
Praeambulum in d, WV 34, 58, 310nn38, 39, 316n21, 323n30, 333n102
Praeambulum in d, WV 35, 57, 307n67, 310n38, 320n36
Praeambulum in d, WV 36, 21, 310nn38, 39, 320nn34, 36
Praeambulum in e, WV 38, 310n38, 320n36
Praeambulum in F, WV 39, 310n38
Praeambulum in F, WV 40, 310n38, 320n36
Praeambulum in g, WV 41, 320n36
Fuga in d, WV 42, 320n36
Canzon in F, WV 44, 56, 84
Praeambulum in G, WV 73, 310n38
Canzon in G, WV 74, 311n21
Schenker, Heinrich, 308n10
Schmahls Tablature. *See* Berlin, Deutsche Staatsbibliothek, Musikabteilung Mus. ms. 40295
Seiffert, Max, 1, 236-38, 302n25, 306n47, 307nn61, 62, 310n42, 327n31
Shannon, John R., 31, 64, 152
Sharp, G. B., 306n45
Snyder, Kerala J., 5, 236, 305n32, 319n16, 321n51, 326nn9, 15, 18, 327n251, 332n89, 335n144, 336n166, 337nn186, 189
sources, 1-2, 4, 233, 241, 242, 301n7, 302n10, 303n31, 308n15, 311n11, 325n2. *See also* autographs, hypothesized; tablatures; individual sources listed by city location
Spitta, Philipp, 1-2, 4, 236-38, 253, 259, 262, 273-74, 285, 294-95, 301n7, 326n18, 327n32, 330n71, 331n79, 332n80, 333n93, 336nn159, 160, 168
Stauffer, George B., 314n20, 336n161
stylus fantasticus, 303n1
stylus motecticus, 303n1
synthesis, defined, 115

tablatures, 1, 233-38, 302nn10, 11, 331n73. *See also* autographs, hypothesized; sources
temperament, 5, 241, 276-77, 291-94, 336n167, 337n186
tempo indications, 241, 276-77, 291-93, 295-96, 320n46, 329n46, 333nn98, 110
three-part form. *See* form, three-part
toccata
 as a genre, 23, 25, 44, 57, 61, 100, 125-26, 205, 309n31
 as a term. *See* praeludium, related terms
tonicization chains, defined, 38-39
transposition. *See* keys, original, hypothesized

Tunder, Franz, 20-26, 43-46, 56-61, 62, 65, 84, 100-103, 124-26, 151-57, 199-201, 203, 227-33, 242-249, 251, 254, 267, 299, 302n12, 306n57, 307nn61, 62, 309n27, 310n42, 312n1, 316n21, 318n23, 321nn49, 51, 323n30, 324n47, 329n47, 331n77
individual works:
 Praeludium in F (Beckmann, ed., #1), 61, 124, 310n40
 Praeludium in g (Beckmann, ed., #2)
  reduction, 124
  mentioned, 43, 124, 151-52, 309nn27, 34, 310n40, 323n32, 333n102
 Praeludium in g (Beckmann, ed., #3), 58-60, 100, 124, 151-52, 310n40
 Praeludium in g (Beckmann, ed., #4)
  reductions, 200-201, 227-28
  mentioned, 58-60, 124, 200-201, 227-28, 310n40, 314n27, 323n31, 324n44
 Praeludium in g (Beckmann, ed., #5), 20
 Canzona in G (Beckmann, ed., #6), 56, 84
 Jesus Christus, unser Heiland (Beckmann, ed., #11), 308n7
tuning. *See* temperament
two-part form. *See* form, two-part

Uppsala
 Universitetsbibliotek:
  Ms. 408, 306n49

Vivaldi, Antonio, 61, 280
Vogel, Harald, 4-5, 304n15, 311n8, 336n167, 337n186

Wagener, 236
Wagener Manuscript. *See* Brussels, Bibliothèque du Conservatoire Royal de Musique, U 26659/Wagener
Weckmann, Matthias, 20-26, 43-46, 57-61, 62, 63-65, 84, 91, 100-103, 124-26, 152-57, 201-5, 227-29, 242-47, 267, 299, 305nn40, 41, 306n47, 307nn61, 62, 309nn31, 33, 310n2, 315n44, 320n46, 321nn49, 51, 323n36, 324n47, 328n42, 329n49, 331n77
individual works:
 Fantasia in d (Seiffert, ed., #1)
  reductions, 153-54, 203-4, 230
  mentioned, 23-25, 45, 57, 60, 84-85, 101, 152-56, 201-5, 230-31, 306n55, 309nn33, 35, 317n24, 320n44, 321n49, 324n44
 Fuga in d (Seiffert, ed., #2) 23-25, 45, 57, 61, 85, 91, 101, 152, 201-3, 306nn55, 57, 317n25, 320n43
 Praeambulum in d (Seiffert, ed., #3)
  reductions, 125-26, 229

Leipzig
   Musikbibliothek der Stadt Leipzig:
      Ms. II. 2. 51, 306n55
      Ms. III. 8. 4 (Andreas-Bach-Buch), 233, 236, 239, 267, 298, 327n20, 330n70
Lindemann, Gottfried, 233
Lowell Mason Codex. *See* New Haven, Yale University, Music Library, LM 5056
Lübeck, Vincent, 302n12, 328n42
   individual works:
      Praeludium in d, 331n75
      Praeludium in E, 315n47
Lund
   Universitetsbibliotek, Handskriftsavdelningen:
      Sammlung Engelhardt Nr. 216, 233, 236, 279, 301, 302n10, 327n22
      Sammlung Wenster, 233-41, 264, 295, 298, 301n6, 302n10, 325n3, 328n38
Lüneburg
   Ratsbucherei:
      Mus. ant. pract. KN 147 (Lüneburg Tablatures), 306n47
      Mus. ant. pract. KN 207 (Lüneburg Tablatures), 23, 45, 306nn 47, 49, 50, 60
      Mus. ant. pract. KN 209 (Lüneburg Tablatures), 306n55
Lüneburg Tablatures. *See* Lüneburg, Ratsbucherei, Mus. ant. pract. KN 147, 207, 209

Mason, Lowell, 236, 326n9
Mason, Lowell, Codex. *See* New Haven, Yale University, Music Library, LM 5056
Mattheson, Johann, 20, 305n26
meantone tuning. *See* temperament
metrical relationships, 53, 311n8
modality, 26, 31-32, 42-43, 241, 309n23, 329n46
modular style, defined, 11
Möller Manuscript. *See* Berlin, Staatsbibliothek Preussischer Kulturbesitz, Musikabteilung Mus. ms. 40644

New Haven
   Yale University, Music Library:
      LM 4838, 271, 327nn23, 24
      LM 4983, 327nn23, 24
      LM 5056 (Lowell Mason Codex) 233-36, 238-41, 248, 262-63, 272, 282, 298-99, 302n17, 308n15, 311n11, 321n4, 325n7, 326n9, 328n38, 330n70, 332n83, 336n159, 337n191

opening flourish, defined, 14
"organ recitative," 336n168
original keys, hypothesized. *See* keys, original, hypothesized
overlegato style, defined, 304n15

Pachelbel, Johann, 236
passaggio, 305n26
Pauly, Hans-Jacob, 312n2
Pirro, André, 262, 333nn92, 93
Powell, Kenneth George, 5, 10, 31, 63-64, 233, 241-42, 276-77, 303n29, 304nn10, 23, 313nn4, 5, 325nn2, 4, 327nn21, 26, 328nn45, 46, 330n56, 332nn85, 88, 333n101, 335n134
praeambulum
   as a genre, 21-25, 44, 61, 100, 124-26, 205
   as a term, 2
praeludium
   as a genre, 21-25, 43-44, 57, 61-62, 84, 100, 105, 124-26, 128, 205-6, 223, 309nn30, 31
   as a term, 2, 302n28
   related terms:
      praeambulum, 2
      prelude and fugue, 2, 10, 128, 223, 269-79, 310n46
      preludio, 302n28
      toccata, 2, 10, 303n29
Praetorius, Jacob
   individual works:
      Praeambulum (Seiffert, ed., #3), 314n27
prelude and fugue. *See* praeludium, related terms
preludio. *See* praeludium, related terms

"recitative." *See* "organ recitative"
Reincken, Johann Adam, 236, 261, 302n12, 328n42, 332n89
   individual works:
      An Wasserflüssen Babylon, 261, 332n89
rhapsodic style, defined, 10-11
rhetorical conventions, 5
Riedel, Friedrich Wilhelm, 238, 259, 326nn9, 17, 327nn25, 32
Rinck, Johann Christian Heinrich, 326n9
Ritter, A. G., 328n34
Rohde, Michael, 233

Scheidemann, Heinrich, 2, 20-22, 26, 43, 44, 56-58, 62, 65, 83, 100, 103, 126, 151, 154, 156, 199, 242-47, 249, 267, 306nn48, 49, 57, 309n31, 311n21, 312n1, 316n20, 318n23, 321n47
   individual works:
      Praeambulum in C, WV 30, 310nn38, 39

mentioned, 23-25, 43, 45-46, 57-60, 84, 101, 125, 153, 201-2, 204, 228, 307n62, 310n42, 317n24, 321n49, 324n48, 329nn47, 49, 52
Canzon in C (Seiffert, ed., #4), 88
Canzon in c (Seiffert, ed., #6), 87-88, 320n46, 331n77
Canzon in d (Seiffert, ed., #7), 87, 320n46
Canzon in G (Seiffert, ed., #8), 89
Toccata in d (Seiffert, ed., #9), 25, 306nn46, 47, 317n26
Toccata in d (Seiffert, ed., #10), 57, 86, 315n37, 324n45
Toccata in e (Seiffert, ed., #11), 45, 57, 59, 86, 306n45, 309n30
Toccata in e (Seiffert, ed., #12), 21, 317n26
Toccata in a (Seiffert, ed., #13), 25, 57
Wenster Collection. *See* Lund, Universitetsbibliotek, Handskriftsavdelningen, Sammlung Wenster
Werckmeister, Andreas, 328n42